STRUCTURED DESIGN:
Fundamentals
of a Discipline
of Computer Program
and Systems Design

STRUCTURED DESIGN:
Fundamentals
of a Discipline
of Computer Program
and Systems Design

EDWARD YOURDON

LARRY L. CONSTANTINE

PRENTICE-HALL, INC. Englewood Cliffs, New Jersey 07632

Library of Congress Cataloging in Publication Data

YOURDON, EDWARD.
   Structured design.

   Bibliography: p.
   Includes index.
   1. Electronic digital computers—Programming.
2. Structured programming. I. Constantine, Larry L.,
joint author. II. Title.
QA76.6.Y67 1979   001.6'42   78–24465
ISBN 0–13–854471–9

Printed in the United States of America

10   9   8   7   6

PRENTICE-HALL INTERNATIONAL, INC., *London*
PRENTICE-HALL OF AUSTRALIA PTY. LIMITED, *Sydney*
PRENTICE-HALL OF CANADA, LTD., *Toronto*
PRENTICE-HALL OF INDIA PRIVATE LIMITED, *New Delhi*
PRENTICE-HALL OF JAPAN, INC., *Tokyo*
PRENTICE-HALL OF SOUTHEAST ASIA PTE. LTD., *Singapore*
WHITEHALL BOOKS LIMITED, *Wellington, New Zealand*

Contents

v

Preface

Because the publication of this book marks my exit from the computer field and, therefore, my last opportunity to set the record straight, a brief historical note seems in order. The ideas in this book began taking form in 1963, while I was programming for C-E-I-R, Inc. (later to become part of Control Data). Extraordinarily good luck put me on a corridor where Jack Cremeans had assembled some of the best programmers I would ever encounter. Somehow, despite or even because of the constant fire-fighting in cranking out routine business applications, we found the time to think and talk about what we were doing. The earliest "investigations" of program structure to which I often refer were no more than noon-hour critiques of each other's programs and long afternoon debates of what might have been done differently to avoid difficulties we encountered in debugging, maintaining, or modifying our programs. I emerged as chronicler and organizer of the hard-earned knowledge of others and on numerous occasions since have become aware of how many of my ideas are but reformulations of what Dave Jasper and Ken MacKenzie taught me. In 1964, I first attempted to integrate into an article the principles we had evolved ("Towards a Theory of Program Design," *Data Processing*, December 1965). I also taught my first course, an introduction to LISP, while at C-E-I-R's Washington office, becoming hooked on the magic of sharing meanings with others and thereby beginning the process of critical feedback from students which would leaven so many half-baked ideas.

Those ideas first were mixed together in notes for "Advanced Program and Systems Design," an Institute for Advanced Technology course, which I was singularly unqualified to teach when I began it in 1966. Along the way I had been influenced by Edsger Dijkstra, by various works on "systems engineering," and by a manuscript on organizational theory by James Emery. In the latter, I saw the first promising intermediate-level application of general systems theory. From it, I gleaned the essential concept of intercomponent coupling and firmed my commitment to a systems-theoretical view of the universe.

Under Ray Wenig at C-E-I-R's Boston office, I continued to stretch my skills, cooking up larger designs, learning the validity of many design principles more from failure to apply them than from anything else. By the time my own consulting firm was launched in 1967, the graphics for picturing program structure and a vocabulary for talking about structural problems had emerged. I had begun to make some original contributions, although I would not have recognized them as such at the time. Technical memos from that era covered such concepts as modularity, hierarchy, normal and pathological connections, cohesion, and coupling, although without the precision or detail now possible.

In July 1968, the landmark National Symposium on Modular Programming was held. The limited-edition *Proceedings,* one of the first large compilations of material on program structure, contained many ideas still fresh today. By that time, I had outlined a strategy for program design, called simply "functional analysis," that significantly simplified the teaching of structural design. With clients' problems I had conducted many experiments, mostly gedanken experiments, comparing alternative structures to arrive at factors contributing to modularity and sound program design.

The collapse of my company overlapped my joining the faculty of IBM's Systems Research Institute (SRI). Fortunately for all involved, Al Pietresanta kept me on the faculty even after half of my first students rated me as one of the worst instructors of all time. At SRI, I learned how to teach, not merely lecture, and in the process fine-tuned most of the basic concepts to their present form. "Functional analysis" proved too difficult to learn and "transform analysis" emerged, first as a simpler alternative, later as the method of choice. One of my couple of hundred SRI students, Glen Myers, paid me the tribute of turning lecture notes from my course into an IBM Technical Memorandum and later submitted a piece to the *IBM Systems Journal* under the title "Composite Design." Still another former SRI student, Wayne Stevens, pulled me into the process. For yeoman service in editing and warding off open warfare, Wayne was awarded senior authorship of the piece that was to usher in "Structured Design," newly retitled by IBM for reasons we can only guess. At times it had seemed to me that the lack of such a trademark for what I was teaching may have been partly responsible for slow, early "sales."

There was, of course, much more to say than was embodied in that May 1974 article. While at SRI, I had begun to write a book, with the working title "Fundamentals of Program Design: A Structural Approach." By 1970, I thought I was about halfway through, with 150 manuscript pages. When I left the computer field in December 1972, I stored some 400 pages in my garage, but I was still about only half-finished!

Eight months later, I returned to teaching systems design in order to pay accumulated bills and to do something to stop being haunted by the dust-laden pile of manuscript notes. My coauthor, Ed Yourdon, not only sieved through these to extract the most essential pieces, but, from teaching the material himself, has added novel methods of explanation and crucial links to more widely known techniques and theories.

Thanks to Ed, and to Bob Brown who called me every month to ask when the book would be done, here it is. It is yours, to use, to build on, or to ignore. No more ghosts in the machine. I can now devote full time to the infinitely more important issues of people in families. *Ciao!*

LARRY L. CONSTANTINE
ACTON, MASSACHUSETTS

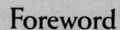

Foreword

In the past few years, the computer industry has been revolutionized by a number of new philosophies and techniques. One of the most popular of these techniques, *structured programming,* in some cases has led to order-of-magnitude improvements in the productivity, reliability, and maintenance costs associated with computer systems.

More recently, though, there has been a recognition that perfect structuring of GOTO-less code may be of little value if the basic *design* of the program or system is unsound. Indeed, there are a number of well-known case studies, including the now-famed IBM system for *The New York Times,* in which maintenance problems have persisted despite the use of top-down structured programming techniques. In virtually all of these cases, the problems were due to a misunderstanding of some fundamental *design* principles.

Concepts like "modular design" and "top-down design" have been circulating through the industry for more than a decade. Yet, if one watches what an average programmer actually *does* (as compared to what he *says* he does), it is apparent that the process of designing a program or system is still art, characterized by large doses of folklore (e.g., "Every program has to have an initialization module, right?"), black magic, and occasional flashes of intuition. To say that the average programmer's design process is organized, or *structured,* would be charitable.

This book is an attempt to provide elements of a discipline of program and systems design. We assume that the reader is familiar with the basic elements of computer hardware, though we rarely make reference to the particular features of specific systems. We further assume that the reader is familiar with the syntax of his programming language, though it does not matter greatly to us whether he programs in FORTRAN, COBOL, PL/I, or assembly language; we will comment on programming languages only insofar as they influence the *design* of a program. Finally, we assume that the reader knows how to code, and is capable of writing "good" code; we will not place much emphasis on structured programming, defensive programming, or the other "styles" of programming.

Our concern is with the architecture of programs and systems. How should a large system be broken into modules? *Which* modules? Which ones should be subordinate to which? How do we know when we have a "good" choice of modules? and, more important, How do we know when we have a "bad" one? What information should be passed between modules? Should a module be able to access data other than that which it needs to know in order to accomplish its task? How should the modules be "packaged" into efficient executable units in a typical computer?

Naturally, the answers to these questions are influenced by the specific details of hardware, operating system, and programming language — as well as the designer's interest in such things as efficiency, simplicity, maintainability, and reliability. The issues of program structure posed above are of a higher order than such detailed coding questions as, Should I use a GOTO here? or, How can I write a nested IF statement to accomplish this editing logic?

Quotation marks are used throughout this book to highlight words that often are thought of as having precise, well-defined technical interpretations. On closer examination, however, many of these terms — such as "modularity" — are often found to be technically undefined or used ambiguously. For example, two programmers may agree that good modular programming requires that each module perform a single service. Unfortunately, they probably will *not* agree on whether a subroutine which reads in a set of control cards but does not validate them is performing one service, several services, or only part of a service. Similarly, we might ask whether the suspension of processing on an end-of-file condition is a "low-level" decision or a "high-level" decision? Some programmers would argue that it is a high-level decision, because it results in "returning back to the operating system"; others would argue that it is a low-level decision, because it "has to do with the detail of reading a magnetic tape." We are left again with a matter open to debate.

The problem is not so much with the words themselves, but rather with the manner in which they are used and defined (or not defined). Indeed, a number of the terms in quotation marks above will be used later in this book but always with the following qualifications: They will be given precise, technical definitions before being used, or the context will clearly indicate that what is meant is the colloquial sense.

In general, terminology is a major problem and occupies a central position in this book. Except to our former students, much of the terminology will be new. There is so much that may be new that the book may appear to be simply a *tour de force* in vocabulary, an attempt to foist an entirely new set of buzzwords on a field already over-burdened with them.

We have, however, endeavored to minimize this burden by adhering to a set of consistent rules. With very few exceptions, a new term is never introduced unless *no* term for a specific concept or idea already exists. Whenever possible, equivalent or related terminology is borrowed from other technical disciplines where it already is established. A well-defined set of concepts usually is described by terms that are internally consistent and grammatically related (thus: coincidental, logical, temporal, communicational, sequential, and functional cohesion, as discussed in Chapter 7). Where common, general, informal words are given specific technical meanings, these are chosen to be consistent with and, if possible, intuitively suggested by the colloquial usage.

In some cases, new terms have been introduced where terms have already existed. This has been done where the new terms are more general, more consistent with other terms in a set, or where prior terminology was strongly associated with a specific language, manufacturer, or machine — with a consequent conflict between the general phenomenon and the highly specialized variant intended by a specific user community.

An example of this type of choice of terminology is the introduction of the term *conroutine* to mean a module activated by another module as a parallel (simultaneous) process. The prefix "con" means "with"; it leads to a consistent set with the older established terms *subroutine* and *coroutine;* it does not conflict with other usage in programming. The terms "parallel routine" or "asynchronous routine" are less desirable because they are both clumsier and inconsistent with the related terms. The term "task" is less desirable because it already has a specific, language-dependent, vendor-dependent definition (e.g., IBM's definition of a "task" in PL/I may not correspond to the use of the word on Hewlett-Packard, Burroughs, or Univac equipment), and because "task" is a word used informally in so many ways.

For the most part, we have avoided usurping such common words for narrow technical meanings. The specific variant will always be qualified (thus, "PL/I task" or "ALGOL procedure"). In no cases has a word with an almost universally accepted meaning been redefined. Thus, a subroutine is still a subroutine as we have all come to know it. Where other authors and computer scientists have provided terminology before us, we have used it if at all possible (thus, "coroutine" after Mel Conway's classic introduction of the term; and "incremental" module after Dove).

Some terminology is only a convenient shorthand. One can get very tired of talking about a "module that obtains its inputs from subordinates and returns its output to its superordinates, thus serving to bring inputs to the process as seen from the superordinate." The term "afferent module" is much shorter, and anyone with a good vocabulary probably could guess at its technical use here.

There are notable exceptions to the above rules, many our sole responsibility; we apologize in advance for such lapses. "Function" and "functional" are used with several distinct specific interpretations, as well as in both the mathematical sense and the broad colloquial sense, simply because no other words seem to work. Similarly, we apologize in advance for the unfortunate implications inherent in such phrases as "pathological connections" (which are not necessarily sick, as we will discuss in Chapter 13), and "logical cohesion" (which is not what it may seem at first glance). The term "pathological connection" has been used with its present meaning in some organizations since 1964, has appeared in more than a dozen published papers and books, and has been learned by nearly 5,000 innocent students — ample reason not to change it now.

In short, the vocabulary is essential; long teaching experience has shown us that the subject matter of this book *cannot* be presented without the building of a concomitant vocabulary.

All of this is reflected in the organization of the book. Section I consists of a number of introductory chapters that discuss certain fundamental concepts and philosophies, which must be understood before subsequent techniques are introduced. Section II lays the foundation for the structured design techniques: In addition to discussing program complexity from a "human information processing" point of view, it contains chapters on coupling and cohesion — two fundamental concepts in structured design. Section III can be considered the "guts" of the book: It discusses transform analysis, transform-centered design, transaction analysis, top-down design, and a number of heuristics commonly used by the program designer.

Section IV covers a number of the pragmatic issues in systems and program design; it contains chapters on intermodular communication problems, packaging, and optimization of modular systems. Section V discusses advanced topics such as homologous systems and incremental systems. Finally, Section VI discusses certain management and implementation issues, including the relationship between structured design and structured programming, as well as "top-down" versus "bottom-up" implementation strategies.

We envision a number of uses for this book, both in academia and in industry. In a university curriculum, this book could be the sole text for a course in program design, one of the texts in a course in software design or systems design, or auxiliary reading in an advanced programming course. If the material is treated in depth, it probably would comprise a second or third course, after the usual introductory programming courses. Many of the basic concepts can be — and have been — introduced into elementary programming courses in such languages as FORTRAN and COBOL. With complete candor, however, we would have to admit that this book does not fit well into most curricula as they are presently organized; in many settings, the questions answered by structural design have yet to be recognized as questions.

In industry, we expect the book to be read by experienced programmers and analysts — people who, unfortunately, already have well-established notions about the proper way to design. We have found that the most successful way of communicating the material to experienced people is through a lecture/workshop course in which programmers/analysts work on a *real* design problem. By selecting an appropriate problem, the instructor should be able to illustrate the advantages of the "structured" techniques over the "classical" techniques. Indeed, most of the material in this book has been influenced by attempts to communicate it to experienced analysts and programmers in several hundred seminars, lectures, and workshops conducted since 1964 throughout North America, Europe, Asia, and Australia.

The feedback from our students has been invaluable. During the years, they have hooted at our bad ideas, pointed out flaws in mediocre ones, and helped us refine and improve the really good ideas. Though we cannot list names, we acknowledge each one for helping us build the beginning of a "science" of design. Equally important, we acknowledge the help of many, our wives among them, who continued believing that there eventually would be a book during the years when the manuscript lay in Larry's garage and at the bottom of Ed's things-to-do list.   We acknowledge our colleagues in the field, whose friendly spirit of competition finally motivated us to put *our* ideas down on paper.   We credit our publishers with helping us avoid the normal two-year delay before a work appears on the booksellers' shelves.

Finally, we owe a very great debt to some of those who taught us.   Kenneth D. Mackenzie and David P. Jasper must be singled out for special thanks, for being superior programming craftsmen who were a decade ahead of their profession, for their professionalism in thinking about the elements of their craft when most others daily reinvented octagonal wheels, and for their patience in explaining it all a third and fourth time to a brash and impatient young man named Larry Constantine.

To the Massachusetts Institute of Technology, we both give credit for beginning it all with a course called "6.41" and liberal access to a PDP-1 with a low serial number.   There, we began to see the world as a system, a system whose behavior is coherent and understandable when viewed from an appropriate vantage point, a system explainable by rules and relationships.   The purpose of this book is to impart a few of the rules of rational behavior for computer programs as designed structures.

LARRY L. CONSTANTINE
EDWARD YOURDON

For most of the computer systems ever developed, the structure was not methodically laid out in advance — it just happened. The total collection of pieces and their interfaces with each other typically have not been planned systematically. *Structured design,* therefore, answers questions that have never even been raised in many data processing organizations. The chapters in this section serve to place the design of systems structure in the perspective of the total systems development process as conventionally practiced with traditional tools and orientations, and to establish the area of discourse for structured program design. Chapters 1 and 2 introduce the basic concept of structured design and locate it in the systems development cycle, relating questions of systems structure to technical and economic goals of systems development. Basic terminology used to describe building blocks and their interrelationships is defined in Chapter 3, and pictorial methods for presenting program and systems structures are developed. In Chapter 4, structure is contrasted with procedure, and the relationship of structure charts to conventional flowcharts is explored.

The lengthy introduction that this section provides is necessary to establish a rich graphic and verbal language for discussing program structures and to avoid confusion with older issues in programming.

I

CONCEPT

Toward
Program Engineering

When most programmers and analysts hear the phrase "structured design," a look of mild bewilderment comes over their faces. "Isn't that the same as 'top-down' design?" they ask. Or, "Does structured design allow us to talk to users more easily? Does it enable us to develop better functional specifications?" Or, considering the recent interest in other "structured" disciplines, they ask, "Isn't structured design just an extension of structured programming? Doesn't it just mean drawing HIPO diagrams?"

The answer to all these questions is no. Structured design is not equivalent to top-down design, though the two have some things in common. Structured design doesn't solve the dilemma of extracting funtional specifications from the user, though it suggests some techniques that have led to the development of a new discipline known as "structured analysis." And, finally, while structured design and structured programming complement one another, structured design is definitely *not* equivalent to drawing HIPO diagrams.

After saying so many things about what structured design is *not,* it obviously behooves us to discuss what structured design *is.* This chapter defines the

3

area of structured design, especially within the context of analysis, programming, and coding — the more familiar steps in the program development process. Having accomplished this, we give some answers to such questions as, What is structured design trying to accomplish? What are its objectives?

1.1 WHAT IS STRUCTURED DESIGN?

Anyone who has been in the data processing profession for more than six months has certainly seen (and probably experienced) the classic approach to systems development: The boss dashes in the door and shouts to the assembled staff, "Quick, quick! We've just been given the assignment to develop an on-line order entry system by next month! Charlie, you run upstairs and try to find out what they want the system to do — and, in the meantime, the rest of you people start coding or we'll never get finished on time!"

Of course, things are not quite so disorganized in the older, larger, more established EDP organizations. Many DP managers will tell you proudly that they have identified a "systems development life cycle" or a "program development process" in their organizations. Chances are that they have developed a seven-volume "cookbook" that will guide the programmer/analysts through the "life cycle" — complete with detailed standards for such things as file layouts, flowcharts, cost-benefit studies, and user sign-off and approval.

In simpler terms, we can think of the systems development life cycle as pictured in Fig. 1.1. We can imagine that it all begins with a user, who suddenly decides that he wants a new computerized system. (In the real world, we know that this is not always so: In many cases, the EDP department comes up with the idea for a new system and foists it upon the unwary user.) Having perceived a need or desire for a new system (or for a major enhancement of an old system), the user carries on a dialogue with a person typically known as a "systems analyst." The systems analyst, in turn, delivers a set of "functional requirements" to a "senior systems designer," who eventually delivers "program specifications" to a programmer. In the larger organizations, the programmer may ultimately deliver a stack of flowcharts to a "coder," who finally writes the COBOL or FORTRAN statements that make the system do what the user wants it to do.

It is instructive to look more closely at the activities we have just described. First, note that many of the terms in the paragraph above have been enclosed in quotation marks, e.g., systems analyst. This is because (a) terms like systems analyst mean something different in every organization, and (b) a person with the title systems analyst may be performing one job, two jobs, or several jobs. We are more concerned with the jobs, or *functional activities,* than we are with the people or their job titles.

Let's consider the systems analyst first. A clue to the real job performed by this person is that many organizations use the title "business systems analyst"; the function being performed, then, is "business systems analysis." The same points apply to the engineering systems analyst, the mathematics analyst, and so forth.

In plain terms, this person has the job of talking to the user and discovering his needs and wants — and then expressing them in sufficiently well-organized terms from which someone can develop an appropriate computer system. As we know from a plethora of textbooks on the subject, the job involves studying the user's current system (if there is one), interviewing hordes of clerks in the user department to find out how they are presently doing their jobs, and using techniques like decision tables to ensure that the user's statement of the problem is not incomplete, redundant, or contradictory.

The final product of the business systems analyst is, ideally, a set of functional requirements (otherwise known by such titles as "systems specifications" or "functional specifications") that describes, in precise terms, the inputs to be supplied by the user, the outputs desired by the user, and the algorithms involved in any computations desired by the user. In addition, the functional requirements generally will include a number of constraints: Examples might be, The XYZ report must be delivered to Mr. Smith's office by 8:00 every morning, or The mean response time to a Type X transaction must be less than two seconds, or The monthly cost of the computer system must be less than two seconds, or The monthly cost of the computer system must be less than $2,000 per month in order for it to be economical.

Ideally, the functional requirements should *not* specify such computer-oriented design decisions as:

- number of job steps, regions, partitions, or control points* involved in the implementation of the system

- record layouts, down to the last bit and byte, with a decision as to whether the file should be implemented with IMS, TOTAL, ADABAS, BDAM, or some other access technique

- number and type of intermediate files to be passed between programs

- programming language to be used in the implementation of the system

The primary reason for suggesting that such decisions should not be found in the functional requirements is that they have nothing to do with the *user's* conception of the application. Why should the user care whether the programs are implemented in COBOL or FORTRAN, as long as they produce the correct outputs within the specified constraints of time and money?

What we are saying, then, is that we do not want the systems analyst to *design*. This is somewhat unrealistic, of course, since many systems analysts were previously programmers or systems designers — and are thus making unconscious design decisions all during their discussions with the user. It is also unrealistic because the "feasibility study" or "cost-effectiveness" portion of systems analysis

---

* These are vendor-dependent terms, used to describe the smallest unit of work recognized by the vendor's operating system.

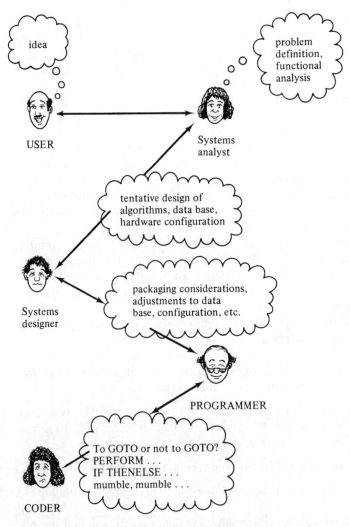

Fig. 1.1 Systems development process.

requires the analyst to make some preliminary decisions about the size, power, and *cost* of the computer equipment required to solve the user's problem.

Thus, we should expect the systems analyst to say, "Aha! It sounds like we'll need a 370/168 to handle that application," or "It sounds to me like the system will have to be on-line IMS system — a batch system just won't satisfy the user's needs." We emphasize, though, that such design decisions should be made as sparingly and as tentatively as possible (so they can be changed later on, if necessary).

We turn next to the "systems designer." It is interesting that some organizations refer to this person as a "computer systems analyst" to distinguish him from the business systems analyst whose role we discussed above. This is the person concerned with what we like to call the "structural design" of the program or system; that is, what are the appropriate subsystems, programs, or modules, and how are they interconnected? To put it another way, the systems designer accomplishes what some organizations call "general systems design": designing the major elements of the data base, the major components of the system, and the interfaces between them. Ideally, the final product of the systems designer is a document describing this structural design; in a later chapter, we will introduce the notion of *structure charts* as a convenient means of documenting the structural design of a program or a system.

Once this step has been accomplished, one would expect that the programmer would get precise specifications of individual "modules" (a term that we will define carefully in Chapter 2) — specifications that include information about inputs, outputs, interfaces with other parts of the system, and the algorithm by which the module is to do its job. Thus, the programmer might be given the task of writing a module to compute the logarithm of an argument found in general-purpose hardware register #1 with its output returned in general register #2. The programmer may not know why it is necessary for the system to include a logarithm subroutine (especially if it is a payroll system), or why it is necessary for the inputs and outputs to be passed through two general-purpose hardware registers (especially if the rest of the system is being programmed in COBOL) — but these are decisions that have already been made by the systems designer, and are presumably beyond the scope of the programmer's job.

Nevertheless, the programmer often finds himself performing some design on his own — or "logic design," as it is often called. In the above example of the logarithm subroutine, the programmer may still be required to determine the best algorithm for computing logarithms, within constraints such as memory and CPU time imposed upon him by the systems designer. He would presumably outline the logical steps through which one must go in order to compute a logarithm. In a small organization, he would then write the appropriate instructions and debug them; in a large organization, he might document his logic design in a flowchart, and turn the job over to a "coder" for final implementation.

Of course, this description of the "systems development life cycle" does not apply to all organizations. We find in some organizations that one person performs *all* of the tasks outlined above. In other organizations, *one* person performs the task that we called business systems analysis *as well as* the task that we called systems design. Alternatively, some organizations allow the programmer to perform the task of general systems design as well as the task of logic design — once the systems analyst has determined the user's needs. In still other organizations, there may be additional intermediate steps in the process, with accompanying personnel and accompanying job titles. Nevertheless, the cycle we have outlined seems a reasonably accurate, albeit slightly superficial, model of the development cycle in most EDP organizations.

The reason for going through this exercise is to identify that portion of the systems development life cycle that we wish to call "structured design." Recalling our earlier diagram of the life cycle, we can now illustrate the areas of "analysis," "design," and "programming"; these are shown in Fig. 1.2. Note that they overlap in the diagram, as in fact they do in the real world. As we pointed out earlier, the analyst find himself making unconscious design decisions; similarly, the systems designer finds himself making decisions that influence the way the user looks at the system — or the amount of money that the user will spend for his system. While the systems designer is not concerned with the details of coding, his decisions obviously influence the manner in which the programmers write their code — primarily because of the interface conventions imposed upon the programmer by the systems designer. Conversely, the programmer may feel that he is being unnecessarily constrained by the systems designer — and he, in turn, may influence some of the systems designer's decisions. Partly because of this, we will often use the phrase "programmer/analyst" when discussing activities that might be carried out by either a programmer or an analyst.

We can summarize this discussion with the following definitions:

Structured design *is the art of designing the components of a system and the interrelationship between those components in the best possible way.*

Alternatively, we can say:

Structured design *is the process of deciding which components interconnected in which way will solve some well-specified problem.*

By introducing a specific formal design activity to describe fully, and in advance, all the pieces of a system and their interrelationships, we have not created a new activity in the program development cycle. Structured design merely consolidates, formalizes, and makes visible design activities and decisions which happen inevitably — and invisibly — in the course of every systems development project. Instead of occurring by guesswork, luck, and default, these decisions can be approached deliberately as technical trade-offs.

By pulling together all of the decisions affecting the choice of modules and interrelationships in a system, we necessarily affect the way in which other decisions are organized and resolved. Thus, some issues which have traditionally been approached in a certain way during the earliest phase of a project may have to be dealt with in an entirely different manner at a much later stage once the designer graduates to a structured design approach.

1.2 OBJECTIVES OF STRUCTURED DESIGN

"Design" means to plan or mark out the form and method of a solution. It is the process which determines the major characteristics of the final system,

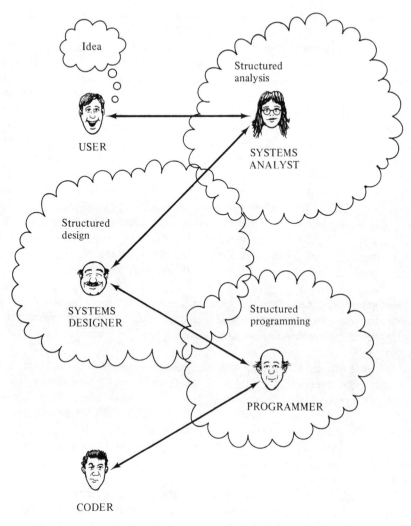

Fig. 1.2 Realm of structured design.

establishes the upper bounds in performance and quality that the best implementation can achieve, and may even determine what the final cost will be. As we suggested in the previous section, design is usually characterized by a large number of individual technical decisions. If we are to make progress toward developing programming into more of an engineering discipline, then we must progressively systematize those decisions, make them more explicit and technical, and less implicit and artful.

All of engineering is characterized by the engineer's dissatisfaction with the achievement of just *a* solution. Engineering seeks the *best* solution in established terms, within recognized limitations, while making compromises required by working in the real world.

In order to make computer systems design an engineering discipline, we need, first of all, to define clear technical objectives for computer programs as "systems." Overall systems goals ultimately determine the criteria by which individual design decisions are made. An understanding of the primary constraints limiting admissible solutions is also essential. To make conscious, deliberate decisions, we must also know that the decision points exist, so that we can recognize them when we encounter them. Finally, we need some methodology or technique which assists us in making decisions that increase objective goals while satisfying design constraints. Given these things — objective goals and constraints, recognized decisions, and effective design methodology — we have some hope of engineering program solutions rather than snatching them out of the air.

Computer programs are just systems, analogous or even equivalent to "hard" systems. Naturally, we would expect to find similar objectives, similar criteria defining quality as in other systems. Unfortunately, most designers are at a stage where if a system appears to work (that is, if it passes a modest acceptance test and does so within tolerable time limits), it is a "good" program. Indeed, many designers today behave as if *a* solution, any solution, were *the* solution. When someone suggests that the programmer/analyst return to the drawing boards to improve the design or develop an alternative design, the reaction often borders on paranoia.

Where quality *is* an explicitly recognized concept, two variations prevail. One is that good programming is what appears to be tricky or non-obvious to another programmer. Thus, the comment, "Wow! I never would have figured out what the loop does," is to be interpreted as an accolade. Although other engineering fields suffer from some of this "cleverness" syndrome, nowhere is it as rampant as in the data processing field. Even if obscurity had no detrimental consequences in terms of external characteristics, its irrelevance to those goals would make it suspect.

The other school of thought associates quality with increased execution speed or decreased memory requirements. These are but superficial aspects of a broad design goal: *efficiency*. In general, we want systems and programs that are efficient — i.e., which make efficient use of scarce system resources. These resources include not only the central processor and primary memory, but also secondary and tertiary storage, input-output peripheral time, teleprocessing line time, on-line personnel time, and more. The narrower view of efficiency is a holdover from the days when the cost of the central processor so overshadowed other costs that any reduction was all but certain to represent an overall savings. Of course, it is *not* a savings to cut weekly run-time by one minute of $600/hour computer time if this adds two hours of $6/hour people time. The system-wide measure of technical objectives is implied throughout this book, and this is nowhere more critical than in the area of efficiency.

One of the reasons why the systems view of efficiency is so important is that the ratio of hardware costs to software costs has been shifting for the past decade, and will continue to shift dramatically for some years to come. In 1971, the United States Air Force estimated that by 1980 only 20 percent of its data processing budget would be spent on hardware — the remaining 80 percent would be spent on the "people costs" of developing and operating the systems.[1] Similarly, a study within General Motors[2] found that by 1970, hardware costs accounted for only 50 percent of the total data processing budget — and the ratio is expected to drop for the foreseeable future.

Reliability is another measure of quality. This is an almost universal criterion for hard systems, but the special nature of failures in software has obscured the importance of developing reliable programs. Mean-time-between-failures (MTBF) can be translated into software terms in a number of ways, the most obvious of which is mean-cycles-between-faulty-data (this approach was taken by Dickson et al[3] in an attempt to derive a mathematical model of software reliability for a large air defense system, and has also been used to analyze the reliability of portions of the software for Apollo Manned Spacecraft missions).

It is essential to see that, while software reliability may be viewed as a debugging problem, it may also — perhaps more productively — be viewed as a problem in design. This view has been growing in popularity in such forums as the 1975 International Conference on Reliable Software,[4] but there is much work to be done before it reaches the level of the average designer in a scientific/commercial environment (as opposed to the military/aerospace environment, where the need for "certifiably reliable" systems is acute).

Closely related to reliability in its effect on system usefulness is *maintainability*. In fact, if we express reliability as MTBF and maintainability as the mean-time-to-repairs (MTTR), then we can define "systems availability" quite simply as:

$$Systems\ availability = \frac{MTBF}{MTBF + MTTR}$$

Again, as with reliability, maintainability seems to mean something different in software than in hardware. We do not repair or replace worn-out instructions, but we do remove and correct residual bugs in the system. A system is maintainable to the extent that it makes the discovery, analysis, redesign, and correction of lurking bugs easier.

This is a very high priority design goal for several reasons. We know that a system will have, throughout its lifespan, a number (generally quite a large number) of residual bugs. While the number of such extant bugs is expected to diminish with time (although that is not *necessarily* so), the difficulty of correct analysis, redesign, and correction has been seen to increase due to a variety of effects. Thus, there is a constant trickle of effort which over the entire lifespan of the system adds up to a substantial cost. The budget of the maintenance department and the steady stream of error and correction notices for systems software attest to this as a significant, although often ignored, systems cost.

Indeed, only recently has the EDP industry been able to attach hard numbers to such phenomena as residual bugs, complexity of fixing bugs, and the cost and difficulty of maintenance. In a classic conference of software engineering, IBM employee M.E. Hopkins remarked that studies have shown every release of IBM's OS/360 contains 1,000 bugs;[5] similar studies have shown that IBM is by no means unique in its propensity for bug-ridden software.[6] Most of the studies concerning vendor-supplied software show the "steady-state" behavior, *after* the majority of initial bugs have been exorcised from the system; the study by Dickson et al[3] suggests the initial experience with most systems is one of increasing bugs, until gradually programmers begin fixing bugs faster than users find new bugs.

This can be illustrated in the "bug detection" graph shown in Fig. 1.3. In the case of the military system studied by Dickson et al, the curve peaked at approximately 900 bugs per month, each of which required modification of an average of 17 instructions in order to fix the bug!

Finally, we note that the programmer's chances of fixing a bug correctly on the first attempt are not very good; according to a study by Boehm,[7] the programmer has a maximum probability of success of about 50 percent if he modifies 5-10 statements in his program, and the odds drop to about 20 percent if he modifies 40-50 statements.

Maintainability affects the viability of the system in a (relatively) constant environment; *modifiability* influences the cost of keeping the system viable in the face of changing requirements. In some areas, both are increased or decreased by the same kind of design and implementation practices; in others, modifiability must be an explicit design goal in itself.

In most contexts, we want a system to perform a variety of tasks without having to undergo any modification, i.e., without having to actually change any of the existing programs. *Flexibility* represents the ease of getting a given system to perform variations on the same theme; *generality* expresses something of the scope or range of the theme. Generality and flexibility have received much more attention than any other design goals except efficiency. However, they are often viewed as appropriate goals only for certain systems, so-called general-purpose

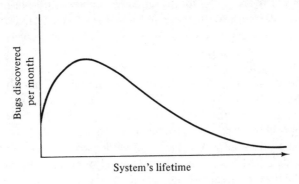

Fig. 1.3   Bug detection rate per unit time.

systems, not as goals applicable to *any* system.   In part, this selective focus stems from myths about the cost of generality and flexibility, and their relationship to efficiency.

Again, the areas of modifiability, generality, and flexibility only lately have been associated with hard figures.   A 1972 survey[8] indicated that the average EDP organization spends approximately 50 percent of its data processing budget on maintenance — which most organizations define as the combination of maintenance (i.e., ongoing debugging) and modification; in some organizations, the figure has been as high as 95 percent.   Indeed, one large organization privately told the authors that they had spent $112 million in programmer salaries during 1974, 75 percent of which was devoted to maintenance and modification of existing programs!

The final test of any system is in the marketplace, which may only mean its actual use (or nonuse) by the ultimate customer.   *Utility* or ease of use is one way to express a key criterion which receives much attention in early analysis, and somehow gets lost in the shuffle of actual design and implementation.   Part of the problem lies with a general lack of understanding of human factors, part with delegation of design responsibility in inappropriate ways.   Internal programming details frequently end up being determining factors for significant features of the user interface (how many computer systems, even today, for example, limit some input fields to eight characters simply because it corresponded to a convenient double-word boundry within the computer?).   Indeed, decisions having a profound impact on systems utility may be made, ad hoc, by a junior programmer.

In short, our overall technical objective function is made up of varying amounts of (emphasis on) efficiency, maintainability, modifiability, generality, flexibility, and utility.   Another way of putting it is that these are components of *objective* program quality.   For them to be usable in an engineering sense by the designer, we will have to develop some objective measure or characterization of each and to show just how each is influenced by various isolated design decisions and overall design practices.   Discussion of the bulk of this task will be deferred until Section VI.

In simple terms, it often is sufficient to state that our primary objective is "minimum-cost" systems.   That is, we are interested in systems that are cheap to develop, cheap to operate, cheap to maintain, and cheap to modify.   The relative priorities placed on development costs, operating costs, maintenance costs, and modification costs will vary from organization to organization, from user to user, and from project to project.   In addition, the priorities will continue to change as evolving technology changes the ratio of hardware costs to software costs.

1.3 DESIGN CONSTRAINTS, TRADE-OFFS, AND DECISIONS

We might view technical design objectives as constituting an objective function, as in an optimization problem — an objective function we want to maximize, subject to certain constraints. As a rule, constraints on the systems design process fall into two categories. Development constraints are limitations on re-source consumption during development, and might be stated in terms of overall cost or in specific components, such as machine time and man-hours. Schedule limitations ("You've gotta be finished by the first of the month.") are also in this category. Computer systems rarely go into mass production in the same sense that hard systems usually do, but analogous to the costs of manufacturing hard systems are the costs of using software systems. Other operational constraints might be ex-pressed in technical terms, such as maximum memory size or maximum response time for an on-line system.

The character of many design constraints is that they are not set limits, but "soft boundaries," which are stretched at varying cost or consequences. Indeed, in the final analysis, objectives and constraints blur. A real-time system may have some fixed upper boundaries on admissible response times and others that merely affect user frustration. This might be translated into a high premium on efficiency, so that the critical response times can be met and the users not left too unhappy.

The very essence of design in the real world and the best characterization of design decisions is *trade-off*. We rarely can have our cake and eat it, too. As we increase one parameter, we almost always decrease another. If we opt for more efficiency, we frequently sacrifice ease of maintenance. Similarly, execution speed can usually be gained at the expense of memory storage or secondary storage. It is the designer's job to be aware of what he is trading off and to select that balance which best reflects his overall goals. Ultimately, the goal is economic, as we have already pointed out — that is, lowest possible net discounted value of all future resource consumption or maximum net present value of future profits. Un-fortunately, the designer almost never has either the tools or the information neces-sary to evaluate this kind of global goal. Moreover, such total economic impact, while it should be an ever-present consideration, is too cumbersome to be applied to each incremental technical decision. It is for this reason that we identify more immediate technical objectives that have some approximate and predictable effect on total economics.

A total design is the cumulative result of a large number of incremental technical design decisions. Though some of these are clearly global, such as random versus sequential file organization, most will be small and isolated (e.g., "Does the end-of-file test go here or there?"). To be able to engineer computer systems, we need to know just how various technical design goals are influenced by the alternatives in the incremental decisions, ideally without having to go through an extensive analysis for each decision. In short, we need a general understanding of which kinds of design decisions influence which design goals, on a case-by-case basis.

Unfortunately, certain trade-offs have been perpetuated in mythological form, relating one design goal to another as if they were locked in a certain rela-tionship when, in fact, the relationship is complex and has many "balancing points" that can be exploited. Examples of these myths are:

- Increasing generality increases development cost.

- Increasing generality decreases efficiency.

- More flexible interfaces are harder to use.

We will not be satisfied with such very general and inaccurate statements.

1.4 SUMMARY

In this chapter, we have attempted to demonstrate that there are a number of important roles in the systems development process — primarily, business systems analysis (understanding the problem), computer systems design (designing the major architecture of a solution to the problem), and programming (putting the design into code). We have concentrated (and will continue to concentrate for the remainder of this book) on the role of design, because we feel it is a critical area that, in many organizations, has been ignored, or delegated to the wrong person (e.g., the junior programmer), or performed by someone incompetent to do the job (e.g., a senior systems analyst whose last *real* experience was with an IBM 650). We have emphasized that it is not sufficient to find just *one* design for a computer system; what we want is the *best* design, given appropriate information about the technical objectives and constraints for the system.

Even more, we want an organized methodology — a "cookbook" — that will help us develop "good" designs and discard "bad" designs as easily as possible. That, in a nutshell, is what "structured design" is all about: a collection of guidelines for distinguishing between good designs and bad designs, and a collection of techniques, strategies, and heuristics that generally leads to good designs — good in the sense of satisfying the common technical objectives and constraints found in commercial and scientific environments.

In the next chapter, we will examine some of the fundamental philosophies and concepts that form the basis of structured design. If it seems that we are placing extraordinary emphasis on philosophies and concepts, have patience: It is critically important if the subsequent chapters on techniques are to make sense. Indeed, we suggest that when you finish Chapter 21, you return to reread the first two chapters!

REFERENCES

1. BARRY BOEHM, "Some Information Processing Implications of Air Force Space Missions in the 1980's," *Astronautics and Aeronautics,* January 1971, pp. 42–50.

2. DR. JAMES ELSHOFF, General Motors Research Center, Warren, Mich. Private communication, April 1975.

3. J.C. DICKSON, J.L. HESSE, A.C. KIENTZ, and M.L. SHOOMAN, "Quantitative Analysis of Software Reliability," *Proceedings of the 1972 Annual Reliability and Maintain-*

ability Symposium, Institute of Electrical and Electronics Engineers, IEEE Cat. No. 72CH0577-7R. New York: 1972, pp. 148–157.

4. *Proceedings of the 1975 International Conference on Reliable Software, ACM SIG-PLAN Notices,* Vol. 10, No. 6 (June 1975).

5. J.N. BUXTON and B. RANDALL, eds., *Software Engineering Techniques,* NATO Scientific Affairs Division, Brussels 39, Belgium: April 1970, p. 20.

6. EDWARD YOURDON, "Reliability Measurements for Third Generation Computer Systems," *Proceedings of the 1972 Annual Reliability and Maintainability Symposium,* Institute of Electrical and Electronics Engineers, IEEE Cat. No. 72CH0577-7R. New York: 1972, pp. 174–183.

7. BARRY BOEHM, "Software and Its Impact: A Quantitative Study," *Datamation,* Vol. 19, No. 5 (May 1973), pp. 48–59.

8. "That Maintenance Iceberg," *EDP Analyzer,* Vol. 10, No. 10 (October 1972).

Basic Concepts
of
Structured Design

CHAPTER 2

In the previous chapter, we saw that design is an activity that begins when the systems analyst has produced a set of functional requirements for a program or system, and ends when the designer has specified the components of the system and the interrelationship between the components. We also saw that it is insufficient, in most cases, for the designer to consider *a* solution, *a* design. He should evaluate several alternative designs and choose the *best* — best in the sense of maximizing such technical objectives as efficiency, reliability, and maintainability while satisfying such design constraints as memory size and response time.

In this chapter, we begin to explore the philosophies and principles of structured design — primarily to see how we can achieve such objectives as reliability, maintainability, and low-cost implementation of systems. We also discuss some general design principles that seem applicable to computer systems as well as to a number of other hard systems.

2.1 HOW DO WE ACHIEVE MINIMUM-
COST SYSTEMS?

When we are dealing with a simple design problem — say, a computer system that can be designed, coded, and tested in less than a week — most of us have little trouble keeping all elements of the problem in our heads at one time. On the other hand, when we are dealing with a complex design problem — say, a real-time management information system that ultimately will involve more than 100,000 lines of code — then it is difficult to believe that anyone would be capable of keeping the entire problem, and its solution, in his head at one time. Successful design is based on a principle known since the days of Julius Caesar: Divide and conquer.

Specifically, we suggest that the cost of *implementing* a computer system will be minimized when the parts of the problem are

- manageably small

- solvable separately

Of course, everyone has a different definition of "manageably small": Some would say that anything that takes more than a week to design, code, and test is too large; most would agree that a problem requiring more than a month to design, code, and test probably should be broken into smaller pieces; certainly everyone would agree that a problem requiring more than a year to implement is too big.

Of course, many designers have made attempts to "chop" a system into manageably small pieces; unfortunately, they have often found that implementation time increased rather than decreased. The key frequently lies in the second part of our stipulation above: The parts of the original problem must be solvable separately. In many computer systems, we find that this is not so: In order to implement part A of the solution to the problem, we have to know something about part B . . . and in order to solve part B, we have to know something about part C.

It is precisely because of this last point that we must eventually halt our attempts to make pieces of the system manageably small. It seems reasonable that a problem requiring one year to implement could be broken into, say, a dozen smaller problems requiring a month each to implement; with the techniques discussed later in this book, we can even be reasonably certain that the one-month pieces are solvable separately. We might then decide to break each of the one-month pieces into four separate one-week pieces. With some extra work, we could break the one-week pieces into separate one-day pieces, and so forth. The problem is that we would eventually reach a point where the microscopic pieces of the system would no longer be solvable separately — that is, the design of microscopic piece A would eventually depend on understanding microscopic piece B. We will have more to say about this in Chapter 5.

In a similar fashion, we can argue that the cost of *maintenance* is minimized when parts of the system are

- easily related to the application

- manageably small

- correctable separately

We recall that maintenance was defined in the previous chapter as ongoing debugging, and we observe that, in many organizations, this thankless task is performed by someone other than the person who designed and coded the system. Thus, when the user calls on the telephone to complain that the third line of the XYZ report is wrong, it may not immediately be clear which part of the system is responsible for producing the third line of the XYZ report. Indeed, it may turn out that *several* obscure parts of the system are involved in producing the third line of the XYZ report. The larger the system, and the more subtle the bugs, the more critical it is that maintenance personnel be able to relate parts of the system to parts of the user's application.

Of course, it is still important that parts of the system be manageably small in order to simplify maintenance. Attempting to find and fix a bug in a 1,000-statement "piece" of a system involves unraveling and modifying a large portion of it; finding and fixing a bug in a 20-statement module are reasonably simple because (a) we should be able to sight-read all 20 statements in a minute or two and comprehend their combined effect, or (b) in the worst case, all we have to do is throw the module away and write a new version. The latter philosophy, nicknamed "disposable modules," was formally employed in a recent Royal Australian Air Force project with great success. Unless the bug could be found in a matter of minutes, the programmer was required to throw the module into the wastebasket and write a new one to accomplish the same job.

Regardless of whether we decide to throw away a piece of the system every time we find a bug, and regardless of how small that piece is, we cannot hope to minimize maintenance costs unless we can ensure that each piece of the system is independent of other pieces. In other words, we must be able to make a correction to piece A of the system without introducing any unanticipated side effects in piece B — and, of course, that is precisely the problem that plagues many maintenance programmers! If we ask the average maintenance programmer, "What makes your job difficult" we are likely to hear answers such as:

- Whenever I get that midnight phone call telling me about a bug in the program, it takes forever to find it. The bug always turns out to be somewhere other than where I expected it.

- Once I find out where the bug is, it takes a long time to figure out how to correct it. This is usually because the code is so tricky and complicated that (a) I can't figure out what it does, except that I know it's wrong, and (b) I can't figure out how to change it to make it right.

- When I correct the bug, I always make some dumb little mistakes — you know, a keypunch error or something like that. It always seems like I have to fix the bug twice before I finally get it right.

- When I fix one bug, it always introduces a new bug in some other part of the system — and it's always in some part of the system that I don't know anything about.

It is this last problem we are concerned about, because it is so insidious. It may be a day, or a week, or a month before we discover that the simple little bug that we fixed has introduced a new bug that resulted in the printing of 100,000 incorrect paychecks.

Finally, we suggest that the cost of *modification* of a system will be minimized when its parts are

- easily related to the problem
- modifiable separately

We recall from the previous chapter that modification involves enhancing existing features of a system, or adding new features — generally at the request of a user who is concerned with the external characteristics of the system rather than its internal subroutines.

Thus, when the user comes to us and says, "I'd really appreciate it if you would change the system to print year-to-date sales totals as well as sales totals for the current month," our first job is to find out which part(s) of the system is involved in the calculation, accumulation, and printing of sales totals. Once again, we point out that this unpleasant job usually is done by someone other than the person who designed and implemented the original system — so it may not be easy. Of course, our earlier comments about independence still hold true: We want to be able to modify one part of a system without introducing any unanticipated side effects in other pieces of the system.

In summary, then, we can state the following philosophy: Implementation, maintenance, and modification generally will be minimized when *each piece of the system corresponds to exactly one small, well-defined piece of the problem, and each relationship between a system's pieces corresponds only to a relationship between pieces of the problem.*

This is illustrated in Fig. 2.1, in which we have represented the problem (application) as a formless amoeba, containing (as is usually true in the real world) subproblems, which contain sub-subproblems (and in that amoeba-like real world, etc., etc.). Thus, if there is a piece of the application naturally known as A, then there should be a piece of the system which implements the A function. Similarly, if there is a natural relationship between part A of the problem and part D of the problem, there should be a similar relationship between part A of the system and part D of the solution — and no other extraneous relationships.

When viewed in this graphic fashion, the problems of the maintenance programmer are even more evident. When a bug in part A of the problem is brought to his attention, it is not immediately clear which part of the system is responsible for dealing with that part of the problem. And when he does finally locate part A of the system (assuming that there is such a well-defined part!), he may not have anticipated the relationship between piece A of the system and piece C of the system (i.e., a relationship of the type that modification to piece A will necessitate a modification to piece C), because there was no such relationship between piece A of the problem and piece C of the problem.

2.2 HOW DOES STRUCTURED DESIGN
LEAD TO MINIMUM-COST SYSTEMS?

In the previous section, we suggested that implementation, maintenance, and modification would be minimized if the system could be designed in such a way that its pieces were small, easily related to the application, and relatively independent of one another. This means, then, that good design is an exercise in *partitioning* and *organizing* the pieces of a system.

By partitioning we mean the division of the problem into smaller subproblems, so that each subproblem will eventually correspond to a piece of the system. The questions are: Where and how should we divide the problem? Which aspects of the problem belong in the same part of the system, and which aspects belong in different parts? Structured design answers these questions with two basic principles:

- Highly interrelated parts of the problem should be in the same piece of the system, i.e., things that belong together should go together.

- Unrelated parts of the problem should reside in unrelated pieces of the system. That is, things that have nothing to do with one another don't belong together.

We discuss the details necessary to achieve this philosophy in Chapters 6 and 7.

The other major aspect of structured design is organization of the system. That is, we must decide how to interrelate the parts of the system, and we must decide which parts belong where in relation to each other. Our objective is to organize the system so that no piece is larger than is necessary to solve the aspects of the problem it includes. Equally important, structured design involves organizing the system so that we do not introduce interconnections that are not part of the interrelationships in the problem.

2.3 THE CONCEPT OF BLACK BOXES

The concept of a black box is a very powerful one, both in engineering and in software design. A black box is a system (or equivalently, a component) with known inputs, known outputs, and, generally, a known transform, but with unknown (or irrelevant) contents. The box is black — we cannot see inside it.

Black boxes have numerous interesting properties, the most important of which is that we can use them. A true black box is a system which can be fully exploited without knowledge of what is inside it. Many of the hard systems we encounter in everyday life are essentially black boxes to their users. To the average driver, an automobile is a virtual black box, transforming fuel, directional, accelerative, and decelerative inputs into motion at the desired speed in the desired direction. Radios, televisions, adding machines, stereos, and a myriad of other common systems are usable as and function well as black boxes. This is fortunate, for if we needed to know the involved electromagnetic, mechanical, hydraulic, and other techniques employed in these systems in order to make use of them, we would be greatly inconvenienced, if not paralyzed, in modern society.

An experienced designer needs only mentally to review his own experience with the programs and modules developed by others to realize that most computer systems only approximate, at best, true black-box behavior. Very often we find that we cannot use or make full use of a subroutine without going inside it and examining its contents. Perhaps it behaves "funny" under some circumstances — e.g., returning a zero for certain values of input, when the results are still fully defined. Possibly there are certain temporary storage areas within the subroutine which must be re-initialized in a special way for each success pass of the file. Or it may be a subroutine that determines whether a character is a "punctuation" character — but when it finds certain illegal punctuation, such as a quotation mark in the middle of a word, it deletes it as well. These may all be characteristics that must be discovered through examination of the code within the module.

Good documentation itself does not make a module a black box. To describe the quirks of some coding trick that result in a loss of precision when the previous result was zero, or to list the 24 cells of temporary storage that may be modified upon reentry to a subroutine in order to alleviate some problem, does not make our "glitchy" subroutine a black box. Indeed, since its contents are now exposed through the documentation, we may properly call it a "white box." A white box is preferable to a mysterious and ill-behaved "kludge," but it is hardly as good as a true black box.

It should be clear that actual computer program modules may vary in the degree to which they approximate ideal black boxes. That is, there are "gray boxes" of varying degrees of black-boxishness; we have not a dichotomy, but rather a continuum, a technical dimension along which modular systems may be distributed.

Program black-box characteristics may be divided into two areas: one static, the other dynamic. A program is more of a black box to the extent that its behavior can be characterized in terms of a set of immediate inputs, a set of im-

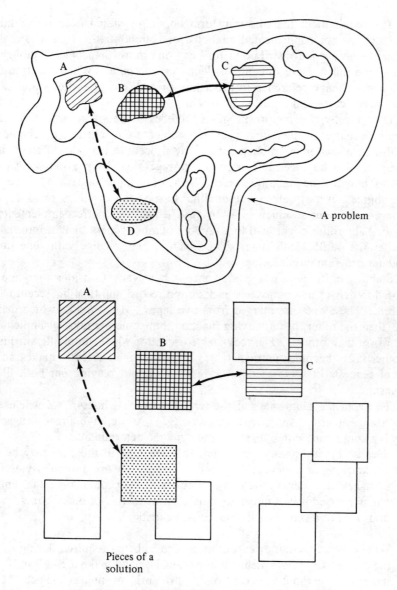

Fig. 2.1   Pieces of a problem and pieces of a solution.

mediate outputs, and a simply stated relationship between the two. Black-box be-havior in program modules is associated with the ability, for each use of the module, to completely specify the sources (i.e., values) and targets for all inputs and outputs and to do this in a simple and consistent manner. Operationally, this is equivalent to saying that the data context of the module is uniquely determinable by the using module for each activation of the module being used.

The requirement that the transform be simply stated need not eliminate difficult functions nor sophisticated methods for computation. It is as simple to state "cumulative normal distribution for" as "one more than twice," though the former may be much more difficult to define or compute. When the transform description must make reference to procedure or code, to side effects and exceptions and special cases, our criterion is missed.

Dynamically, we require program modules to be stable and dependable. This may be a matter of reliability, a separate subject to be taken up in Chapter 19. It may also be a matter of stubbornness. The procedure may do different things depending on what has been left in certain storage areas by previous activations. It may work only for the first 1,023 cases. Some of its input values may come from a remote source. It may deliver output either to specified variables, or to a special exception area without so much as a "by your leave." A perfect implementation of the wrong algorithm might lead to a random number generator that returns only zeroes after the 4,005,236th time. The function may change with time due to intermodular program modification.

Stability of function is a subtle concept, however. Consider a module that is supposed to deliver an employee's background record and then his recent education record. These data are merged from two tapes. *Any* module which delivers first one, then the other, has a varying function, but some methods of implementation are worse than others. The rock-stable oscillator which simply flips from one to the other fails (becomes unpredictable) if its user inadvertently makes an odd number of requests in some section, or restarts without playing out both files in synchronism.

To avoid the clumsiness of the term "black-boxishness," we will use the phrases "static integrity" and "dynamic integrity." As we have already suggested, integrity is a continuum with both static and dynamic determinants.

Because black boxes, or modules, that are high in integrity may be used without our knowing or understanding their contents, they are particularly useful in the design stages of systems development, either as conceptual or actual entities. How they may be used is best understood in terms of a "rule of black boxes," which may be thought of as a general-purpose design heuristic:

> Whenever a function or capability is seen as being required during the design of a system, define it as a black box and make use of it in the system without concern for its structural or methodological realization.

Eventually, of course, each such invoked black box must in turn be designed, a process which may give rise to more black boxes and so on. Finally, the procedure and structure of all will be determined, but in no case earlier than necessary. This increases the likelihood that the information necessary to optimally design any component will be available. It also keeps the designer working on related issues without being sidetracked into consideration of unnecessary details.

While the rule of black boxes is a useful concept and guideline, it is not sufficient unto itself to enable the development of highly maintainable, highly modifiable, minimum-cost systems. In subsequent chapters, we shall see that imbedding such concepts in a formal strategy is the secret.

2.4 MANAGEMENT PARALLELS WITH STRUCTURED DESIGN

One of the fascinating aspects of program design is its relationship with human organizational structures — particularly, the management hierarchy found in most large corporations. Whenever we wish to illustrate a particular point about program design (as we will be doing in subsequent chapters), we often can do so by drawing analogies with a management situation.

Suppose, for example, that you were a management consultant and that you had just been hired to find out why the Fribble Company is not operating efficiently. The company's organizational chart is shown in Fig. 2.2, and a quick glance shows that the president of the organization can look forward to a heart attack or an ulcer in the near future; at the very least, we can expect that his day-to-day work will be error-prone and inefficient. Why? Simply because the president has too many immediate subordinates. Consequently, his job involves too many decisions, too much data, too much complexity — all of which can only lead to mistakes.

The point is this: If we can make such comments about a management structure, why can't we make similar comments about a program structure? If we see that a designer has organized the pieces of a system in such a way that a "control" module has 139 immediate subordinate modules, then we should suspect that the control module is too complex — a phenomenon that will probably lead to bugs in the initial implementation, and will certainly lead to problems during subsequent maintenance and modification.

Similarly, what would we expect a management consultant to say about the management structure shown in Fig. 2.3? The obvious suspicion is that the duties of managers A, X, Y, and Z are relatively trivial and could be compressed into a single manager's job. Again, if we can make such statements about management structures, why can't we do the same for program structures? That is, if we saw a program in which a high-level control module had the sole task of calling one subordinate, which in turn did nothing but call one immediate subordinate, whose only activity was to call one low-level subroutine that finally accomplished some work — if we saw such a program organization, wouldn't we be inclined to think that two or three levels of "manager" modules were trivial and superfluous?

In a similar vein, it is often said (sometimes cynically) that in a perfect organization, no manager ever does anything. That is, all of the work is performed by the lowest-level subordinates. The managers coordinate information between the subordinates, make decisions, and do whatever else would naturally fall under the heading of management. By analogy, it is often argued that the high-level

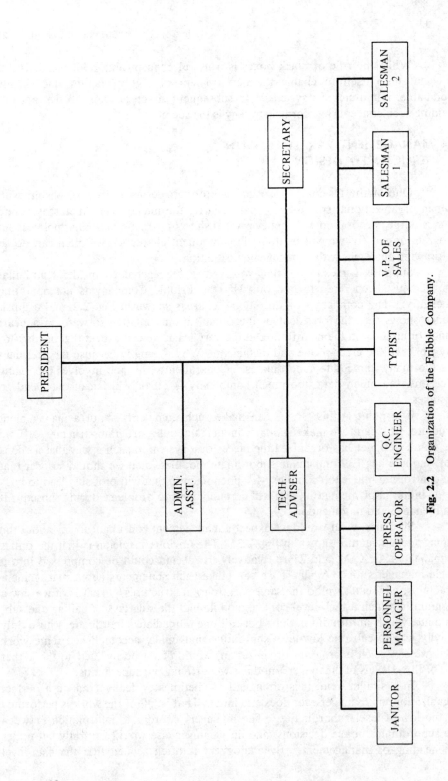

Fig. 2.2 Organization of the Fribble Company.

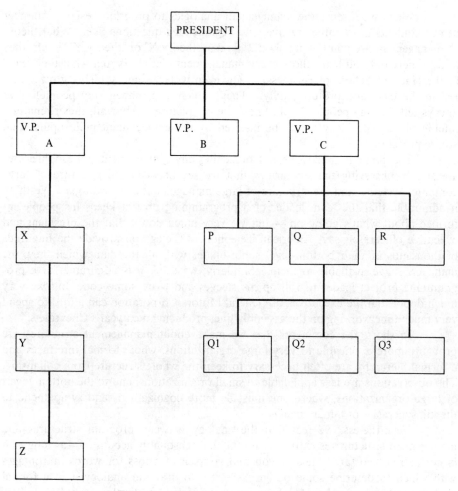

Fig. 2.3 Alternative management structure.

modules in a program or system should merely coordinate and control the execution of the low-level modules that actually perform the computations or other work required of the system.

Finally, we observe that in some organizations, the manager gives only as much information to a subordinate as the subordinate requires in order to perform his job; the subordinate is *not* allowed to see the big picture. This is seen most dramatically in military organizations, where information is provided to subordinates strictly on a need-to-know basis. The philosophy is somewhat more subtle, but equally prevalent, in large commercial and industrial organizations. The analogy in program design is obvious: A subroutine, or module, should only be allowed to access that data which it needs to perform its assigned task. We will deal with this philosophy extensively in Chapter 13.

When we discuss the management analogies to program design, a number of our students grow rather restive, and begin asking questions like, "What theory of management are you talking about? Is that 'theory X' or 'theory Y'?" Or, they ask, "Where did you learn those crazy management ideas? Is that what they teach at the Harvard School of Business?" Or, even worse, some students grow rather red in the face, and protest loudly, "That's not how I manage *my* people! I've always felt that my people should know the big picture. After all, they're mature, intelligent adults! They would be insulted by the management philosophies that you're preaching!"

The point is that we're not preaching any management philosophies; we are simply observing the similarities that we see between the structure of large computer systems, and the structure of large management organizations. We think it admirable that the team leader of a programming project keeps his people informed about what's going on — but we very much doubt that the president and executive officers of, say, American Telephone & Telegraph provide the hundreds of thousands of their bottom-level subordinates with all the data which they, the managers, have available to them. Similarly, we think it is admirable for a programming project leader to roll up his sleeves and write some code, but we very much doubt that the executives of General Motors Corporation can afford to spend very much time working on the assembly line, producing next year's Chevrolets.

In short, the comments that we make about management structures are probably more applicable to very large organizations, where formal interfaces and a formal hierarchy are often necessary to keep the whole structure from collapsing. The observations are less applicable to small organizations, and to the bottom levels of large organizations, where one must be more cognizant of and sympathetic to the idiosyncrasies of human beings.

Nevertheless, we feel that the analogy between program structures and management structures is extremely useful, and reasonably accurate — as long as it is not carried too far. Thus, if you find yourself at a loss for words and images with which to describe some design issue, try to draw an analogy with a formal management organization (perhaps one staffed by emotionless robots!). That should help you decide whether or not your design is reasonable.

2.5 A COLLECTION OF USEFUL TERMS

Throughout Chapters 1 and 2, we have been using terms such as "objectives," "heuristics," and "goals" rather loosely. We pause now for a moment to discuss the implied relationships between these different approaches to the issue of facilitating systems design.

Technical objectives are technically based measures of quality which generally relate consistently to the overall goals of minimum cost or maximum gain. The designer usually evaluates decisions within the framework of technical objectives. Technical parameters of a system are non-evaluative measures — that is, merely descriptions of certain aspects of a system. These are the things under direct control of the designer and which influence technical objectives. Unlike aspects of quality, "more" is not necessarily better; it depends.

The designer is aided by tools, which are models (of the system) that can be manipulated in useful ways. Flowcharts and decision tables are examples of design tools. Design principles, like the ones given in this chapter, are very broad rules that generally "work" in the sense that they favor increasing quality for less development cost. Heuristics, however, are very specific rules of thumb that also usually work but are not guaranteed. A strategy is a procedure or plan in which to imbed the use of tools, principles, and heuristics to specify system parameters in order to increase technical objectives. Any questions?

2.6 SUMMARY

In this chapter we have seen that we can generally minimize the cost of implementation, maintenance, and modification — three of the major technical objectives for current computer systems — by designing systems whose pieces are small, easily related to the application, and relatively independent of one another. We have also seen that structured design achieves this by focusing attention on proper *partitioning* of the application and by proper organization of the pieces of the system. We have also introduced some general design philosophies, such as the "rule of black boxes," which are extremely basic and which will be dealt with later in the book.

Finally, we have seen that a number of our value judgments about the design of a computer system can be expressed by drawing analogies to human organizations. In addition to providing a convenient communications tool between designers, it allows us to draw upon the experience of several hundred years of studying human organizational structures — which, after all, are just another kind of system with many of the same properties as software systems.

The Structure
of
Computer Programs

CHAPTER 3

3.1 PROGRAMS AND STATEMENTS

A computer program is a system. We noted in Chapter 2 that *structure* — components and interrelationships among components — is an essential, often neglected property of computer programs. But just what are the components of computer programs and how are they related?

First, we should recognize that while a program is a system, it is a very special kind of system. It is worthwhile to present a careful definition of "program" and "computer program" as a preliminary to the discussion of program structure. A *program* can be defined as

> *A precise, ordered sequence of statements and aggregates of statements which, in total, define, describe, direct, or otherwise characterize the performance of some task.*

A *computer program* is simply a program which, possibly through intermediate gyrations, can cause a computer to perform the task.

At the most elementary (and safest) level, we observe that computer programs are, by definition, composed of statements. These statements are arranged (another way of saying *structured*) in a sequence. It is thus safe to identify individual statements as the components of computer programs, and the statement sequence as one structuring relationship.

This view of programs as being constructed from statements that are precisely ordered is essentially the classic or "algorithmic" view of programs and programming. By virtue of this characterization, attention is focused on the smallest unit of a program (i.e., the statement), on the sequential arrangement and performance of those statements, and on the required precision with which these are created and sequenced. This view is certainly correct; it cannot be dismissed out of hand. However, the value of such a viewpoint can only be judged fairly in terms of the consequences of highlighting these "algorithmic" aspects at the expense of certain others.

Computer programming is taught to novices and is very often performed by veterans on the basis of a procedural realization of an algorithm. Some function or task is given; an algorithm or "method of computation" is selected, discovered, or created; this algorithm is translated into a language which the computer will accept. This approach to programming is not restricted to mathematical functions or formal algorithms. Generating a weekly payroll is a function; the flowchart or process chart for doing so is an algorithm.

Certain consequences result from this approach. The sequential, procedural, methodological aspects of programs are further emphasized. In this description, the effort is concentrated on two things — on finding a computational method and on the sequential statement-by-statement translation of the method. Programming in the usual use of the term is what we frequently referred to as "implementation" in Chapters 1 and 2. In and of itself, such a conventional view will never lead to considering the whole task in terms of other tasks. The task is considered only in terms of its realization as a sequence of steps and that, in turn, as a sequence of (ultimately) machine-recognizable program statements. Thus, the solution of the whole problem of creating a program is attacked by generating, in order, successively very tiny parts of the solution.

We have not yet said what a statement is. A careful, general definition is more difficult than it may seem at first. Suffice it to say that we mean any small, well-defined, complete instruction, command, declaration or . . . well, anything of that sort. An IBM System/370 machine instruction written in hexadecimal by a programmer making a patch, a COBOL sentence, a FORTRAN arithmetic statement, a symbolic instruction written in the COMPASS assembly language for the CDC Cyber series computers, a PL/I declaration — all of these are examples of statements.

For almost all purposes in this book, it will not matter whether the statement is a machine instruction, an assembly language statement, or a high-level language statement. In almost all cases, we are interested in whatever "line" of code the programmer writes. In many respects, all statements in any programming languages of any "level" are equivalent or comparable.

To reinforce this perspective, we will introduce an ultra-simplified notation for writing programs. A short, straight line will represent a line of code, or a statement — any line of code or statement, in any language. This, of course, vastly simplifies writing programs and presenting examples! Here, for example, is a seven-statement program:

———————
———————
———————
———————
———————
———————
———————

At first, this degree of abstraction probably will be most uncomfortable, especially for programmers with many years of experience. Much of the rhetoric (if not the substance) of programming shoptalk — even of programming litera-ture — has depended on drawing sharp distinctions between high- and low-level languages, on debating this language against that language, or that machine repertoire against another. It will be worthwhile to try to accommodate viewing programs in the abstract, as, very often, features and aspects that otherwise would be missed can easily be seen.

3.2 THE STATEMENT STRUCTURE OF COMPUTER PROGRAMS

If statements are the components of programs, what is the *structure* of those statements? To answer that question, we must distinguish between differ-ent interpretations of the term "interrelationship," on which "structure" is based. Two statements may be interrelated because they are part of the same procedure, or because they involve the same type of operation. Similarly, we may say that statements are interrelated because they are executed in sequence. Finally, some statements are interrelated because they actually refer to each other.

These are examples of very different forms of structure: The first example might be termed *conceptual structure*. Such interrelationships, though important to the programmer doing the detailed coding (e.g., "Jeez, where are all the MOVE CORRESPONDING statements in this program — it turns out, the compiler generates incorrect object code for them!"), can be ignored, for they do not really exist in the program. The associations are mental rather than physical.

Implicit structure, such as that resulting from the sequential execution of program statements, is more objective — though it still depends on context. The structure based on explicit references in one part of a program to things in other parts of the program is the most concrete and, it turns out, the most important from the standpoint of program design. We will call this simply *referential structure*. Other forms of structure will also be of interest to us. The *communication structure* is the structure based on the flow of data between different statements and different parts of the program. *Control structure* is based on the flow of control (successive activation or execution) between different statements or different parts of programs. *Lexical structure* is a special relationship to be discussed later in this chapter.

In terms of writing, understanding, and modifying, a contiguous linear block of code does not behave like many small pieces, but rather like one big, tightly cemented piece. The term *monolithic* refers to any system or portion of a system which consists of pieces so highly interrelated that they behave like a single piece. As a rule, and in the absence of special features which limit the interrelationships, all continuous linear blocks of contiguous code are monolithic.

It is the monolithic nature of contiguous code that is the undoing of the "myth of modularization." Many organizations have undertaken, at great expense, to "modularize" an already completed piece of software. This is done in the hopes of simplifying future maintenance or minimizing slowly spiraling costs of introducing changes. Let Fig. 3.1 represent such a system, perhaps an on-line inquiry system. Any change, however isolated in function, requires dealing with a large percentage of the total code because it is so highly interrelated. Indeed, because this structure is not (and probably cannot be) documented, essentially *all* code must be checked for possible involvement if a change is being introduced simply to identify which lines need not be changed.

The command to modularize this program can only be read as "chop it into more pieces." In Fig. 3.2, the system has been thus modularized. Note that the potential impact of changes has not been reduced by introducing these artificial boundaries between sections. These remain as complex and highly interconnected as before. The program as a whole may be marginally more complex, for the introduction of "module boundaries" introduces new elements into the system, and may require involved coding to accomplish the actual interfacing implied by so many intermodular references. This expensive and disappointing lesson has been learned by many organizations after a substantial investment. While one may not always do as badly as indicated by Fig. 3.2, it is all but impossible to simplify significantly the structure of an existing program or system through after-the-fact modularization. Once reduced to code, the structural complexity of a system is essentially fixed. It is, thus, clear that simple structures must be designed that way from the beginning.

3.3 THE LINGUISTICS OF MODULARITY

Thus far, we have been informal in our use of the term "module" and have often even avoided it by using the words "section" or "part" or "piece" instead. Before we formally define the term, we must do some preliminary work.

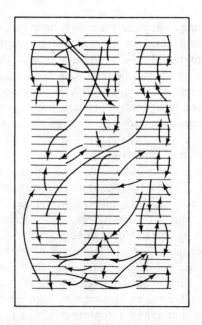

Fig. 3.1 Structure of large program after modularization.

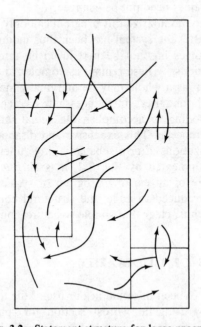

Fig. 3.2 Statement structure for large program.

An analysis of program statements by function in a typical computer program will reveal that some of these statements serve to aggregate statements into larger programming elements. These statements effectively form the boundary of statements which are "within" the larger aggregate. Such statements will be termed *boundary elements,* and the positions in the program that they define are the *boundaries* of the aggregate.

For example, in the following portion of a sample program, the statements with labels A1 and A2 bound the aggregate named A. Statement B is inside A, and statement C is outside A.

A1:   BEGIN A
          _____
          _____

B: _____
          _____
          _____

A2:   END A
C: _____
          _____
          _____

The illustration pictures the program *as written,* in the order and arrangement of statements as input to a translator (e.g., a computer or assembler). This

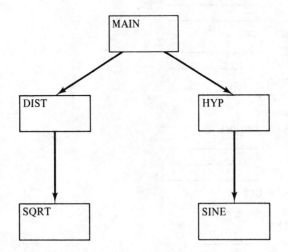

Fig. 3.3 Modular structure consisting solely of subroutines.

order is known as the *lexical order* of the program, and in this context the term *lexical* will always mean "as written" or "as it appears in a listing of the translator input." (The term lexical has other meanings in the context of programming linguistics and languages in general.) Thus, the statement labeled B is *lexically included* in the aggregate named A. The statement C *lexically follows* the statement labeled A2.

It is important to note that the lexical sequence *may* be independent of both the order in which the translation of statements appear in memory and the order in which the statements will be executed. The order of statements can be altered by optimizing compilers or by link-editors (loaders); the sequence of addresses in physical memory may depend upon virtual memory considerations; execution order depends upon conditional and unconditional control transfers.

One purpose that boundary elements serve is to control the lexical scope over which specific identifiers are defined and are associated with specific objects. Thus, in the coding that follows, the identifier B typically would be undefined at statement N3; the reference to A at statement N2 would identify the same object as that at N3 (namely, to the identifier defined in statement N1), while the reference to A at statement N5 identifies a different object — namely that defined at statement N4.

```
N1:    DEFINE A
       _____


L1:    BEGIN
          DEFINE B
          _____

       N2:  USE  A
            _____

L2:    END
N3:    USE  A
L3:    BEGIN
       N4:  DEFINE  A
            _____

            _____

       N5:  USE  A
            _____

L4:    END
       _____

       _____
```

The indentation in the example above serves to highlight the scope defined by the boundary elements BEGIN and END; it serves no other purpose, structural or otherwise.

Note, by the way, that several programming languages — ALGOL, PL/I, and some assembly languages — allow the programmer to formally define the scope of variables in much the way we outline above. In languages like FORTRAN and COBOL, the concept still exists but it is much less formal and general: COBOL subprograms (separately compiled and activated with a CALL) and FORTRAN external subroutines have natural boundary elements that serve to define the scope of variables.

A common problem in identifier definitions is that of "collision of identifiers." This occurs when the programmer uses the same identifier in different sections of his program with the intention of referring to different objects — when, in fact, the *same* object is being referenced. Collision of identifiers may occur, for example, when one aggregate with a local interpretation of, say, X (but without a local definition or declaration of X) is *lexically included* in another aggregate which defines or declares X for its own use. Some or all of an aggregate's set of defined identifiers — its "identifier space" — may correspond to elements in the identifier spaces of other aggregates.

An aggregate may also have associated with it an *aggregate identifier,* an identifier whose object is the entire group of bounded statements, as a whole. Program statements, within or outside the aggregate boundary, may refer to the aggregate identifier.

We are now in a position to define linguistically the terms "programming module," or "module" for short. *A module is a lexically contiguous sequence of program statements, bounded by boundary elements, having an aggregate identifier.* Another way of saying this is that a module is a bounded, contiguous group of statements having a single name by which it can be referred to as a unit.

A bounded aggregate not possessing an aggregate identifier is a *segment.* An aggregate that *also* has an identifier space, which is entirely a subset of that of the sequence in which it is lexically imbedded (its lexical superordinate), may have its boundary elements removed without effect. The boundary elements serve no function whatsoever in that case.

It should be noted that this definition encompasses not only subroutines, in the broadest sense, as modules (provided they are properly constructed linguistically), but also specific language variants such as FORTRAN "subordinates," PL/I "procedures," COBOL "subprograms," COBOL "sections," COBOL "paragraphs," PL/I "tasks," and so forth. Our definition of module includes much more than the conventional subroutine mechanism; it also includes, for example, coroutines and assembler "macros." This may seem like an obvious point, but it warrants emphasis.

Consider the following FORTRAN program. The "main" routine activates GETCHR by using a CALL at statement 20; this transfers control to GETCHR, with the associated condition that GETCHR, on encountering a RETURN statement, will resume execution of the suspended main sequence.

```
                    ──────────────
                    ──────────────
     20   CALL GETCHR
                    ──────────────
                    ──────────────

          SUBROUTINE GETCHR
     30             ──────────────

     40   RETURN
                    ──────────────
                    ──────────────
          END
```

The same result could have been achieved with the problem below, which simulates the behavior of the one above by setting a switch. Note that the subroutine activation mechanism does not explicitly transfer control to GETCHR, but is instead a simple GOTO statement.

```
                    ──────────────
                    ──────────────
     20   ASSIGN 21 TO I
          GO TO 30
     21             ──────────────

     C    BEGIN GETCHR
     30             ──────────────

     40   GO TO I
                    ──────────────
     C    END GETCHR
```

Note that a similar programming mechanism could have been accomplished in COBOL by using the ALTER statement. We will say that a language contains or includes a given type of module if there is a specific linguistic construct which directly realizes the activation characteristics that define the module. Thus, we say that a language contains a "subroutine" type of module if there is a language construct similar to CALL or PERFORM that allows us to activate such a module; a language contains a coroutine type of module if there is an appropriate activation mechanism.

The characteristics of any given type of module always can be simulated in any language that is Turing-complete — that is, which can be used to program any computable function. This is true for virtually any "real" programming language.

3.4 NORMAL AND PATHOLOGICAL CONNECTIONS

We will represent any and all modules (as defined in the previous section) with the graphic notation:

Note that this is the conventional "box" used to represent a procedural step in a flowchart. To avoid confusion, it is necessary to distinguish between a flowchart and a "structural representation." In this book, diagrams consisting of connected boxes will be modular structures unless otherwise stated. To aid in recognizing the exceptions, flowcharts will always begin with a "connector" regardless of context. Thus, we represent flowcharts as follows:

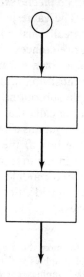

The special status of the aggregate identifier as representing the entire module suggests the graphic convention of having references to this identifier being represented by arrows pointing to the box. Thus, TRANSEDIT below is a module with at least three external references to its aggregate identifier.

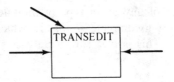

Directed line segments with arrowheads will always be used to indicate such connections; the arrowhead will end at the boundary of the box representing a module.*

Connections that are references to identifier of entities *within* the module boundaries are appropriately represented by directed line segments for which the arrowhead ends within the box representing the module. Below, module PUTLINE has at least one reference to its aggregate identifier, and two references to identifiers defined within it.

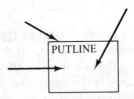

For historical reasons,† intermodular connections to internally defined identifiers are called *pathological connections*. Connections to the aggregate identifier are *normal connections*. The value judgments normally implied by these names should be ignored; they are really just convenient shorthand labels for two structural variations of intermodular references.

The simplest possible graphic for a normal connection, an arrow from one box to another, is reserved for the most ubiquitous (and perhaps most important) form of normal reference: the simple subroutine call. In the structure of Fig. 3.3, module MAIN has within it subroutine calls that reference modules DIST and HYP; DIST contains a call to SQRT, and HYP contains a call to SINE.

We draw an arrow from one box to the other, starting and ending on the boundary, if and only if there exists in the first module one or more calls referencing the identity interface of the second module. In general, the number of such references is not of interest to us, and identical multiple arrows are not usually drawn between the same pair of boxes.

---

* Every effort has been made to make the graphics for program structure simple and intuitive. The rationale for the choice of graphics will usually be presented as an aid to learning. For a complete summary of suggested graphics, see Appendix A.

† See the discussion of terminology in the Preface, and the derivation of minimally connected systems in Chapter 6.

It is important to keep in mind that the existence of a reference does not necessarily mean that a referent will be accessed. For example, the fact that there is a "subroutine call" reference from one module to another does not mean that the subroutine will be called. A subroutine call may or may not involve communication of arguments, and these may be transmitted in either direction. The subroutine LINEEND, for example, might compute the X-Y coordinates of the end of a line of length L, angle A, from initial point X1 and Y1. A call to LINEEND might look like

CALL LINEEND (X1,Y1,L,A,XE,YE)

where XE and YE are identifiers whose values are to be set by LINEEND based on the values of the other identifiers.

In LINEEND, we might find code like that of Fig. 3.4. Note that the only reference in either module FOO or module LINEEND to an identifier defined within the scope of the other is the reference to LINEEND in statement C1 of FOO. Thus,

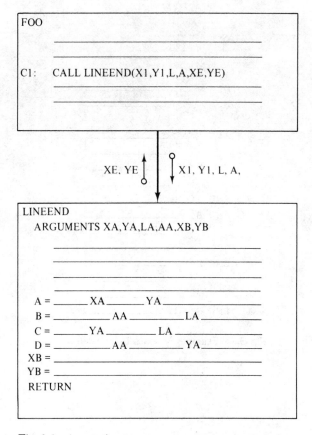

Fig. 3.4 Annotation to represent argument transmission.

argument transmission does not introduce additional connections. Where the existence and nature of arguments is of interest (as it frequently is), these are indicated by small arrows and annotations beside the connection, as in Fig. 3.4.

Pathological connections are distinguished as to whether they are control or data references. A small dot on the "tail" of an arrow always means an element of control is involved, while a small circle means that an element of data is involved. Pathological connections are also drawn beginning within the box in which the reference is found. The rationale for this will be appreciated after you read Chapter 6.

Lexical inclusion presents an unusual problem for graphical representation. In the code shown in Fig. 3.5, A is included within B, which is included within D, which is included within Q. One might reasonably choose to diagram this in a way that directly represents the relationships, as shown in Fig. 3.6. However, this requires many boxes of different size and makes clarification and interpretation difficult, especially when other relationships are involved. The call from B to A, for example, looks rather peculiar.

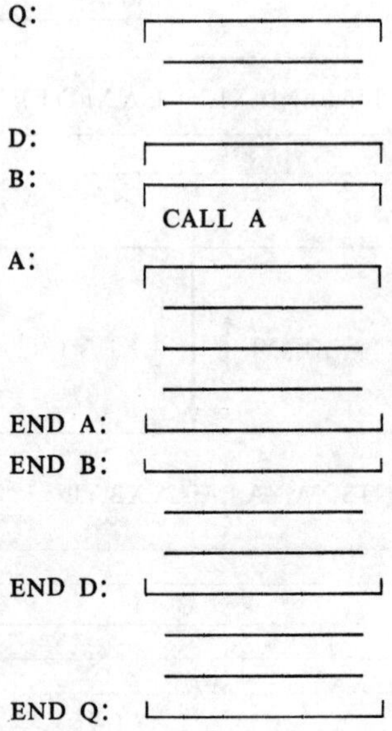

Fig. 3.5   Example of lexically included code.

To overcome these objections, we introduce a special graphic. The structure shown in Figs. 3.5 and 3.6 is much clearer when shown in the form of Fig. 3.7. The graphic is intended to suggest that the box for the lexical subordinate has been pulled out of the lexical superordinate and expanded. Note that the lexical inclusion (or subordination) is independent of all other relationships, which, if they exist, must be shown separately.

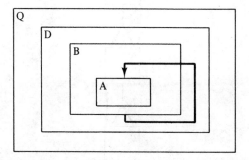

Fig. 3.6   Attempt to diagram lexically included code.

3.5 DATA FLOW GRAPHS

A number of design principles and strategies in this book will require us to study the flow of *data* through the program or system. Hence, we need a method of restating the problem itself (i.e., "functional requirements" or "systems specifications") in a manner that emphasizes the data flow and de-emphasizes (in fact, almost ignores) the procedural aspects of the problem. While it may seem alien at first, it turns out to be rather similar to the high-level "systems flowchart" drawn by many designers as a way of getting started on the design.

The data-oriented technique that we will use is called a *data flow graph.* The same model also is known as a *data flow diagram,* or a *program graph*[1] or even a "bubble chart." The elements of the data flow graph are called *transforms* and are represented graphically by small circles (or "bubbles," to use the colloquial term). As their name implies, the transforms represent transformations of data (which eventually will be accomplished by a module, a program, or even an entire system) from one form to another form. The data elements are represented by labeled arrows connecting one transform bubble to another. Thus, Fig. 3.8 shows a simple transform with a single input stream, and a single output stream.

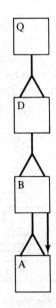

Fig. 3.7 Diagramming lexically included structure.

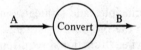

Fig. 3.8 Transform from A into B.

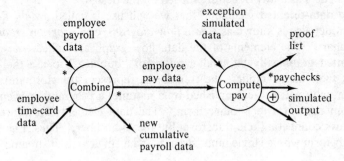

Fig. 3.9 Conjunction and disjunction.

A transform may require (or accept) elements of more than one input data stream in order to produce its output(s). If two adjacently pictured data streams are *both* required for a transform, we draw an asterisk ("*") between the two data streams; by analogy with other mathematical disciplines, we refer to the "*" as an "and" operator, or a "conjunction" operator. Similarly, the "ring-sum" operator ("$\oplus$") is used to denote disjunction — that is, an "either-or" situation. Figure 3.9 illustrates a data flow diagram in which conjunction and disjunction have been used in the input data streams *and* the output data streams.

The amount of detail shown in the data flow graph will vary from problem to problem, and from designer to designer. To illustrate this point, Fig. 3.10a depicts the data flow in a typical "master file update" system; note that it shows very little detail. Fig. 3.10b shows a data flow for the same system — but in much more detail. The diagram of Fig. 3.10a is probably extreme in the sense of not showing enough detail; the bubble labeled "magically transform into transactions" contains

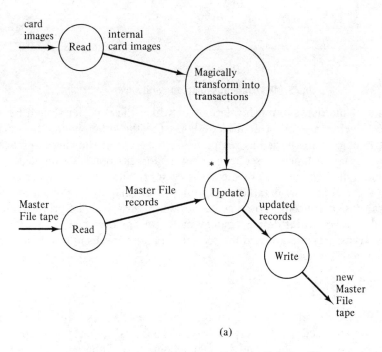

(a)

Fig. 3.10a   Data flow diagram with very little detail.

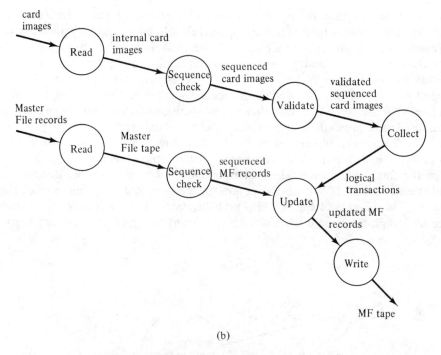

card images

Read

internal card images

Sequence check

sequenced card images

Validate

validated sequenced card images

Collect

Master File records

Read

Master File tape

Sequence check

sequenced MF records

Update

logical transactions

updated MF records

Write

MF tape

(b)

Fig. 3.10b Data flow diagram with excessive detail.

a number of internal subtransformations of which the designer should be aware if he is to develop a good structural design. On the other hand, the diagram of Fig. 3.10b might be regarded as "extreme" in the sense of showing too much detail; the transformation labeled "sequence check," for example, is sufficiently uninteresting that it might be ignored by the designer in his "first crack" at a design.

We will find the data flow graph useful in Chapter 7 in our discussion of a structural design concept known as "cohesion." However, its primary use is that of a tool in a structural design strategy called "transform analysis." Chapter 10 discusses transform analysis and the role of data flow graphs in developing a "transform-centered" design.

3.6 A SUMMARY

We have seen in this chapter that computer programs are systems, and that they can be analyzed in a variety of ways. The most important components of a program are its *statements,* and we can recognize an inherent structure in those statements; indeed, unless *we do* recognize the statement structure, our attempts to modularize a program by chopping it into pieces usually will be unsuccessful.

Most of the emphasis in this chapter has been on the definition of terms and concepts used throughout the rest of the book. In addition to defining terms that are not part of the average designer's vocabulary — e.g., normal and pathological connections — we have attempted a careful, technical definition of words like module.

REFERENCE

1. DAVID MARTIN and GERALD ESTRIN, "Models of Computations and Systems—Evaluation of Vertex Probabilities in Graph Models of Computations," *Journal of the ACM,* Vol. 14, No. 2 (April 1967), pp. 281–299.

Structure
and
Procedure

CHAPTER 4

4.0 INTRODUCTION

Neophytes and veterans alike often find it difficult to comprehend the difference between procedure and structure in computer programs and systems. Even more serious is the failure to understand the relationship between coding and "structural" design. The choice of structure can substantially influence the simplicity of coding. Conversely, selection of a particular coding technique may have predetermined major portions of the structure. This chapter explores relationships between the two by studying examples and by elaborating on various ways of modeling the same system.

The first thing to recognize is that *structure* is not something new that we are adding to the ken of programmers and analysts; it is not a concept or added neologism which systems did not ever have. Every computer system has structure — that is, it is made up of components that are interconnected. Even the degenerate case of the single-module system can be examined in terms of its statement structure (as we did in the previous chapter). Regardless of how a system was developed, whether its structure was designed or determined by accident, we can document the modular structure.

The definitions in the last chapter lead to an obvious discipline for "discovering" the modular structure of an existing system. It is helpful to identify a top-level or main module as a starting point. On a "structure chart," that starting point is represented by the top box. Every reference to an identifier defined outside its scope is an intermodular reference for which an arrow can be drawn to another box. When we have identified the name of the module in which the referent is found, we can insert the module name in the target box. The code for each such box is examined in the same manner as the first module, giving rise to further connections and the discovery of additional modules to be drawn as boxes and analyzed in turn. In most programming languages, this procedure is so straightforward that it can easily be done by a program.

For example, an analysis of the code shown in Fig. 4.1 leads to a diagram

```
BOTTOM:   BEGIN SUBROUTINE
          ARGUMENTS X, Y
          DEFINE BA, BB, BC
          GLOBAL QQ, ST2
          ────────────────
          STORE QQ    (1)
          ────────────────
          STORE Y
          ────────────────
          RETURN
          ────────────────
          FETCH X
          ────────────────
          GO TO ST2   (2)
          END
TOP:      BEGIN ROUTINE
          DEFINE TA, TB, QQ, RR    (3)
          ACCESSIBLE QQ, RR
          ────────────────
          CALL MID    (4)
          ────────────────
          END
MID:      BEGIN SUBROUTINE
          DEFINE MA
          ACCESSIBLE ST2
          GLOBAL RR
ST1:      CALL BOTTOM (RR, MA)   (5)
          ────────────────
          ────────────────
ST2:      ────────────────   (6)
          ────────────────
          RETURN
          END
```

Fig. 4.1   Some code whose structure is to be analyzed.

like that shown in Fig. 4.2. Note especially how normal and pathological connections have been distinguished. A code has been provided to simplify associating the graphic model with the code; in the code, each connection bearing a number identifies the reference with which it is associated.

While any actual code has but a single, valid, complete structural representation, the mapping from a structure chart to code is not single-valued. As any programmer knows, there are an infinite number (well, in any case, a large number!) of ways of coding a module, even when its structural representation has already been determined. All that can be said of the code based on a structural representation is that somewhere within the coding for a particular module, references of a certain type must be present. Thus, based on the structure, we infer certain contents of modules. We know, for example, that a pathological connection directly references a data label defined within some module. If it is shown passing data opposite to the direction of connection, we know it must be accessed as a "load" or "fetch" rather than as a "store." Typical statements or instructions then follow.

4.1 FLOWCHARTS AND STRUCTURE CHARTS

One way of looking at procedure and structure is to consider the relationship between the flowchart (a model of procedure) and the structure chart for the same system. Figure 4.3 is suggestive of a set of flowcharts, one for each module

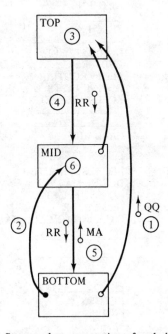

Fig. 4.2 Structural representation of code in Fig. 4.1.

or section of code. This is the standard or "hierarchical" method of flowcharting in which the top-level flowchart reflects the gross overall processing, some of which is expanded in the next level of flowcharts, and so on. In essence, the set of flowcharts is a series of horizontal slices of the system, with time (as a rule) increasing from left to right, and "calling" represented in the dimension into the paper.

As shown in Fig. 4.4, the structure chart is essentially a vertical slice in the plane of the paper; Figs. 4.3 and 4.4 are really just orthogonal views of the same system. It should be recalled, however, that the structure chart is a time-independent model of a system. By convention, we represent subordinations in the same order left to right as they appear lexically. This means that, as a rule, reading across the subordinations emerging from any given module approximates

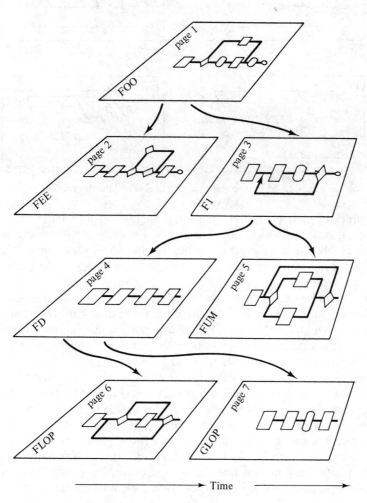

Fig. 4.3 Hierarchical set of flowcharts as a model of a system.

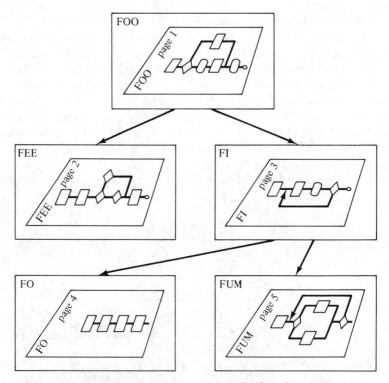

Fig. 4.4 Structure chart as a vertical slice into the system.

the time order of their execution. This can only be a rough indication, however, for the actual order in which calls are accessed on any particular execution may vary considerably due to differing outcomes of conditional statements. Thus, interpreting the subordinating references at any level as a rough flowchart only works well if the procedure is very simple.

It should be emphasized that this is merely a graphic convention. For example, the two structures of Fig. 4.5 are equivalent; they both represent the same information. We stress this point because, among other reasons, we often find that a real-world structure chart is sufficiently complex that we must rearrange the left-to-right placement of modules to avoid a tangle of crossed lines on the chart. Figure 4.6a, for example, shows a structure chart in which we might imagine that module A is executed first, module B is executed second, and module C is executed third (all subordinate to MAIN, of course); Fig. 4.6b shows a structurally equivalent diagram whose connecting arrows are a bit easier to follow.

While it is easy to appreciate that the left-to-right order in a structural representation has no intrinsic implications for the order of execution of the subordinates, it is far less obvious that the vertical dimension of the structure chart is also time-independent. Of course, if we have a complete structure and disregard

52

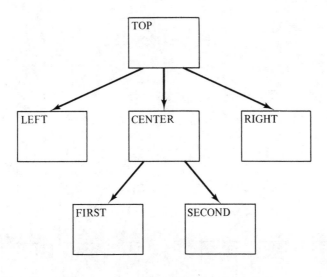

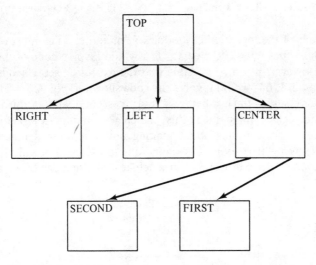

Fig. 4.5 Two equivalent representations of the same structure.

errors, and if A is not superordinate to B and B *is* superordinate to A, then A cannot receive control for the first time until B receives control for the first time. However, in order to fully understand what is happening, we must look at the processing accomplished by a module — its "body" — rather than merely its receipt of control or its activation of other modules.

As an example, suppose we had modules P, Q, and R, and suppose that P is immediately superordinate to Q, which is immediately superordinate to R. The code for PP, QQ, and RR, can be executed in any one of six different orders depend-

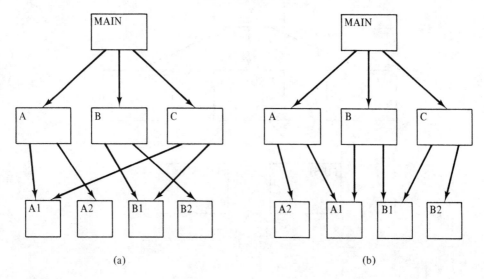

(a)	(b)

Fig. 4.6a. Structure with crossed lines.   **Fig. 4.6b** Equivalent structure.

ing on the details of the logic within modules P, Q, and R. The most obvious order of execution is PP first, then QQ, then RR; this would involve code of the sort shown in Fig. 4.7. However, it is also possible that the execution sequence is PP first, RR second, and QQ third; this would involve the code shown in Fig. 4.8. The other four variations are obvious — the last being RR first, QQ second, and PP third.

So, once again, our point is this: When we examine a structure chart, we should be exceedingly cautious about making any assumptions regarding the sequence of execution. It is somewhat dangerous to assume not only that the modules in a structure chart will execute in a left-to-right sequence, but also that the

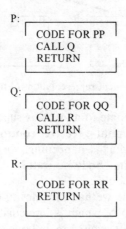

Fig. 4.7   Coding for one sequence of PP, QQ, and RR.

54

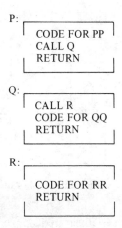

Fig. 4.8 Coding for a second sequence of PP, QQ, and RR.

body of code in a high-level module will be executed before the body of the code in a low-level module. Of course, in a simple structure chart, the top-to-bottom sequence and the left-to-right sequence will frequently occur — but there will be enough exceptions in real-world structure charts that we should learn to read the structure chart for the information it was intended to give: *structural architectural* information.

    Of course, there will be times when the designer wishes to communicate certain important procedural information to those reading his structure chart — not the trivial loops, decisions, and sequencing operations, but the critical ones of which the designer feels others should be aware. Certain major loops or decisions, for example, could have a *major* effect on the efficiency of the program and might well influence the manner in which the designer (or the programmer) "packages"* the modules into physically executable units (e.g., "load modules," "job steps," "overlays," or "segments," depending on the terminology of the computer vendor).

    There are a number of conventions for showing procedural matters in a structure chart. These are discussed in detail in Appendix A, but the major conventions — one-shot executions, iteration, and conditional decisions — can be summarized here. If, for example, we wish to show that a subordinate module is *not* re-executed upon successive activation of the superordinate, we so indicate with a small numeral "one" within the superordinate box and adjacent to the tail of the arrow connecting it to the subordinate. Thus, Fig. 4.9 shows a subordinate module REWIND which is activated as part of an initialization procedure on the first activation of superordinate module MANAGE, but not thereafter.

    Subordinates activated repeatedly as the result of iterative execution of their calls would be shown as in Fig. 4.10. All of the modules activated within a common loop are shown with their references emerging from the same "looping

---

* Packaging is discussed extensively in Chapter 14.

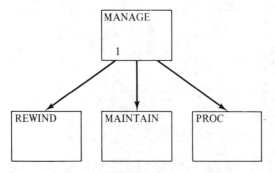

Fig. 4.9 Notation for one-shot modules.

arrow," and the nesting of loops is illustrated appropriately. In Fig. 4.10, PROC and NEXT are executed in a loop which, along with a call to ADJUST, is imbedded in an outer loop.

The familiar diamond figure is used to show conditionally activated calls. Each decision is represented by a separate diamond; alternate outcomes (typically, the binary "TRUE" and "FALSE") emanate from each diamond. Thus, we would expect to see two arrows emanating from the diamond (e.g., a "TRUE" arrow and a "FALSE" arrow) if the code for the diamond corresponded to the classical IF-THEN-ELSE construct of most high-level languages; we would expect to see only one arrow if the code for the diamond corresponded to the degenerate IF-THEN construct; and we could expect to see a multitude of arrows emanating from the diamond if the code for the diamond corresponded to the CASE construct found in languages like ALGOL.

Where several calls are made as the result of the same outcome (e.g., the TRUE outcome), these are shown by allowing the appropriate arrow (e.g., the TRUE arrow) to "split" into a number of branches. For example, in the structure shown in Fig. 4.11, modules A, P, and X are activated based on different decisions. Modules P and Q are the alternate actions of one decision. In the final decision,

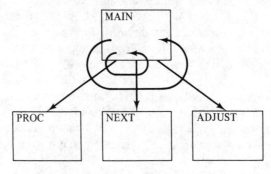

Fig. 4.10 Notation for loops.

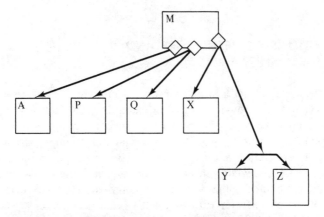

Fig. 4.11   Alternate outcomes of decisions.

module x is invoked on one outcome, and *both* modules y and z are invoked on the other outcome.

The procedural annotations for one-shot, iterative, and conditional access may be used with *any* structural relationship; they are not restricted to subroutine calls, though that seems to be their most common use. For example, we can show a conditionally used pathological data access, as is illustrated by Fig. 4.12.

This could derive from code within the referencing module, such as the following:

```
─────────────
─────────────

IF  C  THEN  FETCH  H

─────────────
─────────────
```

The one-shot, iterative, and conditional indicators should be regarded as annotations which enhance the usefulness of the structure chart as a model for designing and documenting but which are not part of the model itself. They are very useful, however, and the experienced designer often can understand a great deal about the relevant behavior of a system from an "extended" structure chart — that is, a structure chart with procedural annotations.

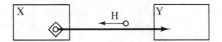

Fig. 4.12   Conditionally used pathological data access.

4.2 INTERACTIONS OF PROCEDURE AND STRUCTURE: AN EXAMPLE

The best way to get a firm grasp on the influence of choice of structure on procedural contents is through a concrete example. Of necessity, this must be a fairly lengthy and detailed example in order to contain interesting design issues, even in rudimentary form. We will first look at this example, known as the Personnel Master Entry Getter, in the context of a simple design problem.

Our task is to develop an afferent subsystem (one that delivers its output upward to superordinates*) that will supply complete, ready-to-process compound items called Personnel Master Entries (PME). Each activation is to result in returning one PME — the next one — until no more exist, at which time an EOF flag is to be set and returned. The module that performs this task, when called, is to be named GETPME; it may have any number of subordinates in any substructure.

Each PME is constructed of from one to ten records: a key record and up to nine continuation records. These records normally have a blocking factor of eight on the incoming file (i.e., eight logical records for each physical "block" on the tape or disk file). However, there are short blocks indicated by a "short block indicator." (Blocking is a physical input-output issue for the purposes of this exercise, and is unrelated to the organization of records into items.)

Deblocked records are combined into PMEs based on several factors. Normally, successive records will contain a "continuation code" indicating that the current record is part of the same PME as the *previous* record. A record containing a "first code" indicates that the previous record was the last in that PME, and that this record is the *first* in the next PME. A record may or may not contain an "end flag," indicating that it is the *last* record of the current PME. The ninth continuation record is assumed to have an "end flag." Obviously, an EOF must be treated the same as a record without a continuation code — that is, it ends the previous Personnel Master Entry with the previous record. Each complete PME must be put through a special process in order to make it ready for further processing.

We will not yet consider how the designer derives an appropriate structure for such a subsystem, but we will consider the consequences of that choice, including some common mistakes.

In skeletal form, the total processing for this function is rather simple. The details of all the individual elements could be comparatively complex. Even if it is possible to code the entire problem in a single module at reasonable cost, it may not be advisable. Certain functions, perhaps the deblocking process or the end-of-PME analysis, might be generally useful in other related applications; as modules, they could be activated by any part of this system or related systems. In any event, we may save significantly on the cost of developing the system because of the advantages of smaller modules.

We may think of the GETPME function as realizable in terms of combinations

---

* Afferent modules are discussed in Chapter 8.

58

of a number of smaller functions, each representing (probably) a non-trivial sequence of code.   The basic functions are:

ADD	add a record to a PME being built.
LOCATE	locate the next record in a block or indicate that there is none in the block; initially there is none.
READ	get the next block of records in the file or indicate that there are no more in the file.
TEST	determine whether a record constitutes the end of a PME, the beginning of a new PME, or neither.
MAKE	make a series of records in the same PME into a processable item.

This overall process is simple enough to identify only two major algorithmic variations on a design.   The "sequential machine derivation" is presented in Fig. 4.13.   The other major variation uses two record areas and always deals with a pair of continuous records.   This avoids duplicating some of the operations as well as some of the sequential decision-making.   As an exercise, you may want to develop the flowchart for this variation.   It is difficult to argue objective overall differences between the two designs and we shall be content, for our discussion, with the flowchart shown in Fig. 4.13.

Of interest to us is the structural representation of the system whose procedural representation was shown in Fig. 4.13.   In order to draw the structure chart, we first recognize that the entire flowchart of Fig. 4.13 is itself a module — that is, the GETPME module.   Also, the ADD, LOCATE, READ, TEST, and MAKE functions described above are modules — subordinate modules to the top-level GETPME module.   The relationship — and, in particular, the data flow — among all of the modules is perhaps easier to see if we write some sample code (in "computer Esperanto") as an implementation of the flowchart; this is shown in Fig. 4.14.

Studying this, we have little difficulty deriving the structure chart shown in Fig. 4.15.   Note that we have chosen to show the *loops* in the structure chart that were present in the original flowchart (and the code, too, obviously) but not the *decisions*.   Why?   Simply a personal decision on the part of the authors: While studying the structural aspects of the program, we felt that the decisions were relatively trivial, but that the loops were of some interest.

Actually, there are several things about the structure chart that are interesting.   First of all, notice its "pancake" structure: That is, it consists of one "boss" module and five immediately subordinate "worker" modules.   When we drew analogies between program structures and management structures in Chapter 2, we suggested that if a boss had too many immediate subordinates, his job probably would become too complicated — and that similar comments could be made about program structures.   We are not yet in a position to decide whether the structure chart of Fig. 4.15 is "bad" in this respect; we simply observe at this point that all of the "control logic" has been put into one *level* of "manager" module — namely GETPME.

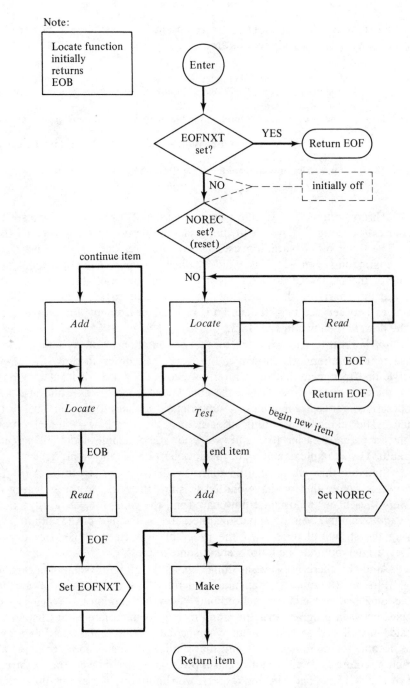

Fig. 4.13 Sequential machine derivation of PME problem.

```
GETPME:         SUBROUTINE, ARGUMENTS ITEM, ENDFILE
                IF EOFNXT GO TO RTNEOF
                IF NOREC GO TO TEST
DE:             CALL DEBLOC (BLOC, REC, EOB)
                IF NOT EOB GO TO TEST
                CALL GETBLOC (BLOC, EOF)
                IF EOF GO TO RTNEOF
                GO TO DE
TEST:           CALL MORTEST (REC, END, NEW)
                IF END GO TO FINISH
                IF NEW GO TO START
                CALL BUILDITEM (REC, ITM, ITM)
NEXT:           CALL DEBLOC (BLOC, REC, EOB)
                IF NOT EOB GO TO TEST
                CALL GETBLOC (BLOC, EOF)
                IF NOT EOF GO TO NEXT
                SET EOFNXT
                GO TO MAKE
START:          SET NOREC
                GO TO MAKE
FINISH:         CALL BUILDITEM (REC, ITM, ITM)
MAKE:           CALL MAKEREADY (ITM, ITM)
                RETURN
RTNEOF:         SET ENDFILE
                RETURN
                END
```

Fig. 4.14   One possible implementation of code for GETPME.

One could argue that this is not entirely true.   In most cases, GETPME acts as the boss — that is, it tells the other low-level modules what to do.   However, there are times when one of the "workers" — DEBLOC — tells the boss what to do. Notice that GETPME passes a block to DEBLOC, with the expectation of receiving a record in return.   However, if the block has been exhausted, DEBLOC sends back

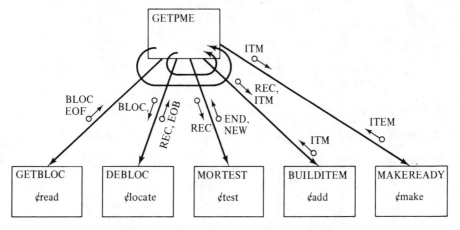

Fig. 4.15   "Pancake" structure for GETPME.

an EOB flag — in effect, DEBLOC tells the boss, GETPME, that it should read another record. We will see in more detail in Chapter 9 that this "inversion of authority" frequently leads to extra flags and switches as well as other undesirable structural characteristics.

Finally, note that the structure that we have shown in Fig. 4.15 has two nested loops. Within the inner loop, the primary activity is to extract a record from a block and add it to a partially constructed PME. The outer loop exists for the purpose of reading more blocks, as required. Unfortunately, the loops are somewhat complicated by the possibility that MORTEST will exit from *both* levels of loops when it discovers that it has a complete PME. At this point, though, we simply observe that there are two levels of loops in GETPME.

While it may appear that we are criticizing the structure of Fig. 4.15, we are doing so cautiously, for we are not yet in a position to state authoritatively what is "good" and what is "bad" about such a design. However, it is safe to speculate that there may be alternative designs, *from a structural point of view,* with characteristics worthy of investigation. The analogies with workers and bosses can lead us to such an alternative structure if we reason as follows: All the boss wants to do is obtain a record and, if it is of an appropriate type, add it to a partially constructed PME. The details of blocking, deblocking, and reading are important, of course, but they should not be of any concern to the boss.

This leads us to the structure shown in Fig. 4.16. Note that the code for the TEST function has been included in the GETPME module itself. Note also that

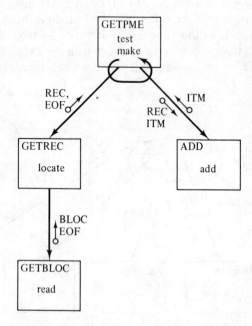

Fig. 4.16   An alternative structure for GETPME.

```
GETPME:        SUBROUTINE, ARGUMENTS ITEM, ENDFILE
               IF EOFNXT GO TO RTNEOF
               IF NOREC GO TO TEST
               CALL GETREC (REC, EOF)
               IF EOF GO TO RTNEOF
TEST:          CODE FOR TEST
               EXIT TO FINISH, START, OR MORE
MORE:          CALL ADD (REC, ITM, ITM)
               CALL GETREC (REC, EOF)
               IF NOT EOF GO TO TEST
               SET EOFNXT
MAKE:          CODE FOR MAKE
               RETURN
START:         SET NOREC
               GO TO MAKE
FINISH:        CALL ADD (REC, ITM, ITM)
               GO TO MAKE
PTNEOF:        SET ENDFILE
               RETURN
               END
```

Fig. 4.17   Possible code for structure shown in Fig. 4.16.

there are more levels of control in this structure than in the previous one — that is, GETREC serves as a "junior manager," hiding the details of blocking and deblocking from GETPME.   Note also that the EOB flag has disappeared as it is no longer necessary.   Finally, note that the new structure has only one loop in GETPME.   Lest you think this a trick, we hasten to point out that there are no loops hidden within GETREC; *each* time that GETREC is called, it determines whether it is necessary to make another call to GETBLOC.

It should be clear from this example that the choice of modular structure does indeed affect the complexity of both internal code and intermodular communication; how much it does so can be appreciated simply by comparing Fig. 4.15 and Fig. 4.16.   The new structure has fewer modules, yet those modules are each simpler and smaller when compared to equivalent portions of the earlier structure. Table 4.1 compares the two structures in terms of a number of objective indications which we might relate to quality or simplicity.   Of special interest is the "span," or communication path length — that is, the number of intermodular connections each data argument must traverse.   We may deduce that "effective" modularity may well be associated with "efficient" modularity, for each unit of total communication path length has some non-zero execution time cost associated with it — indeed, most programmers are aware that passing of data and parameters can be a very expensive proposition in some high-level programming languages.

One of the things we conclude from this exercise is that, in practice, it is not feasible to develop several general total flowcharts — indeed, it usually is not feasible to develop even one — to use as a guideline for evaluating a large number of different structures until one with reasonably good characteristics is found.   The flowchart to serve this purpose generally would be unmanageably large, for it would have to be a totally *detailed* flowchart — not a rough or overall one.   If a high-level

Table 4.1   Comparison of Two Designs for GETPME
System

	FIG. 4.15	FIG. 4.16
Number of Data Input Arguments	5.00	2.00
Number of Data Output Arguments	4.00	3.00
Number of Control Arguments (Flags)	4.00	2.00
Span: Maximum Path Length	3.00	2.00
Average Path Length	2.25	1.33
Number of Switches	3.00	2.00
Number of Duplicated Decisions	3.00	2.00
Estimated Lines of Code	93.00	74.00
(Estimated 80 lines if coded from Fig. 4.13)		

or overall flowchart is used to guide structure derivation, there is just as much chance of running into difficult-to-assess sub-optimal structures as if no guide had been used.

The question of how good structures are to be found, derived, invoked, or otherwise brought into being is one that requires not only substantial knowledge of purely physical aspects of modular structures, but also a technical elaboration of "good." We will thoroughly discuss the characteristics of "good" modular structures and "bad" modular structures in Chapters 5, 6, and 7; beginning in Chapter 8, we will see how "good" structures can be derived for a wide class of program design problems.

4.3 SUMMARY

We have seen in this chapter that a flowchart is a model of the procedural flow of a program, whereas a structure chart is a time-independent model of the hierarchical relationships of modules within a program or system. This distinction is an important one, and needs to be emphasized over and over again to designers who are more familiar with "flowchart-thinking." For example, it is important to emphasize to such designers that one usually cannot infer from a structure chart the order in which modules are executed.

On the other hand, we do have some tools for highlighting certain procedural details on a structure chart. The techniques discussed in this chapter — graphic notations for loops and decisions — will be valuable in the discussions in the following chapters.

Our approach to structured design is based on a formal, though not (as yet) mathematical, theory of the complexity of computer systems and programs. In our view, the cost of systems development is a function of problem and program complexity as measured in terms of human error. For a given problem, the human error production and, therefore, the cost of coding, debugging, maintenance, and modification are minimized when the problem is subdivided into the smallest functional units that can be treated independently. The elements of this theory — comprising definitions of "small," "functional," and "independent" — are presented in this section.

Chapter 5 considers some well-established principles of human problem-solving as they relate to the question of systems complexity. The factors contributing to interactions between systems components are described in Chapter 6 on "coupling." The cohesion of individual systems components is discussed in Chapter 7. Chapters 6 and 7, taken together, represent not just elements of a theory, but also operational methods for evaluating alternative designs in terms of probable cost of implementation, maintenance, and modification. Successive sections rest on the foundation built here.

II

FOUNDATION

Human Information Processing and Program Simplicity

CHAPTER 5

5.1 THE ECONOMICS OF SYSTEMS DEVELOPMENT

An understanding of the basic economic structure of the systems development process is essential in developing better, more efficient methods of systems production — as well as better, more efficient systems. Some of the key figures concerning the costs of systems development — such as the estimate that maintenance accounts for 50 percent of the average organization's EDP budget — were mentioned in Chapter 1. However, the detailed figures, impressive as they may be, should not concern us: They change with time and are subject to debate. What is important are the underlying characteristics, the fundamental phenomena, that give rise to these fluctuating figures.

We might begin by asking where the data processing money goes. Basically, it goes for people and machines — programmer/analysts and computer time — and little else. To a limited extent, person-hours and computer-hours behave reciprocally. There are ways by which we trade one for the other within some narrow range. For the most part, however, they vary together: More programmer/

analyst time to develop a given system means more machine-time used. One should note that it is the programmer/analyst who generates the machine-time — so, it is the programmer/analyst who is the essential link in the economic chain.

It has been documented in a number of places[1,2,3] that testing and debugging account for most of the cost of systems development; the common estimate is that 50 percent of a data processing project is devoted to these activities. While this may be a bitter pill for the proud programmer/analyst to swallow, it is a real one — and if the medicine remains unswallowed, the pain will continue. While "testing" and "debugging" are defined variously by different organizations, we will point out that the true cost of debugging is the cost of everything the programmer/analyst does in the development of a system beyond what would be necessary if he made no mistakes; that is, over and above initial writing of the code, setup, and review of the first compilation or assembly, and setup and review of the last test-run (the one that confirms that the system is acceptable). In other words, the cost of debugging accounts for most of the cost of both the person and the machine.

That most of the cost of systems development today is due to errors is not something to be denied, but rather an insight to be traded upon. Indeed, this is so vital that no theory of programming or programs, no technique or practice for programming or systems design, which does not give central recognition to the role of bugs and debugging, can be of much value in the practical amelioration of the pains in the field.

5.2 THE FUNDAMENTAL THEOREM OF SOFTWARE ENGINEERING

We will attempt, in this section, to develop what may be regarded as a kind of fundamental theorem of systems development. First, we note that it takes longer to write a long program than it takes to write a short one. This is always true if we measure long and short in the proper units. Clearly, "number of instructions" is not quite the right measure since some instructions are harder than others. This borders on the tautological, as we are really trying to say that it is harder to solve a harder problem. If we assume that we have an appropriate measure of the size of a problem P (for an interesting discussion of this area, see Halstead's study[4]), say $M(P)$, then the cost of programming P, which we might call $c(P)$, obeys the rule:

$$\text{IF } M(P) > M(Q) \text{ THEN } c(P) > c(Q).$$

That is, cost is a monotonically increasing function of problem size.

We might try taking two separate problems and, instead of writing two programs, create a combined program. Putting two problems together makes them bigger than the two problems taken separately. The primary reason for not combining problems is that, as human beings, we do not deal well with great complexity. As the complexity of a problem increases, we make disproportionately more mistakes; when problems are combined, we must solve not only each individual problem, but also the interactions between the two (which may involve preventing or avoiding interactions). Thus,

$$\text{M}(\text{P} + \text{Q}) > \text{M}(\text{P}) + \text{M}(\text{Q})$$

and, as we would expect,

$$\text{C}(\text{P} + \text{Q}) > \text{C}(\text{P}) + \text{C}(\text{Q})$$

It is always easier (and cheaper) to create two small pieces rather than one big piece if the two small pieces do the same job as the single piece.

This phenomenon is not unique to the computer field. Indeed, it seems true of any field of problem-solving: mathematics, physics, or naval warfare. In all of these fields, we find that we can increase the complexity of the problem from *very* trivial to trivial to not-quite-so-trivial with a correspondingly small increase in the number of errors — but sooner or later, the errors begin to increase more rapidly. Thus, for program design, systems design, and for all those other problem-solving disciplines that are beyond the realm of this book, we should expect to see an error curve of the sort shown in Fig. 5.1.

The psychologist-mathematician George Miller,[5] in a summary of a very large body of research, first described the human information process limitations that give rise to this effect. It appears that people can mentally juggle, deal with, or keep track of only about seven objects, entities, or concepts at a time. In effect, the immediate recirculating memory needed for problem-solving with multiple elements has a capacity of about 7 ± 2 entities. Above that number, errors in the process increase disproportionately. It matters not what the "somethings" are — people to be managed, state variables to be remembered, subroutine calls to be understood — if there are more than about 7 ± 2 of them, the errors generated rise

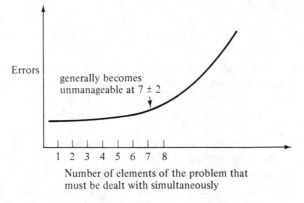

Fig. 5.1 Error curve for normal problem-solving.

sharply and non-linearly. This is a very fundamental and well-established property of human information processing that underlies all strategies for segmenting, factoring, or decomposing problems into subproblems. It is this relationship between problem elements and error generation that assures us that

$$c(P + Q) > c(P) + c(Q)$$

Clearly, once the problem becomes non-trivial, there is a great incentive to break the problem into smaller pieces. We can state this rather dramatically by making the appropriate substitutions in the equation above and writing what we (tongue in cheek) will call the Fundamental Theorem of Software Engineering:

$$c(P) > c(\tfrac{1}{2}P) + c(\tfrac{1}{2}P)$$

Basically, this just says that we can win if we can divide any task into independent subtasks. If the subtasks are not truly independent of one another, then we are not solving just the two subtasks — for in the solution of non-independent parts, we also are simultaneously dealing with some aspects of the other parts.

This last point is crucial. Unless we deal with it, we will always have to contend with the objection that the authors have heard from several hundred skeptical designers: "Yeah, but the problem of chopping a system into small modules (sic) is that I can introduce even *more* bugs — I always get the calling sequence wrong, or pass the wrong arguments to the module . . . and besides, it takes so much time to write out all the details of the calling sequence!"

Suppose we have factored a problem P into two parts of equal complexity; let us call the two parts $P' = \tfrac{1}{2}P$ and $P'' = \tfrac{1}{2}P$. If they are not independent, then the cost of solving the entire problem is

$$c(P' + I_1 \times P') + c(P'' + I_2 \times P'')$$

where I_1 is a fraction representing the interaction of P' with P''. Whenever I_1 and I_2 are non-zero, it is obvious that

$$c(P' + I_1 \times P'') + c(P'' + I_2 \times P'') > c(\tfrac{1}{2}P + c\tfrac{1}{2}P)$$

If I_1 and I_2 are both small — which we would expect if the designer has done a good job of modularizing his system — then we should still expect that

$$c(P) > c(P' + I_1 \times P'') + (P'' + I_2 \times P')$$

Clearly, there are also sufficiently pessimistic solutions, which would make a divided task cost much more than a combined task.

It is a pleasant fantasy to consider chopping a task into more and more pieces, and — if they are independent — reducing the cost to the vanishing point. However, it is obvious that we cannot create a system from an infinite number of nothings. For reasons that we discussed in Chapter 3 (when we looked at the statement structure of a program), the limiting case of a system developed as a very large number of separate and increasingly interdependent pieces is that it behaves precisely like the same system developed as a single piece.

The introduction of modularity into design introduces its own source of bugs. The programmer/analyst frequently finds himself making mistakes when coding the LINKAGE SECTION of a COBOL program; he finds himself writing the wrong argument declarations in a PL/I procedure or a FORTRAN subroutine; he finds himself saving and restoring the wrong general registers in an assembly language program.

We might counter that this is because the designer was never properly trained to use those features of his language (which is generally true in most organizations), but that is not the point. Of course, the designer will make mistakes when designing and coding the references and connections between modules! Writing a subroutine call is subject to the same error probabilities as writing other statements. Along with all of the potential errors listed above, we still have to contend with keypunch errors, spelling errors, and a variety of other errors so trivial as to be dismissed with a wave of the hand.

If we factor a problem into pieces that are relatively independent, we will find that the "chopping" process introduces some errors, but they tend to be relatively straightforward and obvious — and most important, relatively local in nature. In return, we greatly reduce the insidious, non-trivial errors found in big modules — e.g., the sort of error that occurs when the 3,279th statement in the module destroys, through three levels of indirect addressing, a storage area carefully set up by the 13th statement in the module. What we are saying, then, is that the factoring process — if done well — tends to "flatten" the non-linear rise of errors that we saw in Fig. 5.1; in fact, we would expect to see an error curve of the sort shown in Fig. 5.2.

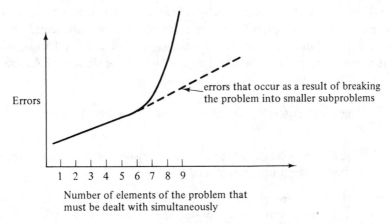

Fig. 5.2 Error curve when problems are broken into pieces.

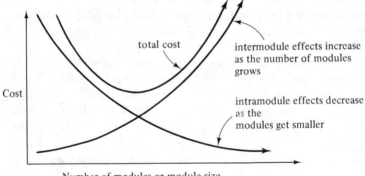

Fig. 5.3 Opposing influences of intramodule errors and intermodule errors.

As we have already suggested, chopping a system into a thousand one-statement modules is likely to cost as much as (and possibly even more than) a single 1,000-statement module to accomplish the same task. Clearly, these two alternatives are at the extreme ends of a spectrum of choices: We could imagine 10 modules of 100 statements each, or 20 modules of 50 statements each, or 100 modules of 10 statements each, and so forth. As the modules get smaller and smaller (assuming, once again, that they are independent of one another), we would expect them to become simpler internally; as we get more modules, we would expect that the problems due to intermodule bugs would increase. The total number of errors we commit (and thus, to a large extent, the cost of developing the entire system) is the sum of these two opposing influences, as illustrated in Fig. 5.3.

At this point, we are not prepared to predict the size of the "optimally small" module. Indeed, it is very doubtful that we ever will be able to make precise statements like, The optimal size for a module is nine statements. However, in Chapter 9 we will discuss a number of guidelines and heuristics that should prove sufficient to guide the designer in most cases. All we have done in this section is to emphasize the following:

- The cost of developing most systems is largely the cost of debugging them.

- The cost of debugging is essentially equivalent to the cost of errors committed by the programmer/analyst.

- The number of errors committed during the design, coding, and debugging of a system rises non-linearly as the complexity (which may be thought of as roughly equal to the size) of the system increases.

- Complexity can be decreased (and, thus, errors and the cost of developing the system) by breaking the problem into smaller and smaller pieces, so long as these pieces are relatively independent of each other.

- Eventually, the process of breaking pieces of the system into smaller pieces will create more complexity than it eliminates, because of inter-module dependencies — but this point does not occur as quickly as most designers would like to believe.

A final word of caution is in order: Whenever we talk of improvements in design, or potential savings in costs, there will always be an implied qualification. We assume equal quality of implementation. It is possible to do a sufficiently poor job of implementing a plan or design so as to exceed any arbitrary limit in cost, time, or any measure of dysfunctionality of the solution. That is to say, there is always some programmer bad enough to screw up even the best design!

5.3 COMPLEXITY IN HUMAN TERMS

We have suggested in the previous section that most of our problems in programming occur because human beings (we are obviously making the charitable assumption that all programmers and analysts *are* human beings) make mistakes, and that human beings make mistakes because of their limited capacity for complexity. This leads to an obvious question: What is it that humans consider complex? In specific terms, what aspects of systems design and program design do programmers consider complex? And, by extension, what can we do to make systems less complex?

We have already suggested that the *size* of a module is one simple measure of complexity; generally, a 100-statement module will be more difficult to understand than a 10-statement module. There is obviously more to it than that, since some statements are more complex than others. Halstead[4] and others, for example, feel that decision-making statements (e.g., IF statements) are one of the prime contributors to complexity in a module. Another possible contributor to complexity is the "span" of data elements — i.e., the number of program statements during which the status and value of a data element must be remembered by the programmer in order to comprehend what the module is doing; thus, a module is made more complex if a data element is loaded into an accumulator in the second instruction, and the data element then is not used until the 147th instruction.

Another related aspect of complexity is the span of control flow — the number of lexically contiguous statements one must examine before one finds a black-box section of code that has one entry point and one exit point. It is interesting to note that the theories behind structured programming[6] provide a means of reducing this span to an almost minimal length by organizing the logic into combinations of "sequence," "IF-THEN-ELSE," and "DO-WHILE" operations.

All of these measures recognize that the human-perceived complexity of program statements varies, influencing the apparent *size* of a module. Three factors, implicit in the above approaches, have been identified as affecting statement complexity:

- the *amount* of information that must be understood correctly

- the *accessibility* of the information

- the *structure* of the information

These factors determine the probability of human error in processing information of all kinds. While the complexity of all types of program statements can be evaluated in these terms, we will focus our discussion on examples of statements that establish intermodular interfaces.

By "amount" of information, we mean the number of bits of data, in the information-theoretical sense, that the programmer must deal with in order to comprehend the interface. In simplest terms, this is correlated with the number of arguments, or parameters, that are being passed in the call. All other things being equal, a subroutine call that involves 178 parameters will be more difficult to comprehend than a subroutine call with three parameters. When the programmer sees a module reference (e.g., a subroutine call) in the middle of a module, he must know what the reference will accomplish, and what information is being transmitted.

Consider, for example, the programmer who has just been assigned to finish testing and debugging an undocumented 20-statement module written by another programmer. Imagine that the new programmer finds, imbedded within the 20-statement module, the statement

CALL SQRT(X)

Chances are, he would immediately decide that the square root of data element x was being computed, and that the result was being returned in x — presumably destroying the original contents. If in his 20-statement module, the programmer found

CALL SQRT(X,Y)

he would probably conclude that the SQRT module must compute the square root of its first argument, returning the answer in the second argument, although he could be wrong if the input and output arguments were inverted. But, suppose that the programmer found the statement

CALL SQRT(X,Y,Z)

At this point, he might pause, scratch his head, curse the memory of the departed author of the program, and then assume that SQRT computes the square root of its first argument (X), returning the answer in its second argument (Y), and an error flag in its third argument (Z) if the first argument (X) was negative. Here, there are still more ways in which the statement could be misinterpreted.

At least, that is what one might infer . . . but what if the author of a square root subroutine had decided, out of sheer spite, that the first argument (X) should be the error flag, the second argument (Y) should be the output from the SQRT module, and the third argument (Z) should be the input to the module? Needless to say, the new programmer could insert a number of errors into the code while trying to come to grips with this entirely unexpected interface.

While the above example was contrived, the reader must admit that it smacks of reality. One could argue that the problem could be solved by providing appropriate documentation, but aside from the fact that such a suggestion is basically unrealistic (almost all detailed documentation in the real world is written *after* the code has been debugged; if the programmer is forced to write the documentation before the code, it will surely be obsolete by the time the code is debugged; in any case, the documentation will be obsolete and incorrect within a month after the code is debugged), it evades the basic question — what kind of information concerning the intermodule interfaces is least complex and least prone to errors?

Since we will be stressing highly modular structures throughout this book, the question we have posed is an important one. While we agree that there are well-established standards for narrative documentation of intermodule interfaces (see, for example, Gray and London's discussion[7]), we shall confine our attention to the interface *as written in the code*.

The programmer often argues that there is nothing he can do about the number of parameters: "If subroutine GETINPUT requires eight input parameters, then it requires eight input parameters — it doesn't help much to tell me that the interface would have been simpler if there were only seven parameters!" While this may be true, the presence of a large number of parameters in a calling sequence is often a clue that the called module is performing more than one task. By splitting the module into smaller pieces, each of which accomplishes only one task, we may be able to reduce the number of parameters. Thus, instead of having to study the call

CALL GETINPUT(A,B,C,D,E,F,G,H)

We would find ourselves studying the following sort of code:

```
_____

_____

CALL GETTRANSACTION(A,B,C,D,G)

_____

_____

CALL GETMASTER(B,E,F,G,H)
```

Note that each module now has five parameters in its interface; both GET-TRANSACTION and GETMASTER require parameters B and G in order to perform their tasks. Cutting a module in half does not necessarily mean that the total number of parameters in the interfaces will be cut in half. The techniques for recognizing those modules that accomplish more than one task, and dividing them into smaller modules that accomplish only one task will be discussed in Chapter 7.

Perhaps more important than the amount of information is its *accessibility*. Certain information about the use of the interface must be understood by the programmer to write or interpret the code correctly. There are four issues here:

- The interface is less complex if the information can be accessed (by the programmer, not by the computer) *directly;* it is more complex if the information refers *indirectly* to some other data element.

- The interface is less complex if the information is presented *locally* — that is, presented with the subroutine-calling statement itself. The interface is more complex if the needed information is *remote* from the interface statement itself.

- The interface is less complex if the necessary information is presented in a *standard* manner; it is more complex if the information is presented in an *unexpected* manner.

- The interface is less complex if its nature is *obvious;* it is more complex if it is *obscure*.

To illustrate the use of these concepts, consider the following example: We are to write a subroutine, LENGTH, which is to compute the distance between two points on a sheet of graph paper. The coordinates of the first point will be called x0,y0; the coordinates of the second point will be called x1,y1. The computation that must be performed by LENGTH is thus the simple calculation.

$$\text{LENGTH} = \text{SQRT} \left((y1 - y0)^2 + (x1 - x0)^2 \right)$$

Suppose we were then asked to select one of the following interfaces:

Option 1. CALL LENGTH(x0,y0,x1,y1,DISTANCE)

Option 2. CALL LENGTH(ORIGIN,END,DISTANCE)

Option 3. CALL LENGTH(XCOORDS,YCOORDS,DISTANCE)

Option 4. CALL LENGTH(LINE,DISTANCE)

Option 5. CALL LENGTH(LINETABLE)

Option 6. CALL LENGTH

Which interface is the least complex to a human who must use it?   On the basis of established results in human information processing, Option 1 is the simplest, least error-prone.   At first glance, it may appear that Option 1 involves the most complex interface; after all, we suggested earlier that the complexity is increased by the presence of large numbers of parameters.   We did, however, insert a small qualification that may have gone unnoticed: "all other things being equal."

Option 1 involves parameters that are presented in a *direct* fashion; the name "x0" is indeed the identifier of the data element containing the value of the x-coordinate of the initial point.   By contrast, Option 2 involves information that is presented in an *indirect* fashion; in order to comprehend the interface, we would probably have to turn to some other part of the program listing to find that ORIGIN is defined in terms of the subelements x0 and y0.   One might argue this point — after all, according to some programmers, ORIGIN is perfectly meaningful in the direct sense, and one would not have to look any further to find out what it means.

On the other hand, suppose that the module that calls LENGTH is concerned with *several* different points on the sheet of graph paper — that is, there may well be variables x2 and y2, x3 and y3, . . . , xn and yn defined in the program.   If such is the case, then *which* points are implied by the identifiers ORIGIN and END?   Obviously, we will have to look at that part of the program that defines ORIGIN; if we are lucky, we might see something akin to the COBOL concept of levels of data in the DATA DIVISION:

```
05    ORIGIN
      10        x0
      10        y0

05    END
      10        x1
      10        y1
```

However, it is just as likely that we will find a definition of the sort

05	ORIGIN	
	10	BEGINNING-X-COORDINATE
	10	BEGINNING-Y-COORDINATE
05	END	
	10	FINAL-X-COORDINATE
	10	FINAL-Y-COORDINATE

in which case, we will have to look through the entire program to see the last point at which some data was moved into ORIGIN and END prior to the call to LENGTH which we are currently studying. In any case, some indirect references are certainly necessary, and there is no doubt that it makes the interface somewhat complex.

It can be argued that Option 3, which takes the form

CALL LENGTH(XCOORDS,YCOORDS,DISTANCE)

is even more complex. Obviously, the parameters XCOORDS and YCOORDS represent required information indirectly. In addition, the information is being presented to the programmer in a nonstandard way; this alone makes the interface somewhat more complex. That is, the standard way (by convention) to present information about two points on a sheet of graph paper is

ORIGIN = (X0,Y0)

END = (X1,Y1)

while the following is less common:

XCOORDS = (X0,X1)

YCOORDS = (Y0,Y1)

A small matter, to be sure, but enough to increase the likelihood of the programmer inserting one or two bugs into his code before he *really* understands the interface.

The degree of conglomeration is further increased in Option 4. Still fewer things can vary independently. With any option in the general case, each use requires the setting up of computed values, possibly with some fixed ones. The basic issue is whether these are set up integrally with the call on LENGTH, as in Option 1, or remotely, as in the other options.

Option 5, which suggests an interface of CALL LENGTH(LINETABLE), is still more complex. The identifier LINETABLE is obscure. How many programmers would instantly recognize that such a variable would include not only the x-co-ordinates and y-coordinates of the initial and ending points, but also the returned length? Once again, there conceivably could be mitigating circumstances: It is possible that throughout the entire program, the code requires all five, and the *same* five, elements of the quintuplet (x0,y0,x1,y1,DISTANCE) for its computations. However, this hardly seems a credible argument; at the very least, it makes it much less likely that LENGTH can be used as a general-purpose subroutine in some other system.

Finally, we consider Option 6, which suggests an interface of CALL LENGTH. At first glance, it may appear that such a subroutine call has *no* parameters — but we know better. LENGTH still requires initial (x,y) coordinates and final (x,y) coordinates to perform its task, and it must still leave the DISTANCE information some place useful — and presumably both LENGTH and the module calling it know where that information will be stored. The problem is that the programmer doesn't know — at least, not by looking at the statement CALL LENGTH. In other words, the parameters are not *local* to the subroutine-calling statement; all the information is provided *remotely*, in a place whose whereabouts cannot be determined by look-ing at the CALL LENGTH statement.

If all the arguments were set up immediately preceding the call to LENGTH, it would be obvious. However, it is hardly safe to assume that all programmers us-ing the CALL LENGTH statement will adhere to such discipline. Eventually, the pro-grammer begins taking advantage of the fact that some of the parameters naturally are set up 23 statements earlier in the code.

Adequate documentation itself increases the accessibility of information and decreases the probability of errors in use. And standardization (see, for example, Gray and London[7]) further improves things. But, remember that all documenta-tion is less accessible, when dealing with the code, than the code itself. An undocu-mented but intrinsically simple sequence may be preferable to a well-documented, complicated one.

It will be immediately obvious to the COBOL programmer that the PER-FORM statement forces Option 6. This is an inadequacy of the language that can only be avoided at the present time by using the CALL statement. It is interesting to note, though, that the CODASYL X3J4 Programming Languages Committee is studying changes to COBOL that include, among other things, parameter lists on PERFORM statements.[8] Similarly, the FORTRAN programmer is familiar with the practice of placing arguments in COMMON to avoid passing data through a param-eter list; the PL/I programmer and the ALGOL programmer accomplish the same thing by defining data in a global fashion. In all of these languages, the program-mer often *consciously* avoids passing data explicitly through a parameter list — either by using COMMON in FORTRAN, by using global variables in PL/I or ALGOL, or by using PERFORM instead of CALL in COBOL.

Why the aversion to passing data through a parameter list? There seem to be three objections: It appears to require more work on the part of the programmer; coding the parameter list is an error-prone process in itself; and it is less efficient than accessing data in a global fashion.   The first objection seems to be an example of the "penny wise-pound foolish" phenomenon: It may take a few more minutes (at most) to explicitly code the parameters as part of the calling sequence, but it could save far more in debugging and maintenance.   We have already discussed the second objection: Of course, errors can be introduced when coding the parameter list in a calling sequence, but such errors tend to be simpler and more direct than the subtle errors that occur when one module begins destroying the global data that belongs to another unrelated module (we will deal with this problem in detail in the next chapter).

The last argument — that passing data through a parameter list is inefficient — is probably the most common one, and the one in which programmers believe most passionately.   Since efficiency is still a major problem in some computer systems, and since programmer/analysts *do* feel so passionate about the subject, it is not an objection to be brushed away lightly; indeed, a good part of Chapters 13, 14, and 15 deals with various aspects of efficiency.   Suffice it to say at this point that argument-passing is usually a serious problem in only a few isolated cases; in most cases, a subroutine call will be executed only a few times, and the wasted microseconds of CPU time can safely be ignored.   In those rare instances in which the overhead is bothersome, the programmer always has the option of changing the calling sequence back to a more efficient one.   To keep things in proper perspective though, we emphasize once again that *people*, not *machines*, are the primary cost of today's computer systems; we should be prepared to waste *hours* of computer time, if it will save us months or years of people time.

As a final comment on the complexity of intermodule interfaces, we observe that the "structure" of information can be a key issue.   The primary point here is that information is less complex if it is presented to us in a linear fashion, more complex if it is presented in a nested fashion.   Similarly, information is less complex if it is presented in a positive fashion, more complex if it is presented in a negative fashion.   For example, consider the following *nested* English sentence:

The girl the boy the dog bit hit cried.

The average person would have to study such a sentence for several seconds before comprehending its meaning; eventually, he would draw mental parentheses to recognize that the structure of the sentence is

(The girl (the boy (the dog bit) hit) cried.)

Though it may seem clumsier, the following statements would probably be regarded by the average person as less complex:

The dog bit boy A.   Boy A hit girl B.   Girl B cried.

The human limits in processing nested information are even sharper than in dealing with linear, sequential information. Whereas one can readily deal with about 7 ± 2 distinct entities presented in a linear or parallel fashion, the human "push-down stack" can get overloaded at only two or three levels of nesting.

Now, imagine that we were trying to describe the scene involving two girls, one of whom cried and one of whom didn't; two boys, one of whom exhibited hostile, aggressive tendencies, and one of whom didn't; and two dogs, one of which was prone to biting moving objects, and one of which slept through the entire scene. We could describe it thus:

The boy the girl the dog did not bite did not hit did not cry.

Needless to say, such a statement involving *negative* qualifiers is generally more complex than one involving positive qualifiers.

Both of these concepts have primary application in the details of writing code. For example, it is well-known that certain forms of nested IF statements are considerably more difficult for the average person to understand than an equivalent sequence of simple IF statements. Similarly, it is known that Boolean expressions involving NOT operators are generally more difficult to understand than an equivalent expression without the NOT operator.

There are times, though, when the philosophies of linear thinking and positive thinking are important for intermodule references. Suppose, for example, that the programmer decided to compute the distance between two points on a sheet of graph paper by writing the statement

DISTANCE = SQRT (SUM(SQUARE(DIFFERENCE(Y1,Y0)),SQUARE
(DIFFERENCE(X1,X0))))

There is little doubt that the average programmer would write out the linear equivalent of this statement in order to comprehend what it does.

Similarly, there are times when the programmer/analyst builds some negative thinking into his intermodule interfaces. Suppose, for example, that the programmer has designed a module called SCAN, which will search through a string for a specified delimiter; if sucessful, SCAN will indicate the position in the string where the delimiter was first found. When designing the calling sequence, though, the programmer/analyst may be thinking more of the negative case — that is, the situation in which SCAN does *not* find the specified delimiter. Indeed, when he first conceived of the notion of a SCAN module, he may have been dealing with a portion of the problem in which it was very likely that the specified delimiter would *not* be found — that is, the problem might have called for the programmer to scan through a string of normal English text, looking for the presence of "&" characters.

With this in mind, the programmer/analyst might decide to design SCAN as a logical function — that is, one that has the value true or false when invoked.

Expecting failures from SCAN, he might design it in such a way that SCAN returns a value of true if the delimited is *not* found, and false if the delimited *is* found. This would allow him to write code such as:

```
(IF SCAN(TEXTSTRING, '&')     (are there any "&" characters?)
   _____             (deal with the normal case of no "&" characters)
   _____
   _____
ELSE                         (deal with the unusual case where "&" characters exist)
   _____
   _____
```

Elsewhere in the system, though, other designers would presumably expect SCAN to be involved in the *positive* act of looking for delimiters; finding such delimiters normally would be considered a success — and the designer instinctively would assume that SCAN would return a value of true when the specified delimiter was found. It is somewhat naive to suggest that the problem could be solved by asking the author of the SCAN module to document the interface in a memorandum for all the other designers. Even if the other designers read the document, there is still a good chance that the other designers — in the heat of the moment, when they are actually writing the code — will follow their instincts, and think *positively*. We should not be surprised to find that the use of SCAN, as we have defined it, will lead to an inordinate number of bugs. Indeed, one of the authors, having designed such a negative SCAN module in the early days of his career, can confirm it from experience!

5.4 SUMMARY

Although it may seem that this chapter is heavy on philosophy and light on practical advice, the philosophy actually forms the basis for almost all of the practical advice in Chapters 6 and 7 — not to mention a large portion of the rest of the book. It is absolutely essential that the designer realize that the major cost of developing computer systems is the cost of debugging, which, in turn, is the cost of *human* error.

And, it is essential that we be aware of the limitations of the human mind when we design computer systems (or any other complex system). Unless we realize that the cost of systems development can be reduced by partitioning systems into smaller pieces, we will be limited to developing systems of 100,000 lines of code or less. On the other hand, there is nothing to be gained from partitioning a system into modules of one instruction each; at some point, the simplicity of each individual module is outweighed by the complexity of the intermodule interfaces.

REFERENCES

1. EDWARD YOURDON, *Design of On-Line Computer Systems* (Engelwood Cliffs, N.J.: Prentice-Hall, 1972).

2. PHILIP W. METZGER, *Managing a Programming Project* (Englewood Cliffs, N.J.: Prentice-Hall, 1973).

3. FREDERICK P. BROOKS, JR., *The Mythical Man-Month* (Reading, Mass.: Addison-Wesley, 1975.

4. M.H. HALSTEAD, *The Elements of Software Science* (New York: American Elsevier, 1977.

5. GEORGE A. MILLER, "The Magical Number Seven, Plus or Minus Two: Some Limits on Our Capacity for Processing Information," *Psychological Review,* Vol. 63 (1956), pp. 81–97.

6. CORRADO BOHM and GIUSEPPE JACOPINI, "Flow Diagrams, Turing Machines and Languages with Only Two Formation Rules," *Communications of the ACM,* Vol. 9, No. 5 (May 1966), pp. 366–371.

7. MAX GRAY and KEITH R. LONDON, *Documentation Standards* (Philadelphia: Auerbach, 1969).

8. HENRY P. STEVENSON, ed., *Proceedings of CODASYL Programming Language Symposium on Structured Programming in COBOL—Future and Present* (New York: Association of Computing Machinery, 1975).

Coupling

CHAPTER 6

6.0 INTRODUCTION

Many aspects of modularity can be understood only by examining modules in relation to one another. In Chapter 5, we introduced a notion that is useful in the context of this discussion: *independence*. Two modules are totally independent if each can function completely without the presence of the other. This definition implies that there are no interconnections between the modules — direct or indirect, explicit or implicit, obvious or obscure. This establishes a zero point on the scale of "dependence" (the inverse of independence).

In general, the more interconnections between modules, the less independent they are likely to be. Of course, this is only an approximation; and before we can judge whether more is worse, we must ask whether the various connections between modules are identical, similar, or different. If two modules require six distinct, completely unique connections in order to function together, then they are more highly interconnected than if six connections of the same form would suffice. Similarly, six connections must generally lead to more dependence than three comparable ones.   The key question is: How much of one module must be known in order to understand another module?   *The more that we must know of module B in order to understand module A, the more closely connected A is to B.*   The fact that we must know something about another module is a priori evidence of some degree of interconnection even if the *form* of the interconnection is not known.

Unfortunately, the phrase "knowledge required to understand a module" is not very objective; we need an operational method of approximating the degree of interconnection.   As we have already suggested, a simple accounting of the number and variety of interconnections between modules is insufficient to fully characterize the influence of the interconnections on the system's modularity.   At the very least, we must be able to account for the fact that a long, involved calling sequence that interfaces with many internal control variables makes two modules less independent of each other than two equivalent modules with only a few basic input-output parameters passed in the call.

The measure that we are seeking is known as *coupling;* it is a measure of the *strength* of interconnection.   Thus, "highly coupled" modules are joined by strong interconnections; "loosely coupled" modules are joined by weak interconnections; "uncoupled" or "decoupled" modules have *no* interconnections and are, thus, *independent* in the sense that the term was used in Chapter 5.   Obviously, what we are striving for is loosely coupled systems — that is, systems in which one can study (or debug, or maintain) any one module without having to know very much about any other modules in the system.

Coupling as an abstract concept — the degree of interdependence between modules — may be operationalized as the probability that in coding, debugging, or modifying one module, a programmer will have to take into account something about another module.   If two modules are highly coupled, then there is a high probability that a programmer trying to modify one of them will have to make a change to the other.   Clearly, total systems cost will be strongly influenced by the degree of coupling between modules.

To see how coupling can be an important factor in total systems complexity, consider a system that processes records from a "customer master file"; we would expect such a file to have information about a customer's name, street address, city, state, ZIP code, telephone number, and the various financial or business data with which the system is primarily concerned.   Now, suppose that one programmer is assigned the task of writing a module to edit the "telephone number" field within the record — that is, to check the ten-digit field to ensure that it does, in fact, consist of all numeric digits, and that the field is nonzero.   To "simplify the interfaces" (as several of our students have phrased it), the designer might decide to pass the entire customer record to the TELEPHONE-EDIT module, rather than just the field it requires.

Now for the consequences of such a design: Suppose that Charlie, the programmer who designs and implements the TELEPHONE-EDIT module, is very aggressive and eager to do a good job.   It occurs to him that he can do a better job of editing the telephone number by cross-checking the "state" field within the customer record with the "area code" portion of the telephone number. Without telling anyone else in the programming team about this brilliant move (after all, he is writing a black-box module, so why should he have to tell anyone what the module does internally?), he sets up an area code/state code table internally in his module, and uses that to cross-check the telephone number in each customer record.

The first thing that goes wrong is that the TELEPHONE-EDIT module begins rejecting telephone numbers because they don't correlate with the state code — and later analysis shows that the state code was incorrect, not the telephone number! As a result, Charlie inserts a little extra coding to make sure, as best he can, that the state code is reasonable before he attempts to cross-check it with the telephone area code. Meanwhile, the word spreads through the rest of the programming team, "Apparently, Charlie has some weird code in his TELEPHONE-EDIT module that does something with the state code."

The coupling aspect of the problem becomes obvious when the *user* of the system suddenly announces that he wishes to change the state code in the customer record from the standard two-character abbreviation (e.g., NY, TX, and so on) to a full character string representation (e.g., NEW YORK, TEXAS, and so forth). Everyone on the programming team immediately panics: Which parts of the system will be affected? The point is obvious: In order to comprehend an aspect of the system that, on the surface, has nothing to do with telephone numbers, we must be familiar with Charlie's TELEPHONE-EDIT module. Why? Because, ultimately, Charlie's module was coupled with other modules in the system.

6.1 FACTORS THAT INFLUENCE COUPLING

Four major aspects of computer systems can increase or decrease intermodular coupling. In order of estimated magnitude of their effect on coupling, these are

- *Type of connection between modules.* So-called minimally connected systems have the lowest coupling, and normally connected systems have lower coupling than those with pathological connections.

- *Complexity of the interface.* This is approximately equal to the number of different items being passed (not the amount of data) — the more items, the higher the coupling.

- *Type of information flow along the connection.* Data-coupled systems have lower coupling than control-coupled systems, which have lower coupling than hybrid-coupled systems.

- *Binding time of the connection.* Connections bound to fixed referents at execution time result in lower coupling than binding that takes place at loading time, which results in lower coupling than binding that takes place at linkage-edit time, which in turn results in lower coupling than binding that takes place at compilation (or assembly) time — all of which result in still lower coupling than binding that takes place at coding time.

Each of these is important and is discussed separately below.

6.1.1 Type of connection between modules

Recall that a connection in a program is a reference by one element to the name, address, or identifier of another element. An intermodular connection occurs when the referenced element is in a different module from the referencing element. Any such referenced element defines an interface, a portion of the module boundary across which data or control flow. The interface may be regarded as residing at the referenced element; you may think of it as a socket into which the plug, represented by the connection from the referencing module, is inserted. Every interface in a module represents one more thing which is/must be known, understood, and properly connected by other modules in the system.

Clearly, we want to minimize systems/module complexity in part by minimizing the number (and variety) of interfaces per module. We already know that each module must have at least one interface to be uniquely defined and to be tied into a system. But is a single identity interface sufficient to implement real functioning systems? The key question here is: What purpose do interfaces serve? In programs, they can only serve a limited variety of functional purposes. Only *control* and *data* can be passed among modules in a programming system. An interface can serve to transmit data into a module (as input parameters), or out of the module (as output results). It can be a name by which control is received or transmitted. Only these four generic capabilities are required. Any scheme which provides interfaces for all four must, by definition, be sufficient to realize all programmable systems.

By a judicious choice of conventions, we will be able to have a single interface per module serve all four purposes. First, we associate the identity interface of the module with its entry or activation interface; that is, a single unique entry interface serves not only to receive control, but to identify the module. We also can transmit data to the module without adding interfaces by making the entry/identity interface capable of accepting data as well as control. This requires that elements of data be passed dynamically as arguments (parameters) as part of the activation sequence, which gives control to a module; any static reference to data would introduce new interfaces.

With respect to any two modules, say A and B, we have determined that the following familiar structure is sufficient to get control and data from A into B:

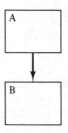

Unfortunately, we cannot use the same approach to get control from B to A, as that would define a system with more than the minimal number of interconnections between modules. We need the identity interface of B to serve as a path for control to be received by A, as transmitted by B; this is a "return" of control to A. We can accomplish this by having the control transfer from A to B be a *conditioned* transfer. B will thus be able to return implicitly to A (or any other activating module) without the introduction of additional interfaces.

This also suggests a mechanism for transmitting data from B back to A without adding extra interfaces: We may associate a value with the particular activation of B, and use this contextually in A (e.g., by making B a logical function, as we did in the SCAN example in Chapter 5). Alternatively, we can transmit to B parameters that define locations for return of results to A.

If all connections of a system are restricted to fully parameterized (with respect to inputs and outputs) conditioned transfers of control to the single, unique activation/entry/origin/identity interface of any module, then the system is termed *minimally connected*. A minimally connected structure has the lowest number of interconnections and interfaces needed to define bidirectional control and information transfer between communicating modules.

It is important to realize that minimally connected structures are minimal in a fundamental sense, and yet are sufficient for the realization of all actual program functions. Minimally connected modules require the least knowledge of discrete, internal features of the module. In addition, such systems have simple, "normal" behavior since the entire data context of a module and its precise return are established and guaranteed by the activating module. The pattern of control transfers into and out of modules must define a symmetric, fully nested set, and all transfers must strictly follow the hierarchical lines so established.

Other control relationships can be admitted which, while not satisfying the requirements for minimal connectedness, still preserve the normal behavior of minimally connected systems. We shall call a system *normally connected* if it is minimally connected, except for one or more instances of the following:

- There is more than one entry point to a single module, provided that each such entry is minimal with respect to data transfers.

- Control returns to other than the next sequential statement in the activating module, provided that alternate returns are defined by the *activating* module as part of its activation process.

- Control is transferred to a normal entry point by something other than a conditioned transfer of control.

Use of multiple entry points to a module guarantees that there will be more than the minimum number of interconnections for the system. On the other hand, if each entry point still functions as a minimal (fully parameterized, conditioned transfer) connection as far as other modules are concerned, the behavior of the system should be every bit as normal as if minimally connected. We note, however, that the presence of multiple entry points suggests that the module is carrying out multiple functions. Furthermore, there is an excellent chance that the programmer will partially overlap the code for each of the functions; this means that the functions within the multiple-entry-point module will be content-coupled (a concept discussed in Section 6.1.3.). However, this can be regarded as an issue separate from that of using multiple-entry-point modules to build normally connected systems.

In a similar vein, *alternate returns* are frequently useful and are within the spirit of normally connected systems. Frequently, a subordinate module wishes to return binary or three-valued results to its superordinate — binary results representing the outcome of decisions in the subordinate. Minimal connectedness would require returning the outcome of such decisions as a datum (e.g., a parameter) to be retested in the superordinate. However, control characteristics would still be simple and predictable if the superordinate module specifices one or more alternate return locations — one of which must be taken by the subordinate upon completion of its processing. Depending on the programming language, the designer can usually provide for alternate returns by specifying a "relative return" (i.e., a return to calling address + 1, to calling address + 2, and so on), or an "alternate return parameter" (where the address of a return location in the superordinate is passed to the subordinate).

If a system is not minimally connected or normally connected, then some of its modules must have pathological connections. That is, at least some of the modules must make unconditioned transfers of control to labels within the boundaries of other modules, or they must make explicit references to data elements outside their own module boundaries. All such situations increase the *coupling* of the system by increasing the amount that we must know about the "outside world" in order to understand how any one module works. All other things being equal, then, coupling is minimized in a minimally connected system; it is likely to be slightly higher with a normally connected system and much higher with pathological connections. The subject of pathological connections is so important that all of Chapter 13 is devoted to it.

6.1.2 Complexity of the interface

The second dimension of coupling is *complexity*. The more complex a single connection is, the higher the coupling. This dimension is necessary to account for the effect of a normal subroutine call with 134 parameters specified as opposed to a call involving the specification of only two parameters.

By "complexity" we mean complexity in human terms, as discussed in Chapter 5. There are various ways to approximate the complexity of an interface, though none is perfect. One simple method, for example, is to count the number of characters in the statement(s) involved in the connection between two modules. Obviously, this is a very rough approximation, since making any consistent substitution of identifiers throughout the program could increase or decrease the character count in the approximate statements without actually affecting their complexity.

A better approximation can be achieved by counting the number of discrete symbols or "language tokens" involved in the interface — that is, names, vocabulary words, variables, punctuation, and so on. In simple terms, then, we would expect that a subroutine-calling interface with 134 arguments in the parameter list would involve more coupling than an interface with only two parameters.

6.1.3 Information flow

Another important aspect of coupling has to do with the *type* of information that is transmitted between superordinate and subordinate; the kinds of information we distinguish are data, control, and a special hybrid of data and control. Information that constitutes data is that which is operated upon, manipulated, or changed by a piece of program. Control information (even when represented by a "data variable") is that which governs how the operations upon or manipulations of other information (the data) will take place.

It can be shown that the communication of *data* alone is necessary for functioning systems of modules. Control communication represents a dispensable addition found in most, but not necessarily all, computer programs. Coupling is, therefore, minimized (all other things being equal, of course) when only input data and output data flow across the interface between two modules. A connection establishes *input-output coupling,* or *data-coupling,* if it provides output data from one module that serves as input data to the other. Not all connections which appear to move data are necessarily of this type: The data might be a flag used to control certain aspects of the execution of the other module, or it might be a "branch-address" to be used if certain conditions arise. These are elements of control disguised as data.

We should emphasize that input-output coupling bears no relationship to input-output devices. Disks, tapes, and other peripheral devices may or may not mediate the connection. What is essential is the *purpose* the connection serves.

Input-output coupling is minimal, because no system can function without it. Modules cannot function as a single system performing an overall purpose, unless the outputs of some modules become the inputs of others. Moreover, any system can be constructed in such a way that the *only* coupling is input-output coupling. The inescapable conclusion is that all communication of control not only is extraneous, but also introduces needless additional coupling.

It is easy to see, at a high level, how a system could be constructed with only input-output coupling.   Consider, for example, an application involving four "transforms" to be applied to a stream of data consisting of student names, in alphabetical order; associated with each student record is a list of other students (presumably from the same educational institution) that he/she likes best.   The first transform involves splitting the stream of data into two separate "substreams"; one substream consists of the student's name (and other biographical data), and the other substream consists of the names that the student has nominated as favorites.   The second transform involves performing some computations on the first substream of student names.   The third transform involves sorting the second substream into alphabetical order — those people who have been named as favorites.   The fourth and final transform is to produce a combined report that lists a student, appropriate biographical information (with the results of the computations performed by the second transform), and a list of all those who named him as a favorite.

The input-output flow, or data flow, structure of this problem is shown in Fig. 6.1.   If we have enough equipment lying around, we can program this as four fully independent programs, each of which reads inputs from paper tape and punches output on paper tape.   Assuming that the paper tape readers have interlocks to prevent the tape from tearing, we could load these machines in the manner shown in Fig. 6.2, and start all four running.   That we have achieved parallel processing is not the central point; what is important is that we have succeeded in constructing a system that is only input-output coupled (you should be able to see that we can always do this), and it consists of maximally independent modules — no control information is being passed.   Q.E.D.!   We will return to this topic, exploring it in terms of more elementary modules in Chapter 18.

In discussing input-output coupling, we noted that communication of elements of control represented a stronger (and, therefore, less desirable) form of coupling.   Since *control-coupling* is nonessential, any system that includes it must consist of less independent modules (other things being equal, of course).   Control-coupling covers all forms of connection that communicate elements of control. This may involve actual transfer of control (e.g., activation of modules), or it may

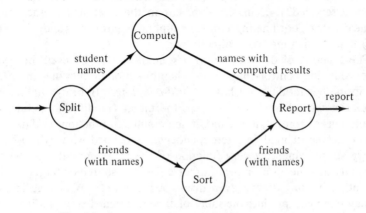

Fig. 6.1 Input-output structure of a small problem.

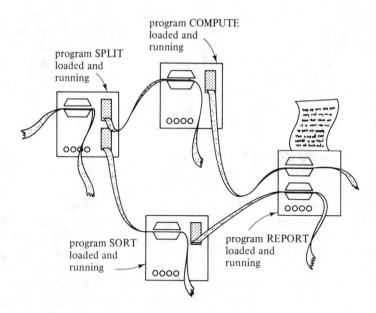

program COMPUTE
loaded and
running

program SPLIT
loaded and
running

program SORT
loaded and
running

program REPORT
loaded and
running

Fig. 6.2   System of Fig. 6.1 with only input-output coupling.

involve the passing of data that change, regulate, or synchronize the target module (or serve to do the same for the originating module).

Such "secondary" or indirect control is termed *coordination*. Coordination involves one module in the procedural contents of another; this may not be obvious in the abstract, but it should be clear in an example. For instance, a subroutine that assembles successive elements of data into compound elements for the superordinate may send a flag to the superordinate indicating whether its return is to request an additional data element or to deliver a completed compound item. The superordinate must contain a decision (in this case, binary in nature), which relates to an internal task of the subordinate module that assembles items (namely: Is the item assembled?). This involvement in the internal activities of another module means that coordinating control-coupling is stronger (and, therefore, less desirable) than "activating" control-coupling.

The function of data and control sometimes may be even more confused than in coordinating control-coupling. When one module modifies the procedural contents of another module, we have *hybrid-coupling*. Hybrid-coupling is simply intermodular statement modification. To the target (modified) module, the connection functions as control; to the modifying module, it functions as data.

The degree of module interdependence associated with hybrid-coupling is clearly very strong, since the very function of the target module can be changed. Moreover, any modification or recoding of either the source or target module may affect the other by an extreme, even disastrous, amount. A change in the target module may eliminate or shift the label of the statement being modified, resulting in modification of the wrong statement; similarly, changes in the source module, which are not based on full analysis of the possible consequences for the target module, can cause it to malfunction in mysterious ways. Fortunately, using hybrid-coupling is a practice that is declining except among systems programmers and those involved in assembly language programming on minicomputers and microcomputers.

Experience has shown that direct modification of data operands, whether intermodular or intramodular, is less serious than modification of programming statements. This seems to affect hybrid-coupling as well.

6.1.4 Binding time of intermodular connections

"Binding" is a term commonly used in the data processing field to refer to the process of resolving or fixing the values of identifiers used within a system. The binding of variables to values — or, more broadly, of identifiers to specific referents — may take place at any of several stages or time periods in the evolution of the system. The time-history of the system may be thought of as a line extending from the moment of writing through the moment of execution. The line may be sub-divided to greater or lesser degrees of fineness by different computer/language/compiler/operating system combinations.

Thus, binding can take place when the programmer writes a statement on a coding sheet; when a module is compiled or assembled; when the compiled or assembled code is processed by a "linking-loader" or "linkage-editor" (interestingly, *this* process is referred to as binding on some systems); when a "core-image" is loaded into memory (this is often indistinguishable from "linkage-editing" on some systems); and, finally, when the system begins running.

The concept of binding time is an important one in program and systems design. When the values of parameters within some piece of code are fixed late rather than early, they are more readily changed and the system becomes more adaptable to changing requirements. In this broad context, let us return to the customer master file system that we discussed at the beginning of the chapter.

Let us imagine that one of the major functions of the system (which we will refer to as the CMF system) is to permit modifications to the "personal data" on the master file — that is, provisions must be made to allow the customer to change his name, address, phone number, and so forth. Further, let us imagine that the transactions specifying these changes are presented to the CMF system in a "free-field" format, and that the data is allowed to be of variable length. For example, if customer Henry Fribble informs us that he has changed his name to John Smith, we would expect a superordinate module to pass control to a subordinate module with a pointer to the beginning of the text string "JOHN SMITH." It is the job of the subordinate NAME-CHANGE module to scan this text string, looking for errors, and then to substitute the new customer name in place of the old one in the master record.

Let us imagine that Charlie has been given the assignment to design and code NAME-CHANGE. While studying the problem, it occurs to Charlie that one of the first things he must do is to scan the text string to ensure that it is terminated properly, that is, to ensure that there is a closing "quotation mark" on the text string "JOHN SMITH." Charlie is aware that the transactions are on punched cards, and he knows that his text string might begin at any character position on the card. Everyone knows that punched cards are 80-columns long; thus, Charlie decides to test, in his NAME-CHANGE module, to ensure that the "JOHN SMITH" text string does not run past column 80.

The first mistake that Charlie makes — from a *binding* point of view — is to code the *literal* "80" throughout his module. Indeed, it is worse than that; his code is liberally sprinkled with references to the literal "79" and the literal "81" — which, of course, *really* represent "80 − 1" and "80 + 1."

It never occurs to Charlie that not all punched cards are 80 columns long; however, the nature of the problem will become clear as soon as the user decides that he wishes to run the CMF system on an IBM System/3 with its 96-column cards! Note that if Charlie attempts to use a sophisticated text-editing package to change all occurrences of the literal "80" to the literal "96", he will miss the literals "79" and "81" . . . and if he willy-nilly changes the references to the literals "79," "80," and "81," he may well end up changing things he did not want.

Of course, this is a simple example of a parameter whose *binding* took place at coding time. It also illustrates the primary reason why this type of binding takes place: naivety. When confronted with the 96-column card problem, Charlie's predictable response is, "Well, you can't blame me for that! How was I supposed to know that you were going to change from 80-column cards. . . ." The situation will hardly be improved if Charlie decides to correct the problem by introducing a parameter into his program called NINETY-SIX, whose value is — surprise! — the literal "96." What we really want is a parameter called END-OF-CARD.

Unfortunately, the trouble is not over yet. Not only does Charlie have an END-OF-CARD parameter in his module, it turns out that all of the other programmers in the CMF system have similar parameters in their modules. Not only do the parameters all have slightly different names (like MAX-CHARS-IN-CARD), but they are all local variables whose binding takes place when each module is compiled. Thus, when the user announces a switch to a Widget computer with 85-column cards, the system's designer discovers that all of the CMF modules are *still* coupled by the "number-of-columns-in-card" data element; that is, he must change the parameter in each module (if he can find it), and then recompile and re-link-edit all of the modules.

Clearly, the solution is to make the aforementioned data element "external" to all of the modules. That is, we easily could build a separate module that contains only declarations of important "systems parameters," such as the number of columns in a card. In this way, the binding of the parameter would be delayed until the link-editing process took place.

In most EDP projects, this degree of caution would be sufficient. However, let us take things one step further: Suppose our user has decided to connect his original IBM System/370, his new IBM System/3, and his even newer Widget computer over telephone lines to a brand-new Frammis computer that will actually perform the CFM processing. To simplify matters, we can assume that only one of the machines — the System/370, the System/3, or the Widget — will be connected to the Frammis at one time. As soon as the connection is established, the CMF system will be started, and it will begin receiving card images transmitted from the remote machine. The point is obvious: Since all three machines had different card formats, the *binding* of the "number-of-characters-in-card" parameter will have to be delayed until the CMF system actually begins executing.

Now we can consider the issue of binding time in relation to intermodular connections, and the manner in which this influences the degree of coupling between modules. Again, an intermodular reference, which becomes fixed to refer to a specific object at, say, definition time, more strongly couples the referencing and referent module than if the connection were not fixed until translation time or later.

Certain commonly encountered examples in design systems will make this clear. Whenever the language/compiler/operating environment permits separate compilation of modules, maintaining and modifying the system are easier than when all modules must be coded, compiled, and recompiled as a single unit. If the linkage of modules is deferred until just prior to execution, implementing changes or even radical restructuring are made even easier.

Because lexical relationships (compare the definitions in the Glossary) are fixed at definition time, the lexical structure of a program can introduce strong interdependencies between modules — even those with no functional interrelationship. Sometimes, these lexical interrelationships are referred to as *content-coupling*. Content-coupling occurs when some or all of the contents of one module are included in the contents of another. Two forms of lexical content-coupling may be distinguished. Lexical inclusion of one module inside another, by itself, is a fairly mild form of coupling. While neither the lexical superordinate nor its subordinate can be used without the other in some form, the process of separating the two into lexically independent units is generally straightforward, unless the lexical subordinate fulfills some position-dependent function. This will be the case if the lexical subordinate is activated in-line (by "falling into" the code) in some circumstances.

Partial content overlap is a more extreme form of lexical content-coupling. Consider the lexical structure of Fig. 6.3 on the next page. Since many programming languages will not permit this structure, we must "invent" one that permits direct declaration of partial overlap. We should emphasize, though, that in many languages, close approximations of this are common programming practice. In the case of Fig. 6.3, both module ARC and module CHORD are intimately tied with the function of the other, and neither can be used independently.

Furthermore, the modifications necessary to decouple the modules are nontrivial. The common sections beginning at statement LL2 must be extracted and made into an independent module, which is activated from both ARC and CHORD in the appropriate places. If there is anything at all clever or tricky in the use of these common sections of code, this procedure could be complicated. The skeletal form of the transformation is shown in Fig. 6.4.

A multiple-entry module is an example of content-coupling, and represents

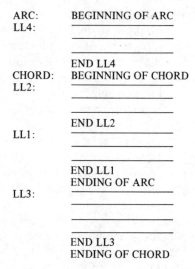

```
ARC:        BEGINNING OF ARC
LL4:        _____
            _____
            _____
            END LL4
CHORD:      BEGINNING OF CHORD
LL2:        _____
            _____
            END LL2
LL1:        _____
            _____
            END LL1
            ENDING OF ARC
LL3:        _____
            _____
            _____
            END LL3
            ENDING OF CHORD
```

Fig. 6.3 Modules with partial overlap form of content-coupling.

```
ARC:        BEGINNING OF ARC
LL4:        _____
            _____
            END LL4
            USE LL2
            USE LL1
            ENDING OF ARC

CHORD:      BEGINNING OF CHORD
            USE LL2
            USE LL1
LL3:        _____
            _____
            END LL3
            ENDING OF CHORD

LL2:        BEGINNING OF LL2
            _____
            _____
            ENDING OF LL2

LL1:        BEGINNING OF LL1
            _____
            _____
            ENDING OF LL1
```

Fig. 6.4 Modules of Fig. 6.3 transformed.

a special case of lexical inclusion in which the identity interface of several modules (the alternative functions) are defined at the same lexical level. It is usually difficult to maintain or modify the various functions of a multiple-entry module independently.

In terms of usage, maintenance, and modification, the consequences of control-coupling are very different from content-coupling. In Fig. 6.5, control-coupling (in this case, activation as a subordinate) is indicated by arrows, and content-coupling is shown by overlapping. We will assume that the figure is a true representation of the system's structure. Note that we can use the module LINE without being concerned with any other parts of the system; that is, LINE is independent of all other modules. Similarly, we can use or manipulate LOOKUP without being concerned with PAGE. The two modules are conceptually and physically independent: Page heading and table searching are disjointed tasks. Because of the subordination relationships shown in Fig. 6.5, the use of PRINT implies the use of PAGE and LINE.

To accomplish printing by using the PRINT module in another system, we must use PAGE and LINE, because page heading and detail printing are part of the same job of report printing. However, what if we wish to do something with STATE and FICA — e.g., use them in another program or change them in this one? The use of STATE requires the use of FICA because of the content-coupling; moreover, some changes to FICA will, in fact, become modifications to STATE as well. Yet, F.I.C.A.

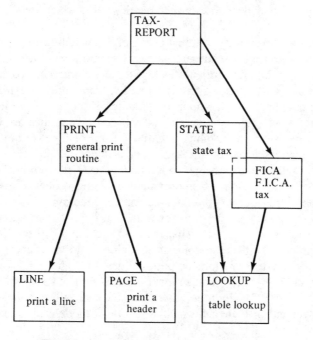

Fig. 6.5 Modular system with content-coupling.

withholding and state tax calculations, *as functions,* really have nothing whatsoever to do with each other.

Why would the designer ever create a program unit coupled by content to another program unit? In the example of Fig. 6.5, we must imagine that both FICA computations and STATE computations have something in common — perhaps they use the same tax table. To save money and duplication of code, the designer decided that STATE should make use of some section internal to FICA. The practice may or may not be justified in this example; as a general design philosophy, it is unwise.

6.2 COMMON-ENVIRONMENT COUPLING

Whenever two or more modules interact with a common data environment, those modules are said to be *common-environment coupled.* Each pair of modules which interacts with the common environment is coupled — regardless of the direction of communication or the form of reference. A common environment may be a shared communication region, a conceptual file in any storage medium, a physical device or file, a common data base area, and so on. The common data areas in primary memory (such as COMMON in FORTRAN, or the DATA DIVISION in COBOL) are the most frequently encountered cases. Note that if two modules both originate or both access an element of data in a common environment, then a change in one module potentially impacts the other. Thus, common-environment relationships go beyond the input-output relationships, which depend on the flow of data.

Common-environment coupling does not fit easily into the schema of coupling strengths that we have already presented. Common-environment coupling is a second-order, rather than first-order, effect. Modules A and B are common environment by virtue of their references to a third entity, the common environment. The severity of the coupling depends upon the number of modules interacting with the common environment. In the limiting case where two modules are being considered, common environment coupling is either a form of input-output coupling (if one originates data accessed by the other) or a minor added factor (if both are transmitting or both are receiving) above and beyond the minimal input-output coupling. In this case, common-environment coupling probably fits, in terms of strength, between input-output coupling and control-coupling.

As an example, consider the system of Fig. 6.6. Let us add a single common environment of a single data element that is common to the eight modules. This results in module U being coupled to module S (and vice versa), even though they may have no control or input-output relationship. The same is true for module U and T, U and V, U and W, and so forth. The complete structure of this system is now that of Fig. 6.7. In total, there are 63 directed relationships. For a common environment of E elements shared among M modules, the total number of relationships, R, is

$$R = E \times M \times (M - 1)$$

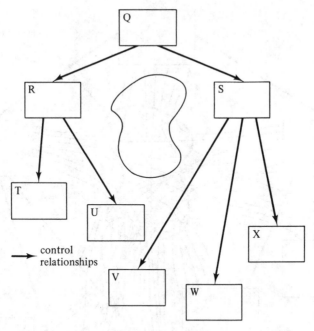

Fig. 6.6 System without common-environment coupling.

Obviously, this rises as the square of the number of modules holding the data environment in common.

The point is not that common-environment coupling is bad, or that it should be avoided at all cost. To the contrary, there are circumstances in which this may be the method of choice. However, it should be clear that a small number of elements shared among a few modules can enormously complicate the structure of a system — from the point of view of understanding it, maintaining it, or modifying it. The functioning (or non-functioning, in the case of bugs!) of any module potentially affects the functioning of every other module sharing the common environment in as many distinct ways as there are elements in that environment.

6.3 DECOUPLING

The concept of coupling invites the development of a reciprocal concept: *decoupling*. Decoupling is any systematic method or technique by which modules can be made more independent. Each of the forms of coupling generally suggests obvious methods of decoupling. The coupling caused by binding, for example, can be decoupled by changing appropriate parameters so that they are bound at a later time, as we saw in the example of the CMF system. Decoupling from a functional point of view seldom can be accomplished except in the early design phase

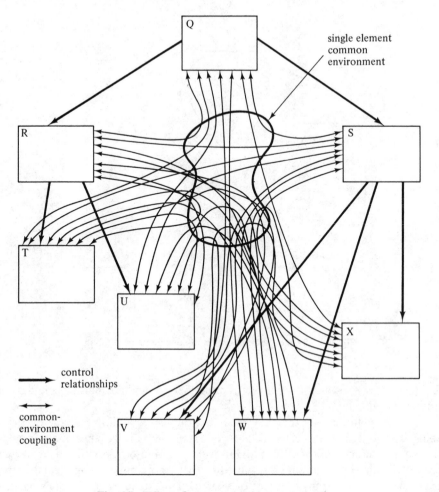

single element
common
environment

control
relationships

common-
environment
coupling

Fig. 6.7 Effect of common-environment coupling.

of a project; as a rule, a design discipline that favors input-output coupling and control-coupling over content-coupling and hybrid-coupling, and that seeks to limit the scope of common-environment coupling is the most effective approach.

Besides these obvious techniques, there are some less obvious approaches to decoupling. Where there are implicit references (one not appearing as distinct references in the code) that are *necessary* to understand the operation of a module or its relationship to another module, then converting the implicit references to explicit references decouples the modules. This works for the simple reason that what can be seen is more easily understood than what cannot be seen. This approach to decoupling is valid only for references, that *must* be dealt with; making explicit any references or relationships that need not be known and understood only complicates the system.

100

Another method to decouple modules is *standardization* of connection. To specify completely a standard connection requires only the specification of the exceptions of incremental information.

The introduction of *buffers* for the elements being communicated along a connection — when it can be done — effectively decouples modules, too. For the purposes of this discussion, a "buffer" can be thought of as a first-in-first-out (FIFO) queue, which preserves the order of elements in the stream. Buffers along communication paths make modules less time-dependent on one another. If the modules can be designed from the beginning on the assumption that a buffer will mediate each communication stream, then questions of timing, rate, speed, frequency, and so forth within one module will generally not affect the design of the other.

For example, it is often difficult to design, as a whole, processes involving complicated ratios of input items to output items. Suppose we have one process that generates three output items for each input item it receives; the output items may become input to a second process, which must deal with them in pairs. The two processes then operate in a cycle — being in and out of step with one another, with a period of six items. While numerous simple tricks can solve this problem, most will make the code for one process dependent on the particular ratio of the *other* process. The situation becomes worse for merge/explosions with several different ratios — particularly if some vary, perhaps dependent on the data itself. In any case, with buffers, each output merely goes into the FIFO queue, and each input simply is obtained from the queue. Timing and ratios can be ignored so long as there is not a cumulative and irreconcilable disparity between inputs and outputs.

One very essential method of decoupling is to reduce the effects of common-environment coupling by *localization*. In a typical real-world system, elements to be communicated via common environments are lumped together into one or a small number of regions. This couples a large number of modules that otherwise would be completely independent of one another. By dividing a single common region into several logical subregions, we often can arrange things in such a way that no module is coupled to any other module except those that it *must* be coupled to by the communication requirements of the problem.

6.4 AN APPLICATION

The coupling between modules in tentative structural designs can be evaluated to guide the designer toward less expensive structures. To illustrate this, consider two alternative modular structures for the same problem. In this application, text as input from an on-line keyboard and text stored on a card deck are to be dissected into words, and combined according to codes from the keyboard and codes contained in the cards. Inputting is to begin with the keyboard and continue, character-by-character, until the ideograph "$RC" is received. At that point the reading of input from cards is to commence, continuing until the ideograph "//" is reached. Input from the keyboard then resumes. An end-of-transmission from the keyboard triggers reading the remaining cards. Last-card under any other circumstances is an error. The continuous stream of text from these two sources is to be broken into separate English words, which are then passed individually to a pre-existing module named PROCWORD.

Once again, Charlie has been called upon to do the programming. Having just returned from a seminar on structured design, he has produced a structure chart for the system, as shown in Fig. 6.8a. When his fellow programmer Nadine looked at the problem, she told him he should structure it as in Fig. 6.8b. Both of these structures are normally connected; each consists of five modules with exactly four interconnections. In each design, all the word-finding logic has been isolated into a single module, but one design is likely to be easier to program, maintain, and modify. The difference must be in the degree of coupling implied by each design. To evaluate this, we will need to look at the information that must be communicated along each connection between modules.

In Charlie's design of Fig. 6.8a, the INKEY module must make available to SCANWORD1 a character read from the keyboard or an indicator that there are no more characters if the user has disconnected the terminal. Note that the indication of presence or absence of a character comprises an element of *control* information even if it is communicated as part of the data. It is not data to be operated upon, but is a control that signals how to operate. There may be many tricks a programmer can use to disguise this fact. A special value for the character parameter may be used to signal end-of-data. This, of course, has its own dangers, as an erroneous or even a legitimate character that turns out to have the reserved value may at some time be input.

The point is that the control information must be known; therefore, it is easier to assess the quality of the design in terms of coupling if we make the fact obvious. No amount of disguising control as data will decouple the modules. This argument suggests that during structural design, it is good policy to regard each distinct type of data and each element of control, flag, signal, or state as if it were communicated via a separate parameter in a calling sequence. Then, counting pa-

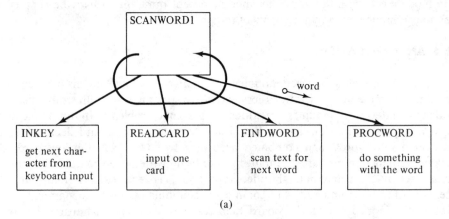

(a)

Fig. 6.8a Charlie's design for the word-scanning problem.

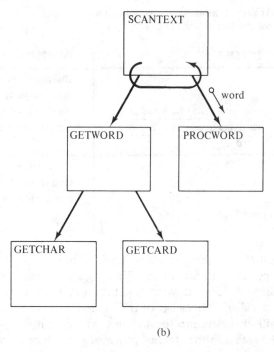

Fig. 6.8b Nadine's design for the word-scanning problem.

rameters will allow the designer to assess degree of coupling.

The remainder of the comparison now becomes easier. The coupling between INKEY and SCANWORD1 is the same as between GETCHAR and GETWORD in Nadine's version. Likewise, READCARD and GETCARD are coupled equally to their superordinates. However, Charlie's FINDWORD module must accept either a character or a card image as input data, plus control elements for end-of-transmission and last-card conditions, and an indicator of which data are being passed.

Like Nadine's GETWORD, Charlie's word-separating module must be able to return the next word in some form, but it will also have to pass control information specifying whether it is returning to deliver a word or to get another card image, or to request another keyboard character. Since the final end-of-text logic is tied up with the card and character reading logic, both the FINDWORD and the GETWORD modules would have to be capable of signaling end-of-process to superordinates. The required parameters for the two systems are listed in Table 6.1. Note that Charlie's design involves two more data parameters and six more control parameters than Nadine's.

An interesting consequence of the greater coupling in Charlie's design is that SCANWORD1 includes coding to test and dispatch on the request by FINDWORD for more input. This is an example of an "inversion of authority"; that is, the subordinate is telling the boss how to do some detail of the subordinate's job, comparable to a janitor telling the office manager to fetch a roll of towels from the stockroom so the janitor can put them in a holder in the washroom. Another complication in Charlie's design not found in Nadine's is that the FINDWORD module

Table 6.1 Data and Control Information Needed in Two
Designs for the Same Problem

MODULE	INPUTS	OUTPUTS
INKEY		character, end-of-transmission
READCARD		card image, last-card
FINDWORD	character, end-of-transmission, card image, last-card, source	word, end-of-words, get-character, get-card, here-is-word
PROCWORD	word	
GETCHAR		character, end-of-transmission
GETCARD		card image, last-card
GETWORD		word, end-of-words
PROCWORD	word	

must be coded so that it remembers where it left off in scanning for a word when it returned to its superordinate for input.   There could be many different loops or branches within the code for FINDWORD, and the correct one must be resumed when FINDWORD is next called.   Because GETCHAR and GETCARD are subordinate to GETWORD, they will always return to GETWORD wherever it left off.   The need for special facilities to maintain the state of processing in Charlie's design may be regarded as a defect of this particular arrangement of subroutines.

6.5 SUMMARY

This chapter has introduced one of the most important criteria for judging the goodness of a design: *coupling*.   The next chapter discusses a related concept known as cohesion; together, these two concepts form the central theory of structured design.

As we have seen, there are several factors that influence the coupling between modules: the type of connection, the complexity of the interface, the type of information that flows between the modules, and the binding time of intermodular connections.   In addition, the use of "global" data greatly increases intermodule coupling.   Attempts have been made to *quantify* the strength of various types of coupling,* but it will probably be several years before such quantitative measures are accepted within the data processing profession.

* See, for example, Glenford J. Myers, *Reliable Software Through Composite Design* (New York: Petrocelli/Charter, 1975), or Christopher Alexander, *Notes on the Synthesis of Form* (Cambridge, Mass.: Harvard University Press, 1971).

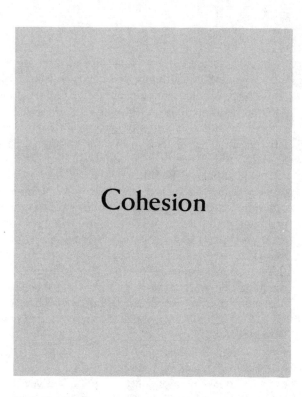

Cohesion

CHAPTER 7

7.0 INTRODUCTION: FUNCTIONAL RELATEDNESS

We already have seen that the choice of modules in a system is not arbitrary. The manner in which we physically divide a system into pieces (particularly in relation to the *problem* structure) can affect significantly the structural complexity of the resulting system, as well as the total number of intermodular references. Adapting the system's design to the problem structure (or "application structure") is an extremely important design philosophy; we generally find that problematically related processing elements translate into highly interconnected code. Even if this were not true, structures that tend to group together highly interrelated elements (from the viewpoint of the *problem,* once again) tend to be more effectively modular.

Let us imagine, for the moment, that there is some measure of functional (problem-defined) relatedness between pairs of processing elements. In terms of this measure, the most effectively modular system is the one for which the sum of functional relatedness between pairs of elements *not in the same module* is minimized; among other things, this tends to minimize the required number of intermodular connections and the amount of intermodular coupling.

"Intramodular functional relatedness" is a clumsy term. What we are considering is the *cohesion* of each module in isolation — how tightly bound or related its internal elements are to one another. Other terms sometimes used to denote the same concept are "modular strength," "binding," and "functionality."*

In the real world, a single, isolated element of processing may be functionally related in varying degrees to any number of other elements. As a result, different designers might see different interpretations of the problem structure, and hence different, least-costly modular structures for the solution. The cohesion of these modules (and, hence the intermodular functional relatedness, or coupling) may vary considerably for these different interpretations of the problem; small shifts in elements among modules may substantially change the total cohesion of a module. There is another real-world problem that adds to the variety of interpretations of problem structure and program structure: In many cases, it may be difficult to identify or evaluate the strength of functional relatedness of one element to another.

Module cohesion may be conceptualized as the cement that holds the processing elements of a module together. It is a most crucial factor in structured design, and it is a major constituent of effective modularity. The concept represents the principal technical "handle" that a designer has on the relationship of his system to the original problem structure. In a sense, a high degree of module cohesion is an indication of close approximation of inherent problem structure.

Clearly, cohesion and coupling are interrelated. The greater the cohesion of individual modules in the system, the lower the coupling between modules will be. In actual practice, these two measures are correlated; that is, on the average, as one increases, the other decreases; but the correlation is not perfect. Maximizing the sum of module cohesion over all modules in a system should closely approximate the results one would obtain in trying to minimize coupling. However, it turns out to be easier both mathematically and practically to focus on cohesion.

Mathematically computing the intramodular functional relatedness among elements involves fewer pairs of processing elements to which the measure would have to be applied than to compute total intermodular functional relatedness. Practically speaking, it just turns out to be more useful to be able to answer the questions, Does this make sense as a distinct module? and, Do these things belong together? than to be able to tell whether or not to chop something at a particular point. Both coupling and cohesion are powerful tools in the design of modular structures, but of the two, cohesion emerges from extensive practice as more important.

---

* We prefer the term "cohesion," as this is the accepted term for the identical concept in sociology, another discipline in which cohesion — in that case, the cohesion of groups — is important. Cohesion is used in a variety of engineering and other scientific disciplines as well, and it almost always has the same connotation as our use of it in this book.

Cohesion represents an operational refinement over earlier concepts about functional relatedness.   Many writers and teachers in the field have long pleaded for highly functional modules without tackling the fundamental problem of how to recognize a functional (or for that matter, a nonfunctional) module.   Development of a practicable means of assessing functionality was frustrated until a direct investigation was undertaken to find out why programmers and systems analysts put things where they did.

Although a definition, or at least a characterization, of what is functional is essential for a full understanding of cohesion, we will continue to use the terms function and functional informally until much later in the chapter when we will be able to treat the problem more adequately.

Cohesion can be put into effective practice with the introduction of the idea of an *associative principle*.   In deciding to put certain processing elements into a module, the designer, in effect, invokes a principle that certain *properties* or *characteristics* relate the elements possessing it.   That is, the designer would state things like "Z is associated with this module containing X and Y, because X, Y, and Z are all related by virtue of having the 'glop' property."   (Lest you think that this is entirely academic, be assured that we will spend several pages in Section 7.1 discussing some very specific glop properties!)   Thus, the associative principle is *relational,* and is usually stated in such terms (e.g., "It's OK to put Z into the same module as X and Y, 'cause they're all related in such-and-such a manner."), or in terms of membership in a set (e.g., "It's OK to put Z into the same module as X and Y, 'cause they're all members of the glop set.").

Ironically, this important design concept had to be developed after the fact — when it was too late, politically or pragmatically, to change designs — by asking the designer/programmer why a certain processing element was combined with others into a module.   It must be kept in mind that cohesion applies over the whole module — that is, to all pairs of processing elements.   Thus, even if the designer has said, "Well, it's OK to include element X in this module, because it's strongly related to elements Y and Z," the module could be low in cohesion, as X may be unrelated to elements A, B, and C in the same module.

We have intentionally used the term "processing element" throughout this discussion, instead of the more common terms, instruction or statement.   Why? First, a processing element may be something which must be done in a module but which has not yet been reduced to code.   In order to design highly modular systems, we must be able to determine the cohesion of modules that do not yet exist. Second, *processing element* includes *all* statements that will or do appear in a module — not only the processing accomplished by statements executed within that module, but also that which results from calls on subordinates.   The individual statements or elements of processing found within some module, FOO, which is called by module FUM, do *not* figure into the cohesion of module FUM any more than we would say that the instructions in one subroutine are "in" another subroutine which calls it.   But the overall processing accomplished by the call on subordinate FOO is clearly one element of processing in the calling module, FUM, and therefore will have to be figured into the cohesion of FUM.

For clarification, suppose we have a module A which consists of elements X, Y, and Z. Suppose that element X is really a call to subordinate module X, and that the elements of X — say X_1, X_2, and X_3 — are highly *unrelated*. It may turn out, however, that X_1, X_2, and X_3, while apparently unrelated to one another, are, taken together, essential to the performance of A's function, which includes Y and Z. Thus, A might be highly cohesive even though one of its subordinates is quite uncohesive — and the *associative principle* would allow X_1, X_2, and X_3, to be included from A's viewpoint. Even so, there will probably be some disagreeable consequences of the artificial attempt to combine X_1, X_2, and X_3 into module X (as we will see in Section 7.2), and this may degrade the design as a whole.

7.1 LEVELS OF COHESION

The first attempts to learn why designers associated things into modules* resulted in distinguishing only three levels of cohesion. Over the years, the list has been expanded and refined through experiment, theoretical argument, and the practical experience of many designers. The associative principles that we will discuss are those which, with a single exception noted below, have stood the test of time and which in all cases may be given more or less precise, technical, mutually exclusive definitions. Recently, additional asosciative principles or different names for the same principles have been proposed, by Myers[1] among others. The "new" levels, however, are found to reduce to special cases of the basic principles. The names we will use are those established as standard by Stevens, Myers, and Constantine.[2]

There are seven levels of cohesion distinguishable by seven distinct associative principles. These seven levels are listed on the following page in order of increasing strength of cohesion, from least to most functionally related.

- coincidental association
- logical association
- temporal association
- procedural association
- communicational association
- sequential association
- functional association

These seven points do not constitute a linear scale There are no data now extant that would permit assigning more than a rank to each level. However, when applied to systems design, they have been found to behave as if the first three (coincidental, logical, temporal) constituted very low and generally unacceptable levels

* Undertaken in 1964 and 1965 by Constantine while at C-E-I-R, Inc.

of cohesion, suggesting a poor, costly design, while the last three (communicational, sequential, functional) produced generally acceptable levels of cohesion. We will return to the question of measuring cohesion in Section 7.3. Each of these seven levels is discussed in detail below, with examples for each.

7.1.1 Coincidental cohesion

Coincidental cohesion occurs when there is little or no constructive relationship among the elements of a module; one is tempted to refer to such a situation as a "random module." Coincidential cohesion essentially establishes a zero point on the scale, or hierarchy, of cohesion. Fortunately, a module that is purely coincidentally associated is a relatively rare occurrence. It is more likely to result from "modularization" of code that has already been written — that is, when the programmer sees an opportunity to convert multiple occurrences of a random sequence of statements. For example, the following code contains the same three-statement sequence in two different places:

```
        _____
        _____
        _____

R:      IF TRAN-TYPE > 5 OR VALUE < 0 THEN DO TR-ERROR    /edit transaction
        READ MASTER INTO Q
        ADD 3 TO REPT-LINES    /bump count for 3-line entry

        _____
        _____
        _____

S:      IF TRAN-TYPE > 5 OR VALUE < 0 THEN DO TR-ERROR
        READ MASTER INTO Q
        ADD 3 TO REPT-LINES

        _____
        _____
```

One may be tempted to modularize the above code by creating a module that does the following:

```
DO-FOO:    SUBROUTINE (TR-TY, VAL, M-Q)
           IF TR-TY > 5 OR VAL < 0 THEN DO TR-ERROR
           READ MASTER INTO M-Q
           ADD 3 TO REPT-LINES
           RETURN
```

with the appropriate calls at R and S.   But suppose we had unintentionally written the second sequence, in the original version of the program, as

```
S:    READ MASTER INTO Q
      IF TRAN-TYPE > 5 OR VALUE < 0 THEN DO TR-ERROR
      _____

      _____
      ADD 3 TO REPT-LINES
```

Our DO-FOO function has disappeared!   Indeed, the three steps probably have no relationship whatsoever with one another, and we may find that two of the three statements are used in other parts of the code.

It must be stressed that coincidental cohesion of modules is not being presented as a taboo; we are not suggesting that lightning will immediately strike the programmer when he creates a coincidentally cohesive module.   Indeed, a system with coincidentally bound modules may be more modular than a comparable system without them!   Certainly, it would be a smaller system in terms of memory requirements.   If a sequence of code was not repeated and was instead put into something like our DO-FOO module above, then it could be understood, debugged, and *possibly* modified in only one place.

However, problems begin to arise when each use of the coincidentally cohesive module does not mean the same thing in application-related terms.   In this case, a change to the module that makes sense in terms of the general case — that is, in terms of the module's purported function — may not make sense in each of the specific uses.   Of course, this is a possibility with any module, but it is obviously more probable if each use of the module exists only because of the coincidental association of several processing elements.

Problems of this sort arise particularly frequently when a maintenance programmer attempts to track down a bug in an unfamiliar program.   For example, report page breaks may sometimes occur in the middle of three-item groups.   In pursuit of the bug, the programmer might start reading through the new modularized version of our code above, which now reads:

```
P:    _____
      _____
      _____
R:    CALL DO-FOO (TRAN-TYPE, VALUE, Q)
      _____
      _____
      _____
S:
S:    CALL DO-FOO (TRAN-TYPE, VALUE, Q)
```

Naturally, when he reaches statement R, his curiosity will turn to the appropriate part of the program listing (probably several pages away) to see what the mysterious DO-FOO does.* Suppose, for the sake of argument, that he finds the bug in DO-FOO. "Aha!" he says, "What I really should be doing here is adding only 2 to REPT-LINES instead of 3." If he is a typical programmer, chances are that he'll change the appropriate statement in DO-FOO, and then put the modified program into a six-hour production run — only to find that he has exchanged one bug for another, because the processing at statement S still wanted DO-FOO to behave in its original fashion. Once again, we observe that this can happen to *any* module — but it is far more likely to occur in a coincidentally cohesive module.

Modules of this type have a propensity to appear at an early point in classroom introductions to "subroutinization." The practice was prevalent (and sometimes justified) in the early 1960's, when the available computers tended to have severe memory limitations. Unfortunately, even in today's world of multi-megabyte computers, some designers persist in developing coincidentally cohesive modules in an attempt to save memory. Another contributing factor to the creation of a vast new supply of coincidentally cohesive modules is the introduction of mini-computers and microcomputers into EDP organizations. Not only do these machines have limited amounts of memory, but they also have memory addressing problems (e.g., the designer may find that he can directly address only 128 memory locations), which tempt the designer into creating coincidentally cohesive modules such as the one we saw above.

There is a more recent influence that has tended to increase the number of uncohesive modules: structured programming. Structured programming has been credited with everything from reductions in dental caries to improvements in one's sex life — and there is no question that it has substantially improved the quality of detailed logic design and coding in many organizations (for technical discussions

---

* This is an extremely important point, though somewhat tangential to our current discussion. Since DO-FOO does not perform a cohesive *function*, but is instead a random collection of processing elements, it will be difficult (if not impossible) to practice "top-down debugging." If the programmer thinks there is a bug somewhere in the sequence of code between P and S (and he must think that — otherwise, why would he be looking at the code?), then he would like to finish searching through the P-to-S code before becoming distracted with some other code — particularly if that code, like DO-FOO, is several pages away in the program listing. This would be possible if DO-FOO were performing a function — say, for example, a square root. In that case, the programmer could say to himself, "Aha, there's a call to the square root routine, the one that some idiot named DO-FOO. I'll assume for now that it works correctly; but I guess I'd better check my P-to-S code to make sure that it really should be calculating a square root at this point, and that I'm passing the right parameters to the subroutine." If the programmer could not find any bugs in his P-to-S code, then he might suspect that the problem lay in his DO-FOO code, and *then* he could turn to the appropriate place in the listing to examine the code. Unfortunately, since our version of DO-FOO is *not* a function, the programmer must look at it as soon as he sees its invocation in the P-to-S code. At the very least, he will find this mildly distracting; indeed, it could easily become intolerable, since DO-FOO may call another subordinate coincidentally cohesive module, which could call another one, and so forth. (Note that this has nothing to do with the infamous GOTO statement, which is usually blamed for the evils of "rats nest" code.) For further discussion, see Yourdon,[3] and Chapter 20.

of structured programming, see[3,4,5]). However, in their rush to cast out their GOTO statements and begin writing structured code, a number of programmers have misinterpreted some of the basic tenets of structured programming (not the least of which is the notion that code cannot be structured if it contains any GOTO statements), and they have applied other rules blindly.

One such situation occurs when the programmer designs logic of the form shown in the flowchart in Fig. 7.1. In the "old days," the programmer would have coded the transfers of control (represented by the arrows in the diagram) with GOTO statements. Using structured programming, though, the programmer is told he should rearrange the logic into the form shown in Fig. 7.2.

Naturally, he complains about the increased memory requirements caused by the duplicated (or triplicated, or quadruplicated . . .) sequences of code. And voilà! He creates modules for all of the duplicated sequences of code and inserts subroutine calls at the appropriate points. Such newly created modules are often uncohesive, even coincidentally cohesive in nature. The newly created modules are frequently only three or four statements whose relationship to one another is nil.

This is particularly ironic since the new modules were created in the name of structured programming — and, of course, everything associated wth structured programming must be "good"! It may turn out that the code would have been

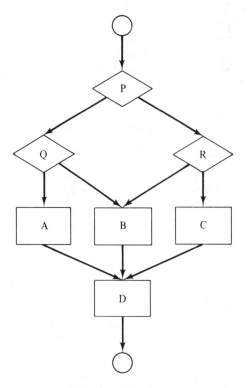

Fig. 7.1 Flowchart.

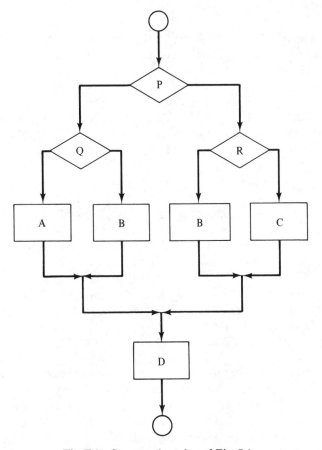

Fig. 7.2 Structured version of Fig. 7.1.

better if it had been left in its original form, shown in Fig. 7.1. If the duplicated sequences of code seen in Fig. 7.2 are each coincidentally associated or low in cohesion, a better design might result if they are physically duplicated in the code — not with a COPY statement (as in COBOL) or a %INCLUDE statement (as in PL/I) or an in-line macro facility, but by actually writing the code two times, three times, or as many times as necessary in the program.* If the duplicated code wastes enough memory to be bothersome, the programmer should search for highly cohesive modules with which to make efficient use of memory.

---

* We observe that the optimizing compilers on many computers are now clever enough to recognize duplicated sequences of code — and they should be responsible for generating a subroutine call, if the programmer has requested memory optimization. Note that if the programmer changes a statement in one of the multiple occurrences of the duplicated code, and then recompiles his program, the compiler will be clever enough to recognize that the sequences of code are now different. Compilers are tireless and error-free in such matters; programmers aren't!

We conclude this discussion by observing that while few modules in the real world are wholly coincidentally cohesive or even largely coincidentally cohesive, there are *many* that contain *some* coincidentally cohesive elements. This is especially true of initialization and termination operations, which could just as easily be placed in the superordinate (initialization and termination modules will be discussed in more detail in Section 7.1.3). Again, the coincidental association of a few elements with a module is not so much a problem in itself, but it is a possible deterrent to effective maintenance, modification, and widespread use.

7.1.2 Logical cohesion

The elements of a module are *logically* associated if one can think of them as falling into the same logical class of similar or related functions — that is, ones that would logically be thought of together. This is best illustrated by examples.

We could combine into a single module all processing elements that fall into the class of "inputting" — that is, logically related by virtue of being input operations. Thus, we could have a single module, INPUTALL, which performs the functions of reading a control card, reading exception transactions from cards, obtaining normal transactions from magnetic tape, and obtaining "old" master records from a disk file. All of these are input operations — and the module INPUTALL is logically cohesive.

Another example is the module that edits (validates) all incoming data, regardless of source, type, or use. Similarly, a module that performs all calculations or computations for a system is logically associated; indeed, one often finds modules in real-world systems whose name is simply COMPUTE. Similarly, a general-purpose error-routine is typically logically associated; depending on the specific type of error, it will print one of several different error messages, reject some of the input currently being processed, restart other processes, or possibly shut down the entire program.

Logical cohesion is generally stronger (that is, more cohesive and thus more desirable) than coincidental cohesion, because it represents *some* minimal problem-oriented basis for associating the elements in the module. However, it should be recognized that a logically cohesive module does not perform a function. The module INPUTALL does not perform a *single* function, but rather one of several different (but logically similar) functions, depending on whether the caller wishes to read a control card, an exception transaction, a normal transaction, or an "old" master record. The potential disadvantages of logically associated modules are easier to see in relation to temporally associated modules, which are discussed below.

7.1.3 Temporal cohesion

It is a common programming practice to bring into a single place — sometimes forming an actual subroutine — all elements having to do with "start-up."

Thus, we typically find an initialization module that reads the control cards, rewinds tape drives and opens disk files, resets counters, sets accumulator areas to zero, and so forth. Such a module may be said to be logically associated; it is also *temporally* associated. Its elements are related by time. However, this particular class association has special properties that render a module more cohesive than other forms of logical cohesion; hence, it is given a special name. Temporal cohesion means that all occurrences of all elements of processing in a collection occur within the same limited period of time during the execution of the system. Because the processing is required or permitted to take place in a limited time period, temporally associated elements of processing may be combined into a module that executes them all at once. This property simplifies the behavior of the module to its superordinate: A single call at a particular time causes all related activities which should take place at that time to occur together.

Not all logically cohesive modules consist of temporally associated elements. For example, elements of the INPUTALL module may have no predictable or bounded time relationship at all. We can get a better clue to the consequences of logical and temporal cohesion by asking how a programmer typically would implement the INPUTALL module. Assume that we have a relatively clever programmer. His module must perform several distinct functions, performing the right one on a given call. How does the module choose the right type of input operation to perform?

First, the programmer notes that control card input will be required only once — and that this will be the first request. So, he writes the first few statements of INPUTALL to perform this function and then sets a switch to bypass these statements on subsequent calls. He also knows that exception transactions are obtained only after certain normal transactions are completed. Similarly, the programmer knows that disk references immediately follow a normal or an exception transaction and that there will be at most one such disk reference for each transaction. Finally, he knows that all calls for exception transactions occur late in the processing, and will thus be higher memory addresses. Slowly, he puzzles out the various combinations and develops a "clever" module that always does the right thing.

Of course, much later (after the programmer has left the organization), the exception transaction coding somehow ends up in low core (where it doesn't work so well), and two successive "type 1" exception transactions will be called for, and a series of consecutive disk references will be required. This "clever" solution is then found to be very difficult to maintain and modify.

A simple-minded programmer, on the other hand, would take a different routine and simply input everything in one magnificent blast — on the first call to INPUTALL. Veteran number-crunchers, experienced in organizing FORTRAN programs, are known for this kind of INPUTALL. But it is obvious that one cannot deal with all input processes in this one-shot fashion — and it would be particularly clumsy for INPUTALL if all transactions and master records were read as a block. Most programmers would recognize the basic contradictions between reading of control cards, reading of exception transactions, reading of normal transactions, and reading of old master records — and they would probably require the superordinate module to supply a flag indicating which type of input function was desired. But then one wonders why the programmer didn't organize four separate modules in the first place. In fact, an examination of the code would reveal four essentially distinct and independent sections of code entered on the basis of an initial four-way test. This seems to be a general property of logically cohesive modules.

The implementation difficulties arise whenever processing elements in a module are logically associated but not (necessarily) associated in time. Computer programs are intrinsically sequential, time-ordered processes. Logical cohesion without temporal cohesion almost always leads to tricky, obscure, or clumsy code which is difficult to maintain and modify. We will say more about the consequences of this a little later.

Thus is a crucial point for the designer. It often is easy to specify what appears to be a function (e.g., edit, calculate, input, transaction-processing, and so on) and find instead that one is specifying a *class* of functions; if such a design is translated into code, the result will be a logical and/or temporal cohesion in modules. But it is also fairly easy to develop the ability to distinguish the levels of cohesion implied by a given design; that is, logical and temporal cohesion can be discovered and discussed a priori — not after the code has been written. The designer then can modify his design, compensate for the effects of low cohesion, or simply take the consequences into account.

Temporal cohesion is stronger than logical cohesion for reasons implicit in the foregoing discussion. Time-relatedness, because of its process orientation and relationship to essential properties of programs, more strongly relates processing elements. Given a choice, then, one would prefer a temporally cohesive module to a logically cohesive module — and both are preferable to coincidentally cohesive modules.

But temporal cohesion is still quite low in cohesion and implies complications to systems with resulting higher expected cost of maintenance and modification. For example, suppose we had an initialization module whose jobs included opening two files, setting a counter to zero, and setting the elements of two arrays to zero. The clever programmer, when combining these activities into one module, might be tempted to write code of the sort shown on the following page:

```
DECLARE A AS ARRAY WITH 20 ELEMENTS
DECLARE B AS ARRAY WITH 30 ELEMENTS

―――――――
―――――――

USE SAME BUFFER AREAS FOR FILE P AND FILE Q
―――――――

OPEN FILE P
OPEN FILE Q

―――――――
―――――――
```

SET COUNTER1 TO ZERO

    _____

    _____

    _____

DO LOOP VARYING I FROM 1 TO 50 IN INCREMENTS OF 1
    MOVE COUNTER1 TO A(I)
END LOOP

    _____

    _____

It should be evident that the programmer has managed to created a number of interdependencies between elements of his code. First, he has arranged that file P and file Q will share the same input-output buffer — presumably because he thinks that the program will not be doing input-output on the two files at the same time. Second, he has cleverly arranged for one loop to initialize the elements of the A array, and then to "fall through" the bottom of the A array and initialize the B array (such a trick actually works in several versions of FORTRAN and COBOL). Finally, note that he is not really setting the array elements to zero, but setting them equal to the contents of COUNTER1 — which happens to have been set equal to zero. We can imagine the sort of problems that will occur if, at some later time, we decide that (a) it is necessary to perform input-output on files P and Q at the same time, or (b) we decide to initialize COUNTER1 to a value of -1, or (c) we decide to change the appropriate DECLARE statement to make array A forty elements long without remembering to change the LOOP statement.

As before, we observe that this kind of code could be written by *any* programmer in *any* module. The problem really occurs when the maintenance programmer wishes to change one *function* without destroying any other function — and, if the functional processing elements have become intermingled within a module, this task will prove to be difficult.

7.1.4 Procedural cohesion

Early in the evolution of measures of module cohesion, it was noted that when the designer used a flowchart of an overall process as the basis for deciding where to chop it into subroutines or other modules, the results were highly variable — but tending towards characteristics typical of low cohesion. No precise definition of what might constitute this *procedural* association was forthcoming, and an adequate technical explanation of the variability of results continued to elude the authors for years. The key turned out, once again, to be the separation of data relationships (which show up in the stronger forms of cohesion discussed below) from control features.

Procedurally associated elements of processing are elements of a common procedural unit; they are combined into a module of procedural cohesion because they are found in the same procedural unit. The common procedural unit may be an iteration (loop) or decision process, or a linear sequence of steps. The latter relationship, a simple succession of steps, is the weaker and shades into temporal cohesion. A temporally cohesive module may include various steps which may be executed in a particular time span, but not necessarily in a particular sequence. Initialization is an obvious example. The very fine distinction here is not of overwhelming importance, and we shall limit our discussion to the more important cases of iteration and decision units.

As always, to say that a module achieves *only* procedural cohesion, the elements of processing would have to be elements of some iteration, decision, or sequencing operation — but not also be elements of any of the stronger associative principles discussed in subsequent sections of this chapter. Procedural cohesion associates processing elements on the basis of their procedural or algorithmic relationships. Although this level of cohesion can result from many practices that emphasize sequence, method, and efficiency, it commonly results when modular structure is derived from flowcharts or other models of procedure, such as Nassi-Shneiderman charts[6] (sometimes termed "Chapin charts"[7]).

Consider the top-level flowchart in Fig. 7.3 and the modular structure suggested by the bracketing shown there. This organization is shown in Fig. 7.4; note that TYPDECID is immediately subordinate to PLANLOOP, which is immediately subordinate to SIMPRO. Note also that in this organization, module PREP is temporarily cohesive (why?), TYPDECID is procedural because its elements are those of the main iteration. The elements within PLANLOOP and TYPDECID are related not only in time, as in the case of temporal cohesion, but by additional procedural dependencies. The procedure chosen to solve the problem is more strongly dependent on the structure of this *particular* problem than are the general, abstract categories and classes of logical cohesion.

Although stronger than temporal and logical cohesion, procedural cohesion has its problems. As an intermediate level of cohesion, we would expect that procedural modules would tend to be fairly strongly coupled and be somewhat clumsy to use as independent entities. This is clearly exhibited in the SIMPRO system. Elements of the manufacturing plant simulation algorithm are found in both PLANLOOP and TYPDECID; the steps that are shaded in Fig. 7.3 have been split between these two modules. We expect complex, subtle interdependencies among these steps with the result that most changes or bugs in the simulation algorithm will probably require dealing with both modules. Neither PLANLOOP nor TYPDECID performs a task that stands alone very well; neither is very likely to be easily used "as is" in another system or in a future version. PLANLOOP, for example, does not perform the complete function of simulating all plants, as the initialization of the loop control condition is found elsewhere (temporally associated with other initialization in the PREP module).

The general point is that procedural cohesion often cuts across functional lines. A module of only procedural cohesion may contain only part of a complete function, one or more functions plus parts of others, or even fragments of several functions. It also might be found, by chance, to encompass exactly one complete,

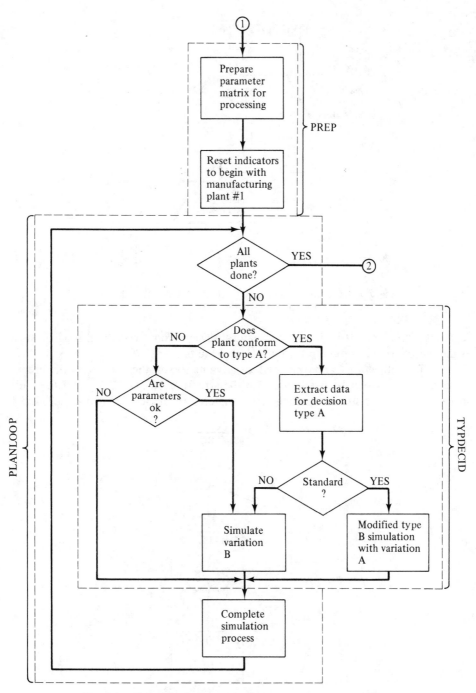

Fig. 7.3 Flowchart for a multi-plant manufacturing simulation program, SIMPRO.

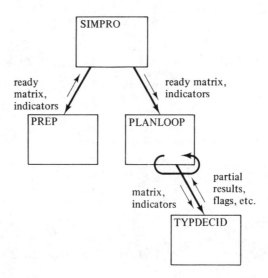

Fig. 7.4 Modular structure for SIMPRO based on the procedural partitioning of Fig. 7.3.

separable function. It is thus that structural design from procedural models, such as the flowchart, leads to such highly variable results.

The objections and potential disadvantages of the SIMPRO structure in Figs. 7.3 and 7.4 can be overcome with the structure of Figs. 7.5 and 7.6. This structure includes a SIMALL module that completes all simulations and a SIM1PLANT

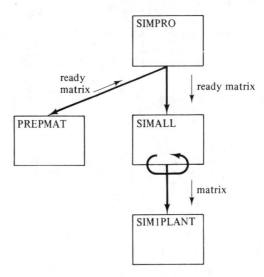

Fig. 7.5 Another SIMPRO structure based on the partitioning of Fig. 7.6.

module that performs the complete simulation of one plant.   While this structure might have been derived from the flowchart, there is nothing in the flowchart that would tell the designer how to accomplish this.

It should be emphasized again that procedural cohesion is not necessarily undesirable in all circumstances.   A further subdivision suggested by the dotted line in Fig. 7.6 might lead to the structure of Fig. 7.7.   The TYPANALYZE module probably is properly described as achieving only procedural cohesion, but it implements the (potentially) useful, distinct task of figuring out which type of plant (whatever that means) is being presented.   This also permits the isolation of the actual simulation computations into a separate single module, PLANCOMP.   The cohesion of that module cannot be evaluated until we have completed the discussion of levels of cohesion.

7.1.5 Communicational cohesion

None of the levels of cohesion discussed above is very closely tied to the structure of a particular problem.   *Communicational* cohesion is the lowest level at which we encounter a relationship among processing elements which is intrinsically problem-dependent.   To say that a set of processing elements is communicationally associated means that all of the elements operate upon the same input data set and/or produce the same output data.   Communicational cohesion is thus defined in terms of the problem structure as represented in the data flow graph introduced in Chapter 3.   In the data flow graph of Fig. 7.8, two such partitionings are shown. One, PROCESS RECORD, is communicationally associated on the input side; the other, GET-A/B-DATA, is communicationally associated on the output side.

The data flow graph of a problem can serve as an objective means for determining if the elements in a module are communicationally associated.   Communicational cohesion, though not maximal, is sufficiently high as to be generally acceptable in the absence of strong counterarguments or lacking an identifiable alternative structure with higher cohesion.

Communicational association is common in business and commercial applications.   Often, it is the result of thinking in terms of all the things that can be done with a given item or piece of data once it is obtained or generated, or, on the other side, in terms of all the things that must be done to create a given result, say a detail line in a report.   Putting such collections together results in a module of communicational cohesion.   Typical examples would include

- a module to print and punch the transaction file

- a module that accepts data from several sources, transforming and assembling them into a report line

The associative principle of communicational cohesion actually covers a wide range of degrees of relatedness, as the elements of data comprising a stream or

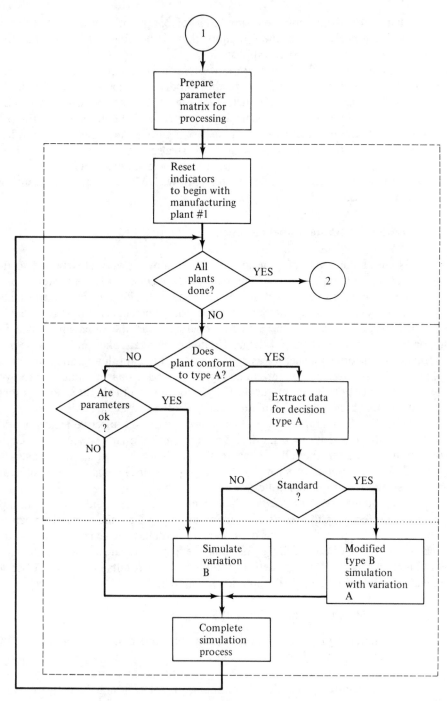

Fig. 7.6 Another partitioning of the SIMPRO problem, corresponding to the structure of Fig. 7.5.

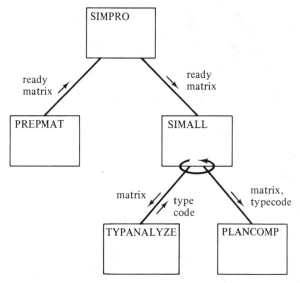

Fig. 7.7 Further refinement of the SIMPRO structure that includes a useful procedural module, TYPANALYZE.

set of data may themselves be interrelated in various degrees. If the designer places in one module all the first transformations for the various records found on a master input tape that intermingles all possible input to some system, the elements of processing will be no more related than are the elements of data in the file. It appears that communicational association based on both input from and output to the same data set is somewhat weaker than association on only one side. Conceptually, this may be seen in Fig. 7.9. Computations A, B, and C are more closely related to each other than to conversions X, Y, and Z. And vice versa, of course.

Some mixed or equivocal cases are found in common programming practice. A familiar example might be the MASTERFILECONTROL module, which reads and writes master file records, opens or closes the file, rewinds, and backspaces. Looking at the elements of processing that would have to be actually programmed within MASTERFILECONTROL, one can see that the reading and opening processing elements are communicationally associated on the input side with the writing and (possibly) the closing on the output side, but rewind and backspace have completely different inputs and outputs in terms of the actually programmed processing elements. Thus, some of the associations are only logical, and this will show up at the interface of the module. It is probable that the superordinate would be required to pass a flag to MASTERFILECONTROL indicating *which* of its functions (opening, closing, rewinding, backspacing, reading, or writing) should be performed. This might be acceptable. We can imagine, for example, that the most likely modification to be made to MASTERFILECONTROL would concern the defini-

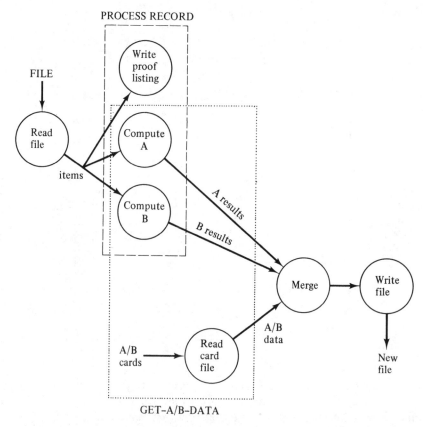

PROCESS RECORD

FILE

Read
file

items

Write
proof
listing

Compute
A

Compute
B

A results

B results

Merge

Write
file

A/B
cards

Read
card
file

A/B
data

New
file

GET–A/B–DATA

Fig. 7.8 Data flow graph with two communicationally associated partitionings superimposed.

tion or attributes of the master file itself — and this would probably affect most or all of the functional processing elements in about the same way.

Of course, we still can imagine a number of situations that would cause serious problems for the maintenance programmer. The most serious problems are often of a timing nature — that is, the programmer assumes that he can share the same input-output buffer areas (or queue areas, or control blocks, or whatever) among the many functions in the module. Sometimes this is based on the simple assumption that the various functions will not be utilized at the same time (which, from an operational point of view, may not be true if one is dealing with a buffered, blocked file); sometimes it is based on the more complex (and more dangerous) assumption that the various input-output functions will be used in a certain sequence (e.g., the programmer assumes that a "close" function will not be invoked until one or more "read" functions has been invoked). Once the programmer begins acting on such assumptions, the various functional processing elements become interdependent, thus decreasing the effective modularity of the entire system.

124

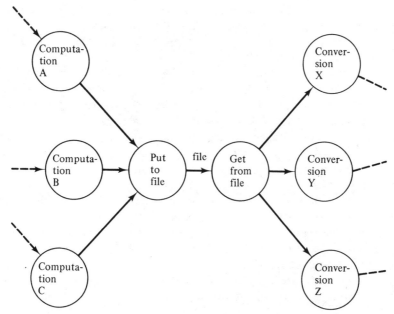

Fig. 7.9 Data flow graph showing the relationship of input, output, and input-output association in communicational cohesion.

7.1.6 Sequential cohesion

Next higher on the scale of cohesion is *sequential* association in which the output data (or results) from one processing element serve as input data for the next processing element. In terms of the data flow graph of a problem, sequential cohesion combines a linear chain of successive (sequential) transformations of data. This is clearly a problem-related associative principle. That it is stronger than communicational association rests primarily on experience and a series of small-scale experiments.* The data flow graph for a problem will make it obvious that sequential cohesion in general results in fewer, simpler intermodular relationships, which would be the expected case if it is taken to be a higher level of cohesion than communicational.

As with lower levels, sequential cohesion can also result from "flowchart thinking." We have noted before that the module structure for a system is often derived from initial flowcharts drawn by the programmer/designer. One or more contiguous steps in the flowchart is combined into a module to be made as a subordinate to the process represented by the flowchart as a whole.

* Conducted by Constantine in 1968 and 1969 while at IBM's Systems Research Institute.

The curious thing about flowcharts as used is that they often confuse *data flow* and *control flow*. The arrows in the flowchart represent flow of *control;* control flows, for example, from "step" A to "step" B in the flowchart shown in Fig. 7.10. If it represents the highest level of a system, the programmer/designer will often refer to it as a system's flowchart. However, especially at this abstract level, the control flow in the flowchart of the system is likely to be more or less related to *data* flow. That is, step A (which might eventually be realized as a subsystem, a job step, a program, or some appropriately large package of code) may involve internal loops, decisions, and complex procedural sub-steps. Sooner or later, it finishes its work and delivers some output (perhaps a sorted, edited transaction file), *which immediately becomes input to the next step of the system.* At least we hope that we perform procedural steps in a system in an order bearing some relationship to the data flow — though, as we saw in Chapters 3 and 4, there are many procedural implementations for a given set of data flow relationships.

Indeed, there are a number of modular structures that the designer might specify for the flowchart of Fig. 7.10. Let us imagine that somehow we know for certain that the flowchart represents two *functions,* one realized by steps A and B, the other by steps C, D, and E. Depending on the designer's mood, he may specify any of the following module organizations:

- A module for each of the steps in the flowchart — that is, a module for A, a module for B, and so forth

- A single module that incorporates all five steps — that is, a single module that includes all of the code for A, B, C, D, and E

- An organization in which module 1 consists of step A, module 2 consists of steps B and C, module 3 consists of steps D and E

- An organization in which module 1 consists of steps A, B, and C, module 2 consists of steps D and E

- And so forth

The same results are possible, though less probable, in derivations from a true data flow graph. The obvious point is that a sequential module may contain more than one function, only part of a function, or parts of more than one function.

For this reason, sequential cohesion is weaker than the ideal functional *cohesion,* even though it is stronger than the five levels we have already discussed. The potential weakness of the sequential module is similar to one of the problems of coincidental, logical, temporal, procedural, and communicational modules: In attempting to modify the code for one function found in whole or in part in a module, the programmer may find that he is inadvertently modifying, or that he must consider, code for another function that happens to be in the same module. Similarly, if we find that each module contains only part of a function (as may sometimes be the case with sequentially cohesive modules), then arguments of

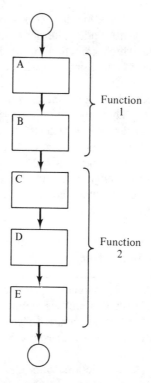

Fig. 7.10 High-level flowchart for a system.

coupling apply: In order to understand what one module does, we must understand what another module does — and the second module may contain other processing elements that have nothing to do with the function performed by the first module.

7.1.7 Functional cohesion

At the upper limit of functional relatedness is functional association. In a completely functional module, every element of processing is an integral part of, and is essential to, the performance of a single function. This definition, taken by itself, is every bit as circular as it appears to be. However, in the company of the (more or less) precise and independent definitions of the lower six levels — sequential down through coincidental — we have an operational definition:

> *Functional cohesion is whatever is not sequential, communicational, procedural, temporal, logical, or coincidental.*

Thus, a module which is purely functional contains no extraneous elements related only by sequential or weaker associative principles. It would be comforting to say

127

that the definitional problem is solved by this bit of legerdemain, but unfortunately, the hole left unplugged by any truly adequate definition of function is a structural defect in the theory through which camels and Mack trucks could readily pass. Fortunately, some examples and much practice will help the practical structural designer deal with this limitation easily.

The clearest and most easily understood examples of functional association come from mathematics. Thus, the ubiquitous *square root* module is certain to be highly cohesive, and is probably completely functional. It is unlikely that any surplus elements are present beyond those absolutely essential to realize the mathematical function for square root — and it is unlikely that (nonempty) processing elements can be added without changing the computation to something other than square root. In contrast, a module which computes either square root or cosine is unlikely to be entirely functionally associated. A sine/cosine subroutine is more ambiguous.

In addition to such obvious examples from mathematics (including logarithm, exponential, and third Bessel functions), we can usually recognize functional modules that are "elementary" in nature. Thus, a module called READ-MASTER-RECORD would presumably be a functionally cohesive module — as long as it did not contain additional code for reading records from the transaction file. Similarly, a module called EDIT-ALL-TRANSACTION-TYPE-13 would probably represent functional cohesion, whereas EDIT-ALL-TRANSACTIONS would undoubtedly be a logically associated module.

Except for these low-level functional modules, we often identify functional modules by comparing functional cohesion with the lower levels of coincidental, logical, temporal, procedural, communicational, and sequential cohesion. That is, if we can demonstrate that a module is better than coincidentally associated, better than logically asssociated, then it must be functionally cohesive.

Thus, it appears that we must identify functional modules by a process of elimination — which may appear to the designer to be an unsatisfying way to go about things. In practice, though, it is not as bad as it seems: It is usually a fairly easy matter to examine a design for potential "defects" in the form of low cohesion.

The task is to determine whether a module has elements of coincidental, logical, temporal, procedural, communicational, or sequential cohesion. We find that an effective way of doing this is to describe, fully and accurately, the module's function in a single English sentence. Naturally, there is a variety — perhaps an infinite number — of English sentences that would accurately describe any given module. However, if the module is functional in nature, it should be possible to describe its operation fully in an imperative sentence of simple structure, usually with a single transitive verb and a specific non-plural object. Furthermore, the following guidelines can be used to help distinguish nonfunctional modules:

- If the only reasonable way of describing the module's operation is a compound sentence, or a sentence containing a comma, or a sentence containing more than one verb, then the module is probably less than functional.   It may be sequential, communicational, or logical in terms of cohesion.

- If the descriptive sentence contains such time-oriented words as "first," "next," "after," "then," "start," "step," "when," "until," or "for all," then the module probably has temporal or procedural cohesion; sometimes but less often, such words are indicative of sequential cohesion.

- If the predicate of the descriptive sentence does not contain a single specific objective following the verb, the module is probably logically cohesive.   Thus, a functional module might be described by "Process a GLOP."   A logically bound module might be described by "Process all GLOPS," or "Do things with GLOPS."

- Words such as "initialize," "clean-up," and "housekeeping" in the descriptive sentence imply temporal cohesion.

To illustrate the use of this guideline, let's consider a number of examples. BESORT, for example, has been described in the following way by its designer: "Before sorting, write a proof tape, add dummy items for control, and check totals." The key word "before" gives us the clue that BESORT is probably a temporally cohesive module: These are all things done in the time period before sorting.   It might reach as high as procedural cohesion if the module were described in the following way: "First write a proof tape, then add dummy items for control, then check the totals, and finally perform a sort."   BESORT is probably not sequential because the proof tape is probably not the input to "adding dummy items."

Next, consider the module JOBREPT.   It has been described by its designer as: "Produce job control reports: library file listings, operator summaries, and customer run report."   The key word in this description is "reports"; JOBREPT is not producing a single report, but rather a *class* of similar reports.   Hence, we conclude that JOBREPT is probably logically cohesive unless its designer can convince us otherwise.

Similarly, suppose the module RUNSTAT were described to us in the following terms: "Collect run statistics for an application program executing on the system: number of system's commands executed, input-output usage, errors, and CPU time used."   Once again, we conclude that the module is logically cohesive.   It is interesting to note that several programmer/designers have suggested that RUNSTAT is *temporally* cohesive because it consists of a number of functions that must be executed at a certain point — *after* the application program (the one for which the statistics are being gathered) has finished executing.   This may be true, of course, and it illustrates some of the difficulties in evaluating a module's cohesiveness based on a superficial examination of a descriptive English sentence.

RUNSTAT, it might turn out, collects some statistics *during* the program's execution, as well as *after* its execution.   In any case — whether RUNSTAT is logically or temporally cohesive — it is fairly clear that the module is *not* functional, and that is the primary purpose of the exercise.

Suppose the module TIMECARD were described to us in the following way: "Update the master time clock record, the employee time record, and the current pay entry — all from the time card." Again, it appears that the module is not performing a single function, but rather a collection of functions. In this case, the functions are related by the input data: All of them involve the time card. Hence, we would conclude that TIMECARD is primarily communicationally associated.

Next, consider the module UPNOUT, described as: "Update the current inventory record, and write it to the disk." Clearly, the output from the "update" function serves as input to the "write" function. Hence, the module is sequentially cohesive.

It is important to remember that there are a variety of ways to describe the task of a module — and some of the descriptions may make the module sound as if it is functional when it is not (or vice versa). However, if the designer is careful in constructing a concise, descriptive English sentence which, nonetheless, fully and unambiguously represents all of the processing accomplished by the module, then the guidelines above will usually suffice to differentiate levels of cohesion.

7.2 COMPARISON OF LEVELS OF COHESION

We will use the problem represented in Fig. 7.11 to illustrate a variety of partitionings of the same problem, corresponding to different levels of cohesion. In this application, items from a tape and a card file are validated, merged in a one-and-two discipline to create a proof listing and to compute various quantities, which are then summarized and delivered as two different reports. The structure of this problem is presented as a data flow graph in sufficient detail to consider different partitionings.

It is easy to present examples of coincidental and logical cohesion by partitioning this data flow graph; the partitions have essentially no relationship to the structure of the problem. DOSOMETHINGS in Fig. 7.11 is an example of coincidental cohesion; any relationship among its processing elements is purely coincidental! The proposed modules EDITNVALIDATE and FORMATREPORTS are good examples of logically associated collections of functional activities. Note that the validation inherent in the central computation is implied to be included in EDITN-VALIDATE. Note how this cuts across functional lines.

Because the data flow graph is inherently nonprocedural, it is somewhat difficult to illustrate temporal and procedural cohesion in relation to it. Two possibilities are shown in Fig. 7.12. STARTIT is an initialization module, which incorporates parts of several transforms: those parts necessary to get them to work correctly the first time. It would contain the file opening portions of the "get" transforms, the elements of processing necessary to initialize the merge for the first comparison on membership number, and the initialization of the loop control and

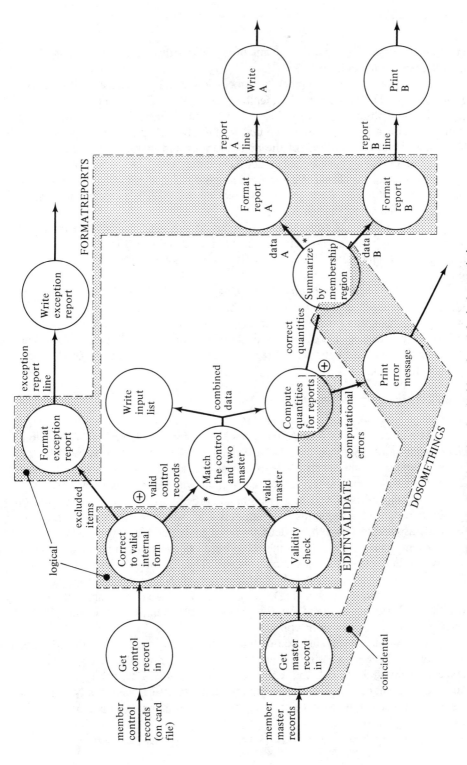

Fig. 7.11 Relationship of coincidental and logical association to problem structures.

accumulators for the "summarize" transform. From this description, STARTIT is, obviously, temporally cohesive.

SUMLOOP combines elements of processing in the procedural unit comprising the iteration that summarizes by membership region. This potentially could include portions of all the transforms "upstream" of the "summarize" transform. The partitioning shown is reasonable; included in the module with the looping logic itself are the continuing portions of the computations and merge logic. The report formatting and printing have been excluded since they take place after (outside) the loop. It is not accidental that the temporal module STARTIT goes hand in hand with a procedural partition. Both levels of cohesion are based on time, procedure, sequence-oriented associative principles.

Communicational and sequential cohesion are very easily represented on the data flow graph, as they are directly problem-oriented. In Fig. 7.13, DOCOMBO is a communicationally cohesive module; GETVALIDMASTER, a sequentially cohesive one.

Illustrating functional cohesion once again presents difficulties. At a superficial level, functional cohesion is roughly the same as each transform on the data flow graph corresponding to one module, but the particular arrangement of these in a hierarchy influences the actual cohesion of the modules. These problems can best be understood through the strategic concepts to be introduced in the next chapter of this book.

7.3 MEASUREMENT OF COHESION

Any given module — whether proposed or completely coded — is seldom a clear example of only one associative principle. Its elements may well be related by a mixture of the seven levels of cohesion. This gives rise to a continuous measure of module cohesiveness rather than a scale with seven discrete points.

It should be observed that the smaller processing elements constituting a single function are *also* sequentially, communicationally, procedurally, temporally, or logically associated (though, by definition, not coincidentally associated).

Where there is more than one relationship between any pair of processing elements, the highest level of cohesion applies. Thus, if module FOO consists of a collection of processing elements, all of which are examples of the same logical class of operations (say, validity checking), but are also *all* related communicationally in that they check various kinds of validity of one type of item, then FOO is evaluated as having communicational cohesion among *all* its elements.

What would be the cohesion of this module, FOO, if it also contained some completely unrelated processing elements? In theory, it would be some kind of average of communicational and coincidental cohesion. For debugging, maintenance, and modification purposes, a module behaves as if it were "only as strong as its weakest link."* The effect on long-term programming costs is closer to that

---

* We are indebted to our colleague Robert G. Abbott for this pithy observation.

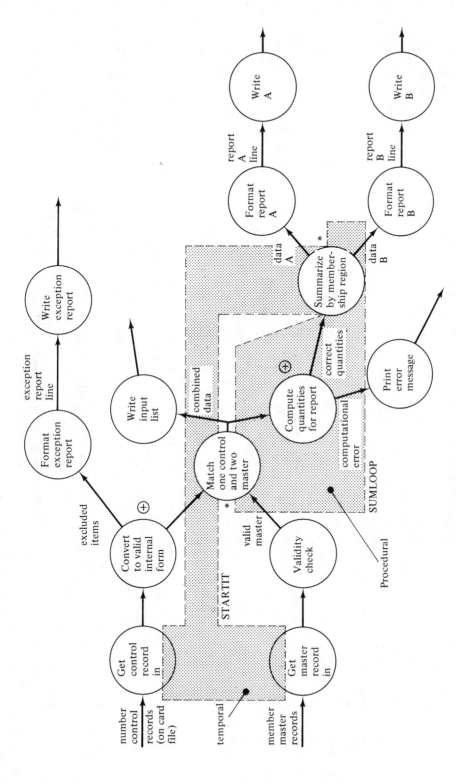

Fig. 7.12 Relationship of temporal and procedural association to problem structure.

133

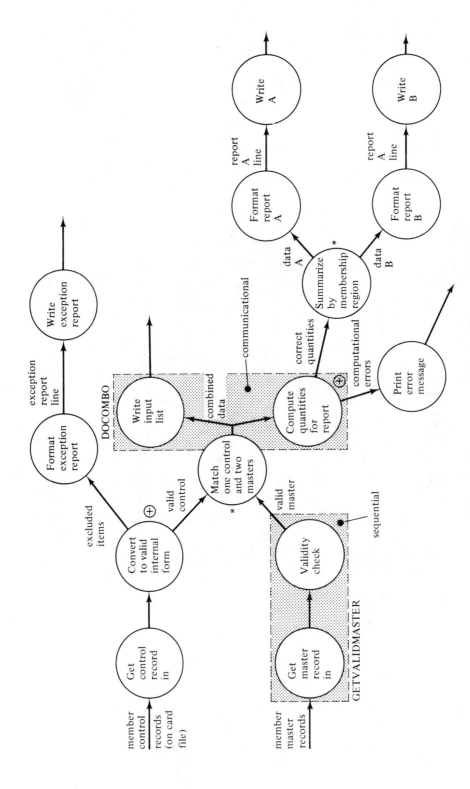

Fig. 7.13 Relationship of communicational and sequential association to problem structure.

of the lowest level of cohesion applicable within a module than to the highest. That is

> *The cohesion of a module is approximately the highest level of cohesion which is applicable to all elements of processing in the module.*

(Which the really astute reader will note is the same as saying the lowest of the highest level relating any pair of processing elements. Whew!)

Other factors can reduce the cohesion of a module, including the number of weak (less than functional) associations among processing elements, whether the module has "side effects" (to be discussed later), and whether the module associates fragments of functions or whole functions.

A module may consist of several logically related *complete* functions. This is definitely more cohesive than a module that logically binds fragments of several functions. For example, compare the cohesion of the following two modules:

- Module 1 is a logically cohesive module that performs sales tax computation, income tax computation, and property tax computation.

- Module 2 performs the multiplication/division computations associated with sales, income, and property taxes.

Module 1, while pretty "loose" functionally, is considerably simpler to understand than module 2. Indeed, if the programmer implements module 1 perfectly (the probability of which is discussed in Section 7.4), it may present only minor maintenance and modification problems.

It is not crucial for the designer who uses cohesion as a guide to simpler, less expensive program structures to know exactly how cohesive a module is, to tell whether it has a "cohesion factor" of 6.7 or 6.8, for example. But the relative magnitude of the cohesion of the various levels, even if not that of specific modules, is of fairly wide interest. As we stated earlier, the lowest three levels are generally indicative of unacceptable partitions, the highest three suggesting simple and inexpensive designs. There have been many requests for and a few suggestions of precise values that could be assigned to each level. Myers,[1] who assigns higher numbers to lower cohesion, suggests that functional cohesion should have a value of 0.2, and coincidental cohesion a value of 0.95. However, Myers admits, such figures

> ". . . are based on educated guesses. . . . All of these aspects of the model must be verified and refined based on data collected. . . . Unfortunately the proper historical data to validate the model is (sic) not readily available."*

---

* Glenford J. Myers, *Reliable Software Through Composite design* (New York: Petrocelli/Charter, 1975), p. 149.

Even presuming that a sample of structures correlated with cost were available, the definitional problems would remain. Deciding which level actually applied to a module would require the judgment of human raters.

We do have extensive experience and a few careful comparisons of alternative solutions to the same problem on which to base some judgments about the relative differences between various levels. Best established is that sequential cohesion is very close to maximal, closer to functional, than it is to communicational cohesion. Similarly, there is a bigger break between logical and temporal than between coincidental and logical. Distinguishing to orders of difference between the ranked levels seems to be fully justified and useful to the designer. For example, the designer knows that he gets a substantial improvement in going from logical to temporal organization, but only a modest one in making the transition from sequential to functional. If numbers are to be assigned, whether for purposes of research, mathematics, or mystification, this would suggest the following scale* of cohesion:

```
 0 : coincidental
 1 : logical
 3 : temporal
 5 : procedural
 7 : communicational
 9 : sequential
10 : functional
```

No more precise measurement can be justified by the available data and experience. You must use any such numbers cautiously, paying heed to what constitutes appropriate and inappropriate use.

To introduce such numbers now (when we have so little hard experience to go by) might introduce an element of magic into the whole field of structural design. What concerns the authors most is that programmer/designers being introduced to structural design for the first time could be offended by the hocus-pocus of artificial values being assigned to levels of cohesion, and thus conclude that the very *concept* of cohesion is suspect.

The hierarchy must thus be recognized for what it is: an incomplete tool in the process of evolutionary development. It represents a useful, proven way to deal constructively with cohesiveness. It is cohesion which can be regarded as an

---

* This is an improvement over a simple ranking that achieves only what is called *ordinal* measurement. Being able to rank the differences between ranks results in so-called *ordered metric*. It still would be inappropriate to add or subtract such numbers, as that would require interval measurement. Coincidental association is taken as a zero point precisely because it is defined as the absence of any (but chance) relationship.

intrinsic property of modular systems; the hierarchy of associative principles only attempts to make the property visible.

7.3.1 Side effects

Some modules have simple purposes as viewed from the outside; they have a single, simple function; they are highly cohesive. These are three ways of saying essentially the same thing. Sometimes, however, a module may do some things "on the side" which do not normally complicate the picture, but enter in only under special circumstances. These so-called side effects to a module's basic purpose marginally lower the effective cohesion of that module.

For example, consider a module GETNEXTTRANSACTION, which always returns the next transaction, ready to process, to its superordinate: a simple, probably functionally cohesive module. So what if it also has the side effect of producing an "80-80" list of transactions obtained for processing! Under most circumstances, the programmer of the calling module (or any other module) would not need even to know about this side effect to make correct use of GETNEXTTRANSACTION — not unless the programmer also were using the printer, which was to be loaded with expensive forms!

Side effects operate as if they marginally lower the cohesion of any module that includes them. There are ubiquitous examples. All direct printing or logging of errors constitutes a side effect of the functions of computations in which the errors are detected. If you ever saw a payroll check with SYS-ERR 126 – ZERO ARG, MATH*PAK printed across its face, you know what we mean!

Side effects cannot be completely avoided, as they often are intrinsic parts of the problems designers try to solve. Their influence on cohesion must be taken into account, however, and this suggests that the designer should, if possible, limit the scope (in terms of number of modules) over which the side effect operates.

7.4 IMPLEMENTATION AND COHESION

When the designer specifies modules of low cohesion, he creates potential problems during the implementation phase of the project. We invoke Murphy's Law of Programming — "if the programmer can, he will" — to analyze the consequences.

Consider the limiting case of two functions, F and G, which are absolutely and totally unrelated. Let us imagine that the designer is trying to decide whether he should create two separate modules, F and G, or a single module FG. If we assume that there are no timing problems and that F and G may execute together, there would appear to be no basis for choosing one over the other. If F and G are logically associated, one might even prefer the single FG module, since one logically expects to find these functions associated and in the same place.

However, this tacitly assumes the programmer will implement functions F and G separately and independently and simply drop them into a container named

FG. This is shown schematically in Fig. 7.14. In the real world though, we find that a single module, FG, affords the opportunity for (indeed, even encourages) casual interactions between the code for F and the code for G. Thus, final implementation is likely to be that shown in Fig. 7.15. But remember: F and G are functionally unrelated. Hence, the common code, or interactions between sections of code, can only be a procedural trick. While it may have been easier to code, the chances are that the code "F and its interactions with G" is more difficult to debug. In any case, F and G are now interdependent: future modification or independent use of either F or G is hindered.

Another cogent example involves the widespread practice of clustering all "edit and validation" processes into a single module. This module does the checking and editing necessary to ensure that all data is in the form (e.g., proper format, range, sequence, and so on) for later processing within the main system; this is represented schematically in Fig. 7.16.

Note that each of the elements of EDIT relate to one (or more) functional element of MAIN. Thus, editing and checking have been "conveniently separated" (to use

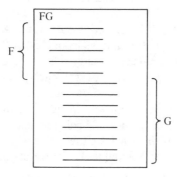

Fig. 7.14   Module with two unrelated functions.

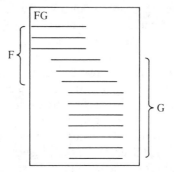

Fig. 7.15   Most likely implementation of a module with unrelated functions.

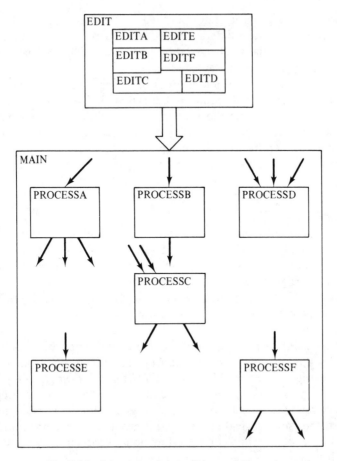

Fig. 7.16 System involving editing and processing.

the words of some designer friends of ours) from the "guts" of each processing function. Moreover, editing can be done as early as possible (upstreams in terms of data flow), making it easier to relate errors to the sources of input. Also, this type of structure may enable one-time validation of data that eventually will be processed by many different modules within MAIN. So, it would appear that the structure suggested by Fig. 7.16 does have some advantages.

However, we should observe that the validity of an input data element is usually intimately dependent on the definition of processing within MAIN. If we find it necessary to change the way in which we *process* an input element, we generally will have to change the manner in which we *validate* the element. In many cases, EDIT actually will duplicate in whole or in part some of the functional processing required in MAIN.

Thus, even if all validation elements are programmed independently within EDIT, future maintenance and modification probably will require treatment of both

139

PROCESSA within MAIN, and its edit operation EDITA within EDIT. On large, complex systems with intricate validation processing, there may be a considerable divergence — even on initial implementation — between what is functionally acceptable within MAIN and what is accepted by EDIT.

With time, inaccuracies and laziness inevitably will lead to such divergence; each functional change would require modifications in two different subsystems — which may well have become the property of two different maintenance groups. The low cohesion of the logically associated EDIT module is merely indicative of the *stronger* bonds between its internal elements and the internal elements of MAIN — that is, between EDITA and PROCESSA, EDITB and PROCESSB, and so on.

7.5 SUMMARY

From the discussions in this chapter, you should *not* conclude that all logical modules are bad, nor that editing and validation always should be distributed throughout a system; nor should you attempt to derive any other black-and-white rules of thumb. High cohesion is not "good," nor is coincidental cohesion "evil." Module cohesion is associated with *effective* modularity; it has certain predictable effects on transparency, programmability, ease of debugging, ease of maintenance, and ease of modification.

Other things being equal, these qualities will improve as cohesion is increased. This does not mean that losses will not be incurred in other areas. For example, the designer may be able to save CPU time or memory, simplify the data flow, divide the programming task more easily, or reduce apparent duplication of effort by using relatively uncohesive modular organizations. The designer may save design effort, too, since logical and temporal groupings are comparatively easy to identify and describe — while complete functional cohesion may require extensive analysis and study.

The obligation of the designer is to know the effects of varying cohesion — especially the cost in terms of modularity — and to be prepared to trade this off against potential benefits in other areas of interest. Unless he gains more in decreasing CPU time than he loses in achieving long-term viability of a program, for example, he must choose a more functional organization.

REFERENCES

1. GLENFORD J. MYERS, *Reliable Software Through Composite Design* (New York: Petrocelli/Charter, 1975).

2. W.P. STEVENS, G.J. MYERS, and L.L. CONSTANTINE, "Structured Design," *IBM Systems Journal,* Vol. 13, No. 2 (May 1974), pp. 115–139.

3. EDWARD YOURDON, *Techniques of Program Structure and Design* (Englewood Cliffs, N.J.: Prentice-Hall, 1975).

4. EDWARD YOURDON, "A Brief Look at Structured Programming and Top-Down Program Design," *Modern Data* (June 1974), pp. 30–35.

5. J.R. DONALDSON, "Structured Programming," *Datamation,* Vol. 19, No. 12 (December 1973), p. 52–54.

6. I. NASSI and B. SHNEIDERMAN, "Flowchart Techniques for Structured Programming," *ACM SIGPLAN Notices,* Vol. 8, No. 8 (August 1973), pp. 12–26.

7. N. CHAPIN et al., "Structured Programming Simplified," *Computer Decisions,* Vol. 6, No. 6 (June 1974), pp. 28–31.

The chapters in this section all deal with methods by which the concepts of the preceding chapters can be put to use to design the structure of complex systems. Chapter 8 describes features of the shape of systems structures found to be related to development costs. The next chapter, on design heuristics, deals with rule-of-thumb methods for designing systems structures. Simple rules of thumb, although useful in identifying certain types of design flaws, have generally proved to be inadequate for large problems without the use of a strategic framework for deriving an acceptable design, which then can be improved. Chapters 10 and 11 develop two interdependent step-by-step methods for deriving acceptable, initial structured designs. The method of Chapter 10 was developed by Constantine to yield systems of the type described in Chapter 8. The method discussed in Chapter 11 analyzes a shortcoming of the previous method; and derives from a technique originated by a group within Bell Telephone Company. Chapter 12 compares and contrasts our approach to other major models and methods of structured design.

III

TECHNIQUE

The Morphology
of
Simple Systems

8.0 INTRODUCTION: ORGANIZATION AND MORPHOLOGY

In the context of program design and systems design, we use the word "organization" to describe the *way* in which structure is used to realize a desired function. Another way of putting this is to say that organization is the relationship between function and structure. Thus, a system *structured* as a hierarchy may be *organized* with control processing at the bottom of the hierarchy. To draw an analogy, a football team could be considered a hierarchical structure, with the quarterback serving as the "control module" during the plays; nevertheless, the team uses various organizations (e.g., split-T, flying-T, and so on) to realize its basic function of winning a game.

"Morphology" refers to the *shape* of a system, with respect to structure. For example, the depth of a structure (the number of levels of subordinate modules) is a visible morphological feature; the width of a modular structure — or of certain parts of the structure — is another morphological feature.

Our purpose in this chapter is twofold. First, we wish to examine *common* organizations of modular systems, and *common* systems morphologies. Second, we wish to make some comparisons between common organizations and "good" systems — that is, systems with low coupling and high cohesion. This serves as a prelude to Chapters 9 through 12, in which we explore design *techniques* that will produce systems with recognizable organizations and recognizable morphologies, as well as low coupling and high cohesion.

8.1 ORGANIZATION OF MODULAR SYSTEMS

On what basis does the designer decide on a particular division of his program or system into modules? How does he decide which portions of the total processing should go into a given module?

We already know that modules combining functionally related elements are more cohesive (and thus result in more modular systems) than, say, modules whose elements have only coincidental cohesiveness. While the designer must be aware of the effects of cohesion, it is seldom practical for him to use this as his only organizing concept. A trial-and-error approach that combines pairs of processing elements and then evaluates the cohesion is certainly not a very orderly way to design a system — if nothing else, it would require an enormous amount of work!

What we find is that a modular system usually is *centered* around various specific aspects of its function. Regardless of whether the designer explicitly recognized a particular modular structure, we usually can identify an implicit organizing concept or criterion. In many cases, the structure literally is centered around a module with a very distinctive purpose or function. Thus, we can speak of *transaction-centered* design, or a *transaction-centered* system. Such a system is developed around modules that perform the various actions associated with transactions; generally, there is a module (or small group of modules) that passes all transactions to the subordinate transaction modules for processing.

Some types of modular organizations have been reflected in strategies — formal systematic procedures for developing, from a problem description, the modular structure of systems of the desired type. Thus, there is a scheme known as transaction analysis (to be discussed in Chapter 11), which gives rise to transaction-centered systems, although they may be developed by the programmer/designer without benefit of the strategy. Other strategies have been developed on an ad hoc basis; let us look at two of them briefly.

Procedure-centered design is derived from procedural representations (e.g., flowcharts) of a system's operation. This usually results in a top-level module whose coding and whose calls on subordinates directly implement the overall systems level processing, defined initially by the systems analyst.*   While every system may be regarded as ultimately procedure-centered, some systems have more emphasis placed on the "procedure orientation" than do others — and some designers apply "procedural analysis" earlier in the design process than do others.   If the module organization was developed from program procedures (e.g., flowcharts) that were developed as a *first* step in the design, then it is fair to say that the system is procedure-centered.   One could develop a formal strategy, called *procedural analysis,* to develop procedure-centered structures.†   One reason for *not* discussing procedural analysis in this section of the book is that procedure-centered systems generally achieve only temporal or procedural cohesion (recall the discussion in Section 7.1.4) and are thus, by definition, less cohesive than they might be.

Device-centered design, which is common in portions of operating systems but otherwise relatively rare, focuses on a physical input-output device and its interfaces.   Of course, it makes sense in almost any program to use one module to interface with a disk and a different module to interface with a magnetic tape drive.   Although the bottom levels of any system will involve some device-oriented modules, this focus usually does not permeate up through the higher levels of the structure.   When the entire design revolves around such device-centered modules, then we say that the design itself is device-centered.

Every system may be thought of as involving one or more *central transforms:* major systems functions that take relatively "digested" data as input streams and create major output streams.   Accepting this statement, we can have *transform-centered* systems; a formal design strategy known as *transform analysis* (to be discussed in Chapter 10) can be used to derive such systems.   In practice, transform-centered design does *not* begin by identifying the transforms as the central modules in the systems.   It is easier to identify everything else, and then call the remainder the "essential" or "major" transform of the system.

For example, consider the simple process shown in Fig. 8.1.   The functions A and B basically are operations that, when performed in sequence, obtain the main data for the system.   Up to the vertical dashed line marked "I," data are still flowing into the system; after line "II," however, data would be thought of as flowing out of the system.   The remaining parts of the process can be neither input nor output — hence, C is a central transform of the system.   Indeed, we would describe the basic purpose of this system as computing the inverse of matrices.

---

* Recall that in Chapter 1 we suggested that the primary job of the systems analyst is to derive the functional requirements of the system by carrying on a dialogue with the user. By drawing a systems flowchart, however, the analyst is participating in the *structural and procedural design* of the system — sometimes with disastrous effects.

† We will cover some of the elements of *procedural analysis* in Chapter 14, when we discuss packaging of modules into efficient executable units — e.g., job steps, partitions, overlays.   Our emphasis there will be on the use of procedural analysis for efficient *segmentation* of an already designed system, rather than as a tool for effective design of the system.

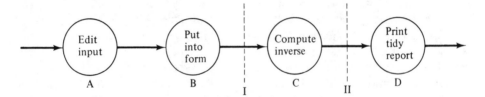

Fig. 8.1 Model of a simple process.

8.2 SPECIFIC MODELS OF SYSTEMS ORGANIZATION

Occasionally, designers make use of a specific functional or structural model as a guide to structural design. In a sense, such use represents a technical preconception about what a system will look or what it *should* look like. This technical prejudice may be productive insofar as the specific model is both *simplifying* (in terms of reducing the labor of design) and *general* — two ostensibly conflicting criteria. However, the limitations of these specific models often outweigh their advantages; indeed, most of the problems in this area are the result of the designer interpreting the model *literally* rather than using it as an approximation.

One specific model of systems organization is shown, in two variants, in Fig. 8.2. One could take the CIPO version as the literal structure of a system; in this case, only four modules would be implemented, regardless of the size of the problem. Note that an INPUT module, literally implemented, probably would be only logically cohesive.

In some organizations, this literal interpretation is taken even further. The designer is told that if INPUT (in Fig. 8.2) has three immediate subordinates, then PROCESS and OUTPUT each also must have three immediate subordinates. And, if there are two levels of modules beneath INPUT, then, according to some designers, there should be two levels of modules beneath PROCESS and two levels beneath OUTPUT. The justification for this literal approach is often an appeal to symmetry, which we discuss in more detail in Section 8.5.

Another problem with the literal interpretation of the CIPO method is that the designer is left (as with any use of such a specialized model) with the problem of assigning processing elements to appropriate categories. Is computation of report values in the process category or in the output category? If the model is not interpreted as a literal structure but rather as a characteristic example, a problem still remains: Having such a model represents only marginal progress toward a complete design. What has one accomplished in the total structural design process if one draws the four requisite boxes of Fig. 8.2? The model itself guides only the initial portion of the total design process, leaving the designer to his own devices for elaboration and completion.

In any case, we are faced with the possibility of an application for which

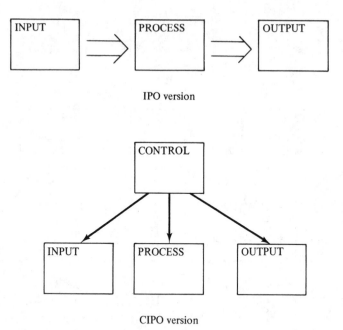

IPO version

CIPO version

Fig. 8.2 Two versions of a popular specific systems model.

the model is inappropriate — such as one with no processing and degenerate out-putting, or with a purely mathematical computation.

This last argument is especially strong for the transaction-centered model (discussed further in Chapter 11) in Fig. 8.3. This model is representative of, and applicable to, many routine business applications. It also may apply to a real-time executive or a dedicated time-sharing application. On the other hand, it is unlikely to be an advantageous structural model for a compiler, and even less beneficial for a large number-crunching application.

As we have already suggested, the general usefulness of these models in-creases if we apply them less literally. To require, for example, that every program have exactly four levels whose functions may be classified as in Fig. 8.3 limits the usefulness of the model as well as the potential modularity of the system. Restric-tions such as prohibiting a second-level module (in Fig. 8.3) from accessing a fourth-level module are equally debilitating and unnecessary.

In general, then, while specific structural models can be developed, their simple — and literal — application to structural design is not recommended. In-deed, the designer must beware of cheap imitations that are being advertised these days as so-called structured design. If a textbook or a consulting firm or a com-puter manufacturing company promotes a packaged approach to structured design, with success guaranteed on the basis of literally following "ten easy steps" — well, perhaps the best advice is caveat emptor.

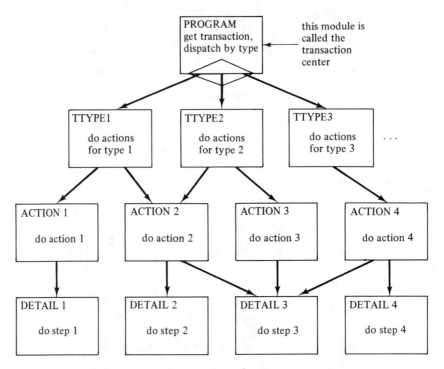

Fig. 8.3   Transaction-centered model of a modular system.

8.3 FACTORING

Design by analogy is widely practiced in software design, and its most common example is the "program-executive" module. Analogous to corporate organizations, the top-level executive module does not perform any of the systems tasks itself, but instead controls and coordinates their performance by lower-level modules to which they have been relegated. In the limiting case, the executive module of a hierarchical system contains *only* calls to subordinate modules imbedded in internal control elements (i.e., iterative and conditional statements). The term "executive module" should be reserved for a module which approximates this limiting case, and for which the iterative and conditional elements within this module correspond to the major loops and decision logic of the system. The purely structural term top-level module should be used when these conditions do not hold.

The executive module accomplishes its task (as viewed from the "outside" — that is, from its superordinate) by using subordinates. The bulk of the actual "work" — if not *all* of the work — is performed by the subordinates and, in turn, by *their* subordinates down to the "atomic" modules. The system is said to be *completely factored* if all actual processing (or computation, or data manipulation) is accomplished by bottom-level atomic modules, and if all non-atomic mod-

150

ules consist only of control and coordination. In a completely factored system, each non-atomic module is an executive with respect to its subordinates.

Where factoring is complete or nearly complete, the non-atomic modules often have near-trivial contents. In a sense, such a system is a summation of trivia. It may be disconcerting to think of a large, complex task being accomplished by a sizable collection of modules, which in themselves are trivial. Actually, nothing could be better; with small, simple atomic modules, we have the best of all possible worlds. Of course, for most real-world programs, the factoring is somewhat incomplete — if it exists at all! Since transform analysis, transaction analysis, and other popular design strategies all favor highly factored systems, we will save our more specific examples of factoring for Chapters 10 and 11.

Similar analogies with corporate organizations have led to some additional rules of thumb for design of the executive module. The *factoring* rule, as we have already seen, states that the executive module should not perform or directly control details. Similarly, the *span-of-control* rule limits the number of immediate subordinates for an executive module; there is an obvious analogy here to the corporate executive who becomes overworked and error-prone if he has too many subordinates reporting directly to him. This and other rules of thumb are discussed in more detail in Chapter 9.

Based on rule-of-thumb design and on systematic strategies, well-designed systems *tend* to show a characteristic distribution of decision processing (i.e., conditional statements). As in Fig. 8.4, the proportion of decision elements decreases smoothly as we move toward the bottom of the hierarchy. The character of decisions should also change: Top-level modules should deal with total, global matters, while the lower-level modules should deal with sub-parts or aspects of the higher-level decisions.

It has also been argued that details should be distributed in a manner inversely proportional to that for decisions shown in Fig. 8.4. The problem, though, is defining exactly what we mean by "detail." If a detailed instruction is manipulative (e.g., shifting the contents of a register two bits to the right), communicational, or computational, then detail is merely equivalent to non-decision. If, on the other hand, detail is conceptually related to low-level operation, then it either defies definition or is tautological; it does us no good, for example, to state that details, i.e. low-level operations, are operations performed at low levels of the hierarchy. Using the distribution of detail either as a design heuristic or as a means of evaluating the goodness of design is seriously suspect. While "decision" is more objective, it, too, makes a poor design guideline. We generally observe this distribution a posteriori in a well-designed system, but we get into trouble if we make it into a *goal*.

8.4 AFFERENT, EFFERENT, TRANSFORM, AND COORDINATE FLOW

In examining the modular structure of a system, we usually observe a few basic *categories* of modules. We note, for example, that some modules obtain

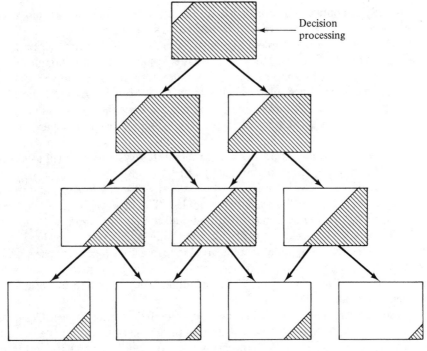

Fig. 8.4 Distribution of decision processing in a hierarchical system.

information from subordinates, and then pass it upward to their superordinate; this is illustrated in Fig. 8.5. We refer to this as an *afferent flow* of data, and we refer to the module itself as an *afferent module*. Others have drawn analogies to engineering and physics, referring to Fig. 8.5 as a "source flow" (see, for example, Myers[1] and the paper by Stevens, Myers, and Constantine[2]). The term afferent is taken from the field of biology by way of general systems theory;[3,4] afferent neurons carry sensory data from the bodily extremities inward and upward toward the brain. Efferent nerves carry motor signals from the brain downward and outward. In general systems terms, a sink has *no* output and a source *only* output. The analogy with the nervous system may seem a bit farfetched, but the terms *afferent* and *efferent* are descriptive of a useful distinction in a manner that is not only graphic but also unlikely to be confused with other overworked programming terms like input and output.

If Fig. 8.5 represents an afferent flow, then it makes sense to refer to Fig. 8.6 as an *efferent flow;* the module shown in the diagram is referred to as an *efferent module.* Clearly, it takes information from its superordinate, and passes it to its subordinate. One can imagine that the efferent module in Fig. 8.6 probably would be involved in the process of outputting, while the afferent module in Fig. 8.5 probably would be involved in the process of inputting.

Note that the modules in Figs. 8.5 and 8.6 pass on the information in exactly the form it was given to them.   That is, the afferent module in Fig. 8.5 calls a subordinate to obtain data element x; it then passes x, unchanged, to its superordinate.   Similarly, the efferent module in Fig. 8.6 receives data element x from its superordinate and passes it, unchanged, to its subordinate.   While this is certainly possible, it is more likely that both the afferent and efferent modules will transform the data they receive.   Thus, a more common form of the afferent data flow is shown in Fig. 8.7; presumably, some computations or manipulations within the module transform x into y before delivering y to its superordinate.   Similarly, the more common form of the efferent data flow is shown in Fig. 8.8.

Even though the afferent and efferent modules are capable of doing some transformations (depending on, among other things, how highly factored they are), we can see that their main purpose is to pass information upward or downward in the hierarchy.   However, other modules exist solely for the sake of transforming data into some other form.   Figure 8.9, for example, illustrates a *transform flow;* the module itself could be referred to as a *transform module.*   Most of the computational modules in a typical system would fall into this category.   The ubiquitous square root subroutine is a simple example of a transform module.

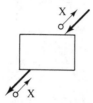

Fig. 8.5   Afferent flow.

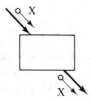

Fig. 8.6   Efferent flow.

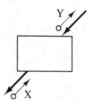

Fig. 8.7   More common form of afferent flow.

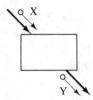

Fig. 8.8 More common form of efferent data flow.

Fig. 8.9 Transform flow.

Fig. 8.10 Coordinate flow.

Finally, we observe that some modules are primarily concerned with co-ordinating and managing the affairs of others.   Figure 8.10 illustrates the *coordinate flow;* obviously, the module is referred to as a *coordinate module.*   Such a module could be found either in the input portion of a system, the central computational portion, or even the output portion.   In a well-designed system, we typically would find a coordinate module relatively high in the hierarchy, since it represents a kind of executive calling upon lower-level junior executives.

Of course, these basic types of modules may be connected and combined to such an extent that we may be unable to tell whether the result is afferent, efferent, transform, or coordinate in nature.   For example, consider the partial structure shown in Fig. 8.11.

What kind of module is A?   To the outside world — that is, to its superordi-nate — A appears to be an afferent module: It has the job of delivering data element Y, which it presumably obtains from a subordinate source (though, of course, the superordinate should not care *how* module A obtains data element Y).   The inside view of A gives us the impression that it is a coordinate module — that much of A's job is concerned with the task of obtaining data element X from a subordinate

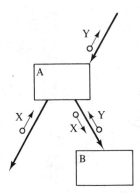

Fig. 8.11 Mixture of afferent and transform modules.

(afferent) module and then passing it to module B, where it is transformed into Y. We probably would conclude that A is a high-level executive module involved in the process of generating input to be used even higher in the system's hierarchy.

At this point, our purpose has been merely to introduce the terms and concepts of afferent, efferent, transform, and coordinate modules. They will be useful in the discussion of systems morphology below, and we will make active use of the concepts in the discussion of transform-centered design in Chapter 10.

8.5 SYSTEMS MORPHOLOGY

Thus far in this chapter, we have looked at modular structures from a number of points of view. We have seen that the designer's orientation can motivate him to develop a transaction-centered design, a procedure-centered design, or one of several other modular organizations. Indeed, we have seen that specific *models* may influence the designer's choice of organization. Further, we have seen that *factoring* considerations influence the arrangement of modules, and the amount of "intelligence" within each module. Finally, we have seen that another way of looking at modules is to characterize them as afferent, efferent, coordinate, or transform in nature.

Now we can put all of the pieces together, and examine the *morphology* — or shape — of the entire structure. We find that some morphological features — width and depth, for example — are found in all systems. Furthermore, we find that certain *values* for those features may be more or less associated with good structural design. That is, we may be able to say that if a modular structure is wider than this design, or deeper than that one, then the overall design might be considered good or bad.

One of the most obvious morphological features is depth — that is, the number of *levels* in the hierarchy. The modular structure shown in Fig. 8.12, for example, has a depth of four. About the only thing we can say about depth is that

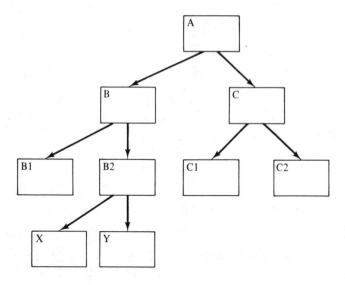

Fig. 8.12 Depth of a system's structure.

it is a rough clue to the size and complexity of a system — just as the number of levels of assistant vice presidents in a management structure gives us a rough clue as to the organization's size and complexity. Obviously, a simple program (consisting of, say, 100 statements) might have a depth of only two or three — indeed, if it were implemented as a single module, it would have a depth of one!

On the other hand, the authors have seen a number of relatively simple 300-statement real-world programs with a depth of five or six — and, in those cases, the time and effort spent by the designer to set up such a hierarchy was more than repaid during the maintenance phase of the project. A system of moderate size and complexity can easily have a depth of ten or twelve — and a truly massive system conceivably could have a depth of fifty or more.

The important thing to realize is that depth, by itself, is not a valid measure of the goodness of a design. As a rule, low-cost, highly factored systems are deep by traditional standards. There are some extremes that generally will stick out like a sore thumb: A 100-statement program with a depth of twenty probably would be an indication of excessive zeal on the part of the designer (most of the executive modules probably would be excessively trivial in nature). Similarly, a million-statement system with a depth of three or four would seem excessively low. As with the factoring of decisions and details, we find that depth is something that usually is observed *after* the system has been designed — but depth generally is not a goal to be kept in mind *during* the actual design process.

Another aspect of the shape of the system might be termed width — that is, how many modules wide is the system? At first glance, it seems that there is not much we can say about width — except for the obvious comment that the larger and more complex the system, the wider it is likely to be. However, we observe that one of the primary influences on the system's width is something that engineers refer to as "fan-out" — that is, the number of immediate subordinates to a given module. In Fig. 8.13, for example, the average fan-out is two (we are ignoring the fact that the bottom-level modules B1, C1, C2, and C3 have a fan-out of zero).

As we suggested earlier, there is reason to suspect that if the fan-out is too high — six or seven seems to be a threshold of some sort — then the executive modules will tend to be too complex (because they contain too much control and coordination logic to look after their many subordinates), and the effective modularity of the overall system will be decreased. There are some exceptions and qualifications to this rule of thumb, as we will see in Chapter 9. In a typical well-designed system, we find an average fan-out of about three or four — but we emphasize once again that this should not be interpreted as a literal rule to be followed by the designer.

Rather than dealing with such primitive measures as depth and width, we might consider the *overall* morphology of the system. Based on observations of a large number of systems during the past several years, we find that most well-designed systems have a shape of the nature shown on the following page in Fig. 8.14. Depending on the vividness of one's imagination, the shape of Fig. 8.14 could be likened to a cigar, a flying saucer, or a mosque.

Indeed, all of those terms *have* been used by designers searching for graphic words to describe a shape they have seen over and over again in their work. Note that the mosque shape characteristically has a higher fan-out in the high-level modules, and a higher fan-in in the bottom-level modules. Still again, we must observe that the overall mosque shape could be a characteristic of a well-designed system, and potentially dangerous if used as a design tool. On the other hand, it is com-

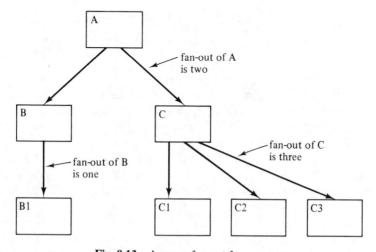

Fig. 8.13   Average fan-out for a system.

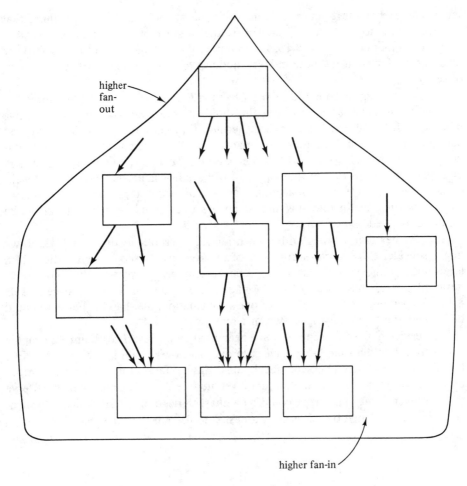

Fig. 8.14 Mosque shape for systems.

forting to note that the strategies of transform analysis and transaction analysis (discussed in Chapters 10 and 11) generally produce the mosque form.

Next, we present morphological features known as "skew" and "balance." Some programmers, for example, might describe the system in Fig. 8.15a as lopsided or skewed. However, since only the topological relationships between modules are structurally relevant (as we discussed in Chapter 4), this structure is equivalent to that of Fig. 8.15b — which does not appear to be skewed. The concept of skew nevertheless may be useful if we can give an appropriate preferred order for drawing subordinate modules beneath the superordinate on a structure chart. Unfortunately, the convention of diagramming the subordinates in the lexical order in which they appear in the superordinate's code makes any inferences on skew procedure-dependent.

The flow of data from the origin of physical input through various transformations to ultimate outputs establishes just the requisite preferred orientation. If, in our example, AA is an afferent module whose output is processed through BB and CC and eventually to GG, then the system of Fig. 8.15a and Fig. 8.15b may be said to be skewed with respect to data flow. We are not suggesting that skew or balance is either good or bad, but merely a way of describing systems with different basic forms of structure. Systems may be skewed in the direction of input, as in the example in Figs. 8.15a and 8.15b, or skewed in the direction of output.

A system highly skewed in the direction of input obtains all of its inputs in elementary (raw) physical form at or near the top of the hierarchy. All of the processing of inputs takes place at lower levels of the hierarchy — and, most important, in branches of the hierarchy that are predominantly efferent. Indeed, the entire system is predominantly efferent. This traditionally has been called an *input-driven* system.

Output-driven code may be viewed as philosophically different. With input-driven code, inputs determine what happens in the process: Items are read first, and then the code decides what to do with them. However, we initially might identify an item that is to be produced as *output* of the system — and, on the basis of that, perform whatever processing is required to develop that item. Of course, events ultimately will occur in the same order, but the system's structure will be very different.

In the extreme case of input-driven or output-driven systems, the system will appear to be highly skewed when viewed at any level. Thus, the efferent branch of an input-driven system will, having obtained its inputs from *above,* deliver them downward to its subordinates — and each of the subordinates will behave similarly.

Balanced systems, with neither elementary input nor elementary output performed at the top of the hierarchy, generally imply that the top level has immediate control over the most significant functions in the system. Balance also could be achieved by having *both* elementary input and elementary output operations take place at or near the top level, but this would violate the factoring rule that we suggested earlier, because it involves the executive in details.

An advantage of the balanced system based on afferent/efferent branches (which in Chapter 10 we call a "transform-centered" system) is that it maximizes the number of *generally* useful modules, at all levels in the hierarchy. We come closer to having all sensible input-like functions and sensible output-like functions when the system is balanced and transform-centered.

Veteran business systems analysts frequently have argued that an output-driven system is less efficient than an equivalent input-driven system. In the final analysis, this is true only for very localized effects or isolated cases. It is true, for example, that a strictly output-driven system will activate all of its afferent modules, down to the lowest level, before obtaining its first input. At first glance, this seems wasteful and unnecessary; on the other hand, the same oscillation up and down the system occurs in the input-driven system — except that it occurs in the efferent side of the system, instead of the afferent side.

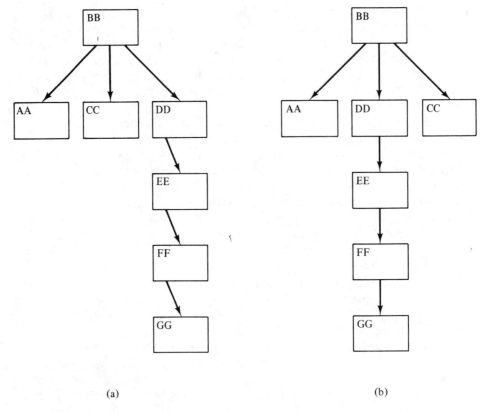

(a)	(b)

Fig. 8.15a One view of a system's structure.   **Fig. 8.15b** Structurally equivalent system.

Equally marginal is the fact that an input-driven system with multiple input streams may obtain the first input for streams that are never used on a given execution of the system. If file attachment, opening, and linking for the first item are complicated processes — as they may well be with certain data base management systems — this cost could become significant. However, neither efficiency argument is convincing, as they both are based on events which occur once per execution of the system.

However, real-time, applications of a certain type may favor the more input-driven organizations. If an elementary input transaction causes a major change in processing, *and* if the resulting action has a critical response time, then the output-driven system may have difficulty responding in time. Imagine, for example, a factory control system that produces reports based on on-line terminal commands. The system has an emergency command (indicated by a first character E from the terminal) that requires an immediate response based on a completely different syntax. In an output-driven system, we would expect the basic terminal input routine to be located deep within the afferent branch; we would also expect the major variations in output to be decided at or near the top of the structure.

Figure 8.16 represents a tentative structure of this type. In the worst case, the E command must travel all the way from INKEY to RETREP, being checked in every intermediate module before it is passed to the next higher level. Thus, EMER may not be activated for quite a long time — that is, quite a few microseconds or milliseconds. It is hard to imagine a subroutine-calling mechanism so slow as to render *this* example critical, but it is prototypical of other real-world situations in which we could have serious response-time problems. In contrast, the input-driven system, illustrated by the transaction-centered structure of Fig. 8.17, does not have this efficiency problem.

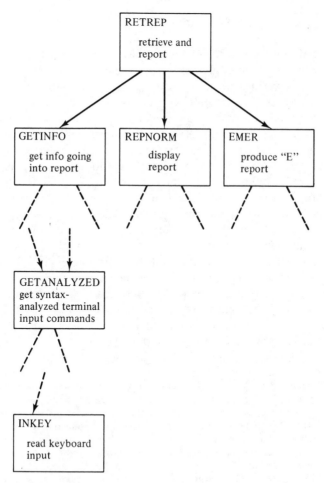

Fig. 8.16 Output-driven real-time system with a deep afferent branch.

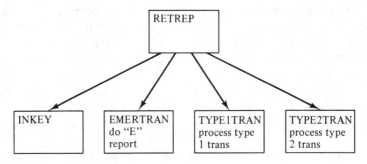

Fig. 8.17 Transaction-centered input-driven system for the problem of Fig. 8.16.

8.6 TRANSFORM-CENTERED MORPHOLOGY

Of the morphological factors relating to systems simplicity, the morphology known as transform-centered organization is the most important. The transform-centered model, shown in the general case in Fig. 8.18, combines several morphological features discussed above. It is highly factored, hence, quite deep for the number of atomic modules. Afferent and efferent branches are somewhat balanced; hence, the model is neither input-driven nor output-driven. Both afferent and efferent branches have a characteristic structure. In the fully factored form, this structure involves at each level a single transformation or set of alternative transformations performed by subordinate transform modules, whose inputs are supplied by the last subordinate afferent modules (on the afferent side), or whose outputs are fed to the next subordinate efferent modules (on the efferent branches).

A model of this subtlety did not spring full-blown from some designer, who on completing his seventeenth structural design, shouted, "Eureka!" It was derived empirically from a careful review of the morphology of systems, comparing systems that had proven to be cheap to implement, to maintain, and to modify with ones that had been expensive. The motivation for the study came from a simple but inspired request from a client, who, lamenting that it was so difficult to learn how to produce good, cohesive, uncoupled designs,* asked one of the authors, "What does the structure of a cheap system look like?"

The original study† required looking at the structure of many programs for

---

* At the time, 1967, the principal technique being taught was a deceptively simple but unreliable strategy called *functional analysis*. Learning to design simple structures was mostly a matter of "sit-by-Nelly." Nelly, you see, knew how to do it! If you were smart and the wind were right, you, too, would be able to do what Nelly does. But you wouldn't know why.

† The research was done by Constantine with the Information and Systems Institute, Inc. Regrettably, the original data and notes were lost or destroyed in the messy demise of the Institute. Cost figures for more than one hundred medium-sized systems from several organizations initially were screened to identify the cheapest and most costly designs. The research design, although sound, was carried out with the informality typical of one-man, small-scale projects. It did not seem at the time worthy of publication or even publicity.

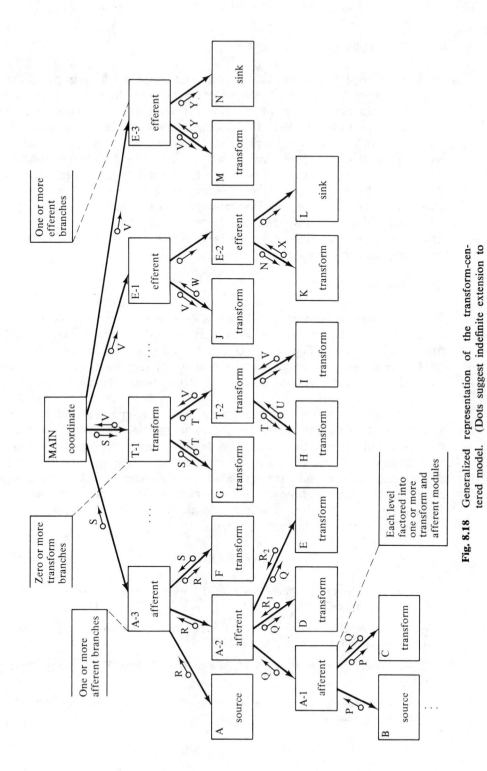

Fig. 8.18 Generalized representation of the transform-centered model. (Dots suggest indefinite extension to more modules.)

which actual implementation, maintenance, and modification costs per delivered source statement were known.   After-the-fact structure charts with their module names omitted were drawn up for the most expensive and least expensive systems obtained from various sources.   The investigator, who did not know which charts represented which programs, simply tried to find ways of sorting the charts into two piles based on morphological features.   The success of the morphological criteria in separating the costly from the cheap systems could be checked by referring back to the separate cost data.   The umpteenth round in this game produced what came to be called the transform-centered model.   Most of the cheap systems had it; none of the costly systems did!   Since then, of course, support for highly factored transform-centered design has become widespread, and is based on both experience and numerous studies.

8.7 SUMMARY

The basic concern of this chapter is the *shape* of systems.   We have introduced a number of terms and concepts regarding systems morphology that are of critical importance in Chapters 9, 10, and 11.   If you read through this chapter quickly, we suggest that you review the meanings of such terms as fan-out, depth, width, skew, input-driven systems, output-driven systems, afferent, efferent, factoring, and span of control.

In addition to the fact that systems have a morphology, we have introduced the notion that most non-trivial systems have an underlying rationale for their shape — usually because the designer has decided to center the design of the system on some aspect that he considers important.   In many cases, this rationale has been informal and intuitive, and often has yielded a system with low cohesion and strong coupling.   The purpose of the next several chapters is to introduce rationales — or design strategies — that are based on considerations not only of systems morphology, but also of coupling and cohesion.

REFERENCES

1. GLENFORD J. MYERS, *Reliable Software Through Composite Design* (New York: Petrocelli/Charter, 1975).

2. W.P. STEVENS, G.J. MYERS, and L.L. CONSTANTINE, "Structured Design," *IBM Systems Journal,* Vol. 13, No. 2, pp. 115–139.

3. LUDWIG VON BERTALANFFY, *General Systems Theory* (New York: George Braziller, 1969).

4. GERALD WEINBERG, *An Introduction to General Systems Thinking* (New York: John Wiley & Sons, 1976).

Design Heuristics

CHAPTER 9

9.0 INTRODUCTON

In this chapter, we develop some selected heuristics with which systems structures may be improved. By heuristics, we mean certain tricks which, on the average, have the effect of increasing the modularity of a system. They are not guaranteed to work, nor do they help much in generating a system's structure in the first place. None constitutes a hard-and-fast rule, nor can any stand alone. So, you might ask: What good are the heuristics?

They are useful because they serve as checks or indicators by which a structure may be examined for potential improvements. Each indicator is a clue that a structure possibly may depart from an optimal configuration. However, we will stress repeatedly, as we did in the previous chapter, that the final judge of whether a heuristic should be applied literally is the intrinsic structure of the problem that the system is supposed to solve. If the system reflects the structure of the problem, then we have an invincible defense against any suggestion that the system's structure should be changed and improved based on the heuristics in this chapter.

9.1 MODULE SIZE

We have already suggested that module size is related to modularity, though not necessarily in the simple manner of "cut it into more pieces, Charlie." That is, technical modularity does not increase when module size decreases, even with other things being equal. For most purposes, though, modules much larger than one hundred statements are outside the optimal range with respect to the economy of error commission and correction. At the low end of the scale, the cutoff is less obvious. Except for the occasional misguided zealots who think that modularity is equivalent to chopping a program into one-statement modules, we find that very small modules have been designed consciously and deliberately — and usually for functional reasons. Normally, though, fewer than five to nine source statements might be a good point at which to start considering alternatives. This is especially relevant when *many* such very small modules are present in a system. However, if the code is either tricky or straightforward, these figures may be adjusted accordingly.

Suggestions for optimal module size have come from a variety of sources during the past few years; an overview of common module sizes may be found in a recent book by Yourdon.[1] One of the best-known suggestions for module size comes from Baker,[2] who suggests that modules should consist of approximately fifty statements to coincide with the number of lines that one can put on a single page of a printer listing; it is ironic that many consider this fifty-statement rule of thumb an "invention" of IBM and a necessary part of structured programming! Still another common number comes from Weinberg,[3] whose studies show that a programmer's comprehension of a module drops quickly if the module is larger than thirty statements. Most organizations have their own home-grown standards in this area. In their travels during the past several years, the authors have found organizations enforcing module sizes ranging from five to five hundred statements (the latter for a U.S. Air Force project).

Of course, very large or very small modules are not bad. Whatever the reasons, though, if the size goes much beyond the optimal range of ten to one hundred statements, we can be assured that the total system's cost will rise above some optimal minimum. On the other hand, the ultimate defense is the structure of the problem. It is possible (though unlikely) that there exists a single self-contained function which is only sensibly realized as a 2,000-statement FORTRAN subroutine. One can envision (though only hazily) a very large, highly involved decision table application or a long, involved mathematical computation, all strung out and segmentable only in an arbitrary and artificial fashion. If that is the structure of the problem — so be it! Cutting up a function simply to stay within an optimal size range is likely to be an injudicious move — particularly if it means sacrificing a problem-oriented structure. It is equally unwise to abolish a widely used character-moving subroutine, because it is implemented with a single FORTRAN statement.

In general though, we should examine and defend separately each case of a very small or a very large module. Let's first consider the very large module. Such

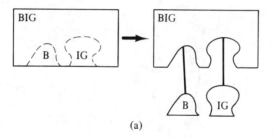

(a)

Fig. 9.1a Reduction of very large module through identification and extraction of subfunctions.

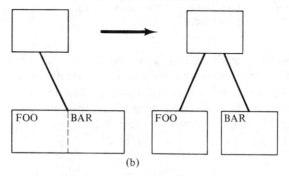

(b)

Fig. 9.1b Reduction of combined functions.

a module is often an indication of an incomplete breakdown into appropriate subordinate modules. Alternatively, we may find that two or more functions have been combined (frequently, with logical cohesion) into the same module. In the first case, we should examine the module to see if we can extract some subfunctions; this is illustrated in Fig. 9.1a. In the second case, we may be able to chop the module into its component functions, as illustrated in Fig. 9.1b. In either case, the structure chart should be used as a tool, and the structural modifications should be tried out on paper. The important thing is to give meaning to the new structure within the context of the actual problem. If it is not possible to make a reasonable interpretation, then the original structure stands.

When dealing with very small modules, we must distinguish two cases: the atomic (bottom-level) module, and the non-atomic module. In the case of an atomic module, the major issues are fan-in* and the ratio of subroutine-calling overhead to useful processing. If there are multiple uses (high fan-in), as in the case of Fig. 9.3, one does not legislate the module out of existence with impunity. With but a single use, as in Fig. 9.2, the designer might consider compressing the module upward into its superordinate ABLE — though each case should be considered on its own merit.

---

* In simple terms, the fan-in of a module is the number of superordinate modules that call upon it. Thus, the fan-in of module STRINGCOMP in Fig. 9.3 is five.

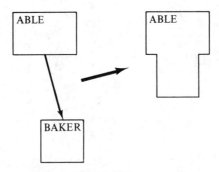

Fig. 9.2 Elimination of very small modules through upward compression.

Eliminating a module like STRINGCOMP in Fig. 9.3 is potentially dangerous, for it means that STRINGCOMP's function will be separately implemented (including coding and debugging) in each superordinate module that formerly used it. This duplicated effort can be expensive, even for simple processes. Moreover, each implementation of the STRINGCOMP function is likely to be slightly different, making maintenance and modification more difficult.

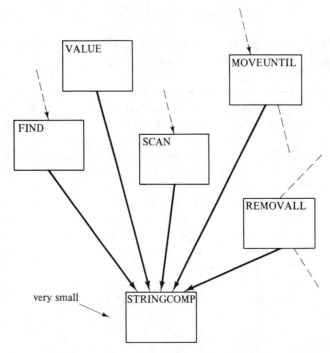

Fig. 9.3 Very small atomic module with high fan-in.

If it appears that the overhead of the subroutine-calling mechanism will be intolerable compared to the useful work performed by the module, the designer has another option. In the case of Fig. 9.3, for example, the designer requires that STRINGCOMP be separately coded and debugged — and then include *in-line* in modules FIND, VALUE, SCAN, MOVEUNTIL, and REMOVALL. Almost all current programming languages provide a feature to facilitate in-line subroutines: The COPY verb in COBOL, the %INCLUDE statement in PL/I, and the macro facilities in most assembly languages are examples.

If the facility is not found in the programming language itself, the programmer often can make use of the macro facilities of preprocessors, text editors, or source program maintenance packages. In any case, it should be evident that the in-line module gives us the advantages of modularity without incurring any overhead at run-time (although there may be a negligible overhead during the compilation or during the assembly process).

This example illustrates our previous suggestions that it is better to go too far in structured design. It is better to extract and identify the common function and have some choice in its implementation than never to have had any choice at all because of an incomplete design. In documenting "decommitments" of this sort, the form of Fig. 9.4 is usually preferable.

When the very small module is non-atomic, the analysis is complicated; the options are to compress upward and to compress downward, both of which should be considered. A special case is that of the so-called dummy module — one that had no contents except a call on its subordinate. It does no work itself and contains no control logic. Dummy modules are obviously the limiting case of very small.

Presumably, the dummy module is there because it reflects some aspects of the problem's structure. For example, Fig. 9.5 illustrates a situation in which IMPAC requires the function "particle velocity"; this is accomplished by module PARVELOC. When the particle velocity function is analyzed, the designer decides that it can be approximated with a square root — so PARVELOC simply calls SQRT. To save CPU time and memory on each call to PARVELOC, one is tempted to have IMPAC call SQRT directly. The temptation to eliminate the dummy PARVELOC is even greater if the module has a high fan-in.

But consider what happens when it is found that, say, an approximation using Yamota multipliers will give better approximations and a more accurate model of the particle velocity. As shown in Fig. 9.6, PARVELOC is no longer a dummy, for it coordinates the operation of both YAMOTA and SQRT, and calculates a formula that combines these results. Had PARVELOC been eliminated, this change would have necessitated modifying IMPAC, PENETRATN, RADIATN, and RMSVELOC to include more complicated, duplicated coding. Preservation of dummy modules often may be justified on the basis of simpler, more obvious future modifications. At the very least, the presence of the dummy module should be noted for future reference.

Throughout this discussion, it has been assumed that the designer knows,

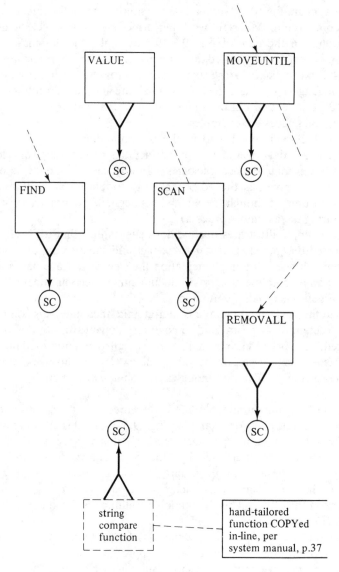

Fig. 9.4 Documentation of imaginary module recreated in-line for each use.

prior to implementation, the approximate size of the would-be modules. Normally, this does not require a separate and substantial estimation process. Experience has shown that the comparatively small size of modules in reasonably modular systems makes the estimation process easy, if not automatic. In addition, the estimation process becomes more accurate because the designer grows more familiar with the

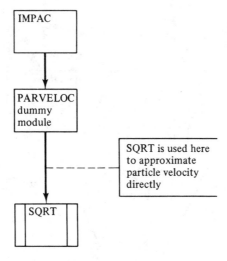

Fig. 9.5 Part of a system with a dummy non-atomic module.

function that various modules are to perform as he pursues the structural design in a systematic fashion. Indeed, we find that it is difficult *not* to be aware of the approximate number of statements as the design process continues.

9.2 SPAN OF CONTROL

Fan-out, or *span of control,* is the number of immediate subordinates of a module; we sometimes refer to this simply as the span of a module. As with module size, very high or very low spans are possible indicators of poor design. In Chapter 2, we drew an analogy with a management structure — and we observed that a manager's function usually becomes too complex if he has more than 7 ± 2 immediate subordinates. In general, we want to check a span of control that exceeds 10, as well as those of 1 or 2; a high span of control is usually more of a danger signal than a low span of control. Frequently, very good designs, especially of the type originating with the strategies in the next two chapters, will include many fully justified instances of fan-out of only 1 or 2.

A low span of control can be increased in most cases either by breaking the module into additional subordinate subfunctions, or by compressing the module into its superordinate; these strategies are illustrated in Fig. 9.7. As before, one should try to give some meaning to the new structure in the context of the specific problem that is being solved. For example, in Fig. 9.8, the first transformation makes more sense, because validation is a useful function whose separate existence as a module is fully justified.

A high span of control could be indicative of an over-zealous breakdown of a module into subordinates, but our experience has shown that this usually is not

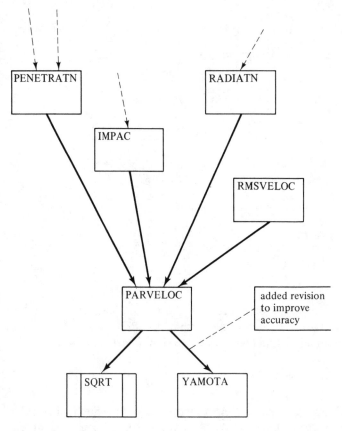

Fig. 9.6 Modified, former dummy module with multiple fan-in.

the case. High fan-outs frequently arise from pancaking, or a failure to define intermediate levels; the structure in Fig. 9.9a illustrates just such a situation.   To solve this problem, we consider various groups of subordinates as potentially forming a combined function. Our knowledge of module cohesion guides this process to help us avoid uncohesive modules.   In the case of Fig. 9.9a, we might introduce the intermediate modules shown in Fig. 9.9b; we might decide *against* an intermediate-level general-purpose COMPUTE-GROSS-PAY module because it would be logically cohesive.

9.3 FAN-IN

Whenever possible, we wish to maximize fan-in during the design process. Fan-in is the *raison d'être* of modularity: Each instance of multiple fan-in means that some duplicate code has been avoided. However, fan-in is not to be achieved

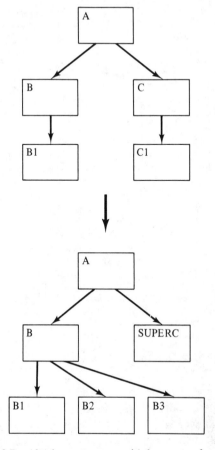

Fig. 9.7 Altering a structure with low span of control.

at any cost. It would be ridiculous, for example, to maximize fan-in by combining many unrelated functions into an uncohesive "supermodule" with a high fan-in.

Fan-in is achieved through an analytical process that accompanies the steps of any structured design procedure. As a new module is about to be drawn on the structure chart, we ask, Is there a module already available which performs the required function? If so, we draw an arrow to the existing box on the chart rather than drawing a new one. From a graphic viewpoint, this sometimes may be clumsy: A module that is used in many widely separated places in the structure results in a number of messy, crossed lines. The graphic convention shown in Fig. 9.10 is suggested as a way of minimizing the risk that the same function is coded twice because the implementer did not recognize that two boxes in the structure chart represented the same module. Specification of fan-in is the designer's job, not the implementer's.

The problem occurs when the designer realizes that his new, would-be

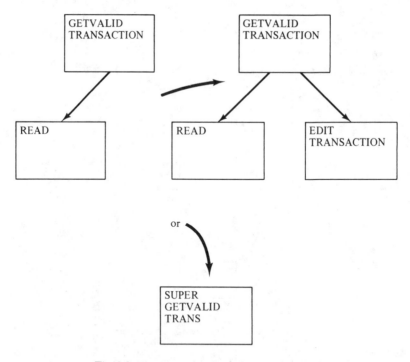

Fig. 9.8   Restructuring for low span of control.

module is similar or related to an existing module, but not identical to it. If he misses the subtle difference between his would-be module and the existing module, things will begin to go wrong during the system's integration. Either the new use of the module will misfire, or the old one will. Further problems will occur when the programmer attempts to make a debugging correction to the common module.

The key is to understand what makes the two instances similar or related — and then isolate that in a separate module. For example, suppose we have a Q1 function that appears to be similar to Q2; let Q represent the processing that they have in common. This suggests, as a first cut, the structure shown in Fig. 9.11a. However, there is a chance that this can be restructured into potentially more appropriate forms. If they are small, either or both of Q1' and Q2' might be compressed upward into their respective superordinates as shown in Figs. 9.11b, 9.11c, and 9.11d. Alternatively, a composite Q1 module could be formed; it would carry out Q1 for superordinate X, and Q for superordinate Y. We might even consider a supermodule, possibly with multiple entry points, which combines Q1, Q2, and Q.

The point is that the designer originally regarded Q2 as similar to Q1 — and he might have forced superordinate Y to call the existing Q1 module in the hope that things would work out all right. We now see that there are a variety of alternatives that do the job efficiently and in a modular fashion.

174

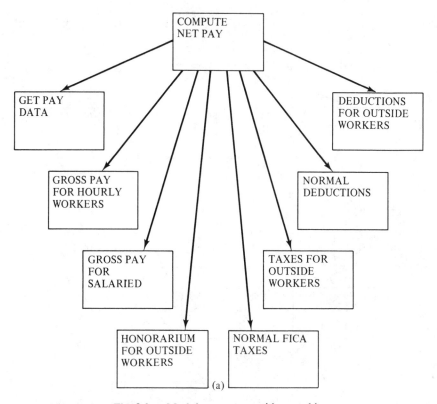

Fig. 9.9a Modular structure with pancaking.

9.4 SCOPE OF EFFECT/SCOPE OF CONTROL

Every decision or conditional statement (e.g., an IF statement) in a system has some consequences: Certain processing either happens or does not happen as a result of the decision. Equivalently, we can say that certain processing is conditional upon the outcome of some given decision. It is important to learn *where* in a modular structure the conditional effects of a specific decision are found. In order to discuss this, we need to introduce two new terms: *scope of effect* and *scope of control*.

The scope of effect of a decision is the collection of all modules containing any processing that is conditional upon that decision. If even a tiny part of the processing in a module is influenced by the decision, then the entire module is included in the scope of effect. If the activation of the entire module is conditional upon the outcome of the decision, then the module's superordinate is also included in the scope of effect: This makes sense when we realize that the superordinate must contain a statement to call the subordinate, and that CALL statement will be executed depending on the outcome of the decision.

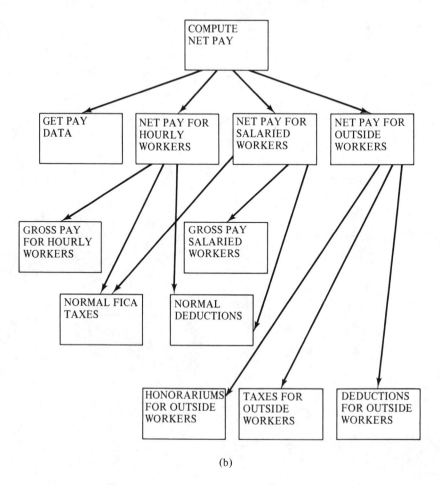

(b)

Fig. 9.9b Solution to the pancaking problem.

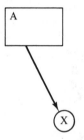

Fig. 9.10 Documenting use of modules in a different part of this structure.

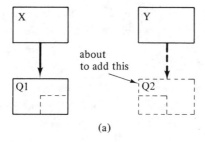

(a)

Fig. 9.11a Analysis of similar modules for fan-in.

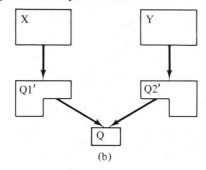

(b)

Fig. 9.11b Alternate restructuring for fan-in.

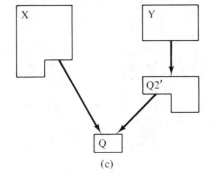

(c)

Fig. 9.11c Alternate restructuring for fan-in.

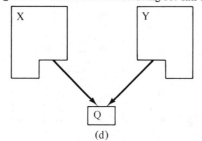

(d)

Fig. 9.11d Alternate restructuring for fan-in.

The scope of control of a module is the module itself and *all* of its subordinates. Scope of control is a purely structural parameter independent of the module's functions.

Now we can state a design heuristic that involves both scope of control and scope of effect:

> *For any given decision, the scope of effect should be a subset of the scope control of the module in which the decision is located.*

In other words, all of the modules that are affected, or influenced, by a decision should be subordinate ultimately to the module that makes the decision. Decision-

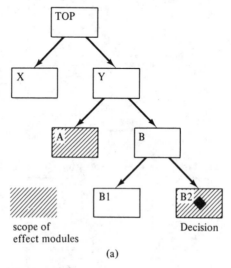

(a)

Fig. 9.12a   Violation of scope of effect/scope of control.

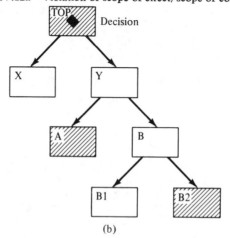

(b)

Fig. 9.12b   Correct scope of effect/scope of control, but with the decision too high in the hierarchy.

making and modular structure are best interrelated when decisions are made no higher in the hierarchy than is necessary to place the scope of effect within the scope of control. Ideally, the scope of effect should be limited to the module in which the decision is made and to those modules that are *immediately* subordinate.

Thus, Fig. 9.12a illustrates a structure in which the scope of effect is *not* a subset of the scope of control; Fig. 9.12b shows a structure in which the scope of effect is contained within the scope of control, although one could argue that the decision is being made too high in the hierarchy; Fig. 9.12c illustrates a structure in which the decision is being made just high enough in the hierarchy to include the scope of effect within the scope of control; and Fig. 9.12d demonstrates the ideal

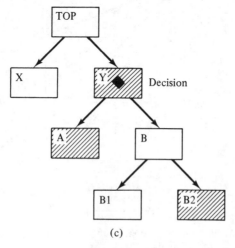

(c)

Fig. 9-12c   Adequate implementation of scope of effect/scope of control heuristic.

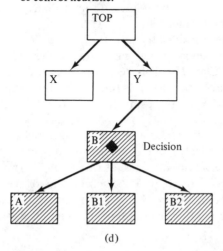

(d)

Fig. 9.12d   Ideal implementation of scope of effect/scope of control heuristic.

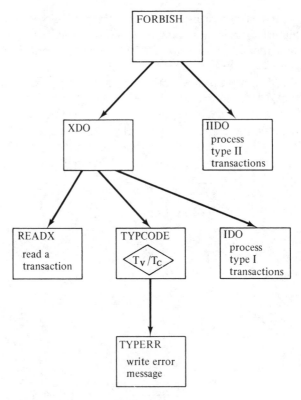

Fig. 9.13 Portion of system with scope of effect/scope of control conflict.

case in which the scope of effect modules are immediately subordinate to the module in which the decision is made.

As an example, consider the structure in Fig. 9.13. Note that a decision has been isolated that validates the transaction code, and divides all legitimate codes into Class I and Class II. This decision, which we abbreviate as Tv/Tc (for transaction valid?/transaction class?), is found in module TYPCODE. Included in its scope of effect are READX (if the transaction code is invalid, read another transaction, otherwise, process this one); TYPERR (which produces an error message if the transaction code is invalid); IDO and IIDO (activated for Type I and Type II transaction codes, respectively), and consequently XDO and FORBISH.

An appropriate question to ask at this point is, How does IDO get done? Or, for that matter, READX? Or IIDO? The outcome of the decision is known to TYPCODE but not, without special provision, to XDO. Somehow IDO must get activated, but only under the right circumstances. One of the following things must always be true:

(1) The decision is repeated in any module with processing in the scope of effect, including a superordinate whose only scope of effect proc-

180

essing is to activate a subordinate. This may not be possible if input information for the decision is unavailable. The Tv/Tc decision might not be possible in FORBISH, because the transaction code is not included in the data made available to FORBISH. Thus, special information may have to be passed in order to duplicate the decision. In other words, there is a certain cost in duplicated processing and a possible communication overhead. Such communication increases coupling.

(2)   The *outcome* of the Tv/Tc decision is encoded (generally, in the form of a flag, that most favored of design gimmicks) and passed to superordinate modules, which retest and act accordingly. This involves some communication overhead and a lesser amount of duplicated processing. However, since it involves passing control information, coupling may be significantly increased.

(3)   During implementation, the structure shown in Fig. 9.13 is violated — with pathological connections or hybrid coupling used to achieve the desired results. Thus, we might find that TYPCODE is programmed in such a way that it modifies code in FORBISH under the right conditions.

Clearly, some revision of the structure is indicated. In general, it is best to perform this in steps rather than to attempt one drastic modification to cure the structure of its ills. The final effect of such a series of modifications is usually that *portions* of the decision are moved upward in the hierarchy until the scope of effect is within the scope of control. We note parenthetically that this usually results in "distributed decision-making" of the sort that we described in Chapter 8.

Let us imagine that validation of the transaction code and classification of the transaction code are separable. We want TYPERR to be subordinate to the module that includes Tv, as only that module will have full, direct information about the nature of an error, and will thus be able to construct a reasonable error message. But we note that READX is also within the scope of effect of Tv, and IDO is in the scope of effect of Tc. Moving Tc up into XDO and making READX subordinate to the module containing Tv leads to the structure shown in Fig. 9.14; note that we have renamed GETVALIDX to reflect the change in its function. Whether the problem with IIDO can be solved gracefully depends on the reasons for having FORBISH; very likely, IIDO can be made subordinate to XDO.

Now, consider that Tc might be a complicated process — perhaps involving a table lookup and some computation. Indeed, it may be so complicated that we wish to make it a distinct module of its own; such a module probably would be subordinate to XDO. While this would violate our scope of effect/scope of control heuristic, the return of a binary flag to XDO is probably tolerable. In Fig. 9.15, a call on TYPCLAS behaves as a two-way conditional instruction to XDO. Two-way flags and three-way flags, as violations of the scope of effect/scope of control heuristic, are much more tolerable than an n-valued flag.

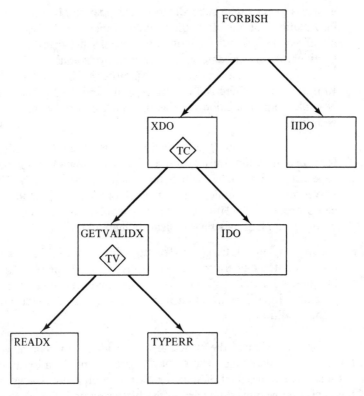

Fig. 9.14 System of Fig. 9.13 after partial resolution of scope of effect/scope of control conflict.

The solutions shown in Figs. 9.14 and 9.15 were derived on the assumption that Tv and Tc could be separated. If Tv/Tc is monolithic (perhaps because validity is determined by a failure of Tc), we could solve the problem by combining GETVALIDX and TYPCLAS of Fig. 9.15 into a module that we call, for lack of a better name, GETTYP-CODEVALIDX.

While the example shown in Figs. 9.13, 9.14, and 9.15 may seem somewhat divorced from the real world, it is nevertheless true that a number of classic data processing problems may be analyzed in terms of scope of effect/scope of control. For example, Fig. 9.16 shows individual records being combined by some discipline into compound items, which are searched for parts to be summarized into groups. The numerical ratio and relationship between groups, parts, items, and records vary. Note that the structure of Fig. 9.16 includes a system-supplied READ subroutine which exits to the operating system when an end-of-file is encountered. The decision, which we will abbreviate as F, is whether the processing of this file is finished; the outcome of the decision is to continue or to quit.

However, suppose that the execution of PHASE2 is conditional on the completion of PHASE1 processing. Thus, it is in the scope of effect of decision F. Un-

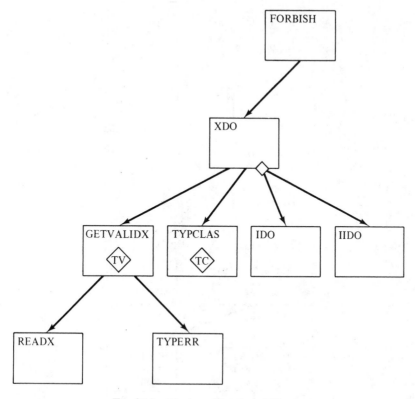

Fig. 9.15 Final modification of Fig. 9.13.

fortunately, ARB never has the opportunity to activate PHASE2 if READ decides to make a "panic abort" to the operating system. What we need to do is

- Change READ so that when it discovers an end-of-file condition, it communicates a "no-more-records" condition to COMPOUND.

- COMPOUND tests for "no-more-record" signal from READ. If it occurs, COMPOUND forces a call to MAKREADY to prepare this last compound item; the item is given to FINDPART. On the *next* call from FINDPART, COMPOUND returns with a "no-more-compound-items" indicator.

- FINDPART tests for "no-more-compound-items" indicator. Upon receiving it, it returns to SUMMARIZEGROUP with "no-more-parts" indicator.

- When SUMMARIZEGROUP receives the "no-more-parts" signal, it uses WINDUP to finish the last group, and returns that to PARSUM. On the next call from PARSUM, it returns with a "no-more-summaries" signal.

- When PARSUM receives the "no-more-summaries" indicator, it activates FINISH and then terminates.

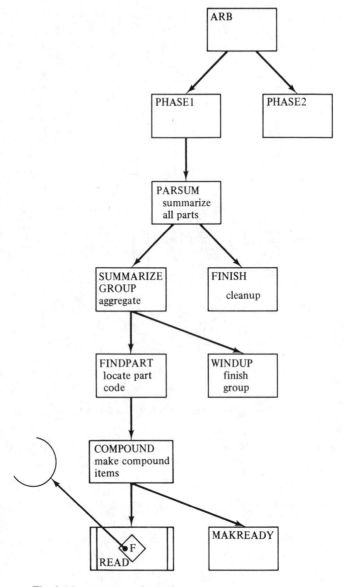

Fig. 9.16 A system with serious scope of effect problems.

It is essential to note that each module is making a different decision (or different parts of the same decision). Each is testing a different condition and informing its superordinate of yet another condition. In the strictest sense, the same information is not merely being passed up the line. Each module deals *only* with decisions and outcomes that are a part of its immediate function. Thus, when

COMPOUND returns an end-of-compound-items indicator, it makes no assumptions about (and has no knowledge of) *groups* and *parts;* no module needs to know how a decision might affect the function of other modules. The fact that a subordinate informs its superordinate when it cannot perform its function is expected behavior — both in computer systems structures and in management structures!

In summary of the discussion in this section, the scope of effect/scope of control heuristic is usually an excellent indicator that a decision has been placed in the wrong part of the modular structure — but it is only a heuristic! The most common example of violations of this heuristic is the occurrence of a relatively important decision (e.g., an end-of-file test or a "fatal-error" test whose outcome may result in returning pathologically to the operating system) at or near the bottom of the hierarchy. Unfortunately, violations of this heuristic are rampant (see, for example, the end-of-file logic in Armstrong's programming examples[4]). As we have seen, the violations usually have one or more negative consequences:

- duplicated decision-making

- increased coupling from additional flags and switches being passed to other scope of effect modules

- pathological control flow or data flow

Scope of effect/scope of control problems that occur early in the design phase almost always can be rectified easily by judicious restructuring. In general, the designer has three options for correcting the problems:

- Compress a low-level module into its superordinate so that the decision takes place high enough in the structure to solve the scope of effect problem.

- Move a scope of effect module down in the hierarchy to get it within the scope of control.

- Remove all or part of the decision from the low-level module and place it in a higher level module.

9.5 SUMMARY

It must be emphasized that this chapter has discussed *heuristics,* not religious rules. Heuristics such as module size, span of control, and scope of effect/scope of control can be extremely valuable if properly used, but actually can lead to poor design if interpreted too literally. Unfortunately, the authors have experienced several cases in the past few years where the design heuristics of this chapter were used blindly — and the results often have been catastrophic.

REFERENCES

1. EDWARD YOURDON, *Techniques of Program Structure and Design* (Englewood Cliffs, N.J.: Prentice-Hall, 1975).

2. F.T. BAKER, "Chief Programmer Team Management of Production Programming," *IBM Systems Journal,* Vol. 11, No. 1, pp. 56–73.

3. GERALD M. WEINBERG, *PL/I Programming: A Manual of Style* (New York: McGraw-Hill, 1970).

4. RUSSELL ARMSTRONG, *Modular Programming in COBOL* (New York: John Wiley & Sons, 1973).

Transform
Analysis

CHAPTER 10

10.0 INTRODUCTON

In Chapter 8, we saw that systems whose morphology — or overall shape — was transform-centered tend to be associated with low development costs, low maintenance costs, and low modification costs. We also observed that such low-cost systems tend to be highly factored; that is, the high-level modules make most of the decisions, and the low-level modules accomplish most of the detailed work.

Transform analysis, or *transform-centered design,* is a strategy for deriving initial structural designs that usually are quite good (with respect to modularity) and generally require only a modest restructuring to arrive at a final design. It is a particular form of a top-down strategy, which takes advantage of overall or global perspective. Applied rigorously, transform analysis leads to structures which are fully, or almost fully, factored. It produces sizable numbers of modules at intermediate levels in the hierarchy, which represent compositions of basic functions (or compositions of compositions). However, even the intermediate modules avoid doing any "work" except to control and coordinate the work of subordinates.

187

Overall, the purpose of the strategy is to identify the primary processing functions of the system, the high-level inputs to those functions, and the high-level outputs. It then creates high-level modules within the hierarchy to perform each of these tasks: creation of high-level inputs, transformation of inputs into high-level outputs, and processing of those outputs. As we will see, transform analysis is an *information flow* model rather than a procedural model.

The tranform analysis strategy consists of the following four major steps:

1.   restating the problem as a data flow graph

2.   identifying the afferent and efferent data elements

3.   first-level factoring

4.   factoring of afferent, efferent, and transform branches

Each of these steps is discussed in detail in subsequent sections of this chapter.

10.1 THE FIRST STEP: RESTATE THE PROBLEM AS A DATA FLOW GRAPH

In order to carry out the strategy of transform analysis, it is necessary to study the flow of data through the system. That is, we must draw a data flow graph for the system we are designing. We recall that data flow graphs were presented in Chapter 3 to illustrate non-procedural aspects of a system; they served that purpose in subsequent discussions of cohesion in Chapter 7. However, the data flow graph typically was presented as an accomplished fact. What we now must do is to ask *how* a data flow graph is conceived.

In certain trivial systems, the data flow may be perfectly obvious to the designer; he instantly may be able to draw a data flow graph of the sort shown in Fig. 10.1. Indeed, even the simple payroll example shown in Fig. 10.2 — which involves both conjunction and disjunction operators — may be intuitively obvious to the designer. But how should we deal with more complex situations?

There are several ways to approach this analytical process. Designers who are experienced in the use of data flow graphs and who are used to non-procedural thinking generally start with the physical inputs (e.g., a card from the card reader, or a message from the terminal) and work their way downstream through successive

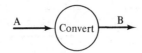

Fig. 10.1   Transform from A into B.

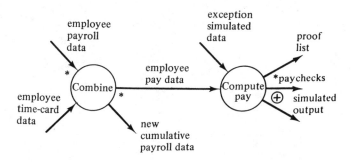

Fig. 10.2 Conjunction and disjunction.

transforms to the physical outputs (e.g., a printed report). Working upstream from outputs toward the inputs works just as well for many designers. It appears to be a matter of taste, rather than a technical issue.

Unfortunately, many newcomers to the use of data flow graphs find that these two approaches tend to lose them in procedural details, which must be set aside at this stage. An alternative is to begin with a single bubble that correctly represents the entire system in terms of inputs and outputs. This trivial data flow graph is then refined by segmenting it into several transforms so that the resulting data flow graph has two to four bubbles of approximately equal size or importance. In turn, this is replaced with yet another more detailed data flow graph for the entire application. This "middle-out" approach is also a useful exercise in top-down thinking.

Whatever approach is used to develop it, the amount of detail shown in the final data flow graph will vary from problem to problem, and from designer to designer, but the beginner is advised to show the data flow in considerable detail until he has a feel for the amount of detail required by various problems. None of this effort will be wasted, as greater understanding of the problem at this stage in the design can greatly simplify some of the subsequent steps.

To illustrate this point, we recall the master file update example that was first presented in Chapter 3. Figure 10.3a shows a data flow graph that is probably extreme in the sense of not showing enough detail; on the other hand, the data flow graph shown in Fig. 10.3b is perhaps extreme in the sense of showing too much detail. If forced to choose between one extreme and the other, we would prefer to show too much detail — that is, we would prefer Fig. 10.3b.

Generally, it is easier to follow through certain "main" data paths dealing with primary inputs; minor inputs and minor outputs (e.g., error paths that emerge from a "validate" bubble) can be ignored at first. Often, it is found that secondary inputs are employed in transforms deep within the data flow, and they will be picked up automatically when those points are reached. A final "clean-up" sweep through the data flow graph can account for any unattached input or output streams.

When drawing the data flow graph, it is essential not to become entangled

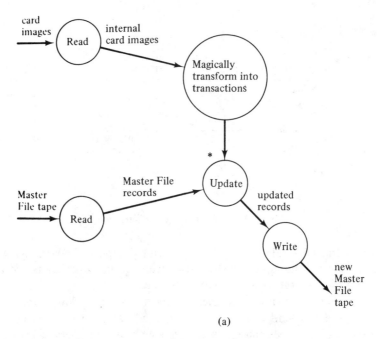

(a)

Fig. 10.3a. Data flow diagram with very little detail.

in aspects of *procedure* or *decision-making*. That is, the graph should not show (and the designer should not worry about) such things as loops, initialization, termination, recovery procedures, or decisions. For example, from an information flow standpoint, an error detection process is not a decision branch, but a *filter,* which separates good data from bad data.

Thus, in Fig. 10.4, we imagine that the process has been running forever, and will continue running forever; we'll get around to the initialization and termination procedures later when we're ready to deal with procedure-oriented design. Similarly, it does not concern us that the bubble labeled "check skill validity" contains a decision (although the module that eventually realizes that transformation obviously will contain one or more decision-making statements). All we care about at this point is that the "stream" of employee skill records has been split into two separate streams of data. Indeed, as we suggested above, we might not even bother showing the "bogus skill" path in our initial data flow diagram, since it is not the primary data stream. Note also, in this example, the fact that many individual employee skill records are required to produce a department skill summary is not represented in the data flow graph. We only see that the "summarize" bubble transforms a stream of valid employee skill records (by some magical process) into a stream of department skill summaries.

To summarize our discussion of data flow graphs, we offer the following suggestions to the designer:

190

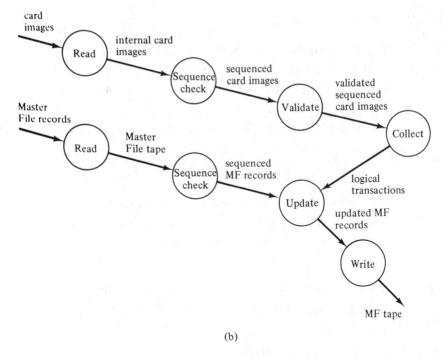

(b)

Fig. 10.3b   Data flow diagram with excessive detail.

- Work your way consistently through the problem, from the input stream toward the output or vice versa, depending on your preference. If you get stuck somewhere in the middle, then switch.   Or, you can use the middle-out approach described above.

- Never try to show control logic.   If you find yourself thinking in terms of loops and decisions, you're on the wrong track.   Specifically, if you find yourself drawing an arrow and thinking to yourself, Now let's go to this bubble and do the process again, you're in trouble.   Remember: The arrows represent the flow of data, not control.

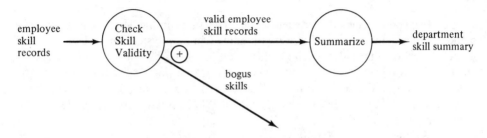

Fig. 10.4   Validity checking as a filter.

- Ignore initialization and termination. Pretend the system all runs at once, and that it continues running forever.

- Omit simple error paths from each bubble to the outside world.

- Label the data elements very carefully as they enter and leave a transform bubble. That is, if a data stream marked A enters a bubble, then the output stream that emerges from the bubble should generally not be marked as A. It may be called "new-A-as-a-result-of-computations" or "the-good-A's-after-we-discarded-the-bad-ones."

- Make use of "*" and " ⊕ " operators as appropriate.

- Make sure that the data flow is correct for the level of detail being shown. If in doubt, show too much detail rather than too little. Don't flowchart!

Typically, the result of this first step of transform analysis is a diagram of the sort shown in Fig. 10.5; this diagram illustrates a manufacturing plant simulation process.

10.2 THE SECOND STEP: IDENTIFY THE AFFERENT AND THE EFFERENT DATA ELEMENTS

In Chapter 8, we introduced the notion of afferent flow and efferent data flow; in that discussion of systems morphologies, we also saw modules that could be termed afferent modules, and others that could be termed efferent modules.
We now define *afferent data elements* as follows:

Afferent data elements are those high-level elements of data that are furthest removed from physical input, yet still constitute inputs to the system.

Thus, afferent data elements are the highest level of abstraction to the term "input to the system." They represent the most aggregated, the most processed, the most "macro-level" inputs.

In general, the afferent data elements will bear the least possible resemblance to the raw input data that were obtained from a physical input device. That is, physical blocking and buffering will no longer be visible; control characters (if any) will have been removed; any necessary formatting and conversion of the input to a standard internal form will have been done; and all editing, checking, and validation will have been accomplished. What remains are good, clean data, ready for processing.

We identify the afferent data elements by starting at the physical inputs to the system and moving inward along the data diagram until we identify a stream

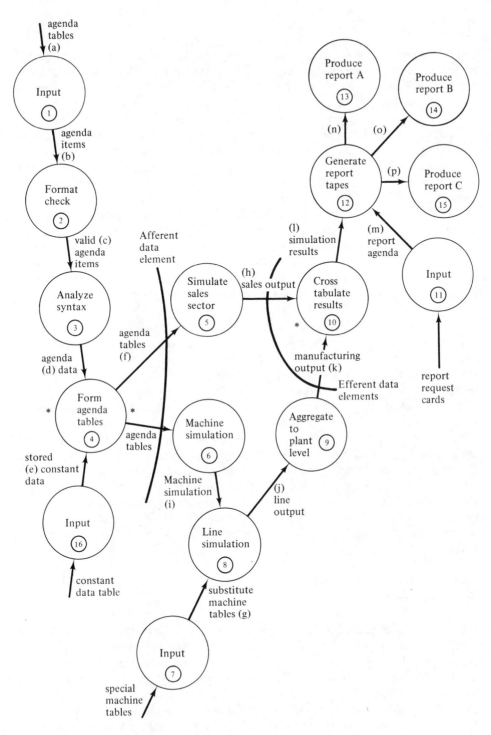

Fig. 10.5 Data flow diagram for a simulation system.

that can no longer be considered as incoming. This represents a value judgment on the part of the designer, but the aim is to go as far from the physical inputs as plausible. Generally, experienced designers will not differ by more than one or two transforms in their judgment of where the afferent transforms end.

This process is performed for each input stream. Often, we find that several physical input streams may end in the same afferent data element. In the data flow of Fig. 10.5, for example, the afferent data element is the "agenda table."

Beginning at the other end with the physical outputs, we try to identify the *efferent data elements*. As the name implies, the efferent data elements are those furthest removed from the physical outputs which may still be regarded as outgoing. Such elements might be regarded as "logical output data" that have just been produced by the "main processing" part of the system and which have had the least amount of processing to convert them to "physical output data." We perform this process for each of the ultimate output streams. In the plant simulation system shown in Fig. 10.5, "sales output" and "manufacturing output" are the efferent data elements. Note that we use brackets to designate the afferent and efferent data elements.

This step usually leaves some transforms in the middle, between the afferent data elements and the efferent data elements. These are designated *central transforms*. They are the main work of the system; they transform the major inputs into the major outputs. Occasionally, the afferent and efferent data elements will be the same, in which case there are no central transforms.

It may be argued at this point that this step is an attempt to model all systems as a trivial input-process-output flow. Indeed, most systems *are* sufficiently trivial to be modeled in this form (for, after all, what else do most systems do but read some input, perform some computations, and generate some output?), but that is not the real point. What is important to us is that many designers do not have the instinct to follow the main input streams all the way in to the afferent data element. As a result, their modular structures tend to be *input-driven* (cf. the discussion in Chapter 8). Even though it may seem trivial at this stage, the process of transform analysis that we are outlining ensures that the structure will be balanced.

10.3 THE THIRD STEP: FIRST-LEVEL FACTORING

Having identified the afferent and efferent data elements of the system, we specify a main module which, when activated, will perform the entire task of the system by calling upon subordinates. For *each* afferent data element feeding a central transform (in the example of Fig. 10.5, there is only one: the agenda tables), an afferent module is specified as an immediate subordinate to the main module. Its ultimate function will be to deliver the afferent data element to its superordinate, that is, to the main module. It should be clear that the afferent modules are *truly* afferent modules in the sense that we defined the term in Chapter 8: They obtain their inputs from below (by calling lower-level subordinate modules), and they deliver that input upward.

Similarly, for *each* efferent data element emerging from any central transform (in the example of Fig. 10.5, there are two), we define a subordinate efferent module that will accept the efferent data element and, ultimately, transform it into the final physical output. Again, it should be clear that such modules are truly efferent modules, in the sense of the definitions of Chapter 8.

Finally, for each central transform or functionally cohesive composition of central transforms, we specify a subordinate transform module (where, once again, we have used the term in the sense in which it was defined in Chapter 8), which will accept from the main module the appropriate input data and transform it into the appropriate output data; of course, this output is delivered back upward to the main module. Thus, we can see that there is a simple (usually one-for-one) correspondence between the data flow graph and the initial first-level factoring.

The main module is the overall control, or executive, for the process. Its function is to control and coordinate the afferent, transform, and efferent modules dealing with the highest-level data of the system. It will call the immediately subordinate afferent modules to obtain major inputs, pass these to the appropriate transform modules, deliver the results to other transform modules, and deliver the final results to the efferent modules. These calls will, in the general case, be imbedded in the major decision and iteration control logic for the overall process.

The first-cut factoring for the system of Fig. 10.5 is shown in Fig. 10.6. The number in each module "box" refers to a transform that is similarly identified in the data flow diagram.

10.4 THE FOURTH STEP: FACTORING OF AFFERENT, EFFERENT, AND TRANSFORM BRANCHES

Three distinct substrategies are used to factor the three types of subordinate modules (afferent, efferent, and transform) into lower-level subordinates. There is no particular reason for starting with the afferent portion of the system, but many designers find it the most natural way of proceeding. It is not necessary to completely factor one branch down to the lowest level of detail before working on another branch, but it is important to identify all of the immediate subordinates of any given module before turning to any other module.

Thus, suppose we have identified MAIN, A, B, and C as a first-level factoring for Fig. 10.7. Suppose that our next step was to begin factoring module A, and that we have identified subordinate A1. We should continue defining and identifying the other subordinates of A (namely A2 and A3) before exploring the subordinates of B, C, or A1.

To see how an afferent module can be factored, look at the top-level afferent module GETAGENDATAB in Fig. 10.6. We know that GETAGENDATAB's function, as viewed from the main module, is to produce agenda tables; thus, our job is to

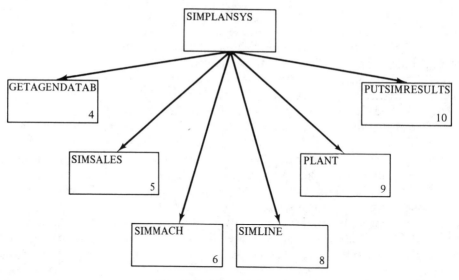

Fig. 10.6 First-cut factoring.

identify the transform (or computations) required to produce agenda tables. This last (in the sense of transformation of data) transform becomes the function of a new *transform* module immediately subordinate to GETAGENDATAB. Obviously, this new transform module requires some input: For each input to this last transform, we specify a new *afferent* module immediately subordinate to GETAGENDATAB. Each of these new lower-level afferent modules is factored, recursively, in the same manner until the ultimate physical input is reached or the process is otherwise terminated (see Sections 10.5 and 10.6 below). The first-cut factoring of the afferent branch for the plant simulation system is shown in Fig. 10.8.

The factoring of efferent modules is essentially symmetrical to that of afferent modules. For a given efferent module, we are looking for the *next* transform to be applied which will bring the data closer to its ultimate "physical" form. The transform module that accomplishes this transformation will be subordinate to the "top-level" efferent module in the system. Thus, the transform module CROSS-TAB is identified as a subordinate to the top-level module PUTSIMRESULTS shown in Fig. 10.6. The output of the transform module CROSSTAB then becomes input to a new efferent module which is *also* subordinate to the original top-level efferent module PUTSIMRESULTS; the process then continues. Naturally, there may be more than one "next transform" and more than one subsequent efferent process. For our plant simulation process, the factoring of efferent modules is shown in Fig. 10.9.

Little is known about the optimal factoring of central transform modules — that is, for modules like SIMSALES, SIMMACH, SIMLINE, and PLANT in our example of Fig. 10.6. Obviously, for each transform, we are looking for sub-transforms that will compose the overall transform. We also are looking for composi-

196

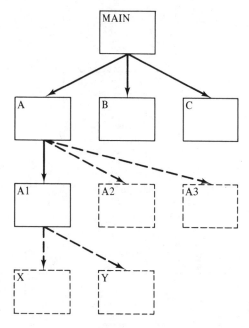

Fig. 10.7 Factoring of subordinate modules.

tions of the functions shown as the central transforms in the original data flow graph (e.g., for the central transforms shown in the data flow graph of Fig. 10.5). These are inserted as intermediate modules in the hierarchy — between the top level and the functions from which they are composed.

Our purpose is to ensure that the subordinates of the main module represent the highest levels of processing and that less important details are relegated to lower levels. The designer's judgment and experience are guided throughout this process by the important considerations of coupling and cohesion, as well as by the various design heuristics that were discussed in Chapter 9. For the plant simulation example, the trial factoring of the transform modules is shown on page 200 in Fig. 10.10.

10.5 THE FIFTH STEP: DEPARTURES

The strategy thus far described assumes an orthodox structure in which the data flow inward or outward in any branch — but not both! Consequently, we expect that afferent modules will have only afferent and transform subordinates; similarly, efferent modules are expected to have only efferent and transform subordinates; and transform modules (regardless of where they are in the structure) should have only transform subordinates.

However, real-world problems frequently require exceptions to these rules if clumsy processing is to be avoided. For example, in our plant simulation prob-

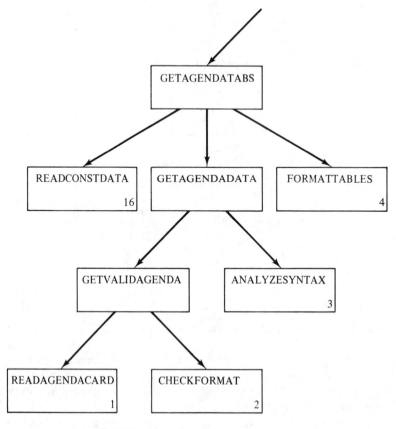

Fig. 10.8 Factoring of an afferent branch.

lem, the "special machine table solutions" could require afferent subordinates to a transform module; similarly, the "report agenda" input could require afferent subordinates to an efferent module.

Let us assume, for example, that the special machine table solutions are used only when some detail in the plant simulation transform detects certain conditions. We would expect this step to be found quite far down in the transform structure, as we have, in fact, shown in Fig. 10.10. To place an afferent GETSPEC-TAB module subordinate to the top-level SIMPLANSYS module would be terribly artificial: It would mean either that the tables must be input in all runs of the system, just in case they are needed, or that the detail step SIMMACHSTEP would have to signal its superordinate, which would signal its superordinate — and so forth — all the way back to the top level to read the tables, and then return all the way back down to continue the simulation.

We must always keep in mind that our objective is to make the program structure reflect the structure of the problem as closely as possible. The detailed

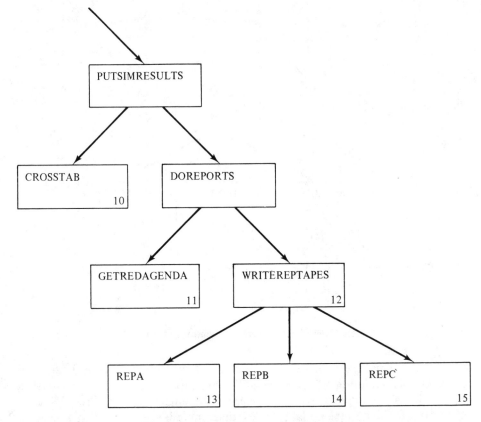

Fig. 10.9 Factoring of an efferent branch.

data flow diagram is a guide to the problem structure, and if the problem requirements necessitate a departure from the orthodox transform-centered organization, it should be apparent in the diagram. Certainly, this is the case in the example shown in Fig. 10.5.

When completed, the trial structural design using transform analysis will bear a simple, straightforward relationship to the data flow. This will be evident in our plant simulation example by comparing the structures shown in Figs. 10.8, 10.9, and 10.10 with the data flow shown in Fig. 10.5. It must be remembered that this is a trial, first-cut structural design. The final structure, which will reflect many design trade-offs and heuristics, will be derived from systematic refinements and alterations of this initial structure. These modifications may be made in a separate phase after completing the initial factoring, or (as many designers prefer) *during* the initial factoring. Especially when similar problems have been exhaustively analyzed before by the designer, this concurrent approach may save considerable effort.

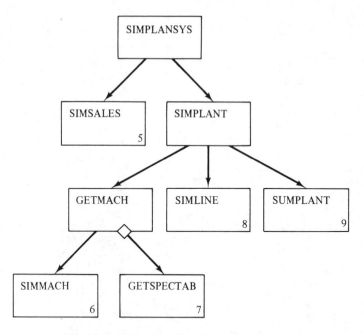

Fig. 10.10   Trial factoring of central transforms.

For example, a final version of our plant simulation problem might look like the one shown in Fig. 10.11 on the following page. Again, carefully study the relationship between this figure and the earlier structures shown in Figs. 10.8, 10.9, and 10.10 — as well as the initial data flow diagram in Fig. 10.5.

10.6 GENERAL COMMENTS ON FACTORING

As we pointed out earlier, *all* of the subordinates of a module should be identified and defined before any one of the subordinates is analyzed any further. Clearly, we are seeking the smallest number of distinct modules which satisfies the appropriate transform. To check whether this step has been completed, we need only to ask whether the available subordinates are sufficient to implement the transform. We must be able to see that there is at least one way to program the current module (which implements the transform currently being analyzed) in terms of the subordinates plus appropriate control and coordination processes (decision-making, looping, communication, and so on). It is not necessary to detail this procedure, nor to consider more than one way of doing the job — as long as we are assured that at least one way exists. Obviously, the designer should regard with suspicion any subordinate module which he cannot see as *necessary* to implement the current module.

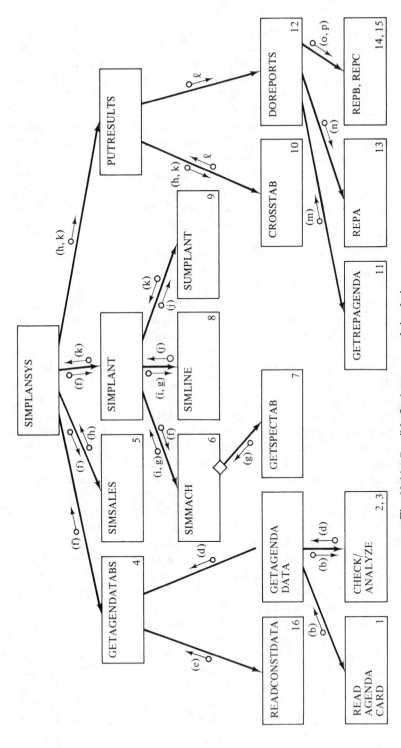

Fig. 10.11 Possible final structure of simulation system.

As subordinate functions are identified, the designer names them. A brief descriptive name or phrase is used to characterize the function of the module. This may be a phrase taken from a description of the superordinate's transform, or it may be a restatement of that description. It should fully and *specifically* describe what the module does with respect to its superordinate — that is, what function it appears to perform from the outside.

Several heuristics concerning *names* of modules are useful in determining their effect on the module structure. Names that identify classes of operations should be avoided, as they frequently are associated with logical cohesion (cf. the discussion in Chapter 7). Names that involve many conjunctions and qualifying conditions are clues to low cohesion. Thus, if the name GET RECORD UNLESS FLAG OR CARD BLANK IN WHICH CASE READ CARD AND PRINT RECORD is the only correct description of the module (as seen from its superordinate), then it probably has very low cohesion.

The consistent use of names that imply inherent communication structure will avoid ambiguity and subsequent unintentional changes in interpretation. Any consistent set will do, but the names shown in Table 10.1 are in fairly wide use and have the added advantage of yielding subroutine calls that read like commands in a high-level programming language. Note that the names consist of verbs followed by a description of the specific process being carried out by the module. Thus, we have names like GET CONTROL SPECS or PRODUCE MONTHLY REPORTS.

Forms of names that do *not* imply a specific procedural implementation are preferred to those names having a more specific connotation. COMBINE is a more general form of MERGE, and is, therefore, preferable. Certain general terms — such as UPDATE and VALIDATE — have specific procedural meanings to particular designers. We would like to avoid such procedural interpretations while we are involved in the structural design of the program. Similarly, device names and physical input names should be avoided until it is clear that the object being dealt with can only exist in actual physical form. READ-TIME-CARD is usually a low-level function, for example, as compared to GET-TIME-ITEM.

References to the term FILE often tempt the designer to commit himself to file-by-file processing or to using more intermediate files than necessary. For example, the two top-level functions DEVELOP-EMPLOYEE-FILE and PRODUCE-EM-PLOYEE-REPORT seem to suggest a structure in which DEVELOP-EMPLOYEE-FILE creates (or outputs) a magnetic tape file of employee data, which PRODUCE-EMPLOYEE-REPORT will read, format, and print as a report. Aggregations of data that are not the fundamental unit of processing should not be referenced. Names that imply processing of a single element of data have been found to leave more room for free choice of a processing algorithm.

By making complete, but succinct, statements of the function of a module, the designer often can identify low cohesion at an early stage in the design. By using a consistent, restricted vocabulary, the designer avoids ambiguity and over-commitment to a single processing methodology. Finally, if the designer has difficulty finding a succinct name for a function, it may be a clue that such a module

Table 10.1 Suggested Module Names

Afferent processes with external sources of data

GET	ACCEPT (usually asynchronous)
OBTAIN	FIND
INPUT	LOAD

Afferent processes with internal sources of data

SETUP	FORM
DEVELOP	CREATE
GENERATE	

Transform processes

ANALYZE	COMPUTE
TRANSFORM	CALCULATE
CONVERT	PERFORM
DO	PROCESS

Specific verbs like SORT, VALIDATE, etc.
Function-oriented nouns like SQUAREROOT, INVERSION

Efferent processes with external targets

PUT	OUTPUT
PRODUCE	STORE
SAVE	WRITE
DELIVER	

Specific verbs like PRINT, LIST, PUNCH, etc.

But some of these are somewhat ambiguous

PROCESS	(could be afferent or transform)
CREATE	(could be afferent or efferent)
GENERATE	(could be afferent or efferent)
DO	(could be anything)
PERFORM	(could be anything)
DELIVER	(could be afferent or efferent)

does not exist, or that it does not make sense in the current context, or that it does not make sense at the current place in the structure.

10.7 TERMINATION

Various criteria may be used to determine when the functional factoring of modules should be terminated. The end may be reached when it is not possible to state a transform with any clearly discernible subtasks. When a vendor-supplied module or library subroutine is reached, factoring cannot proceed because the substructure has already been determined (though it should not be visible to the designer if the library routine is truly a black box). Similarly, reaching a module that interfaces with physical input-output media signals the end of factoring. Finally, when we identify very small modules, it indicates that we have reached the bottom level of the hierarchy — although clearly any such signal is approximate and has exceptions. "Very small" generally means vanishingly small: a few instructions or source statements. The approximate size of such modules is, by definition, obvious — hence, no distinct size-estimating process is needed.

It is preferable to go too far in an initial factoring, and to have recognized processes that are too small, too fractional, and too specialized to constitute distinct modules. The very tiny modules always can be combined later with a full knowledge of the composition of the combined module, and with a full understanding of the structural design consequences; the trade-offs can be weighed, and a deliberate optimal choice can be made. If the design does not proceed far enough, the opportunity for conscious decision may be lost, and the exact nature of any resulting composite modules may never be known.

10.8 AN EXAMPLE: THE FRANK SYSTEM

Consider a system to be used by a meat packer who prepares processed meat products for discount-food stores. The company wants an appropriately headed Buying List report for their hot dogs to tell them which meat products to buy in order to produce frankfurters of a given quality at the lowest possible cost. The company is constrained by Federal standards, state standards, product-consistency requirements, quality standards, and so forth — all of which comprise a matrix of parameters. Some prices and constraints are fairly stable and will be maintained as one set of row definitions in the matrix; others are transient, the row definitions changing almost daily.

In either case, it is necessary to verify the reasonableness of row definitions based on some fairly complex internal consistency checks; an invalid row is corrected by an exception input from an on-line terminal. Both kinds of row definitions (stable and transient) are punched on cards in a "free-field" format, which must be checked and converted to a standard internal form. One, two, or three cards with the same row number constitute a row item.

The two card decks (one for the stable row definitions and one for the transient row definitions) are read from a fast card reader (using a systems-supplied routine READCARD-F) and from a slow card reader (using READCARD-S). Rows are combined by a simple merge on row number to form the parameter matrix. If the row numbers from the two card readers match, the transient row definition is used; row 999 signals the end of input. When the rows have been put into an ordered matrix form, the matrix is used to compute an optimal meat mix for frankfurters. Depending on a sophisticated mathematical test, this computation may sometimes require conversion of the matrix to a "canonical form"; this allows a short subroutine called SIMPLETON to compute the least-cost solution using a linear programming technique that is known as the "simplex" algorithm.

10.8.1 Restatement as data flow

The first step, as we have seen, is to restate the problem in nonprocedural form using the data flow graph. This is done most easily by proceeding systematically from the system's inputs to its output. There are four input streams to the FRANK system; stable parameters, transient parameters, the description file used to produce a readable report, and exception input. The first transform applied to each of these streams is the operation necessary to get them physically into the program. As shown in Fig. 10.12, the data flow graph begins at the left of the page, showing the input transform. Note that the streams are labeled very specifically to avoid confusion among similar streams or different forms of the same stream. Ignoring the description file and the exception input for the moment, the design continues with the sucessive transforms of the transient and stable parameter streams, which must be reformatted and built into complete rows, as shown in Fig. 10.12.

At this point, there is a choice to be made. Ultimately, the FRANK system must have available rows of parameters that are merged (from stable and transient streams) and validated. However, the statement of the problem is ambiguous as to the order in which merging and validation are to be performed. We will

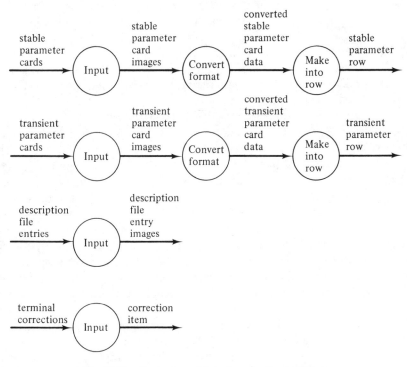

Fig. 10.12 Beginning of data flow for FRANKSYS.

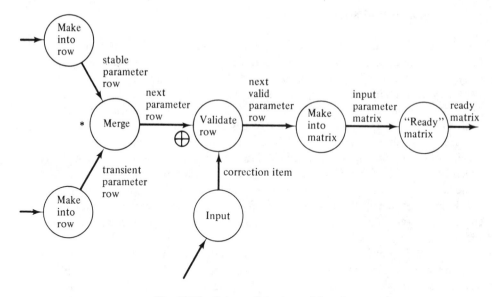

Fig. 10.13 Intermediate stage of data flow.

simply choose to perform validation after the merging operation. The resulting stream must be put into matrix form, and the matrix readied for processing with the simplex algorithm. This results in the data flow diagram of Fig. 10.13. Notice that "*" and "⊕" have been used in appropriate places.

The results of the optimization must be combined with the descriptions of items (from the description file), formatted into a report, and printed. The completed data flow graph is presented in Fig. 10.14.

The next step is to identify the afferent and efferent data elements by locating the points in the data flow that are furthest away from physical input and output forms, yet still comprise, respectively, inward and outward flowing data. This decision may be approached by asking ourselves whether it is possible to imagine a GET module for a given afferent stream, and a PUT module for an efferent stream.

For example, we can easily imagine a GETTRANSIENTCARD process, or even a GETNEXTVALIDROW process, or even a GETPARAMETERMATRIX process — but we probably cannot imagine a GETOPTIMALINGREDIENTS process as an *input* process. Most designers would draw the line defining the afferent data element between the production of the matrix and its use in the simplex calculation. Because the readying of the matrix is functionally allied with the nature of the simplex algorithm itself, we have left the "make-ready" transform out of the afferent portion of the data flow.

On the efferent side, we certainly can imagine an efferent process to PUT a line, and we can imagine a PUTRESULTMATRIX operation — but we would have difficulty imagining a PUTINPUTPARAMETERMATRIX process. The final selection of afferent and efferent data elements is shown in Fig. 10.15. Note that the descrip-

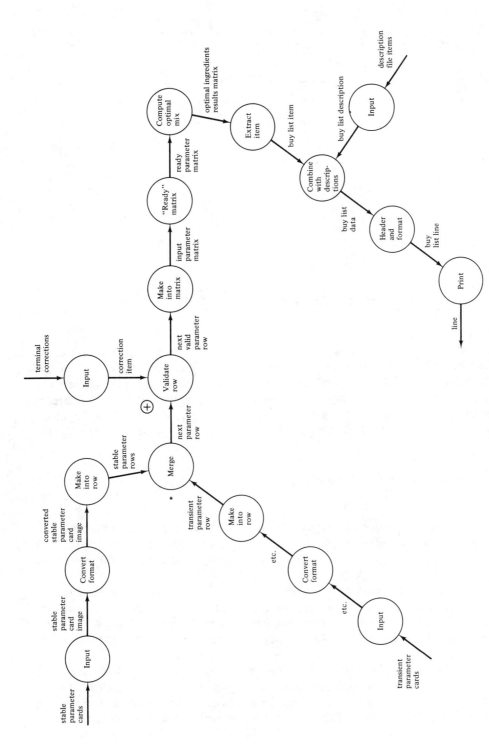

Fig. 10.14 Complete data flow for FRANKSYS.

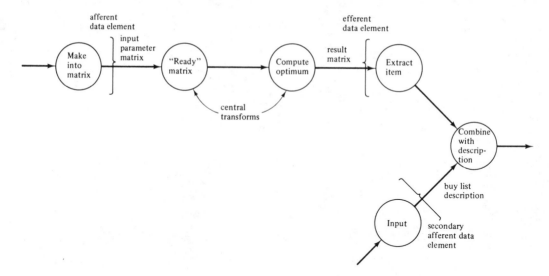

Fig. 10.15 Identification of afferent and efferent data elements.

tion file constitutes an afferent data element — but to a separate transform center for which the efferent data element is the report data line. Note also that much of the detail in the data flow graph was unnecessary for determining the afferent and efferent data elements. However, we have already pointed out that it is better to go into too much detail than not enough, and this extra detail will prove advantageous in later stages of our design.

10.8.2 The structural design

The initial structural factoring includes one module for each central transform, one for each afferent data element feeding the central transforms, and one for each efferent data element emerging from a central transform. For the FRANK system, this inital breakdown is shown in Fig. 10.16.

As we discussed earlier, each of the initially specified modules at the top level is factored into lower-level subordinates according to an appropriate strategy: Afferent modules require one strategy, efferent modules another strategy, and transform modules yet another. Let us begin the factoring of the afferent module GETMATRIX.

In order to factor GETMATRIX, we must look for the last discrete transform to be applied to the data stream in order to produce the afferent data element which GETMATRIX must deliver to FRANKSYS. In this case, the afferent data element is the input parameter matrix and the last transform involves the creation of the matrix

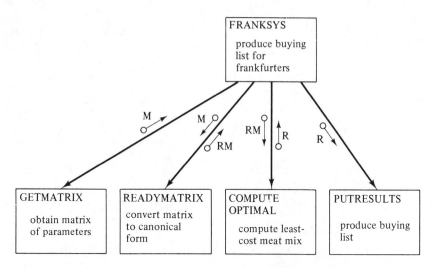

Fig .10.16. First-level factoring of FRANKSYS.

from the same data in non-matrix form — that is, from valid row data. The valid row data must, in turn, be supplied by some new afferent module. The newly identified immediate subordinates to GETMATRIX are modules GETNEXTVALIDROW and ROWTOMATRIX. The latter eventually may prove to be a trivial function to implement, but note that in a functional sense it belongs here — and at this early stage in the structural design, we include it as a distinct module.

Turning to the afferent module GETNEXTVALIDROW, we can see that the last transform required to produce a valid row is simply that of validating the row; the afferent data element required by this transform is the next raw unvalidated row. The structure of the afferent branch thus far is shown in Fig. 10.17.

Next, we examine the GETNEXTROW module. Its function is to merge two streams of data (the stable parameter rows and the transient parameter rows) into one stream of the proper order. The merge discipline is the last transform to be applied. However, note that this last transform has *two* afferent data elements: the latest stable row and the latest transient row. Consequently, there are three subordinates to GETNEXTROW at this stage in the design. We will continue the factoring of one of these three — the GETTRANSROW module.

We can see that the last transform of GETTRANSROW is the completion of the row from one or more valid transient cards. These come from an afferent module that delivers, in a standard internal form, the data of valid (with respect to format) transient row card images. One could complete the factoring as shown in Fig. 10.18a: Card images are obtained, checked for proper format, then converted from card image format (i.e., a character string) to the standard internal representation. The problem is that the format-checking process must duplicate much of the conversion process — e.g., finding the ends of fields, locating decimal points, test-

209

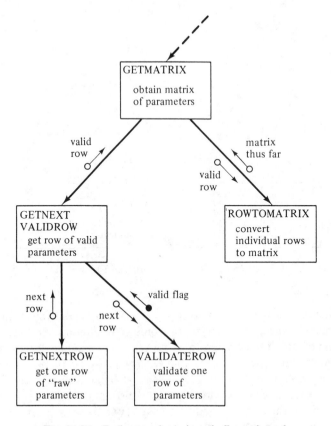

Fig. 10.17 Early stage in design of afferent branch.

ing for alphabetic/numeric character types, and so on. As we can see in Fig. 10.18b, the smallest system results from a single conversion/checking module, which performs all the necessary checking in the process of translating from external to internal format.

With the identification of module READCARD-S, we have reached the bottom of this particular sub-branch — that is, we have located the ultimate source of data in this stream. Along the way, we have identified modules whose substructure we have yet to determine; among these is the CONVERTVALID transform module. CONVERTVALID is defined as a module that detects format errors in transient row card images. The original description of the problem specified that format errors should cause an error message to be printed on the on-line terminal, together with a request for a correction in card-image form. Should the error message be transmitted from CONVERTVALID or from GETVALIDTRANSCARD? Which module should obtain the exception input, in card-image form, from the terminal? The answer suggested by the transform-centered strategy is that either the card image *or* the substitute input from the terminal is the afferent process feeding the last transform (validation) to

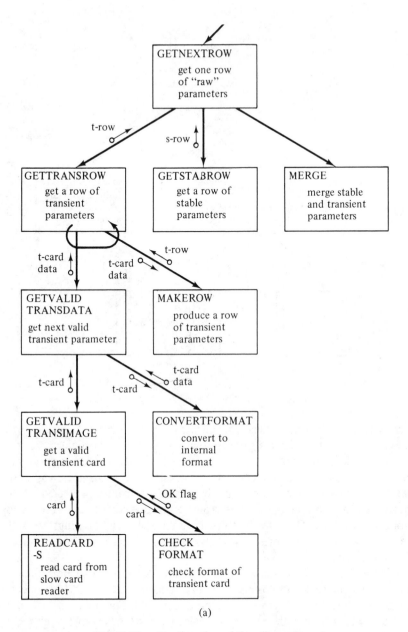

(a)

Fig. 10.18a Continuation of the afferent branch.

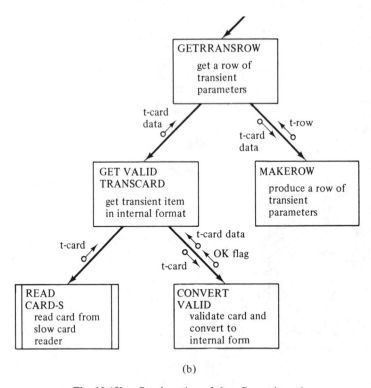

(b)

Fig. 10.18b   Continuation of the afferent branch.

produce a valid row image.   Thus, it seems most straightforward to make GETVALID-
TRANSCARD responsible for getting exception input from the terminal.

What about the error message?   We note that the discovery of an error
situation takes place in CONVERTVALID.   To have the error message output by
GETVALIDTRANSCARD, the message must be passed *up* from CONVERTVALID to GET-
VALIDTRANSCARD, and then back *down* from GETVALIDTRANSCARD to an appropriate
error-printing routine.   This seems to involve unnecessary coupling; we prefer the
simpler alternative of allowing CONVERTVALID to call its own subordinate error-
printing subroutine.

Note that the card image from the terminal must also be validated and
converted; this suggests the structure of Fig. 10.19a.   It would be unnecessarily
clumsy to require SUBSTITUTEVALID to pass a raw line of input *up* to GETVALID-
TRANSCARD, which would then pass it *down* to CONVERTVALID for checking and
conversion.   At some small execution overhead, SUBSTITUTEVALID can make the
call to CONVERTVALID itself, as shown in Fig. 10.19a; note that SUBSTITUTEVALID
contains a loop when valid input has finally been received.   By moving that loop upward into GETVALIDTRANSCARD, we could transform the structure into that shown in
Fig. 10.19b.   However, this is a decision that is better deferred until factoring of the
other afferent sub-branch has been completed.

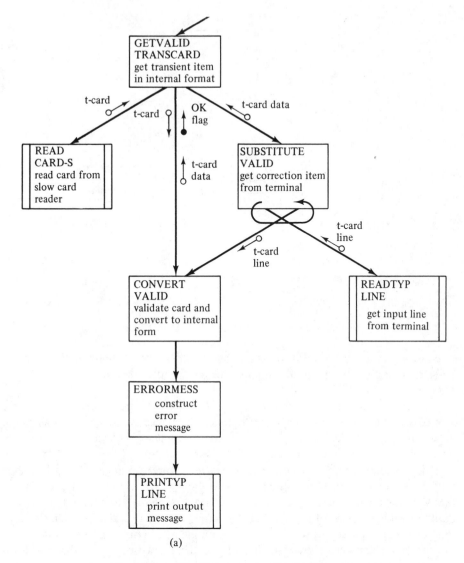

Fig. 10.19a   Handling errors in CONVERTVALID.

When we approach the factoring of GETSTABROW, we immediately wonder whether this isn't the same structure as the one just designed for the transient sub-branch. Before we proceed, it is important to recognize that GETSTABROW and GETTRANSROW perform different, distinct functions in the problem as defined — although this does not prevent us from designing a single module that accepts a parameter specifying which of its two functions is to be performed on a given call. Were we to follow this approach, we would have to recognize that the combined module would not be highly cohesive (in fact, it would have logical binding), and

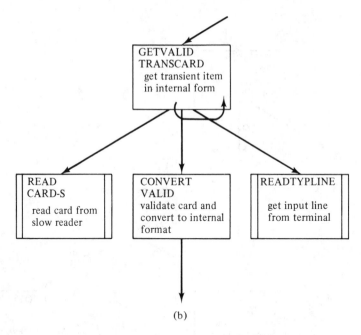

(b)

Fig. 10.19b Alternative design of GETVALIDTRANSCARD.

the control parameter would have to be passed and tested all the way down to the low-level module, which would finally decide whether to call READCARD-S or READCARD-F.

At the other extreme, we could specify totally duplicate structures. Since some of the functional requirements of both sub-branches are identical (such as the convert-and-validate function), it stands to reason that we will have a simpler system if we can specify some shared single-function modules. The structure of Fig. 10.20 is a suitable compromise and will permit future modifications to be made easily to either or both data streams. Note how the availability of the distinct MAKEVALIDCARD module results in a simpler total structure than would have been possible with the design of Fig. 10.19b; if we had followed that approach, the coding in GETVALIDTRANSCARD would have been duplicated in GETVALIDSTABCARD.

Moving higher in the structure of Fig. 10.20, we note that the transform module MAKEROW may prove to be trivial to implement in most high-level programming languages. Thus, we may legitimately compress it upward into GET-TRANSROW and GETSTABROW.

At this point, we should consider the "which-is-next" decision processing implicitly included in the module MERGE of Fig. 10.20. The outcome of this decision determines whether a new transient row, a new stable row, or both (in the case of a match) should be obtained. Thus, GETSTABROW and GETTRANSROW are both within the scope of effect of the decision, though not within the scope of control of MERGE. This conflict (which was discussed at length in Chapter 9) may be resolved by compressing the merge decision upward into GETNEXTROW. Indeed,

214

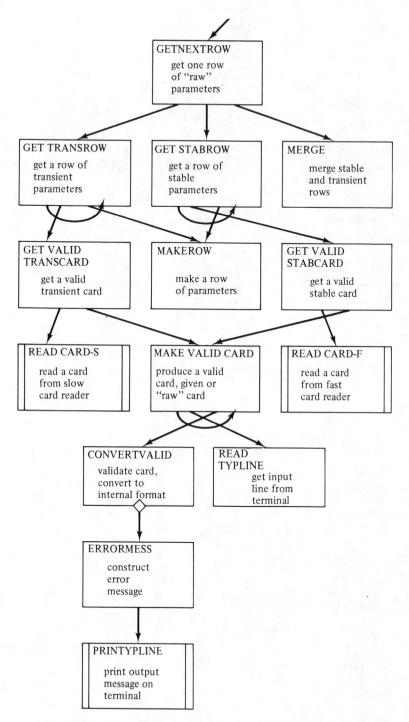

Fig. 10.20 Afferent branch with stable and transient sub-branches.

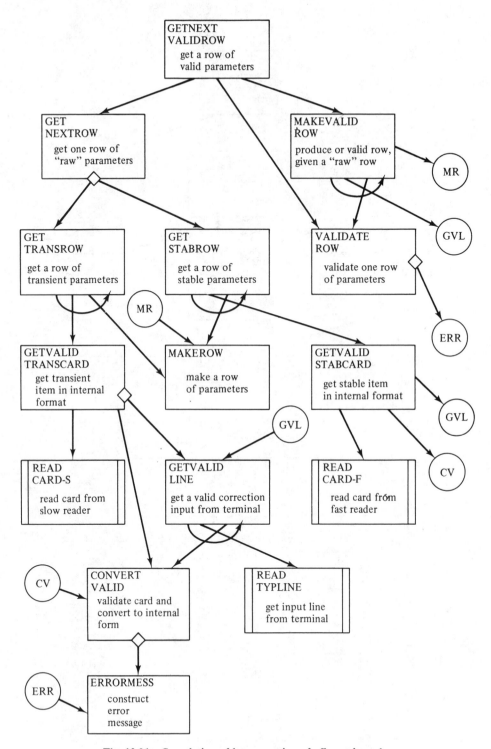

Fig. 10.21 Completion of lower portion of afferent branch.

this kind of structure is common, and the result of our design decision may be reduced to a rule of thumb. A module that represents the merge point of data streams (as shown in a data flow graph) should contain the merging discipline — that is, it should contain the decisions which determine the merging sequence. The merging discipline should not be placed in a subordinate module.

We know that the row validation function is non-trivial. We can be guided in its factoring by our experience with the MAKEVALIDCARD module. The difference here is that we must input one or more card images from the terminal and make them into a row. The function MAKEVALIDCARD of Fig. 10.20 expects to test one set of inputs from above before deciding that it should read some input from the terminal. With this in mind, we see that our requirement is for an afferent module that simply gets a validated line from the terminal, as in the SUBSTITUTEVALID module of Fig. 10.19a. We back up to this variant and complete the structure of Fig. 10.21. At this point, we notice that, although we have avoided most of the duplication of coding, the procedure for combining a series of row images into a row appears in three separate modules — the only difference in each case being the source. It is not hard to convince ourselves that a parameterized combination module would be almost as complicated as the sum of the three individual modules. Such a combination module would be only communicationally cohesive, too.

Having completed the afferent branch, we can begin to factor the central transforms. Obviously, the simplex computation of optional mix is an existing entity in itself. The testing of the matrix for potential conversion to canonical form together with the conversation procedure itself comprises the READYMATRIX function. In factoring central transforms, we also should consider combinations of

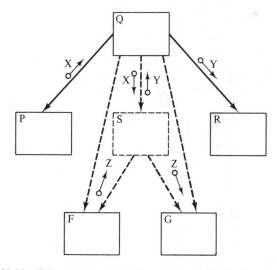

Fig. 10.22 Schematic representation of sequential binding decision.

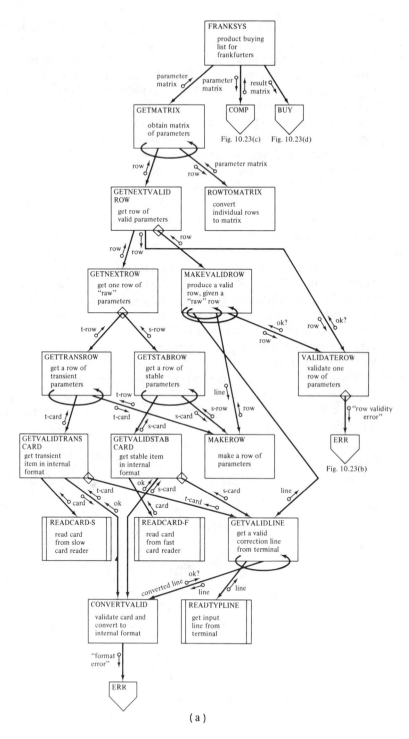

(a)

Fig. 10.23a Complete FRANKSYS structure, first part.

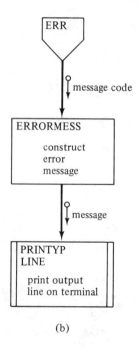

(b)

Fig. 10.23b Complete FRANKSYS structure, second part.

transforms, which might comprise highly cohesive functions — particula the level of detail in the data flow diagram might lead us to miss intermedi functions. For example, SIMPLETON and its mathematically (and computa related function MAKEREADY comprise a function to compute results from matrix. A module for such a function would be at least sequentially cohes functionally cohesive.

Deciding whether we should have a sequentially cohesive modu sentially the same in all cases. Schematically, this is represented in Fig. and G are sequentially related functions due to the data element z. First whether either (or both) of the functions in question is functionally relate contents of any other module. Usually, this would be modules in the designated P, Q, and R in Fig. 10.22. If such a structure exists, it almos would be preferable to a sequentially cohesive module.

Second, we consider the existence, or probable future existence, tional uses of the sequential combination of modules — F-G in this case uses are simplified if the sequentially cohesive module (in this case, m does exist. (Note that a compound F-and-G module is a structure distir modular than one with a superordinate s calling subordinates F and G.)

On the other hand, the superordinate s module adds one level of on each activation; the costs of this overhead are the third consideration must be balanced against the implementation and storage costs of some nu "paired" calls to F and G individually, compared to the same number of sir to s. Finally, a sequentially cohesive module may be elected for its value

219

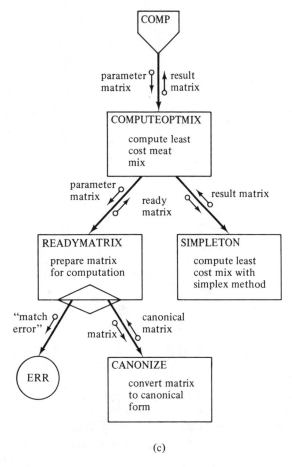

(c)

Fig. 10.23c Complete FRANKSYS structure, third part.

ceptually organizing the problem if there is no functionally cohesive alternative. This final criterion is used to justify the specification of this system's COMPUTE-OPTMIX module; see Fig. 10.23c.

In factoring the efferent branch, we look for the next-to-follow transform, and the efferent process it feeds. In this case, the data for a single buy-order must be extracted from the result matrix, and delivered to a module that will put it into a nicely formatted report. In turn, this module next must combine the buy item with its description from the description file. Recalling that the merge decision function will be in this module, we specify the structure shown in Fig. 10.23d. The next transform is to add heading data (if needed, i.e., if there is a page overflow), and finally to print the line. Printing the header also involves printing lines of data.

The finished transform-centered design for the FRANK system is shown in the four parts of Fig. 10.23. This structure should be studied carefully and compared with the original data flow shown in Fig. 10.14.

220

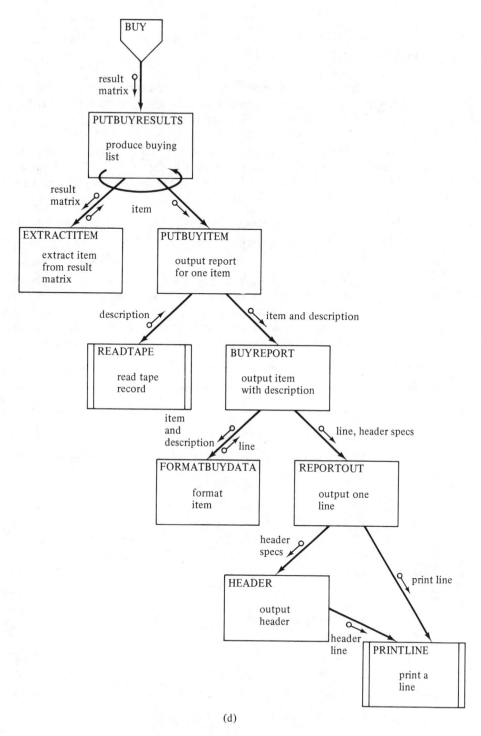

(d)

Fig. 10.23d Complete FRANKSYS structure, fourth part.

10.9 SUMMARY

In this chapter, we have presented one of several design *strategies* available to the designer. The next two chapters present other design strategies, but three things should be emphasized before we go on:

1. The transform-centered design strategy is based on an analysis of data flow, as is the approach presented in the next chapter. Some of the strategies discussed in Chapter 12 are based, instead, on data *structure*.

2. The transform-centered strategy still requires judgment and common sense on the part of the designer; it does *not* reduce design to a series of mechanical steps.

3. The transform-centered strategy is based on the assumption that the resulting system will consist of one hierarchical structure. As we will discuss in Chapter 18, that is not always necessary; it sometimes is possible to stop as soon as the data flow graph has been drawn, with each bubble being implemented as a distinct task in a multi-tasking operating system.

Transaction
Analysis

CHAPTER **11**

11.0 INTRODUCTION

In the last chapter, we explored transform analysis as a major strategy for designing well-structured programs and systems. Indeed, transform analysis will be *the* guiding influence on the designer for most systems. However, there are numerous situations in which additional strategies can be used to supplement — and occasionally even replace — the basic approach of transform analysis. One of these supplementary strategies, known as *transaction analysis,* will be discussed in this chapter. The strategy is derived from the SAPTAD structure[1] originated by Vincent and others at Bell Telephone of Canada. Transaction analysis is a more flexible, more sophisticated updating of the SAPTAD technique.

Transaction analysis is suggested by data flow graphs resembling Fig. 11.1 — that is, where a transform splits an input data stream into several discrete output substreams. In many systems, such a transform may occur within the *central* transforms (as defined in Chapter 10); in others, we may find the transform shown in Fig. 11.1 in either the afferent or efferent branch of the structure chart.

223

The phrase transaction analysis suggests that we will be building a system around the concept of a "transaction" — and, of course, the word transaction implies to many programmers that we are dealing with a business-oriented data processing system. Indeed, it is true that many commercial systems are at least partly transaction-oriented (if we use that term informally); as a result, transaction analysis should play an important part in a *portion* of the design of such systems. However, it also can be applied to portions of many real-time systems, such as process control, data acquisition, and interactive time-sharing systems; to engineering applications; to programmed control of numerically controlled machine tools; and to many others.

A great deal of the usefulness of transaction analysis depends on how we define transaction. In the most general sense,

> *A transaction is any element of data, control, signal, event, or change of state that causes, triggers, or initiates some action or sequence of actions.*

According to this definition, a large number of the situations found in normal data processing applications would be considered transactions. For example, any of the following would be considered a transaction:

- The operator pushing the start button on an input device

- Some input data to a commercial system designated as add-shipment-to-inventory

- An escape character from a terminal, indicating a need for special processing

- A hardware interrupt on an out-of-bounds subscript reference within an application program

- A customer replacing the phone on the hook, thereby terminating a telephone conversation being monitored by a computer system

We are not suggesting that *all* data processing systems are transaction-oriented; we might be able to stretch our imaginations to think of a number-crunching program as transaction-oriented, but it would be awkward and artificial. Similarly, we are not suggesting that all parts of a typical business data processing system are transaction-oriented. As we saw in Chapter 10, a significant part of the analysis of typical business data processing systems involves the tracing of afferent and efferent data items through the system. Nevertheless, it is clear that a great deal of the work in many systems *is* involved in the identification and processing of transactions; hence, the transaction analysis strategy should prove useful in a wide variety of applications.

11.1 TRANSACTION ANALYSIS STRATEGY

11.1.1 Transaction center

The transaction analysis strategy simply recognizes that data flow graphs of the form of Fig. 11.1 can be mapped into a particular modular structure. A transaction center of a system must be able to

- get (obtain or respond to) transactions in raw form

- analyze each transaction to determine its type

- dispatch on type of transaction

- complete the processing of each transaction

In its most fully factored form, the transaction center may be modularized as in Fig. 11.2. The head of this subsystem structure, TRANS, might be subordinate to any part of some much larger system. Each of the modules GETTRAN, ANALYZE-TRAN, DOTYPE1, DOTYPE2, and so on could itself be the head of an entire subsystem. Less-factored variations of this structure are readily derived from Fig. 11.2 by compressing one or more modules upward into its superordinate, leading, for example, to the pancaked structure of Fig. 11.3.

In orthodox form, the substructure below the dispatching module may be modeled as a four-level system. This structure is shown in Fig. 11.4. The four levels are called:

- transaction processor (or P-level)

- transaction level (or T-level)

- action level (or A-level)

- detail level (or D-level)

Problems can arise if an attempt is made to shoehorn an entire application into the model of Figs. 11.2 and 11.4. These will be taken up fully at the end of this chapter.

The span of control of the transaction processing module (whatever module contains the dispatch logic) should be noted. The span of control here is potentially quite high: one for each transaction type. However, *if* each transaction processing module is required to complete independently all processing of a particular transaction before returning, the dispatching logic remains simple and the module containing it still will appear small to the programmer looking at it. The transaction processor module, TRANS in Fig. 11.4, typically is relatively uncohesive, ranging from logical to communicational in cohesion depending on the application.

225

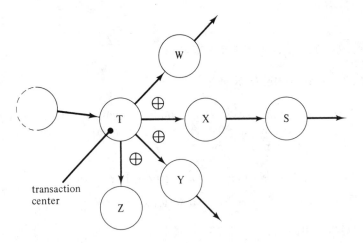

Fig. 11.1 Data flow graph of a typical transaction of an application.

Thus, the dispatching itself may profitably be partitioned into strongly related sub-classes in some systems.

In the orthodox form, the transaction processor (TRANS in Fig. 11.4) would expect to receive a transaction from its superordinate when it is activated. A system may include any number of transaction centers. A transaction center may be located in an afferent branch of the system, in a transform branch of the system, or

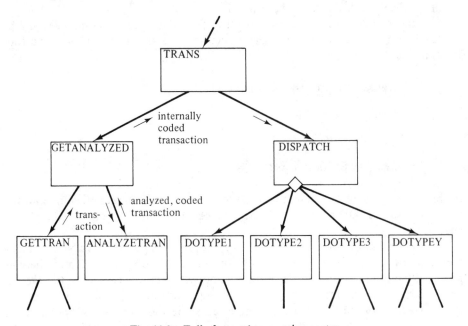

Fig. 11.2 Fully factored transaction center.

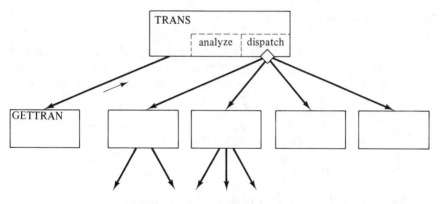

Fig. 11.3 Pancaked transaction center.

in an efferent branch of the system. The outputs of the transaction center might consist of

- A converted, formatted version of the input transaction — which can be passed upward to feed higher levels of the afferent process

- A simple flag indicating whether the input transaction was valid. We would expect to encounter such a validate form of TRANS frequently in the afferent branch of a system.

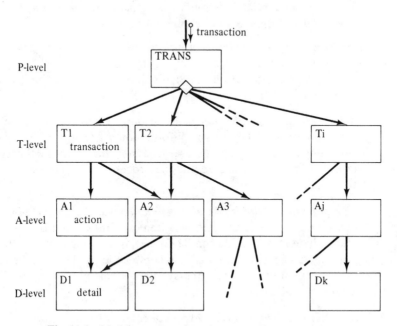

Fig. 11.4 Model structure chart for transaction-centered system.

- Computed results based on the processing of the input transaction. The results would be passed upward to the superordinate to be used in other central transforms — or to be passed downward to lower levels of an efferent process.

- An updated (modified) form of an element or elements of some data base, whether internal or external

11.1.2 The strategy

Using Figs. 11.2 through 11.4 as models, we can outline the steps of a transaction analysis strategy as follows:

1. *Identify the sources of transactions.*   In many cases, the transactions will be mentioned explicitly in the problem definition, in which case it usually can be assumed that the transactions will come from the physical input media.   In other cases, the designer may have to recognize afferent, transform, or efferent modules that generate transactions; this may be more obvious after the first few steps of factoring of a transform-centered design.   More than one transaction stream may feed the P-level module, and these may have to be merged from different directions (e.g., afferent and efferent).   Transaction streams may also have to be merged with non-transaction data streams.

2. *Specify the appropriate transaction-centered organization.*   Figure 11.2 usually will be a good model, but the designer should feel free to alter it as appropriate, based on the theory and the heuristics introduced in earlier chapters.

3. *Identify the transactions and their defining actions.*   Again, we often may find that all of the requisite information is provided in the problem definition; if the transactions are generated internally in the system, the designer must define carefully the processing to take place for each transaction.

4. *Note potential situations in which modules can be combined.*   As in the case of transform analysis, we often can find situations in which an intermediate-level module can be created from a functionally cohesive group of low-level modules.   This combination is likely to be appropriate in situations in which the syntax or semantics of various transactions is similar.

5. *For each transaction, or cohesive collection of transactions, specify a transaction module to completely process it.*   Because the transactions in a system are often similar, there is a temptation to group the processing of several transactions into one module.   This should be avoided if the resulting module has low cohesion; we want to avoid

modules with only communicational or lower cohesion and, especially, logically cohesive modules.

6. *For each action in a transaction, specify an action module subordinate to the appropriate transaction module(s).* In essence, this is the factoring step that we discussed in Chapter 10. Note that there may be many opportunities for transaction modules to share common action modules.

7. *For each detailed step in an action module, specify an appropriate detail module subordinate to any action module that needs it.* Clearly, this is a continuation of the factoring process. Note that for a large system with complex transactions, we may have several levels of detail modules. In addition, keep in mind that similar action modules should share common detail modules whenever possible.

Throughout this process, the designer should be guided by the principles of cohesion, coupling, and the design heuristics discussed in Chapter 9. In addition, the designer should remember the fundamental design principle mentioned repeatedly in earlier chapters: The form of the systems structure should reflect, as closely as possible, the form of the problem.

It is especially important for the designer to recognize that there is nothing magical about processing transactions in exactly four levels. (Remember, 7±2 is the only magical number!) Some transactions may be fully factored with only a transaction-level module; others might take nine or ten levels. Nor is there anything particularly sacred about the processing assigned to each level. If one transaction can be implemented as the composition of other transactions, by all means do so structurally, even though this makes some modules serve on both transaction and action levels. For example, an OPENACCOUNT transaction module might also be used as an A-level subordinate to the OPENBLOCK module, which opens a unique block of sequential account numbers.

11.2 AN EXAMPLE OF TRANSACTION ANALYSIS

11.2.1 Statement of the problem

Consider a portion of a system that is designed to update selected fields in specified records of a Customer Master File. We will assume that the Customer Master File is a serial file occupying several reels of magnetic tape, and that the file is sorted in ascending order on a five-digit numeric customer account number.*

---

* That we are using a sequential tape file is a packaging assumption that the designer should not be making at this early stage of the design effort; more of the consequences of packaging will be discussed in Chapter 14. In the meantime, we will continue to assume a sequential tape file for the sake of simplicity; most of our attention will be focused on a transaction center in the system.

Updates to the Customer Master File will be supplied to the system from cards (or card images) in a free-field format described below. Each card will specify the account number of the customer whose record is to be updated; this will be followed by a specification of one or more fields to be updated. For historical reasons, the user's data preparation group has always supplied update cards that already are sorted by customer account number.

Our system, which we will call MFUP, will read the update cards, make certain checks for reasonableness, and then proceed to update the Customer Master File. The system is required to print a brief report of any errors found during its processing, as well as a copy of any and all records that have been successfully updated.

We may assume that every customer has one record on the Customer Master File. Each record is a fixed length of 142 characters. The layout is shown in Table 11.1.

Table 11.1   Structure of the Customer Master File

FIELD	TYPE OF INFORMATION	LENGTH	ALPHA OR NUMERIC	MAY BE UPDATED
1	Account number	5	numeric	no
2	Customer name	30	alphanumeric	yes
3	Customer street address	30	alphanumeric	yes
4	City	20	alphanumeric	yes
5	State (abbreviated, standard U.S. Post Office code)	2	alphabetic	yes
6	ZIP code	5	numeric	yes
7	Phone number (with area code)	10	numeric	yes
8	Customer status: active/inactive	1	alphabetic	no
9	Salesperson handling this account	5	numeric	yes
10	Date of last transaction	6	numeric	no
11	Date of last payment	6	numeric	no
12	Current balance	8	numeric	no
13	Total volume of business, YTD	8	numeric	no
14	Credit limit, in dollars	6	numeric	no

Updates to the Master File will be supplied from cards whose format is as follows: Card columns 1-5 will specify the account number of the record to be updated; columns 6-9 are always blank and should be ignored; beginning in column 10, there will be a variable number of fields of the form

$$xxabcd...pqr*xxabc...stu*xxabc...uvw**$$

where xx represents a two-digit integer that specifies which of the 14 fields in the Master Record is to be updated, and abcd...pqr represents the corresponding field in the Master Record.

Note that each field is terminated with an asterisk (*), and that the last field on each card is terminated with a double asterisk (**); thus, it is conceivable that we should see an update card containing the information

$$12345 \quad 07abcd*02pqrs*03ijk**$$

Note that the character string, which has been represented above as abcd . . ., may consist of alphabetic characters, numeric characters, or a mixture of both. The definition of the Master File in Table 11.1 tells us whether the appropriate form of data has been received. Note also that it is possible to have multiple cards updating the same Master File record. That is, the following sequence is legal:

$$12345 \quad 02abcd**$$
$$12345 \quad 04pqrstuvw**$$
$$12345 \quad 03ijk**$$

Thus, there is a great deal of flexibility in the input format. However, the user has specified one important restriction: A field may not extend past the end of the card. That is, a field may not be split between one card and the next. Obviously, this means that *each* card should have a double asterisk on or before columns 79-80 (recalling the experiences of the unfortunate Charlie in Chapter 6, we must admit that we are somewhat wedded to the traditional eighty-column card!).

As MFUP performs its updates, it should check for a number of possible errors; if any are detected, they should be printed in a report whose format has not been specified by the user. If, for example, the account number of a card is out of sequence, or cannot be matched against any Master File record, then the entire record should be rejected and an appropriate error message should be printed.*

Similarly, if any of the updates contain an illegal field number, an appropriate error message should be printed. Since there are 14 fields defined in the Master Record, the update cards must specify field numbers between 1 and 14. If the field number is out of range, it should be rejected; however, subsequent fields on the same card should be processed normally. That is, the presence of a bad field on a card does not invalidate the rest of the fields on that card.

Naturally, the system should check to ensure that each field is of the correct type. That is, certain fields are specified to be of an alphabetic type, while others are numeric, and so on. If a field is not of the proper type, it should be rejected — but subsequent fields on the same card should be accepted, if they are correct.

Table 11.1 also indicates that MFUP is not allowed to update certain fields in a record. We may assume that those fields are established (and possibly up-

---

* Among other things, this means that the MFUP system will not be capable of adding new records to the file. This restriction, although not a terribly realistic one, is made for the sake of simplicity; for the same reason, we will assume that MFUP does not allow records to be deleted from the file.

dated) by other systems — but, in any case, an attempt to use MFUP to update fields 1, 8, 10, 11, 12, 13, or 14 should be considered illegal.

Since the update cards supply variable-length input in a free-field format, it is possible that an update field will be shorter than the corresponding field on the Master File; in some cases, the update field may be exactly the same length as the corresponding Master File field; and, of course, it is possible that the update field will contain a field that is longer than the corresponding Master File field. The user has specified that if a field is too long for the Master File, it should be rejected if the field is of a numeric type, and truncated if the field is of an alpha or alphanumeric type. In any case, an appropriate message should be generated. If the update field is shorter than the corresponding Master File field, then the update field should be right-justified and zero-filled if it is numeric, and left-justified and blank-filled if it is alphabetic or alphanumeric. There is one exception: The ZIP code field (field 6) must be supplied as a five-character numeric field — anything longer or shorter will be considered an error.

11.2.2 Structural design for MFUP

From our discussion of transform analysis in Chapter 10, recall that the first step in the design is to draw a data flow graph. For MFUP, a first approximation of the data flow graph is shown in Fig. 11.5. This data flow graph is quite detailed, as it is preferable to show too much detail rather than to show too little at this stage (cf. Fig. 10.3b).

However, the transform labeled "edit field" is a bit superficial. Since there are 14 distinct types of fields, it is more precise to represent the data flow in the form shown in Fig. 11.6. Now, it is apparent that the data flow graph is similar to the prototype for a transaction-oriented system shown in Fig. 11.1. We still have the job of identifying the afferent data element, the efferent data element, and the central transforms — but the important point is that we have recognized in the data flow graph the presence of some transaction-oriented processing.

The normal process of transform analysis might lead to the structure chart shown in Fig. 11.7. You may want to verify that we have factored the afferent branch of the structure in the manner presented in Chapter 10, but we will not dwell on this aspect of the design. Similarly, we will not concern ourselves with the details of GETVALIDMFRECORD, or UPDATEMF, or WRITEMF, or PRINTUPDATEREC. What concerns us is the design of the module labeled EDITFIELD. From our previous discussion, we can see that it is a module similar to the DISPATCH module in Fig. 11.2. As input, it receives a transaction (which may have one of 14 valid field codes); and as output, it produces a flag indicating whether the field should be accepted.

A tentative design for the EDITFIELD module is shown in Fig. 11.8. Since there are 14 different fields on the Master Record, we specify 14 transaction modules immediately subordinate to EDITFIELD.

At this point, it might occur to the designer that several of the transactions are similar — or even identical — and therefore could be combined. We note, for

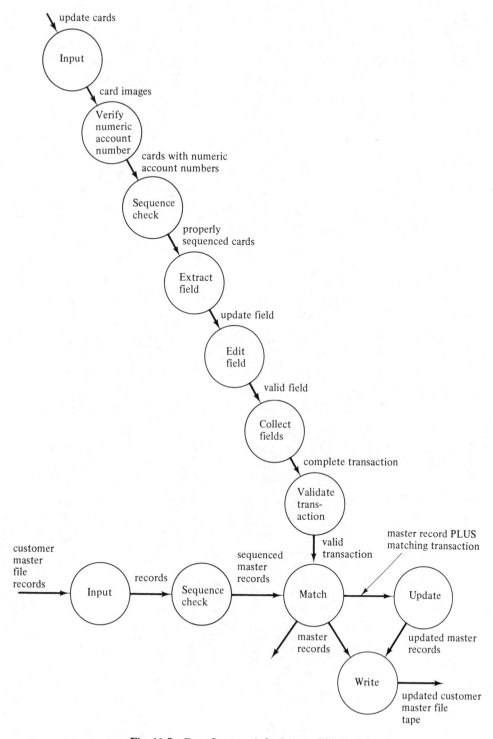

Fig. 11.5 Data flow graph for Master File Update.

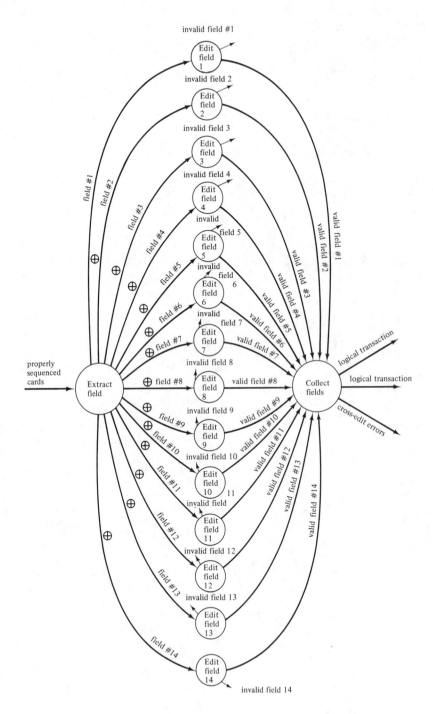

Fig. 11.6 Expanded data flow graph for Master File Update.

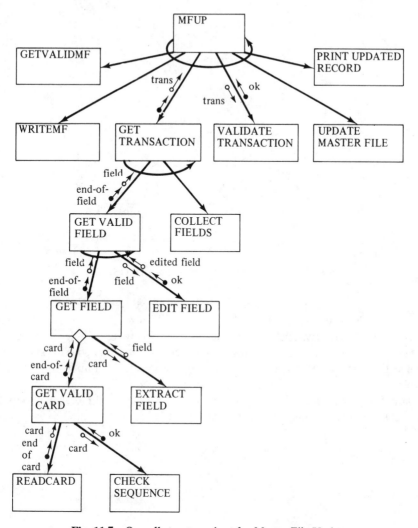

Fig. 11.7 Overall structure chart for Master File Update.

example, that the "customer name" field and the "customer street address" field are both defined as thirty-character alphanumeric fields. Why not have a single module that will edit either or both fields? Similarly, we note that fields 10, 11, and 14 are defined as six-character numeric fields that are not allowed to be updated by MFUP. Why not process them with a single combined transaction module? The same argument could be made for fields 12 and 13, which are defined as eight-character numeric fields. Indeed, the designer might even go one step further and process fields 1, 6, and 9 with a combined module, since they are defined as five-character numeric fields. If we were to follow these instincts, we might end up with the refined structure shown in Fig. 11.9.

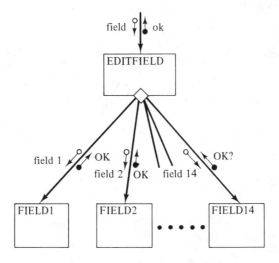

Fig. 11.8 Initial structural design of EDITFIELD.

Of course, there is a small detail that we have overlooked. We have decided, in Fig. 11.9, to process fields 1, 6, and 9 with a module now labeled TYPE1, because they are all five-character numeric fields; however, Table 11.1 indicates that MFUP *is* allowed to update fields 6 and 9 but is *not* allowed to update field 1 (a perfectly reasonable restriction: Field 1 is the account number and is the key by which the serial Customer Master File is sequenced). Thus, in addition to the normal processing required to edit a five-character numeric field, we have to make a special check to prevent an attempt to update field 1. In fact, things are even worse:

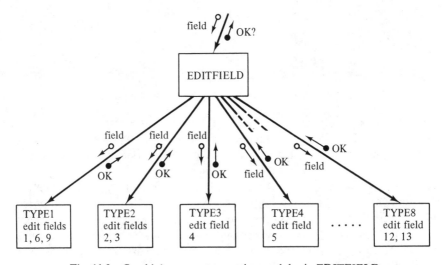

Fig. 11.9 Combining some transaction modules in EDITFIELD.

We recall from the problem definition that short numeric fields are generally right-justified and zero-filled — but field 6 is a special case. Field 6, the ZIP code field, must always be *exactly* five characters of numeric data; if the update field is either shorter or longer than five characters, it always must be rejected.

We could reject the TYPE1 module outright on the basis of cohesion; it is only logically cohesive. But some designers still would argue that this could be handled in a single TYPE1 module. When asked about the special requirements of fields 1, 6, and 9, they probably would reply, "Oh, that's no problem — a couple of flags will keep all the logic straight." Our counter-argument is obvious: Why go to the trouble of making a complicated combination module when three perfectly trivial modules will do the job? Indeed, we would use the same argument for TYPE2, TYPE3, and all the other TYPEn modules: Why go to the labor of combining the modules when doing so may lead to insidious problems of the sort found in TYPE1?

Of course, there are no apparent problems combining the "customer name" field and the "customer street address" field into a single TYPE2 module; they both are thirty characters in length and alphanumeric, and they both may be updated by MFUP. However, what happens if six months from now the user decides that the "customer name" field should be strictly alphabetic, instead of alphanumeric? All of these problems can be precluded by processing each transaction with a separate module; hence, we return to the initial structure chart shown in Fig. 11.8.

One might be tempted to form the structure of Fig. 11.9 because of common processing in the various transactions. We still can reap the benefits of common processing by using common subordinate action-level modules that could be called, as needed, by the 14 transaction-level modules. The common subordinate modules can be described in terms of the *actions* required to process each transaction: From time to time, we need to reject a long field, reject a short field, adjust the length of a field, reject non-alphabetic fields, reject non-numeric fields, and so forth. This suggests the structure shown on the following page in Fig. 11.10.

In turn, the action modules have details in common. For example, the modules REJECTLONG, REJECTSHORT, and ADJUSTLENGTH all need to determine the length of a specified update field. Similarly, we can imagine that REJECTNON-ALPHA, REJECTNONNUMERIC, and REJECTNONALHANUMERIC accomplish their tasks by checking the update field on a character-by-character basis to see if there are any offending characters present. Thus, it would seem that all three modules could use a subordinate CHARTYPE module to determine the type (alphabetic, numeric, or special character) of a single character. In addition, it occurs to us that one of the details involved in rejecting a field is the printing of an error message; hence, another detail module, ERRORMESS. This leads us to the structure presented in Fig. 11.11.

Note that there is no action or detail module designed to reject attempts to update fields that, according to Table 11.1, are not supposed to be updated by MFUP. That logic is a function only of transaction code and would be contained within the transaction module; it would be the *only* coding found in those modules. For example, we know that attempts to update field 1 should be rejected; hence,

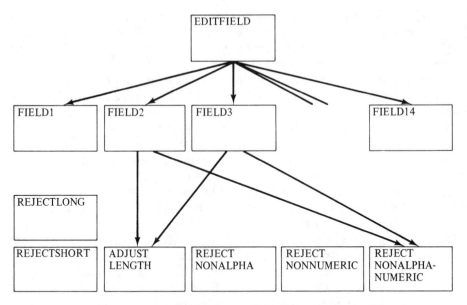

Fig. 11.10   Action modules for EDITFIELD transaction modules.

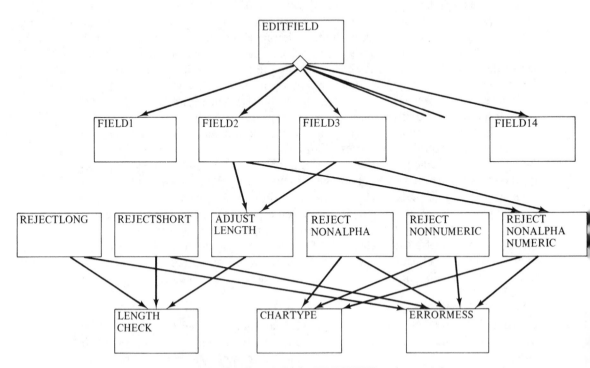

Fig. 11.11   Detail modules for EDITFIELD action modules.

238

the logic in module FIELD1 could consist simply of printing an error message (via ERRORMESS) and passing an error flag back up to EDITFIELD.

Thus, it seems that FIELD1 — as well as FIELD8, FIELD10, FIELD11, FIELD12, FIELD13, and FIELD14 — are dummy modules, and the designer may be sorely tempted to eliminate them. This could be accomplished by moving the check for non-updatable fields into EDITFIELD, resulting in the structure shown in Fig. 11.12.

11.3 SPECIAL CONSIDERATIONS IN TRANS-ACTION PROCESSING

The ideas behind transaction and transaction-centered systems are so familiar to most EDP professionals that many are tempted to use these organizing principles to structure entire systems and applications. Extensive experience with various transaction-centered design techniques has established that such systems may be easy to organize in the first place, but distinctly harder to implement and modify thereafter.

In the limiting case, the top-level executive module of a system can be made into *the* transaction center; that is, the system as a whole would be organized along the lines of Fig. 11.4, with each transaction subsystem having appropriate action and detail subordinate modules. Thus, all transactions would be consolidated at the executive module in an input-driven oganization. This might well mix transactions of various types and various levels of importance to the system, as viewed by the executive. The executive routine itself would be quite uncohesive, as it combines some elements of processing that are related only in that they deal with a particular *class* of data elements, namely transaction, and are thus only logically related.

An executive, which is also a transaction center, does not control the overall flow of processing, but rather is involved in procedural details needed to accomplish some parts of the overall task. If it "sees" transactions directly in input form, rather than as derivatives of an afferent subsystem, it becomes an even better example of a president handling shipping orders.

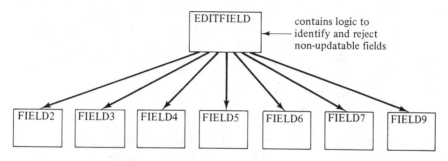

Fig. 11.12   Alternative structure for EDITFIELD.

11.3.1 State dependency in transaction processors

A special case arises whenever the transaction processing incorporates so-called state-dependent or sequential decision processes. In a state-dependent decision process, the outcome of each application of the decision procedure depends not only on the incoming data presented at this application of the procedure, but also on what has gone before. The decision outcome depends on the *state* of the decision procedure, including the state of processing invoked by previous applications of the decision procedure. For example, one transaction, type X, might be processed as a type X or type Y, depending on whether a type A was successfully completed. Or, an end-of-file transaction may require completion of certain other transactions *if they occurred* during the processing.

It is easy to see that state-dependent decision procedures run counter to the basic requirement that each transaction-level subsystem independently complete the processing of a given transaction so that the transaction processor (dispatch) remains simple. Within the purely transaction-oriented organization, none of the possible alternatives is particularly attractive. The state dependency can be removed from higher levels only at the expense of complicating lower ones. If the transaction processor for the example mentioned above always invokes transaction-level module DOTYPEX for a type X, then the transaction, action, or detail modules of that subsystem will require interactions and control-coupling with both the DOTYPEY and DOTYPEA subsystems. Alternatively, details of the processing (of type A transactions) may be communicated back up to the transaction processor (added control-coupling), and the dispatch made state-dependent (more complicated). This could even require an extra flagged call to DOTYPEA to find out if the type A has been finished.

The difficulty with state-dependent decision procedures is a fundamental defect in the transaction-centered structure. If all transactions are consolidated around a single high-level transaction center, the interactive effects can become very substantial and may span many levels of detail, involving the executive decision-making in minute details of minor transactions. By factoring and distributing transaction processing appropriately, the interactive effects are localized at appropriate levels and removed from the ken of the executive (or subexecutives). In a system of substantial size, the results of careful factoring could be to create a series of several transaction centers distributed throughout the system as in Fig. 11.13, where transaction centers can be found on afferent, efferent, and transform branches.

11.3.2 Syntactic and semantic processing of transactions

The structure first shown in Fig. 11.2 has the property of separating syntactic from semantic processing. By syntactic elements we mean, of course, those aspects of processing related to the *form* that transactions take. By semantics, we mean the resulting *actions:* the "what" and "how," so to speak. This is a most fortunate partitioning. By validating format and converting to an internal code in the afferent branch, the remainder of the system — DISPATCH, TRANS, and the superordinates of TRANS — can be written to operate independently of the form that transactions take. Thus, it is easier to change the appearance and the processing of transactions independently of each other. In addition, the transaction-processing modules can be used to operate correctly on transactions obtained in other formats from completely different sources.

A careful and comprehensive transform analysis of a typical transaction-processing application can yield an even more factored generalized structure. We would again begin by noting that the broad *class* of operations denoted by edit and validate transaction covers various distinguishable types of validation. Note the following four points:

- Some validation applies to transactions directly as inputted.

- Some validation applies to the internal, converted form of transaction contents.

- Some validation is completely defined on a transaction alone; other validation requires data from additional sources.

- Some validation applies to all transactions from a given source; other validation depends on the type of transaction.

The structure of Fig. 11.13 can be considered typical of the most fully factored form for a transaction subsystem. Such a structure maximizes the care with which many types of changes can be introduced. It also suggests convenient places to break the process into pre-edit and run phases while answering many of the technical objections which have been raised against separate edit-and-validation subsystems. More pancaked versions can be readily derived from the structure shown in Fig. 11.13. This subject will be reconsidered in Section 19.2.5.

11.3.3 Effect of placing transaction centers at different levels in the hierarchy

In some cases, the designer finds that he is designing a system with only one transaction center — but with a certain amount of choice concerning the placement of the transaction center within the hierarchy. As we pointed out at the beginning of Section 11.3, it is possible — and sometimes tempting — to make the top-level executive *the* transaction center. Such an extremely high placement of the transaction center is usually a poor idea, for reasons of coupling and cohesion; but if the transaction center is not placed at the top level, where *should* it be placed?

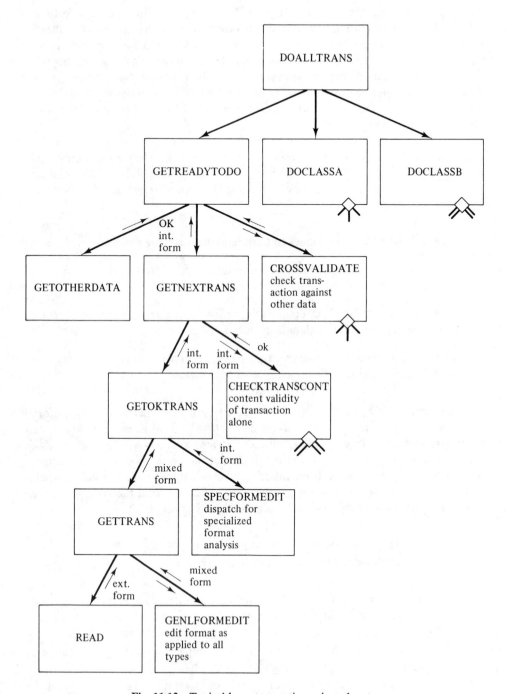

Fig. 11.13 Typical large transaction-oriented system.

Ultimately, coupling and cohesion are the best criteria for deciding what goes where. However, there is a philosophical aspect of this decision that the designer should keep in mind: Placing a transaction center high in the hierarchy reflects the designer's decision to allow the environment (that which exists outside the computer system) to control the computer system. Conversely, placing the transaction center near the bottom of the hierarchy reflects the designer's desire to have the computer system control the environment.

Why is this so? Remember what a transaction center is: a point at which one of several distinct types of processing will take place, depending on the precise nature of an element of data. Thus, if the transaction center (the P-level module) is at the top of the hierarchy, it is analogous to the president of a company saying, "I don't know what kinds of situations will face the corporation in the next few milliseconds, but I will respond appropriately."

If the transaction center is located near the bottom of the hierarchy, then it is likely that the top of the hierarchy will have been organized according to the guidelines of transform analysis presented in Chapter 10. In this case, the top-level module is more analogous to a manager who knows precisely what data he wants from his subordinates, and precisely what he wants to do with the data — that is, it is more analogous to an environment in which the manager controls the environment, rather than allows the environment to control him.

Some designers feel that this question of control over the environment is merely a reflection of the choice of a batch computer system or an on-line (possibly real-time) system. *Not so!* An on-line system may have its transaction center near the top or near the bottom of the hierarchy. If it is placed near the top of the hierarchy, it reflects the designer's desire to be as interactive and responsive as possible; that is, such an on-line system effectively is saying, "I have no idea what the terminal user will type on his terminal next, but I will carry out his commands." An on-line system with its transaction center near the bottom of the hierarchy reflects the designer's desire to have the system lead the terminal user through an orderly dialogue to accomplish what the *system* wants to accomplish. Thus, the top-level modules of such a system will coax, cajole, and harass the user to provide the input that the system wants; low-level transaction centers, unaware of what characters or messages the user will actually key-in next, will carry out the appropriate transaction-centered processing, and pass the results to some higher authority. In a similiar fashion, a batch computer system may have its transaction centers either high or low in the hierarchy, depending on the designer's philosophy of how best to organize the system.

We attach no value judgments to the designer's philosophies — as we have said repeatedly, coupling and cohesion are the final arbiters of good and bad. We do feel, though, that it is useful for the designer to be aware of these philosophical issues, so that his design truly will reflect the degree of control that he wishes his system to exert over the environment. Without such an awareness, it is quite easy to design a system whose basic architecture is quite different from what the designer intended.

A good example of this is an on-line system designed with any commercially available teleprocessing "monitor" package — e.g., IBM's CICS package, PMI/ Informatics' INTERCOMM package, or others of the sort. The sales literature of several of these packages strongly implies that the teleprocessing monitor serves as a P-level module, with the application designer merely supplying T-level modules to carry out detailed processing. If this were the case, then the environment (with the assistance of the teleprocessing monitor) would be delivering transactions to the application subsystem whenever the environment wished to do so — certainly, a clear case of the environment controlling the computer system. To put it another way, application designers usually make the assumption that the transaction center of their on-line system *must* be at the top of the hierarchy, simply because the tele-processing monitor forces them into such a design.

However, it turns out that most teleprocessing monitors *do* give the application designer the option of explicitly *asking* for terminal input; this usually is accomplished with a subroutine call that behaves very much as if one were calling to obtain input from a card reader or a tape file (or any other batch device). With this approach, the designer can arrange his system to obtain input precisely when and where it wants — that is, he arranges his computer system so that it controls the environment. The result of this usually is that the transaction center (if there is one) either is lower in the hierarchy, or is distributed — as we suggested in the previous section — throughout the hierarchy.

11.4 SUMMARY

We have seen in this chapter that the transaction-centered design strategy is based on an analysis of data *flow,* just as was the transform-centered strategy of Chapter 10. We also have seen that the transaction-centered design strategy requires that we define a transaction in the broadest fashion.

It should be emphasized that the transaction-centered strategy presented in this chapter requires some judgment and common sense on the part of the designer. Several similar strategies have failed in the past because they were too rigid and orthodox in their approach.

REFERENCE

1. P. VINCENT, "The System Structure Design Method," *Proceedings of the 1968 National Symposium on Modular Programming,* ed. Tom. O. Barnett (Cambridge, Mass.: Information & Systems Press, 1968, out of print).

Alternative
Design Strategies

CHAPTER 12

12.0 INTRODUCTION

As we have seen in Chapters 10 and 11, systems design can be derived in a fairly methodical fashion by analysis of the data flow graph associated with the problem. Depending upon the nature of the application, transform-centered design or transform-centered plus transaction-centered design usually will yield a design with highly cohesive, loosely coupled modules.

However, these two strategies are not the *only* way of deriving good designs in a systematic manner. A number of other researchers have developed techniques different from the ones that we have presented in this book; in this chapter, we will discuss the strategies developed by Michael Jackson, Jean-Dominique Warnier, and David Parnas.

Over the next several years, we can expect to see several more design strategies — some identified by the name of their inventor, some by the applications for which they are best suited, and some by the general nature of the strategy. We should look forward to any such design strategy with enthusiasm — we need as many as we can get. At the same time, we should remember that coupling and cohesion (as well as the heuristics of span of control, scope of effect/scope of control, and so forth) are the ultimate judge of whether a design strategy produces good designs or bad designs.

It also should be kept in mind that these design strategies — those that we discussed in Chapters 10 and 11, the ones that we will discuss in this chapter, and those that we can look forward to in the next several years — will still require the judgment, experience, and common sense of the designer. The situation is roughly comparable to a cook attempting to use a cookbook in a *haute cuisine* restaurant: There is no way to avoid those standard cookbook phrases of "season to taste," or "stir gently until ingredients are thoroughly mixed."

12.1 THE DATA-STRUCTURE DESIGN METHOD

One of the popular design strategies is based on analysis of *data structure,* rather than *data flow;* it has been discussed by Michael Jackson[1] and by Jean-Dominique Warnier.[2] The strategy is summarized as follows:

1. Define structures for the data that is to be processed.

2. Form a program structure based on the data structures.

3. Define the task to be performed in terms of the elementary operations available, and allocate each of those operations to suitable components of the program structure.

Implicit in the data-structure approach is the fact that most EDP applications deal with hierarchies of data — e.g., fields within records within files. Thus, this approach develops a hierarchy of modules that, in some sense, is a mirror image of the hierarchy of data associated with the problem. For example, Fig. 12.1a shows the structure of a simple sequential file; Fig. 12.1b shows the structure of a program that prints the file.

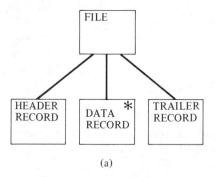

(a)

Fig. 12.1a   Structure of a sequential file.

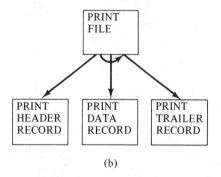

(b)

Fig. 12.1b Structure of a program that prints a file.

It is common for an EDP application to involve more than one set of data; unfortunately, the sets of data sometimes have quite different structures. Jackson emphasizes that if such an application is to be implemented with a single program (i.e., a single hierarchy of modules), then there must be a one-to-one mapping, *at all levels in the hierarchy,* between data elements of *each* of the data sets and modules that are responsible for processing those data elements. For example, Fig. 12.2a shows the data structures for an application that merges financial and non-financial data for employees. Figure 12.2b shows the structure of the output file of composite data for each employee. Figure 12.2c shows the hierarchy of modules that will carry out the desired operation; note the one-to-one correspondence between modules in the structure chart and elements of the data structure.

If a one-to-one mapping cannot be made between corresponding elements

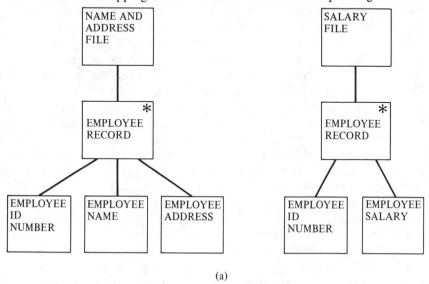

(a)

Fig. 12.2a Data structures merging employee data.

247

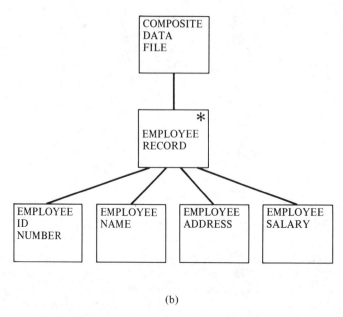

(b)

Fig. 12.2b Structure of output file of employee's composite data.

of the data structure, then a *structure clash* exists. This phenomenon is an important part of the data-structure approach. In practical terms, it means that the application cannot be implemented in a natural way with a single hierarchy of modules. Instead, Jackson proposes an approach (which he refers to as *program inversion*) that involves multiple programs (or, more precisely, multiple hierarchies of modules). As an example, suppose we were required to design a report-writing program which accepted a single input file and produced a single output report — and suppose that the structure of the input file was entirely incompatible with the structure of the output report. The solution, according to Jackson, would involve two programs — one that breaks the input file into more elementary chunks of data (e.g., into individual fields of data), and one that recombines those chunks into a form compatible with the required structure of the output report.

One common example of a structure clash might be termed an "order clash." Suppose, for example that the name-and-address file shown in Fig. 12.2a above was ordered alphabetically by employee name, while the salary file was ordered by employee ID number. We can safely assume that there are the same number of records in each file, but they do *not* appear in the same order; thus, we do not have a one-to-one correspondence at each level in the data hierarchies. An obvious solution is to sort one of the files so that its records are ordered on the same key as the other file — but that is just the point: We need two programs, not just one, to implement this application in a natural way.

The other common type of structure clash is known as a "boundary clash," and usually is caused by the blocking characteristics of physical input-output devices. For example, suppose we wanted to design a program to update the name-and-address file shown in Fig. 12.1a from an on-line terminal; suppose, further, that

248

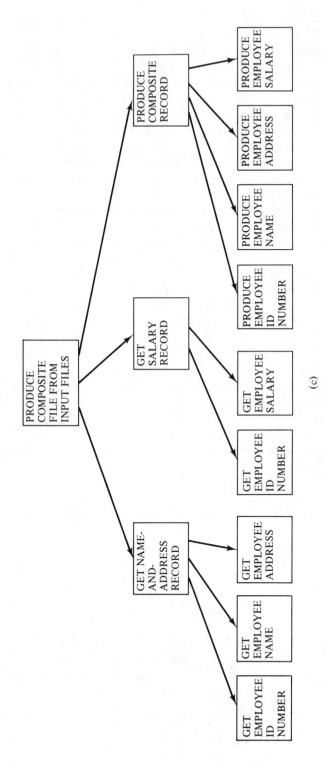

Fig. 12.2c Hierarchy of modules.

(c)

the terminal transmits data to our program in hundred-character blocks, *within which* are contained logical transactions specifying updates to the file. Our program then would deal with the data structures shown in Fig. 12.3. Note that there is *not* a one-to-one correspondence between terminal data blocks and employee records: It is not necessarily true that a block contains an integral number of update transactions, nor does an update transaction necessarily require an integral number of blocks. The solution here would be to have one program (or hierarchy of modules) decompose a terminal data block into its component characters, and then another program could rebuild characters into logical update transactions with the same structure as that of the name-and-address file.

For small design problems, the data-structure method produces systems remarkably similar to those produced by the transform-centered approach discussed in Chapter 10 (see, for example, the comparison made by Plum[3]). However, it is important to note that the data-structure approach requires about the same degree of black magic as the data flow approach. That is, *if* one chooses the proper data structure for a problem, then one presumably will get a good design — just as one can derive a good design *if* one can draw the proper data flow diagram for a problem. Experienced designers probably can use either method with ease; for beginners, though, *neither* approach is likely to be obvious.

It is worth emphasizing that the data-structure approach seems to work best on relatively small systems. On larger systems, the designer must work with several sets of data — e.g., two or three input files, two or three reports, and two or three transaction files. In such a situation, there is an excellent chance that one or more structure clashes will occur. Dealing with multiple structure clashes has, in the authors' experience, made the data-structure approach extremely difficult to use.

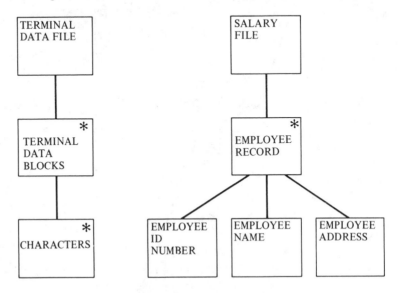

Fig. 12.3 Data structures.

Indeed, this may point out a more fundamental problem: If the designer is forced to deal with the *entire* problem and with *all* of the structure clashes at once, it usually will be difficult for him to see how to decompose the problem into smaller, separately solvable problems. Furthermore, the data-structure method advises the designer to *define the task to be performed in terms of the elementary operations available, and allocate each of those operations to suitable components of the program structure* (italics ours).* By "elementary operations," we mean the COBOL or FORTRAN statements with which the modules eventually will be coded; thus, it seems that the notion of levels of abstraction — being able to express the implementation of a large system in terms of smaller systems — works only when the *whole* problem is small.

Despite our criticism, we're happy to see the data-structure approach included as part of the bag of tricks that the designer has at his disposal. The important thing to remember is that the data-structure approach concentrates on only one part of the overall design process — namely, the *strategy* by which the design can be derived. If it works, fine; however, it must be included with such central concepts as coupling, cohesion, design heuristics, and appropriate implementation/testing strategies. Perhaps the greatest advantage of the data-structure method is its use as a bridge between designs produced by transform analysis or transaction analysis and the actual coding of the resulting modules. Once we have developed a data flow diagram, each bubble usually becomes a distinct module, and the transform-centered design strategy guides us in developing the appropriate hierarchy of modules. The data-structure approach then becomes useful in the microscopic sense: If we know the structure of the data that comes out of a module, then we should be able to determine the structure of the code *inside* that module.

12.2 THE PARNAS DECOMPOSITION CRITERIA

Another interesting modular design approach is described by Parnas[4] as a set of rules for the decomposition of systems into subsystems. To avoid confusion with the very specific terminology already established in this book, we will — simply for the sake of discussion in this chapter — introduce terms somewhat different from Parnas' own — terms which, in some case, were defined by Parnas to be deliberately vague.

Parnas offers guidelines for the decomposition of a total problem into *design units,* or portions of a design problem or work assignment identified by the designer. Design units are related by *design interfaces* (Parnas uses the term "connections") which are *any* sort of interrelationship or interdependency. Design units and their design interfaces may or may not have any relationship to actual modules and connections as they need to be programmed. Parnas even suggests that we

* M. A. Jackson, *Principles of Program Design* (New York: Academic Press, 1975), p. 43.

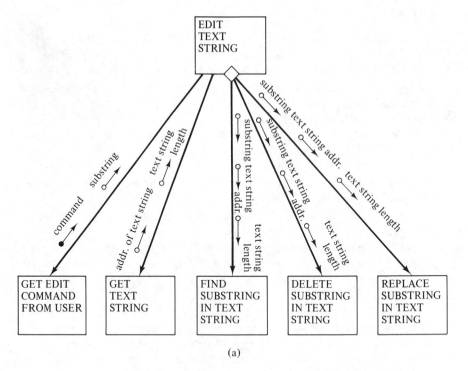

Fig. 12.4a Example of modules with visible format and linkage detail.

"allow a subroutine or program to be an assembled collection of code from various [design units]."

The Parnas decomposition criteria may be paraphrased as follows:

1. Decomposition is *not* to be based on flowcharts or procedures.

2. Each design interface is to contain (require) as little information as possible to correctly specify it.

3. Each design unit is to "hide" an assumption about the solution that is likely to change.

4. A design unit is to be specified to other design units (or to the programmers of other design units) with neither too much nor too little detail.

The first criterion obviously relates to cohesion, identifying negative consequences of "flowchart-thinking." The second criterion clearly is equivalent to a call for reduced coupling, as are the last two criteria (although less directly). Some design decisions that are most likely to change and, therefore, ought to be "hidden" within a given design unit are

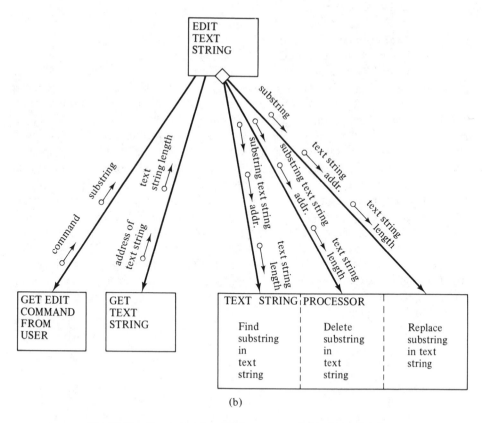

Fig. 12.4b Example of multiple-entry module of communicational cohesion.

1. a data structure along with its format and linkages, as well as its access, storage, and modification procedures*

2. formats of control blocks

3. character codes and collating sequences

4. sequence in which items are processed

In Plum's comparison of major design approaches,[3] it was concluded that these decomposition criteria do not constitute a general methodology for structural design. First, no procedure is offered within which to apply the criteria; and sec-

---

* Note that this is in direct contrast to the Jackson/Warnier data-structure approach: Rather than *hiding* the data structure, Jackson and Warnier strongly argue that the structure of the whole program should reflect the data structure. Thus, Parnas points out a potential weakness in the data-structure approach: If major changes to the data structure occur during maintenance of the system, it is likely that major changes will have to be made to the program structure as well.

ond, the critical problem of translation from design units and design interfaces into programmable, interconnected modules is not addressed at all.

Nevertheless, these ideas are a useful adjunct to structured design. Parnas contributes several broadly useful notions. For example, he draws attention to the dependencies created by "shared assumptions," common to more than one module in a system. The approach suggests isolating each related set of shared assumptions into a cluster of modules to be managed as a unit. This concept, along with specific examples of design assumptions to be hidden, can be used *after* completion of an overall structural design to refine the interfaces and generalize the design, principally by further reductions in coupling.

For example, we might note that several modules in the design of Fig. 12.4a all must share assumptions about the format and linkage structure of "text strings." A more generalized, more readily changed structure results if we treat these as a single design unit and make the format and linkage details invisible to all other modules. Myers[5] suggests a practical way of doing this with what he calls "informational strength" modules — a multiple-entry module of communicational cohesion. An example of this is shown in Fig. 12.4b. Note that more information hiding and

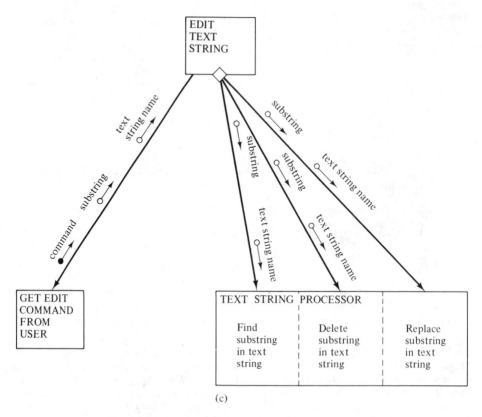

(c)

Fig. 12.4c   Further refinement of multiple-entry module.

decoupling are achieved by further refinement of the interfaces to that of Fig. 12.4c, where only a string index (identifier) is known to any other module.

REFERENCES

1. M.A. JACKSON, *Principles of Program Design* (New York: Academic Press, 1975).

2. JEAN-DOMINIQUE WARNIER, *The Logical Construction of Programs,* 3rd ed., trans. B.M. Flanagan (New York: Van Nostrand Reinhold, 1976).

3. THOMAS PLUM, "Structured Design Case Study Comparison," *The YOURDON Report,* Vol. 1, No. 7 (September 1976), pp. 8–12.

4. D.L. PARNAS, "On the Criteria to Be Used in Decomposing Systems into Modules," *Communications of the ACM,* Vol. 15, No. 12 (December 1972), pp. 1053–1058.

5. GLENFORD J. MEYERS, *Reliable Software Through Composite Design* (New York: Petrocelli/Charter, 1975).

This section takes up matters essential for turning a completed structured design into an implementable, efficient system. Nevertheless, highly modular systems, which are acceptable by standards established in earlier chapters, may include conflicts between the planned structure and required communication of data through the system. Resolution of these conflicts is analyzed in Chapter 13, and the specific issue of normal versus pathological communication paths is explored in detail. The resulting designs are complete in a structural sense; but before they can be coded and executed, decisions must be made as to what physical type of module will be used to implement each required functional entity. Packaging, the subject of Chapter 14, determines the physical implementation of the final system and accommodates the design to constraints imposed by the programming language, operating system, and machine configuration.

The cherished topic of run-time efficiency is addressed in Chapter 15, which presents a systematic approach to optimization of systems. That approach is entirely compatible with highly modular structural designs.

IV

PRAGMATICS

Communication
in
Modular Systems

CHAPTER 13

13.0 INTRODUCTION

In several previous chapters, we mentioned the concepts of *normal* connections and *pathological* connections: in Chapter 3, where we first introduced the notion of systems structure; in Chapter 5, where we discussed the factors that influence systems complexity; and in Chapter 6, where we discussed coupling. Obviously, it is a phenomenon that affects several aspects of structural design; consequently, we will devote the major portion of this chapter to a discussion of normal connections and pathological connections.

We will begin by presenting a brief overview of the problem of pathological connections; as we will see, pathological data connections are quite different from pathological control connections. We then will discuss several different types of pathological data connections, since these are far more common than pathological control connections. We do not intend to portray such pathological connections as an evil that must be avoided at all cost, but we will suggest some steps that the designer should go through in order to justify anything other than normal connections.

Finally, we will make some suggestions for minimizing the coupling caused by pathological connections.

13.1 AN OVERVIEW OF THE PATHOLOGICAL CONNECTION PROBLEM

As we first saw in Chapter 3, a pathological connection is a reference or an identifier or any entity *inside* a module. Such a reference could involve either data or control, or both. While hybrid combinations — pathological connections involving the combination of control and data — still are possible in most programming languages (e.g., the ALTER statement in COBOL), they are sufficiently unpopular in most competent programming organizations that we can ignore them in this discussion. We will examine the pathological data connections first; pathological control-coupling will be dealt with later.

13.1.1 An overview of pathological data connections

In simple terms, a pathological data connection can be represented by Fig. 13.1. As we will see in the next section, there are several variations on this simple theme. A more important question at this point is *why* the designer would want to indulge in this kind of practice.

The answer can be demonstrated by Fig. 13.2. The designer realizes that data element x is created by low-level module A, and must travel all the way to the top of the hierarchy before being passed back to low-level module B. It is apparent to the designer that none of the intermediate- or high-level modules has any interest in data element x. Rather than incurring the overhead of passing the data through so many intermediate levels of modules, the designer decides to pass the data directly — pathologically — from module A to module B. In addition to the argument of efficiency, the designer often invokes an argument of simplicity: Why clutter up the interface of the intermediate- and high-level modules with a data element that is irrelevant to their task?

The technical issues involve the increase in coupling contributed by the pathological connection and the consequences of this in terms of ease of maintenance and modification. Consider, for example, module B in Fig. 13.2. Because a portion of its input data context is determined directly by possible unrelated activities in A (which set up or computed the last value of x), control of module B by

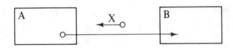

Fig. 13.1   Simple pathological connection.

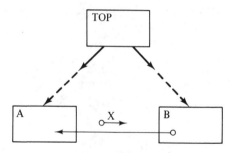

Fig. 13.2 Common temptation for pathological connections.

its superordinate is incomplete. The immediate CALL activity B does not, therefore, completely determine what B will do, as it would were all of B's input and output data communicated normally.

In order to introduce a new use of module B operating on some different value of x, the calling module must reference datum x *in module* A, thus a *new* pathological connection is required. The initial decision to have *some* pathological connections for certain purposes almost invariably generates the need for additional pathological connections for others; they tend to proliferate. Note as well that the choice of pathological communication requires that the programmer of a new module using B also must concern himself with module A, which may well have nothing to do with his problem. Clearly A and B have become coupled, strongly so, despite the absence of any immediate functional relationship between them.

The analogy with management structure may be particularly instructive here. In management terms, Fig. 13.1 can be interpreted as follows: If clerk A wishes to pass data to clerk B, he does so by passing the data through his boss. If the two clerks are in widely separated departments, the data may have to pass through several layers of management before reaching the second clerk. If clerk A had communicated directly with clerk B, we probably would not have referred to his behavior as a pathological connection; instead, we would have said he "went around the boss." What we have called normal communication is referred to in a management structure as "going through channels," or "going through the chain of command." Particularly in the larger and more formalized corporations and government agencies, the normal form of communication is rigorously enforced. The smaller companies and the organizations whose managers consider themselves progressive frequently permit — even encourage — the pathological form of communication.

Unfortunately, there are disadvantages to analogies between management structures and the structures of computer systems. This is particularly true here, since a number of workers and some managers feel quite strongly that the requirement for normal communication is one of the most onerous aspects of modern corporate life. It is worth exploring this feeling in more detail, for it helps us see just how far we can carry the comparison between people and machines. Workers and managers alike quickly will identify three reasons for avoiding the rigorous enforcement of normal communications:

- *Inefficiency.* In a large organization, a worker or junior manager complains that he may have to wait several days, weeks, or even months for his data to filter up to the higher levels of management. Meanwhile, he sits idle.

- *Politics.* Many of the more cynical workers complain that their information is filtered and qualified as it travels upward in the hierarchy. Thus, if clerk A generates datum X, it may be distorted into datum Y as it travels up and down the hierarchy on its way to clerk B in a different department.

- *Human psychology.* In a large organization, the worker often complains that he is a small cog in the machine — and that he is demoralized by not being able to see where his labors fit into the big picture. This is accentuated by the rigid form of normal communication, characterized by the manager who says to his worker, "Here is your input data; don't ask where it came from, or what I'm going to do with your output — just shut up and do your job."

The issue of efficiency is obviously relevant in both management structures and computer systems structures. Our experience with large vendor-supplied operating systems is sufficient evidence that such overhead can be truly monumental within ordinary applications, Knuth's study[1] suggests that the two most expensive statements in a high-level language program are the subroutine-calling statement (particularly when several parameters are passed) and formatted input-output statements. This may only be an indictment of the quality of implementation of these features by compiler writers. On the other hand, a typical computer system has only a few modules that are frequently executed; the overhead in the remaining modules often can be ignored. We will have more to say about this in Section 13.3.2, as well as in Chapter 15 when we discuss optimization of modular systems.

Clearly, modules do not behave in a political fashion; they do not distort data received from subordinate modules that they do not like. However, the programming teams that develop modules often *do* behave in a political manner with respect to other programming teams; they may well distort the data received from subordinate modules implemented by a programming team they do not like. We usually can (although not always) assume that such problems will be exposed and resolved during testing and integration. While the programming teams may continue to behave toward each other in a political fashion, their modules —once debugged and integrated with one another — presumably will behave in an apolitical fashion.

Similarly, we should not have to worry about a module in a computer system becoming demoralized because it does not see the big picture — even though such morale problems may plague the programming team that develops the module! Indeed, one of the objectives of the normal form of communication is that it fosters a black-box approach to modules, so that each one can be considered, debugged, or modified without serious impact on other modules.

It is possible, for example, that module A in Fig. 13.2 also uses datum x in some way other than as a value to be accessed by module B. It could have been written to expect that the value remain constant between calls. (For languages that do not permit "owned" or local data of this sort in subroutines, the same issues can apply to data passed via common or global variables.) Before the programmer can unceremoniously plunk a new value into x for the alternate use of module B, the coding in module A would have to be inspected to insure that no such side effect or competing use of x is made within A. But module A ceases, thereby, to be a black box!

In general, the use of pathological connections reduces the ability of the programmer to treat modules as black boxes. To some extent, normal communication justifies the existence of the managers. Aside from the degenerate cases, we assume that managers (and superordinate modules) exist for a purpose: They control and coordinate the work of their subordinates. To bypass a manager by transmitting data pathologically is to weaken the power, effectiveness, and flexibility of the manager. To suggest that the manager doesn't look at the data anyway and should therefore not have the data pass through his hands is a somewhat subtle form of "inversion of authority": What business does the worker have telling the boss what data he should or should not receive? Furthermore, how does the worker really *know* what data the manager requires in order to make his decisions?

A more specific and relevant argument relates to flexibility. The manager may wish to move a clerk from one department to another, with the clerk still carrying out the same function. Or, the manager may decide that instead of performing services for just one department, the clerk should be able to carry out general-purpose services for multiple departments. All of this is made more difficult if the clerk is transmitting and/or receiving data pathologically with other clerks — particularly if the manager is unaware that such pathological communications are taking place (and since the manager has presumably been "cut out of the loop," there is no reason to expect that he would be aware of such nefarious dealings behind his back!).

Finally, there is the argument of security: Many organizations require that data be communicated normally in order to ensure that it is provided on a need-to-know basis. This is particularly true in certain military agencies, of course, but one finds it in the more sensitive areas (e.g., marketing, research and development, patient work, and so on) of other organizations as well. One occasionally finds unusual cases in which the boss does not have access to certain sensitive information manipulated by his subordinate, but the reverse is normally true: The boss has more global access to data, and decides which subordinates should be granted local access to selected bits of data.

13.1.2 Overview of pathological control connections

Pathological control connections are considerably less prevalent than pathological data connections, but they still occur sufficiently frequently to warrant some discussion. In simple terms, a pathological control connection can be represented in the form shown in Fig. 13.3. Again, our question is not so much, What do pathological control connections look like? as Why do designers use pathological control connections?

Assuming that the system is basically modular in nature (i.e., that it consists of modules, which are called normally and which exit normally), we will find only a few limited uses of pathological control connections. Relatively infrequently, one low-level module transfers pathologically to another low-level module, as shown in Fig. 13.4a. More often, each module has a separate control connection to the other, as shown in Fig. 13.4b, usually because a portion of the code or task of one module is being used by the other. The structure of Fig. 13.4b suggests that the designer may be building a primitive homologous (or one-layer) structure, though he may not recognize it as such. We will discuss homologous structures in Chapter 18.

A more common example of pathological control connections is the "panic abort" exit to the operating system. This is demonstrated in Fig. 13.5a. Such a structure is not necessarily evil, if the designer consciously chooses a panic abort and understands the trade-offs. However, a number of designers do not even recognize that Fig. 13.5a represents a pathological control connection. To emphasize the contrast, Fig. 13.5b shows a structure that accomplishes the same thing as Fig. 13.5a, but with normal control connections.

The difference between Figs. 13.5a and 13.5b illustrates the reason why many designers opt for the panic abort approach: The normal approach involves too much overhead in returning error flags to the top level of the structure. This may appear to be a false issue, since a panic abort presumably would be executed only once. However, if every module has to check for the presence of a "fatal error" flag after each call to a subordinate, a considerable amount of CPU execution and memory overhead *might* be involved. The issue might also be *programmer* time: The programmer doesn't want to spend time and energy coding a fatal error flag into all of his modules. What is needed, of course, are simple and efficient methods of accomplishing this task.

Figure 13.6 illustrates a variation on the panic abort: A low-level module discovers a serious error and decides to transfer control directly to the top module

Fig. 13.3 Pathological control connection.

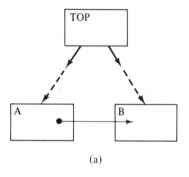

(a)

Fig. 13.4a Simple example of pathological control flow.

— thus circumventing a number of intermediate-level modules that might have been in the midst of some task when the low-level module began executing. This situation often occurs when the designer decides that the fatal error — which is discovered in the low-level module — should cause the system to abort a great deal of processing that was underway. In a business data processing system, for example, the processing of a complex transaction could be terminated in this fashion. Sometimes, the designer carefully arranges things so that the intermediate modules will "flush" the processing they were in the midst of, and ensures that the modules properly reinitialize themselves in preparation for any new processing; sometimes, he simply crosses his fingers and hopes that things will take care of themselves. The normal form of Fig. 13.6 would be quite similar to Fig. 13.5b.

The problem, of course, is that, to each of the intermediate modules, the fatal error flag has some meaning in terms of what aspects of the immediate processing task must be adjusted, reinitialized, and so on. These details should only concern and be known to the programmer of each particular module, and this is only possible when each sees the flag. One can even say that an error becomes fatal by virtue of its being passed up the line without being intercepted and handled to become non-fatal or a non-error by any intermediates. The management analogy is self-evident; the janitor, for example, does not tell the Chairman of the Board that it is time to dissolve the corporation — unless the janitor is also the major stockholder.

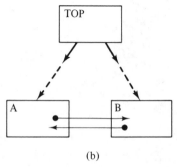

(b)

Fig. 13.4b More common example of pathological control flow.

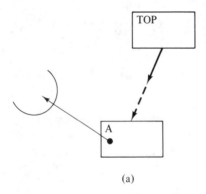

(a)

Fig. 13.5a Panic abort as an example of pathological control flow.

13.2 TYPES OF PATHOLOGICAL DATA CONNECTIONS

We recall that the obvious form of a pathological data connection was shown in Fig. 13.1. Examination of this structure shows us that module A is "loading" some data from B's domain into its own. That is, we would expect that the connection shown in Fig. 13.1 would be implemented with a statement in module A of the following sort:

MOVE B-GLOP to A-GLOP

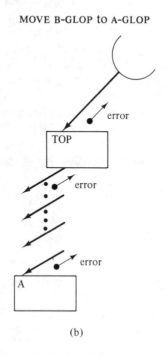

(b)

Fig. 13.5b Normal version of the panic abort.

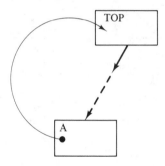

Fig. 13.6 Another example of pathological control flow.

Of course, data may flow in the other direction as a result of a pathological connection; that is, A may store data into B, as shown in Fig. 13.7. Both variations are equally simple from a structural point of view. We often refer to the process as a *direct pathological connection.*

An extremely popular form of pathological connection involves a *common data environment;* this is illustrated in Fig. 13.8. What makes the connection pathological is that A and B are not passing and receiving data through their superordinates. The situation might be compared to two clerks communicating by storing and retrieving data from a publicly accessible file cabinet — but without explicitly informing their boss of the communication. As we discussed extensively in Chapter 6, this form of pathological connection typically leads to greatly increased coupling — not just A and B, but *all* of the modules in the system have access to the common data environment shown in Fig. 13.8. We will make suggestions for minimizing this problem in Section 13.4.

One of the more subtle forms of pathological communication involves a so-called communicator module, as shown on the facing page in Fig. 13.9. Technically, this does not involve a pathological *connection,* since neither A nor B is explicitly referring to anything internal to TABLEIT. However, the *communication* is pathological in the sense that A is passing data to B without the explicit awareness of its superordinate. In addition, TABLEIT has relatively low cohesion; depending on the nature of the call, it will either store or retrieve a specified data element — and is thus communicationally cohesive.

We might compare this situation to the following management scenario. Manager P awakens clerk A from his slumbers and gives him a job to do. In the midst of performing his job, clerk A creates data element x. Clerk A knows that the

Fig. 13.7 Another form of direct pathological communication.

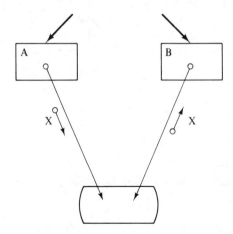

Fig. 13.8 Common data environment pathological connection.

nature of his job is such that his friend, clerk B who works down the hall in another department, eventually will be awakened to carry out a job that will require access to data element x. At the same time, A knows that his boss has no explicit interest in x. Consequently, clerk A awakens a junior clerk who has the peculiar surname of TABLEIT, and asks him to file data element x in a file cabinet *whose location is known only to* TABLEIT.

At some later time, clerk B is awakened by his boss to carry out some task. In order to perform the task, B knows that he will require data element x; he also knows that A was active at some previous time and that he arranged for TABLEIT to store the vital information away. Thus, B immediately calls upon TABLEIT to retrieve x; this allows B to perform his job, and he is able to return the appropriate output to his boss. Note that neither A nor B knows explicitly where TABLEIT has

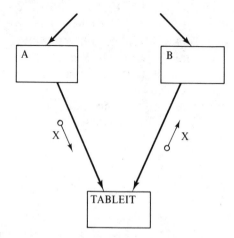

Fig. 13.9 TABLEIT form of pathological communication.

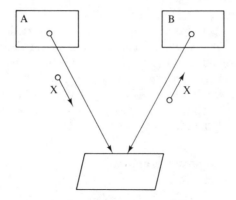

Fig. 13.10 Device-coupled pathological communication.

hidden data element x. They don't have to — they know that TABLEIT is trust-worthy and can be counted upon to store and retrieve information upon command.

It is obvious that the management has been circumvented to some extent; it should be obvious that a reorganization at the upper levels of the organization could seriously disrupt the cozy communication between A and B. Suppose A is informed that, from now on, he will be awakened by one of several different man-agers; he is expected to perform the same basic function for each. If manager P calls on him to perform a job, then we know that clerk B ultimately will be activated and will require data element x; however, if manager Q awakens A, then it may well turn out that clerk B will *not* be awakened — in which case, data element x should be stored and retrieved via TABLEIT.

The points to recognize in this hypothetical example are (a) if clerk A does not know explicitly which manager is awakening him — that is, if it is an anonymous subroutine call — then he does not know whether or not to store data element x, and (b) if the higher levels of management are not aware of the shenanigans being carried on by A, B, and TABLEIT, they will assume that their organization can be implemented without any trouble.

The final form of pathological communication is known as *device-coupled* communication and is shown in Fig. 13.10. This can be regarded as a variation on the common data envionment shown in Fig. 13.8. The form involves primary memory as the communication medium, while the latter involves secondary storage of some form — typically, tape or disk. Once again, this often is regarded as an innocent practice by veteran designers because the modules involved are not med-dling in each other's internal affairs: A should not know that its execution is in any way connected to, or coupled to, subsequent execution of B.

13.3 JUSTIFICATION OF PATHOLOGICAL COMMUNICATION

As we have said several times, pathological connections are not to be considered evil — despite the obvious pejorative connotations of pathological. We do know that, all other things being equal, a system with pathological connections will tend to be more difficult to maintain and modify — particularly if such work is performed by programmers other than the original development programmers. Nevertheless, the designer often is influenced by other constraints and pressures, and these may be sufficient to justify the pathological connections.

Our purpose in this section is to discuss the justifications for pathological connections. This can be accomplished by simply asking a few questions, each of which is listed separately below.

13.3.1 How much extra programming time is involved?

Much of the reluctance to use normal communication between modules may stem from the coding required for the interfaces. Programmers complain that it takes a great deal of extra work to code the passing of parameters, and to check fatal error flags and all the other encumbrances of normal communication.

While each case deserves to be judged on its own merits, we should make a few observations about the amount of time typically spent in the *coding* of a typical program. Aron,[2] Metzger,[3] and others have reported that coding typically occupies only about one sixth of the person-hours of a typical programming project — design accounts for one third of the project, and testing accounts for about one half. Once we have figured out what we want our system to do, we tend to spend a minimal amount of time coding it, and a large amount of time trying to make it work! Thus, a small amount of extra time to code the intermodule interfaces required for normal communication hardly can have much impact on the overall project schedule. Indeed, we suspect that the basis of the programmers' objection in this area is a combination of laziness and impatience to begin testing the program.

Knuth's study[1] indicates that CALL statements account for only 4 percent of all the statements in a typical FORTRAN program. The authors' observations of large numbers of programs, even highly modular ones, suggest that these statistics are probably valid for a variety of other programming languages as well. If only 4 percent of the statements written by a programmer involve activation of other modules, can it really take that much extra work to pass and return the parameters required for normal communication?

There will certainly be some cases in which the answer is yes. All we ask is that the designer and the programmer take the time to consider whether the extra coding time will be significant.

In the final analysis, this probably is a false issue. Since the highly modular approach of structured design has been proved to *reduce* programming, it is extremely unlikely that a central feature — namely normal subroutine calling — should increase programming over all. The truth is that the *functions* served by parameterized subroutine calling are necessary features of any solution. Whether spread around and buried as side effects in other code or concentrated and made highly visible in a long subroutine argument list, the programming effort is still there.

13.3.2 Is the overhead of normal communication too high?

Perhaps the strongest, certainly the most commonly heard, argument in favor of pathological communication is that of efficiency. Still, the designer should ask himself whether the cost of normal communication is truly unbearable compared to the total cost of pathological communication. If so, and if efficiency is an important issue in the system, then pathological communication may well be justified.

We should point out, however, that the cost of normal communication is not so terribly excessive in most high-level programming languages. The statement

$$\text{CALL GLOP } (\text{A},\text{B},\text{C},\text{D}, \ldots ,\text{X},\text{Y},\text{Z})$$

generally involves passing one *address* for each of the parameters, regardless of whether the parameter is a triple-precision floating point number or a 256-character text string. If the parameter must be passed up and down through several levels of the hierarchy, this may amount to a considerable overhead. On the other hand, considerable overhead may be expended in any case — regardless of the number of parameters passed — because of the "prologue/epilogue" processing associated with the entry and exit to modules in a high-level language: saving and restoring general registers, setting base address registers, and so forth. Thus, passing one or two extra parameters may represent only a small incremental overhead.

Ultimately, the proper method in which to assess communication efficiency is not to measure the cost of subroutine calls, which is to implicitly compare the cost of normal communication to the cost of doing nothing, but to compare the costs of the alternative. Despite prevailing programming mythology, pathological communication, say, via common or global variables,[4] does not come completely free.

On the average, each use of a module requires establishing special or unique values for the major portion of its inputs and targeting the resulting outputs to the proper places. Where pathological communication has been elected, this will require, in many instances, the actual moving of data from sources into the global input variables and, on return, moving results from where they were generated by the module to where they ultimately are needed. Thus, the typical code is most likely to resemble the code below with respect to some or all of the inputs and outputs.

```
MOVE Q INTO IN1
MOVE R INTO IN2
CALL FOO
MOVE OUT1 INTO S
```

While it is true that many programmers do not always cluster these data-shuffling statements in the immediate vicinity of the CALL, where they would be painfully obvious, a thorough perusal of the code will reveal their presence. Note that such separation of the statement that activates the module from those that determine what it does can only complicate the program and increase the probability of error.

The hidden, or at least often ignored, cost of pathological communication is increased when a new, alternative use of a module is introduced and the programmer must avoid a possible conflict with other usage of input and output data variables, as introduced earlier. The required coding then resembles the following:

```
MOVE X INTO TEMP
MOVE NEWX INTO X
CALL B
MOVE TEMP INTO X
```

The saving and restoring is necessary to assure that a still-needed value of x is not accidentally lost.

When one considers that normal communication in most programming languages automatically establishes a complete, unique input and output data context for each CALL by passing *pointers* (which are "address site" entities), then it is not surprising that this often can be *more* efficient than the actual moving of data required in pathological communication.

In any case, we would recommend that the designer begin with the assumption that normal communication will *not* be unduly expensive — unless he has some strong evidence to the contrary. Having implemented the system, the designer/programmer can gather statistics to see if a few of the intermodule references are causing excessive overhead. We will touch upon this philosophy again in Chapter 15.

13.3.3 Are future alternative uses likely?

Perhaps the strongest argument *against* pathological connections is that they make future modification of the system more difficult. However, if the designer is relatively certain that the system will be stable (a brave designer indeed!), then he perhaps can justify the use of pathological communication. There are two aspects of future modification that concern us: future general-purpose use of the modules that currently are communicating pathologically, and future uses for data elements that are currently being transmitted pathologically.

Thus, in Fig. 13.8 (or in any of the other forms of pathological communication), we are concerned with possible future uses of modules A and B, as well as possible future uses of the data element x. When the system is first designed, we can imagine that A and B each have only one superordinate; thus, the fact that they are communicating pathologically does not bother us too much. However, we should ask ourselves whether there is any possibility that module A (or B) will ever be used by other superordinates if some future modification to the system is made. Similarly, we observe that data element x is hidden from the higher levels of modules in the pathological structure shown in Fig. 13.8; since the superordinate modules apparently have no explicit need to access data element x, this may not bother us. However, we should ask whether some future modification to the system will require x to be transmitted to, or used by, some other part of the system; if so, the data should be communicated normally. Note that any other value of data element x requires substitution of any other value into location x in the pathological connection.

This question and the others raised in this section require some deliberate judgment on the part of the designer. If the designer feels that every minute of coding time is precious, that nary a microsecond of CPU time can be wasted, and that future modifications to the system are unlikely at best, so be it! We are concerned only with the fact that many pathological communications are designed unconsciously or casually — or they result from a long-standing prejudice that all normal communications are bad because they require too much CPU time.

13.4 SUGGESTIONS FOR MINIMIZING COUPLING IN PATHOLOGICAL CONNECTIONS

If we assume that pathological communication is sometimes justifiable in terms of the criteria discussed above, we should distinguish between good and bad pathological communications. In particular, we would like to choose pathological communications that aggravate intermodule coupling as little as possible.

Perhaps the most important suggestion is that a pathological connection or other direct communication should be used only for communication: Local, internal uses of a pathologically communicated data element should be avoided wherever possible. Thus, we may be prepared to accept the simple pathological connection of Fig. 13.1 as long as it serves only the purpose of transmitting a useful parameter from A to B. Module A should not use data element x for local purposes internally — e.g., it should not at some later point use x as a temporary storage area for saving intermediate results of calculations. Although *any* pathological connection is likely to be more obscure than a normal connection to the maintenance programmer, a pathological connection involving internal uses and side effects is *considerably* more obscure. To assure safe use of a pathological connection that has a side effect, the programmer must look inside modules; in this particular case, they are *not* black boxes.

Since common data environments are such a prevalent form of pathological communication, we offer another suggestion: Whenever possible, common environments should be regionalized. In general, a module should not be given access via a common environment to any data element that it does not require in order to perform its job. Recall that this suggestion was made in Chapter 6; coupling can be greatly reduced by careful regionalization of common environments.

Finally, we suggest that the designer and the programmer extensively document any pathological communications. Assuming that a structure chart is used as one form of documentation, the appropriate notation should be used to highlight any pathological connections that may be present. Similarly, the flowcharts or narrative documentation that accompanies each module should indicate any of its pathological connections. Finally, the documentation that accompanies each data element (e.g., a data dictionary) should indicate whether the data element is transmitted or used pathologically.

13.5 SUMMARY

As we have seen, there are many different types of pathological data connections and pathological control connections. It is especially interesting that so many analogies can be drawn between this aspect of software design and the structure of human organizations; we recommend that you keep these in mind when discussing such questions with your fellow designers.

The issues behind the use or nonuse of pathological connections are fairly obvious: efficiency, convenience, and future maintenance. There are indeed circumstances that justify a pathological connection; however, in today's environment of cheaper hardware and increasingly complex software, there are fewer and fewer cases really justified on rational grounds. Unfortunately, remembering the days when hardware was expensive and software relatively cheap, many designers continue to defend pathological connections on emotional grounds.

REFERENCES

1. DONALD E. KNUTH, "An Empirical Study of FORTRAN Programs," *Software—Practice and Experience,* Vol. 1, No. 2, pp. 105–133.

2. J.D. ARON, "Estimating Resources for Large Programming Systems," *Software Engineering Techniques,* NATO Scientific Affairs Division (Brussels 39, Belgium: April 1970), pp. 68–79.

3. PHILIP W. METZGER, *Managing a Programming Project* (Englewood Cliffs, N.J.: Prentice-Hall, 1973).

4. W. WULF and M. SHAW, "Global Variables Considered Harmful," *ACM SIGPLAN Notices,* February 1973, pp. 28–34.

Packaging

CHAPTER 14

14.0 INTRODUCTION

In this chapter, we consider two very practical steps in the design of a working modular system. Ultimately, we must make a system fit into the available physical memory (or occupy units of a reasonable size, for storage management purposes), and we must implement the various input-output processes of the system on actual devices. Both of these steps are concerned with the physical realization of a modular system on an actual computer.

The term *packing* refers to the assignment of the modules of a total system into sections handled as distinct physical units for execution on a machine. Each such unit will be called a *load unit,* and will be considered a portion of the system processed as a unit by the operating environment. For some systems, *programs* are the load units; in others, we see the terms "overlays," "load module," "job step," and so forth. Load unit boundaries and module boundaries are independent theoretical constructs, though, in practice, they are highly correlated.

The relationship between functional module structure and packaging may be considered in either order. Traditionally, the mechanical requirements of space and time are weighted relatively highly as inputs to the process of modularization. In other words, execution speed and memory constraints traditionally have guided the modular design. The early intrusion of such unequivocally nonfunctional aspects of the problem may — and often does — substantially reduce the effective modularity of the system. On the other hand, we *must* pare the system to fit into memory, or limit the load-time packages to a manageable size.

As a general rule, we cannot simultaneously minimize memory and execution time. The most useful expression of the problem is to find a packaging arrangement that will minimize execution time while just satisfying an actual or arbitrary limit on load unit size. Packaging within this framework *can* be done after a complete modular structure has been determined. This is *desirable,* too, for it allows us to focus our attention on increasing the modularity of the system, provided satisfactory execution speed can be achieved.

When the modules of a system are small, we almost always can perform packaging while leaving the module boundaries intact. With small modules, the probability is high that the boundary of a package will be at or near a modular boundary. As suggested in Chapter 9, high technical modularity relates to small module size — thus, prior modular design emphasizing technical modularity makes after-the-fact packaging feasible.

With a complete structural design, we will have additional information: the procedural skeleton and the communication structure. This is precisely the information we need to make a *good* segmentation of the system into packages. Indeed, neither the procedural skeleton nor the communication structure (i.e., the flow of data back and forth between modules) would be known with nearly as much accuracy or detail before the structural design. By deferring packaging to the end of the design process, we (potentially) improve both the efficiency and the technical modularity of the system.

Using a strategy known as *procedural analysis,* we will study the problem of organizing systems into efficient load units. The emphasis thoughout this chapter is on *memory* requirements of the system. The discussion of optimization in Chapter 15 will concentrate largely on execution speed, which is best done after the system has been implemented and put into production.

14.1 PROCEDURAL ANALYSIS

Procedural analysis consists of a set of criteria to determine which modules must be in the same load unit for the sake of efficiency. The criteria derive originally from ideas of Emery[1] as refined for packaging purposes. To use this as a technique for designing the modular structure is technically undesirable, but it is precisely the approach needed for efficient packaging. Application of these criteria generally leads to overdetermined systems — that is, the requirements conflict in such a way that the only way to satisfy all of them is to have a single load unit for the entire system, which would be a contradiction. In other cases (although less frequently), the packaging is undetermined, with some "don't-care" boundaries. In either case, we are left with an art, not a science. The designer must cleverly juggle conflicting desiderata.

Procedural analysis involves three steps:

1. Determine the expected size of each module in the structure. This first step is actually easier than it sounds, for with a complete modular design we have a good idea of the module size in most cases — and when we don't, the small size of most modules makes estimation easy.

2. Apply each of several criteria discussed below to determine preferred groupings and a priority among preferences.

3. Find groupings of modules such that splitting of preferred groupings by load unit boundaries is minimized without bringing the size of the load unit above the allowable maximum. This will be the most efficient packaging for the given structure within given memory constraints.

The general concept is very simple: In the same load unit, we want to include modules connected by a reference that is used or accessed many times during an execution of the system. We do this because references *between* load units cost something in overhead above the basic modular overhead; where the operating environment becomes involved, this cost can be substantial indeed. Between programs or job steps, communication usually will require use of intermediate files, an even more expensive matter.

There are several distinct guides for recognizing high-frequency references between modules. First, we look at the *iteration* structure — that is, the imbedding of subroutine calls or other intermodular references within loops. The rule of thumb is that, wherever possible, we want to place a module referenced within an iteration in the same load unit as the referencing module. Since iterations often are nested either within the referencing module or by virtue of subordination, the preference for grouping modules into a load unit must be given to inner (lowest-level) loops over outer (higher-level) loops.

In the structure of Fig. 14.1, the highest priority is to include modules B and E in the same load unit. The next priority is to include B and D in the same load unit; the only way of accomplishing this without violating the first priority is to include B, D, and E in a common load unit. By a similar argument, the next lower priority would include A, B, D, and E in the same load unit.

Because other grouping criteria will be added to the one involving iteration, it is more useful to begin by showing the groupings of modules in pairs. For example, if we discover later that there is a very high priority for associating module Q (shown in Fig. 14.1) with module B, we do not want to be misled into thinking that the highest priority overall grouping is B, D, E, and Q — when in fact it is B, E, and Q.

Sometimes, it may be efficient for two modules to be in the same load unit

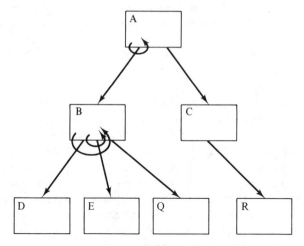

Fig. 14.1 First-cut packaging based on iterative structure.

even if there is not an obvious, or even explicit, iterative relationship. For example, we may know that module C in Fig. 14.1 is invoked for every record of a 27,000 record file. Thus, a reference from A to C is made 27,000 times during the execution of the system. Indeed, the estimates of *volume* of references often are more useful than the iterative structure by itself.

We may find, for example, that the loop in module A (within which there is a call to module B) iterates an average of three times, *if it is executed at all*. Subsequent analysis might show that a decision within module A causes the loop to be executed only once out of every four times the system is run. If this is the case, the priority obviously would be given to the grouping of modules A and C rather than to A and B.

The decision structure shown on an extended structure chart is a useful rough guide to the *frequency* of references. Clearly, a conditional reference reduces the frequency by an amount proportional to the fraction of time that the relevant condition is false; an unconditional reference means that the referenced module and the module making the referral are executed with equal frequency. Where frequency of reference or communication is the observable criterion, the rule of thumb is that modules related by high-frequency references should be in the same load unit.

Another somewhat less useful packaging criterion is the *time interval* between references from one load unit to another. In most cases, this means that we are interested in the amount of time that passes between the execution of one module and another. The longer the time interval, the less overhead will be incurred in switching from one load unit to another. For example, we can think of module C in Fig. 14.1 as an intermediary between module A and module R. If C requires a long time to execute, we would not mind at all having A, C, and R in separate load units. On the other hand, if c executes quickly, it is preferable to have A, C, and R in the same load unit. Otherwise, the ratio of overhead to useful processing jumps considerably.

This criterion is relevant only when volume or frequency information is not available. Clearly, the same analysis should apply to an "atomic" module, based on its expected execution time.

Two special cases exist when we do *not* want to include modules in the same load unit. We define an *optional function* as one that, for some executions of the system, may not be needed at all — *and* one whose use (or nonuse) can be decided in advance of the situation in which it might be required. *Run optional functions* are those whose use (or nonuse) can be determined when the system initializes itself. Clearly, wherever feasible, optional functions should be placed in separate load units by themselves. The advantage of isolating optional functions is that under some circumstances (i.e., the circumstances in which the function is not used) our use of modularity costs us absolutely nothing — for the optional function will not even be loaded into memory.

The other special case is for "one-shot" functions. These are used only once per execution of the system, or once for some well-defined segment of the system. Obviously, a one-shot function should be in a load unit by itself; once it has been executed, it need no longer be kept in memory.

An exceptional case occurs whenever a *sort* is required in a structure. Sorts represent natural breakpoints to separate load units. Indeed, this often has been a criterion invoked in traditional design work.

When separation into physical packages may require the use of distinct programs or job steps, special attention must be given to the volume or communication on any transition between load units. The designer should try to identify points with the lowest volume and simplest data to break the structure. If the communication were to be accomplished via input-output devices (device-coupling), then intermediate files can be kept small and with simple structure. When an overlay communication region in primary storage is used, the size and complexity of tables in that region are reduced.

Table 14.1 summarizes the criteria for efficient packaging of modules with the rules for priority of application. When applied, these criteria typically will yield a complex set of overlapping alternate groupings. The designer's task is to juggle possibilities until a group of distinct load sets has been identified. One way of looking at the problem is to draw load unit boundaries so as to minimize the number of grouping preferences that must be cut (properly weighted by priority). When sufficiently well defined, this process is analogous to certain graphic theoretical problems. Since we lack the space in this book to pursue such a formal graphic theoretical approach, the designer will have to regard this step as an art.

In resolving conflicting requirements, there is one trick that frequently is useful. In Fig. 14.2, the designer has used the iteration structure to lead to two load units with a single conflict, in the form of the common subordinate module MM. Let us imagine that the maximum permissible load unit size is 450 units

Table 14.1. Criteria for Packaging by Procedural Analysis

	GROUPING CRITERIA	**PRIORITY RULES**
ITERATIONS	Include in the same load unit modules connected by iterated reference.	Inner loops take precedence over outer loops. Loops nested within a module take precedence over nesting by subordination.
VOLUME	Include in the same load unit modules with high volume of access on connecting references.	High volume (many activations or many items passed) takes precedence over low volume. The volume criterion is preferable to the iteration criterion, if volume information is known.
FREQENCY	Include in the same load unit module with high frequency of access on connecting references.	Frequent transfers of control or data take precedence over infrequent transfers. If known, volume and/or iteration criteria are preferable.
INTERVAL	Include in the same load unit as the superordinate (or the subordinate) any module with short interval of time between activation.	Short execution time has precedence over long execution time. This is a low-priority priority criterion.
	ISOLATION CRITERIA	
OPTIONAL FUNCTIONS	Put into a separate load unit any optional function.	
ONE-SHOT FUNCTIONS	Put into a separate load unit any module used only once.	
SORTS	Put modules applied on input and output sides of a sort into separate load units.	

(bytes, words, pages, or whatever — we really don't care in this discussion). Thus, we cannot combine HH-JJ-LL-MM with KK-NN into a single load unit to solve the problem. However, all of the requirements can be met if we provide duplicate copies of MM for each load unit. This generally is feasible when the common subordinate(s) is (are) small. Of course, we do not wish to duplicate the design and coding of MM, so the modular structure remains as in Fig. 14.2. All that we have done is make two *physical* copies of the same module.

Actual realization of a preferred packaging is another matter altogether

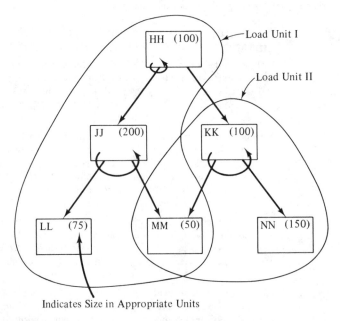

Indicates Size in Appropriate Units

Fig. 14.2   Conflicting load unit grouping with common subordinate.

and generally will depend on the programming language, the operating system, and the computer hardware. Thus, the designer may have to transform modular load units into physical overlays. Or, he may find that the operating system handles each module separately and will not permit several modules to constitute a single load unit. In such cases, the designer may have to lexically include subordinates within the superordinate (if that is possible). In some systems, compiling several modules together may cause a single load unit to be created by the compiler. Separate compilations produce separate load units. Or, there may be a distinct link-edit process which combines separately compiled modules into load units.

The person making the packaging decisions should have a complete catalog of packaging options within the language-compiler-operating environment in use. Such a catalog should identify, for each available type of package, the functional characteristics and limitations, the operating overhead, and any peculiarities or special advantages. For example, a module on a structure chart may be packaged in full ANSI COBOL in many forms: as a paragraph or section of a main program or callable subprogram; as a main program; or as a callable subprogram, managed either dynamically or statically. All of a program or subprogram may constitute a load unit, or sections can be handled as overlays. The use of a section saves the prologue/epilogue required by a called subprogram, but makes all communication into and out of the module pathological via the common environment comprising the data division. On the other hand, COBOL subprograms can only pass data normally except by device-coupling.

14.2 PACKAGING IN PRACTICE

Obviously, a realistic example of packaging involving division into more than a few load modules would be far too tedious to present in detail here. But some of the subtleties of packaging, especially of the advantages of deferred packaging, can best be appreciated through concrete example. For this reason, we will summarize the techniques of procedural analysis and packaging of modular program systems by a lengthy, but, we hope, not excessively tedious example.

The MULTISM system employs a data bank of simulation parameters to define a variety of simulations of chemical processes for the United Sodium and Sugar Company. The updated contents of specified entries from the data bank are combined with a series of simulation instructions (an agenda) calling for that data. Represented in suitable form, the agenda becomes input to simulation calculations, which execute the agenda step by step. The results calculated by each agenda step are plotted. A summary for a complete agenda is to be entered into one of two reports depending on the yield in the simulated results. These reports are to appear in another sort-order based on codes in the agenda itself.

An extended structure chart for a highly factored, transform-centered version of this complete system is shown in Fig. 14.3. The afferent branch headed by GETSIMULATIONAGENDA delivers one complete agenda with its required parameters. The simulation transform, DO1AGENDASTEP, and the two efferent branches for plotted results (PUTINTERIMRESULTS), and the summary reports (PUTTOSUM) are called in an inner loop of MULTISIM for each step. A transaction center is found at GETCOM/DATA in the afferent branch. The system as originally specified is assumed to be a single load unit using a callable sort routine with separate entry points for putting to and, after completion of the sorting, taking from the sort subsystem.

A typical run involves about 2,000 transactions at the point identified as (1) in Fig. 14.3, about 1,400 of which might be updates to the data bank. About half of the usual 600 individual agenda instructions require parameters from the data bank items that are being updated, the remaining involve other items. The volume of items at points (2) and (3) is about 600 in each case, but the data at point (3) are more compact, less complex. Since an average agenda comprises about three steps, the volume at point (4) averages only 200 items, but each item involves many fields or subitems. As each agenda step produces output, the volume at point (5) is, again, typically 600. The agenda summaries represented at point (6) total only 200, each resulting in a page-long report. Most often, only one in ten simulations has a high yield and thus would appear in the high-yield report; the volume at (7) would be about twenty items.

This information, along with the procedural annotations on the structure chart, permits us to establish some preferences for grouping and separating. In Fig. 14.4, solid lines enclose the higher-priority groupings based on iterations; dashed lines identify points where the presence of optional or one-shot functions favors separation of load units. Low-priority groups have been omitted. Clearly,

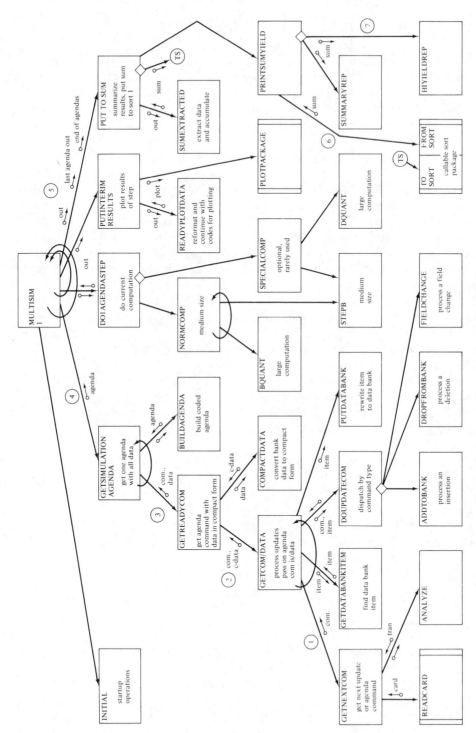

Fig. 14.3 Structure chart for the MULTISIM system.

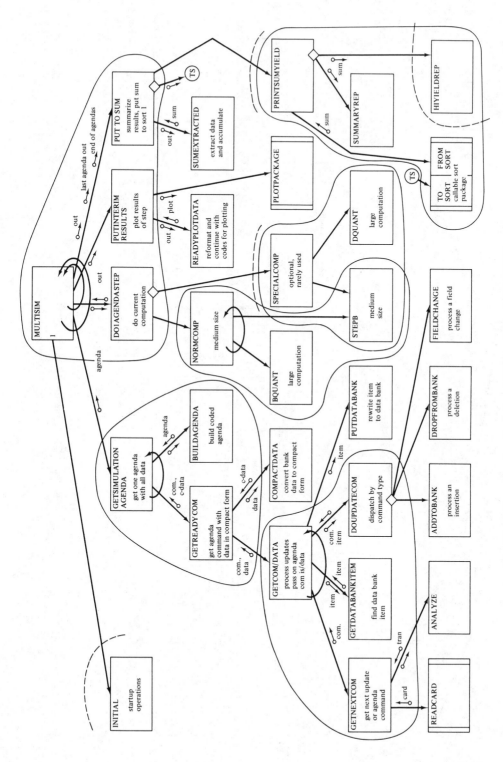

Fig. 14.4 Procedural analysis for packaging of the MULTISIM system.

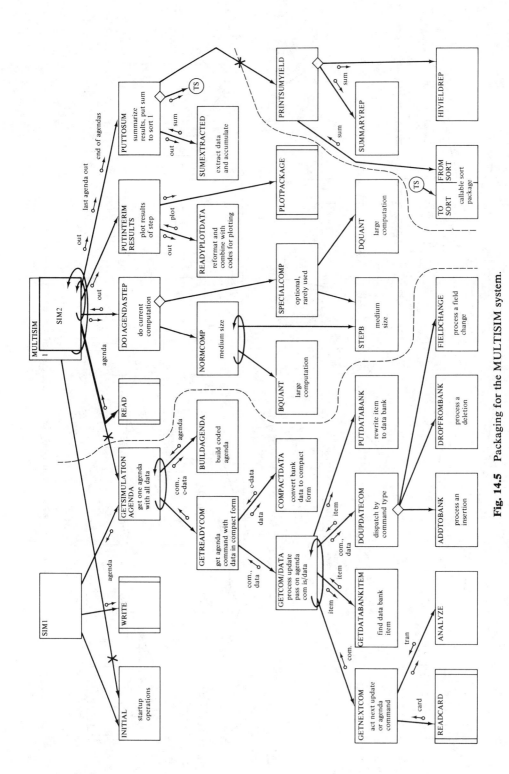

Fig. 14.5 Packaging for the MULTISIM system.

the highest-priority groupings are the ones headed by GETCOM/DATA and NORM-COMP. The ultimate enclosure of both these subsystems in nested loops within MULTISIM suggests a single large program; but what if together the two subsystems exceed memory limitations? The procedural analysis indicates the preferred point of separation to be between GETSIMULATIONAGENDA and MULTISIM. This cannot be done without reprogramming (really, alterations in the procedural design); the question is, how much? Fig. 14.5 suggests a realistic compromise that creates three main programs: SIM1, SIM2, and PRINTSUMYIELD. The soundness of the highly factored design is proven in the minor clerical nature of the changes that would be required. Indeed, SIM2 differs from MULTISIM only in dropping the call to INITIAL and in substituting a call to an input routine for the original call to GET-SIMULATIONAGENDA.

The declarations for PUTSUMYFIELD will be different if it is to be a main rather than a subordinate program and if the call to it is omitted from PUTTOSUM. SIM1 constitutes new coding required by the packaging, not the problem, but even it is a mere clerical procedure, a trivial subprogram. Most, perhaps 95 percent, of the original design has been preserved. A problem is posed by making SPECIAL-COMP a callable subprogram. If STEPB is another callable subprogram that is designed to be used from both load units, and much-used NORMCOMP inner loop could be significantly slowed. However, the alternative is two copies.

Until performance statistics lead us into a post-development optimization (to be described in Chapter 15), the simpler option of a callable subprogram would be the choice. In COBOL or a similar language, all other subroutines might be packaged as PERFORMed SECTIONS at some loss in modularity due to the required pathological communication; thirty normally communicating callable subprograms in this size application would very likely be far too costly both in storage and in execution overhead.

The chosen packaging requires an intermediate file (the coded agendums) of small size and moderate complexity. Disk storage might be ideal for this purpose. The first pass, SIM1, is essentially an update and proofing run to generate ready-to-simulate agendums; error detection and processing have been omitted to simplify the structure for expository purposes. The addition of a listing of the finalized agendums that are written to the intermediate file would make it more practical to use SIM1 and SIM2 separately.

How did we fare? Compare our packaging to the conventional one shown in Fig. 14.6, which a systems analyst drew up based on the problem description. The division into runs in Fig. 14.6 is absolutely standard. Because it was based on presumptions about what form the solution *should* take rather than a thorough understanding of the functional structure, each full use of the traditional system will be *more expensive* than each use of our packaged structured design by (1) about 300 disk search-and-reads; (2) two passes (write and read) on 600 uncompressed rather than compressed agenda items; (3) two passes (write and read) on the 600 item output file; (4) sorting of 600 instead of 200 items; and, if one includes as a feature of the conventional design the standard use of a separate sort program op-

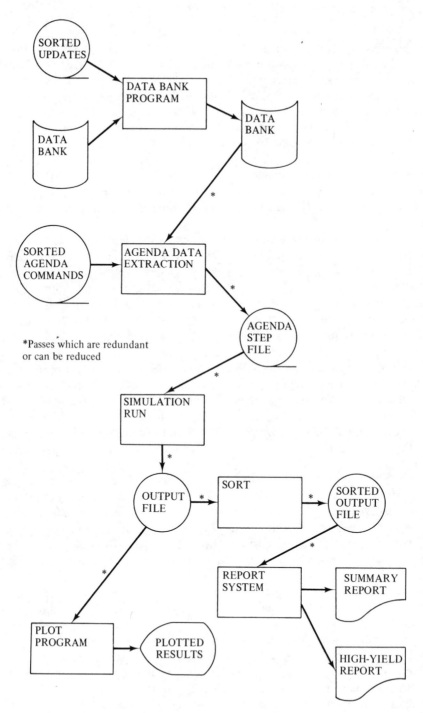

*Passes which are redundant
or can be reduced

Fig. 14.6 Systems flow or conventional packaging for the
MULTISIM system.

erating from and to files instead of a callable sort subsystem with first and last pass own coding, (5) three passes on 600 items being sorted.

It *might* be possible for a sharp and unconventional systems analyst doing prepackaging to come up with our system, but how much easier and more likely is the identification of efficient packages after complete structural design. Finally, it should be obvious that a repackaging of the structure of Fig. 14.3 to have the same intermediate file structure as the traditional packaging would be trivial were this deemed necessary or desirable, but it is not likely that the programs of the traditional design could be easily transformed from five separate runs into a single nest of subroutines!

14.3 SUMMARY

In general, we attempt to satisfy mechanical restrictions on memory size or execution time through packaging, rather than through modular structure. This helps us maintain the discipline of a highly modular system through the design phase of a project, and allows us to maximize such worthy design goals as maintainability and modifiability. As a rule, this *can* be done. Indeed, experience indicates that packaging done in this manner leads to significantly more efficient and more manageable systems than when packaging precedes and guides the structural design.

This is a more significant point than it may seem at first. In many organizations, packaging is done by the systems analyst — not by the *designer*. This means that the sequence of steps in such organizations is often: packaging first, flowcharting second, and structural design (of the most primitive sort) last. This frequently leads to a proliferation of intermediate files that are passed back and forth between the various load units specified by the analyst. The problem is aggravated by the fact that some systems analysts are obsolete technicians. Thus, in the late 1970's, analysts still specify a new payroll system consisting of an edit package, an update package, a sort package, and several report-writing packages — with intermediate tape files passed between the various packages. Why? Because that's the way analysts accomplished the job in the early 1960's on an IBM 1401 — and if it worked then, it should work now!

It is difficult to impress upon many such analysts that they currently are working with a fourth-generation computer that has four million bytes of physical memory, plus the sophistication of virtual memory and a vast array of drums, disks, and other fast storage devices. In many cases, the entire system could be implemented as one load unit, with all data passed through memory in the form of arguments to modules. In any case, we cannot overemphasize that packaging should be done as a last step in the structural design — *not* as the first step!

REFERENCE

1. J.C. EMERY, "Modular Data Processing Systems in COBOL," *Communications of the ACM*, Vol. 5, No. 5 (May 1962).

Optimization
of
Modular Systems

CHAPTER 15

15.0 INTRODUCTION

As its title makes clear, this chapter is devoted to the optimization of modular program systems. The authors' decision to discuss optimization in Chapter 15, three fourths of the way through the book, was deliberate: Optimization is something that should be considered *after* the system has been designed, and should not be an influence on the design process itself. It is demonstrably cheaper to develop a simple working system, and speed it up, than to design a fast system and then try to make it work. The savings possible by delaying optimization are even greater when the design is highly factored and uncoupled. At the same time, it is appropriate that the chapter be placed in the section on pragmatics: Many systems do *have* to be optimized to reduce their use of CPU time, memory, use of peripheral devices, or other limited systems resources.

The previous chapter on *packaging* discussed techniques for developing reasonably efficient systems within given memory contraints. However, this chapter assumes that such a priori techniques may not have been sufficient — i.e., we still may be dealing with a daily system that requires 25 hours of computer time.

Therefore, the primary emphasis in this chapter will be on the reduction of CPU time, since that is still the most precious of systems resources in the majority of organizations. Several of the techniques can be applied, with some modification, to the optimization of disk accesses, I/O channel usage, and so on.

Before discussing the techniques themselves, we will discuss some impor-. tant philosophies of optimization. Those readers who feel they understand the proper role of optimization in systems development are free to skip the next section to get to the meat of the chapter. However, even the battle-scarred veteran is advised to reread these statements of "apple pie and motherhood" to reinforce the discipline that so often slips away in a real-world project.

15.1 PHILOSOPHIES OF OPTIMIZATION

An interesting paradox comes to light in most discussions about the optimization of modular systems: Many programmer/analysts are convinced that the techniques discussed in this book contribute significantly to the inefficiency of their systems, yet they have no idea *how much*. A few crude experiments suggest that a highly modular system usually requires 5–10 percent more memory and CPU time than do systems implemented in the traditonal fashion; on the other hand, there have been occasions when modular systems have been considerably *more* efficient than classical systems.

To make an accurate statement about the overhead and inefficiency of modular systems, we would need an experiment with several thousand pairs of identical twins — with one twin of each pair developing a highly structured modular system, and the other twin developing the same system with the classical approach. Lacking the resources for such an experiment, we are content to use the rough approximation of 5–10 percent for the overhead of the modular approach.

The estimate of 5–10 percent is small enough that many EDP professionals would prefer to ignore it — particularly in light of the overhead associated with modern operating systems, data base management systems, teleprocessing monitors, and other vendor-supplied software packages. However, in a large number of real-world computer systems, optimization is a serious business —proper tuning of a system can save an organization millions of dollars. Similarly, there are still many real-time systems — particularly on the growing number of minicomputer and microcomputer systems — in which each microsecond of computer time is critically important. Nevertheless, optimization should be discussed from a rational point of view: Not *every* microsecond of computer time has to be optimized! The following philosophies are important for us to keep in mind as we discuss the optimization techniques in the subsequent sections of this chapter.

15.1.1 The efficiency of a system depends on the competence of the designer

There is not much point in talking about efficient systems or optimization if the system is being designed and/or programmed by people of only mediocre talent. Of course, this is a rather sensitive issue. One's ego makes it difficult to deal with one's own mediocrity, and one's manners make it difficult to accuse colleagues of mediocrity. Nevertheless, it is a fact that should be faced squarely: A surprisingly large number of analyst/designers design *stupid* systems, and an even larger number of programmers write horribly *stupid* code.

These are blunt words, to be sure. However, a classic study by Sackman et al.[1] pointed out that, among *experienced* programmers, we can find a 25:1 difference in design time and debugging time. Equally disturbing is the fact that the resulting code can vary in speed and size by a factor of ten. The most depressing fact of all was that Sackman's study indicated that there was no correlation between programming performance and scores on programming aptitude tests. H.L. Mencken observed that nobody ever went broke underestimating the intelligence of the American public. After visiting programming organizations around the country, the authors have concluded, somewhat sadly, that a similar statement could be made about programmers and designers.

Our point is simple: There is no substitute for competence. If you want a system designed and implemented efficiently, make sure it is done by people who know what they are doing — which, by the way, has very little to do with the number of years they have been working in the computer field!

15.1.2 In many cases, the simple way is the efficient way

A number of programmers take it for granted that efficiency in a computer program only can be achieved with intricate, sophisticated, obscure techniques and language statements. Thus, the assembly language programmer feels obligated to use instructions with multilevel indirect addressing (with indexing at the same time, of course!) in order to achieve an efficient program; the PL/I programmer feels compelled to use built-in functions that probably have never been used by anyone else in his organization; the FORTRAN programmer and the COBOL programmer may feel equally obliged to indulge in programming tricks that are beyond the ken of their vendor's software representatives.

All of these sophisticated statements have their place, but many programmers have found that such sophistication can gobble up large amounts of CPU time and memory. Quite often, the simple statements are the most efficient. More important, the simple modular *structures* often are far more efficient than the rat's-nest structures. One of the authors had the opportunity to observe a large rat's-nest payroll system with serious efficiency problems. Analysis showed that, among other things, the system recomputed the payroll tax for each of the 100,000 employees each time it was executed. Since the tax algorithm was a third-degree polynomial involving only the employee's salary, there was no need to recompute it unless the employee's salary changed — and the unnecessary recalculation wasted a large amount of computer time when applied to 100,000 people! A simple modular design probably would have made it perfectly obvious that the computation needed to be done only once.*

The point that we are making is that a simple system does only what it has to do, without any wasted or redundant motion. A large, disorganized rat's-nest system frequently performs the same computations multiple times, or performs computations totally irrelevant to the task at hand — all because the structure is so complex that the designer could not see what was happening.

15.1.3 Only a small part of a typical system has any impact on overall efficiency

Many a programmer has been heard to mutter, "Jeez, 90 percent of the code in this system deals with exceptions!" Perhaps the most dramatic example of this phenomenon comes from AT&T's Business Information System. It is estimated that 98 percent of the modules in that vast system consume less than one second *per year* of execution time. Similarly, Knuth's classic study[3] indicated that approximately 5 percent of the code in a typical program consumes approximately 50 percent of its execution time.

From this viewpoint, it is obvious that the way to win the game of efficiency is to find that critical 5 percent and optimize the hell out of it! The problem is that we don't know which 5 percent of the code will be the critical 5 percent *until after we have implemented the system and put it into production.* Of course, it will be obvious from the beginning that certain portions of the system will be executed frequently. Nevertheless, it usually is true that the run-time behavior of the system is quite different from the designer's expectations. Thus, we often see a programmer/analyst gather run-time statistics on his system, and then exclaim, "I can't believe that the system is spending 50 percent of its time in *that* module!"

15.1.4 Simple modular systems can be optimized easily

Throughout this book, we have stressed that highly modular systems have the advantage of being easily maintained and modified. It is worth noting that optimization is a kind of modification: We have to modify the code within individual modules, or possibly modify the structure of the complete system, in order to improve its efficiency. Thus, it is entirely appropriate to the theme of this book to suggest that a modular system should be optimized more easily than a monolithic system. In a system with high cohesion and low coupling, we should be able to

---

* This was only one of several inefficiencies in the system. A redesigned version of the payroll system ultimately reduced the run-time by approximately four hours out of a nine-hour run on a Honeywell 8200 computer. For more discussion of this interesting project, see Yourdon.[2]

change the code in one module without creating any adverse effects in another module. If the overall structure of the system is simple and well documented, then we easily should be able to make structural changes (of the sort discussed in Section 15.3).

15.1.5 Overemphasis on optimization tends to detract from other design goals

As we have stated, a great deal of optimization can be accomplished simply and easily. However, a number of programmers tend to be fanatics when it comes to efficiency: Every possible byte of memory must be pruned. If taken too far, this fanaticism has serious adverse consequences. The code within modules becomes too complicated for mere mortals to maintain, and the coupling between modules becomes too complex for even an Einstein. Indeed, the fanatical approach to optimization often backfires. In an attempt to optimize a system by introducing complex flags and sophisticated instructions, the programmer sometimes ends up with a *less* efficient system.

These problems are much more serious if they occur during the design process. Once the system has been designed and built, the natural "firewalls" of modularity will tend to minimize the negative effects (in terms of maintainability) caused by fanatical optimization. However, if the designer is strongly influenced by optimization during the design phase, the overall modularity of the system probably will suffer significantly. It is likely that the resulting system will have high coupling and low cohesion. Its modular structure may bear very little relationship to the inherent problem structure.

15.1.6 Optimization is irrelevant if the program doesn't work

It may seem facetious to suggest that an efficient program with a bug is less valuable than a somewhat inefficient program with no bugs. However, the authors have found it quite difficult to impress this upon some supposedly professional programmers and analysts. Actually, our point is a bit less trite: Optimizing a system usually requires a large amount of time and energy — especially since the optimization of code affords the programmer an excellent chance to introduce new bugs into the system!

Hence, it would appear that the best strategy is to get the system working first — even if it is inefficient. Users may howl and complain about the inefficiency, but they will be happier with a slow system that works than with a fast system that isn't finished. Besides, the system may not turn out to be inefficient after all! Or it may take such a small amount of computer time that nobody really cares whether the system could be optimized. *If* the system turns out to be large and time-consuming, and *if* there are indications that it could be optimized, *then* the programmer can work on the problem.

15.2 AN APPROACH TO OPTIMIZATION OF MODULES

If our system needs to be optimized, there are two ways of approaching the problem: optimizing the code within modules, or changing the overall structure of the system to improve its performance. We will discuss the former in this section; the techniques of structural changes for efficiency will be discussed in Section 15.3.

The specific techniques for optimizing code within a module are largely outside the scope of this book. We know that optimizing compilers are becoming increasingly significant. If so directed, the compilers can produce object code that is optimized for memory and/or CPU time. In addition, several vendor-supplied proprietary packages are capable of examining the object code produced by compilers in an attempt to eliminate unnecessary instructions. We also can use a variety of hardware monitors and performance measurement packages to help determine where a module is spending its time — i.e., to find the critical 5 percent that we discussed earlier. Finally, we know that most programming textbooks and vendor-supplied programming manuals devote entire sections of the devious tricks for writing the world's most optimal code. Since these tricks are highly machine-dependent, language-dependent, and vendor-dependent, and since they are constantly changing, it would be inadvisable to deal with the subject, even in a general way, in this book.

However, we can suggest an organized plan of attack, first published by Constantine,[4] for optimizing the code within modules of a large system. Our approach is based on our belief that most code (recall the 5 percent phenomenon) is not worth optimizing because it contributes very little to the total system overhead; nevertheless, we probably will have to continue optimizing modules until our systems have achieved some reasonable measure of efficiency. Thus, we need a way of assigning priorities to modules from the point of view of optimization. Any organized plan will suffice; however, the following approach has been used successfully by the authors in a number of projects:

1. *Determine the execution time for each module or load unit.* The hardware monitors and the performance measurement packages mentioned previously should be adequate for this step; lacking these, the programmer/analyst should be able to build his own instrumentation. Note that this is not a process of estimation as was done for the packaging strategy in Chapter 14: We are capturing *actual* statistics from a *real* system. For simplicity, we will refer to the execution time of the ith module in the system as T_i.

2. *Examine each module to estimate potential improvement.* This step *must* involve estimation unless the programmer wishes to recode each module to see how much improvement can be achieved. While it is thus an art, it depends upon the programmer's knowledge of his language, his operating system, and his hardware — as well as upon his

ability to perceive better implementations of the module. It should be obvious that this estimation process is made more accurate when dealing with small, independent modules. We will refer to the estimated potential fractional improvement in the execution time of the ith module in the system as I_i.

3. *Estimate the cost involved in making the improvement.* By cost, we mean programmer/analyst salaries, computer test-time, and other costs that might be involved in producing a new, optimized version of the module. Clearly, this is only an estimate, and its accuracy will depend on the ability of the programmer/analyst to forecast such work. It should be clear, once again, that the estimating process has a better chance of being accurate when we are dealing with small, independent modules. We will refer to the dollars-cost of making an improvement to the ith module in the system as C_i.

4. *Establish priorities for making improvements to modules.* We will refer to the priority of the ith module in the system, from the viewpoint of selecting it to be optimized, as P_i. From the discussion above, we see that we can rank the priorities in the following manner:

$$P_i = A \times I_i \times T_i - B \times C_i$$

where A and B are appropriate weighting factors.

5. *Optimize the modules with the highest priority.* The priority scheme is intended to help the designer optimize those modules from which he will realize the largest improvement in machine efficiency for the smallest amount of work. It may be entirely uneconomical to make a 50 percent improvement in the run-time of a module if it is going to take three person-years of effort.

The priority-ranking scheme listed above probably would indicate that it is not worth the effort to improve the efficiency of a module by 50 percent if it uses only three milliseconds of computer time. Note that our ranking scheme not only indicates the optimization priority of one module relative to another; it also indicates that certain modules may have a *negative* optimization priority (depending on the selection of weighting factors A and B). That is, it may indicate situations in which the cost of making an improvement to the module exceeds the savings in reduced execution time. In such cases, we are clearly better off leaving the module alone.

15.3 STRUCTURAL CHANGES FOR EFFICIENCY

In a small number of cases, optimization within module boundaries may not be sufficient to achieve the desired level of efficiency. It then may be necessary to modify the structure of the system. Before indulging in this kind of optimization, it is important that the designer identify the source of the inefficiency: Even though the structural modifications discussed in this section are relatively straightforward, one does not want to go through them needlessly. Thus, it is important that the designer gather statistics concerning intermodule transitions (e.g., subroutine calls and passing of parameters) as well as statistics concerning intramodule execution time (as suggested in Section 15.2).

It is interesting to note that the intermodule transition-time statistics probably are easier to capture than are statistics for execution time within each module. Indeed, the cost (or overhead) of subroutine calls often is published by the vendors of selected operating systems, programming languages, and computer hardware.

Fortunately there is only a small set of structural modifications that make noticeable improvements in execution speed (and perhaps, in memory). We will discuss each in the subsections that follow.

15.3.1 Macros or lexically included code

Before looking into actual changes in the structure of the system, the designer should consider changes in module *type* which preserve module *structure*. In particular, the designer should remember that macros and subroutines represent trade-offs of execution speed versus memory. The "transmission" of parameters to a macro is accomplished during compilation time or assembly time, and context-switching (otherwise known as prologue/epilogue, or more simply as the saving and restoring of the machine) may be optimized by the compiler/assembler. Also, since the macro body becomes part of the lexically superordinate sequence of code, any optimization of hardware registers applied by the compiler within the sequence of code also should be applied across the macro-subordinate boundary. Finally, if the module is referenced only once or a few times in the structure, or has a small body compared to the prologue/epilogue, the use of macros probably will save *both* execution time and memory: Argument transmission, context-switching, and other types of intermodule overhead consume memory as well as CPU time.

15.3.2 Pancake structures

A general rule is that deep structures* have more overhead than broad, shallow structures. However, the exceptions are so numerous and so subtle that it is never safe to apply this rule indiscriminately. Only after analysis reveals that the inefficiency of a given system may be resolved by "flattening" or "pancaking" the structure can techniques for doing so be applied.

Let us consider, as an example, a structure of two levels. These two levels

---

* Recall the definition of depth in our discussion of systems morphologies in Chapter 8: The depth of a system is the number of levels in its hierarchical module structure.

consist of a control module and its subordinates. Each call to a subordinate module represents some overhead; when these are imbedded in an iterative control structure, the cumulative overhead can indeed be substantial. If the procedural logic in the superordinate is not very complex, a structure of this type can be converted to one homologous* level joined by unconditional transfers. Thus, in Fig. 15.1a, a simple endless loop is transformed into the structure of Fig. 15.1b, in which each module simply transfers directly to the next step. Note that this process implants in GETC, COMPI, NEWM, and REPU elements of the overall task once realized by DOINU. Thus, the GO TO COMPI which must appear in GETC has nothing whatsoever to do with the function GETC. Such pancaked structures always result in some reduction in cohesion as well as some increase in coupling.

Pancaking to a homologous structure works for two reasons. First, unconditional transfers generally can be implemented with much greater efficiency in most languages and operating systems than can conditioned transfers (e.g., subroutine calls). Second, there are few intermodule transitions involved in the homol-

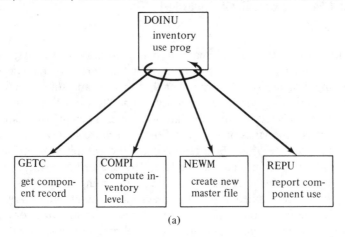

(a)

Fig. 15.1a   Hierarchical structure.

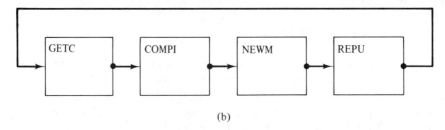

(b)

Fig. 15.1b   Pancaked homologous structure with coordinating procedure imbedded in modules.

* Homologous systems are discussed in greater detail in Chapter 18. For now, they may be defined loosely as non-hierarchical systems — that is, systems in which control and data do not flow strictly up and down in the hierarchy.

ogous structure.   For example, the hierarchical structure of Fig. 15.1a requires eight intermodule transitions for each iteration of the loop; the homologous structure of Fig. 15.1b requires four.

Pancaking to an equivalent, flat, hierarchical structure from a deeply nested one is much less likely to improve efficiency, because the above reasons do not apply. The conversion shown in Fig. 15.2 may, however, be the first step in an ultimate conversion to a homologous structure.   In some cases, a few modules disappear in the process of pancaking as shown in Fig. 15.2.   This will happen when modules in a fully factored hierarchy consist only of code to coordinate the subordinate modules.

15.3.3 Compression

The most ubiquitous of all structural manipulations to improve efficiency might be called "demodularization," since it consists of compressing all of one module (or, less often, part of one module) into another.   In the simplest possible case, this is done through lexical inclusion of the module, intact, in a superordinate.

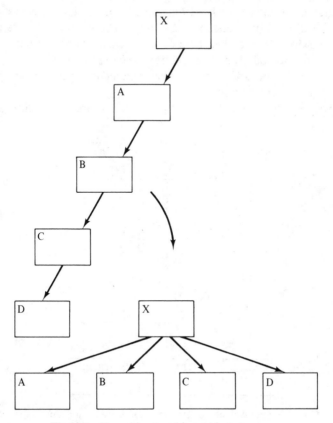

Fig 15.2   Pancaking to a hierarchical structure.

Depending on the programming language and the operating system, the gain in efficiency from this simple maneuver is likely to be marginal; it consists of the difference in overhead between a call to a lexically included subordinate, and a call to an external subordinate.

The subordinate code may be imbedded in the superordinate code with the boundary elements removed and the linkage elements removed or simulated. If the body of the subordinate is actually copied in-line at each point where the superordinate previously contained a subroutine call, then there may be an increased memory requirement; obviously, the analysis is similar to that required for macros. If we intend to include only one copy of the body of the subordinate module, some substitute for subordination may be used to force the one copy to function in several contexts. The most popular substitute is a switch mechanism.

The effect of compression — even of the simplest form — varies tremendously, depending on whether the compression is accomplished before or after the system has been implemented. For example, the compound module AB, defined by the compression of B into its superordinate A, may be implemented with the code for A and the code for B intermingled — perhaps not even distinctly identifiable as A and B. If this takes place during the implementation of the system, then it is possible that separate uses of B within A will not be recognized as such — and each use of B will be solved, coded, and debugged separately. While there would appear to be no duplicated coding (the code for each use of B differs, and may be intermingled with the code for A in different ways), this obviously is an illusion. The possibility of this occurring is a further argument for optimization as a post-design or post-implementation process.

As we can see in Fig. 15.3, compression upward and compression down-

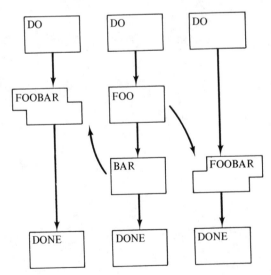

Fig. 15.3 Equivalence of upward compression and downward compression of whole modules.

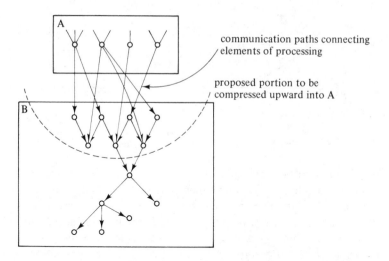

Fig. 15.4   Partial compression upward to reduce communication.

ward are equivalent when the entire module is involved. Most manipulations for efficiency involve compression downward in the hierarchy, as the goal is to reduce the number of intermodule transitions. Upward compression usually is only indicated when communication paths may be reduced or eliminated. For example, upward compression might improve the efficiency of the structure shown in Fig. 15.4. The meaning of such a move would have to be carefully considered: The "function" resulting from the compression might be meaningless. Furthermore, structures that have high cohesion and low coupling generally are fairly efficient to begin with — so upward compression is seldom necessary or successful.

Lateral compression is analogous to the pancaking discussed earlier. It combines two or more (procedurally) adjacent subordinates into a single module. As illustrated in Fig. 15.5, this is equivalent to partial extraction of the coordination procedure from the superordinate (FOO), plus two (or more) complete upward compressions. Here again, the aim is to reduce the overhead of subordinations.

15.3.4 Changing communication techniques

A great deal of the overhead in intermodule transitions is involved in the passing of data; consequently, some of the most popular optimization techniques involve minimizing the passing of such data. For example, if a data element is used in only one module — generally a low-level element is used in only one module — the designer may wish to *change* the communication of that element from a normal scheme to a pathological scheme. The ramifications of pathological communications were discussed extensively in Chapter 13. As we saw, one of the designer's greatest concerns should be the possibility of future modifications to the system.

301

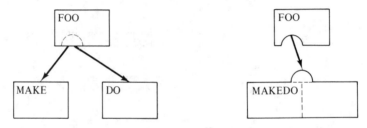

Fig. 15.5 Lateral compression of modules.

Wherever there are multiple uses of a module that receives or transmits some data pathologically, the designer may find that it is more efficient to switch from a pathological communication scheme to a normal communication scheme. This would also be the case if a data element was being transmitted pathologically to several different modules — a situation that we would not expect to occur in the course of normal structural design. Recall that normal communication most commonly involves passing of locators (addresses), while pathological communication usually involves passing of data. Thus, the size of a datum relative to the size of a locator can determine which mode is more efficient.

Another possibility is to change the communication from an intermediate file to an internal flow of data through primary memory. As we suggested in Chapter 14, unnecessary intermediate files are a common consequence of premature packaging by the analyst/designer. Thus, this form of optimization may simply be a rectification of a poor design decision. When packaging is done properly, the designer still may elect the use of intermediate files in order to make the system fit into a specified amount of memory; this usually means that various modules in the system will execute as overlays. Thus, optimization represents a trade-off between CPU time and memory. By expanding the available memory for the system, the designer makes it possible for all of the modules to reside in primary memory simultaneously — enabling them to transmit data through memory rather than through tape or disk files.

In several high-level programming languages — FORTRAN, COBOL, and PL/I in particular — another source of overhead is the conversion of data from one format to another. The superordinate module, for example, may transmit a floating point number as an argument, while the subordinate module may be expecting an integer as its argument. In some cases, the only question is whether this conversion should be performed explicitly (by the programmer) or implicitly (by the language or operating system); that is, it may turn out that the natural form of the data in the superordinate is the floating point, and the natural form of the data in the subordinate is integer. In many other cases, though, the conversion process is the result of laziness or sloppiness on the part of the designer — a phenomenon that unfortunately is encouraged by the features of many popular high-level programming languages.

In some cases, the designer also may increase the efficiency of his system by passing arguments by *value* rather than by *name*. "Call by name," as interpreted in most programming languages,* means that the *address* of a parameter is passed from the superordinate to the subordinate module; "call by value" means that the parameter itself is passed, usually through an accumulator or hardware register. For the subordinate module, the difference is one of addressing speed: The call-by-name approach requires an additional level of indirect addressing in order to access the parameters. The assembly language programmer obviously has the option of passing arguments by value or by name. In some implementations of FORTRAN, the programmer can specify that certain parameters in a subroutine parameter list be passed by value. In all implementations of COBOL known to the authors, all parameters in a CALL XYZ USING . . . . statement are passed by name.

15.3.5 Recoding

An option that the designer/programmer should always keep in the back of his mind is that selected, independent modules can be recorded into more efficient language. We can imagine, for example, that certain portions of a commercial application may involve extensive computations; the appropriate modules could be recoded in FORTRAN. Similarly, we can imagine that various input-output operations would be more efficiently coded in assembly language. Indeed, we can even imagine recoding various modules in microcode if efficiency requirements are particularly stringent.

The danger here is that many designers — and many programmers — have preconceived notions about the portions of their system that should be coded in a particular language. It is a common feeling, for example, that computational logic is highly inefficient in COBOL, and that input-output logic is highly inefficient in any high-level programming language. While this may be true, we must remember that we are only concerned about the efficiency of a module relative to other modules in the system. The fact that a module's processing time can be cut in half is probably irrelevant if the module's current processing time accounts for only 0.0001 percent of the total processing time of the system.

15.3.6 Analysis

Experience has shown the value of actually drawing structural changes and considering their consequences incrementally. Visual devices that suggest the nature of what is changing — such as Figs. 15.3 and 15.5 — are very useful. The structure chart is an extremely powerful tool in this regard. After each manipulation of the structure, a careful analysis should be performed to see what actual, demonstrable gains in efficiency and what probable sacrifices in modularity have been made. It often is possible to see what kind of future changes will be more

---

* We will not concern ourselves here with the subtle distinctions between "call by name," "call by reference," and "call by value" in such languages as ALGOL.

difficult and which procedures will be more complicated to debug and maintain as a result of the optimization.

15.4 SUMMARY

We have tried to make several points in this chapter. Perhaps the most important is that efficiency is something that must be considered in the proper perspective — that is, efficiency means more than just recoding a module to save a few microseconds. As we have pointed out, such optimization is irrelevant if the system doesn't work; and since it is becoming more and more difficult to make our complex EDP systems work, we believe that the emphasis should be shifted from optimization to development of correct systems. At the same time, we observe that highly modularized systems usually are easier to optimize than monolithic rat's-nest systems.

Most optimization can be accomplished in the simple manner suggested in this chapter. An analysis of the system will determine where the greatest improvements in efficiency can be achieved for the least cost, and will dictate which module(s) should be recoded. Only if this approach proves inadequate should the designer consider changing the *structure* of the system to gain efficiency.

REFERENCES

1. H.H. SACKMAN, W.J. ERICKSON, and E.E. GRANT, "Exploratory Studies Comparing On-Line and Off-Line Programming Performance," *Communications of the ACM,* January 1968, pp. 3–11.

2. EDWARD YOURDON, "A Case in Structured Programming: Redesign of a Payroll System," *Proceedings of the 1975 IEEE Computer Society Conference,* Institute of Electrical and Electronics Engineers, IEEE Cat. No. 75CHO988-6C. New York: 1975, pp. 119–122.

3. DONALD E. KNUTH, "A Empirical Study of FORTRAN Programs," *Software — Practice and Experience,* Vol. 1, No. 2 (April-June 1971), pp. 105–133.

4. LARRY L. CONSTANTINE, "A Modular Approach to Program Optimization," *Computers and Automation,* Vol. 16, No. 3 (May 1967).

Many problems, indeed broad classes of problems, become significantly simpler to eliminate when conventional modules are employed in slightly unconventional structural arrangements, or when subroutines are replaced by less familiar types of modules. This section, destined to be one of the most controversial, extends structured design beyond the status quo. In Chapter 16, a typology is developed not only to encompass existing module types but also to highlight areas for future development of novel kinds of modules having highly desirable features. Recursive structures are discussed in Chapter 17 as a special case in structured design. One implication of this discussion is that recursion may be of broader utility than previously assumed by most designers.

Chapter 18 defines and explores, in detail, two exotic types of modules, the coroutine and the subcoroutine. Used appropriately, these modules permit the decoupling of modules more completely from one another, and can eliminate many of the problems associated with state maintenance in nested subroutines.

Substantial payoffs can result from adding to the designer's tool kit for the relatively simple mechanisms that are suggested in this section. We are convinced that some of these apparently offbeat proposals will become standard in the near future.

V

EXTENSIONS

A Typology
of
Systems Components

CHAPTER 16

16.0 INTRODUCTION

When modularity is first introduced, one frequently hears, "Oh, you mean using subroutines." It is true that the subroutine is the most ubiquitous type of module within computer systems; fortunately, it is not the *only* type! In fact, there is a whole array of modules available to the designer/programmer. Not to make full use of this array is to do oneself a disservice.

By "type" of module, we are not referring to *function*. A complete functional clasification of modules would be difficult — and the exercise would have very little value if it were not exhaustive. Establishing functional categories of modules — e.g., inputting, calculating, housekeeping, and so on — and then saying that modules in the same category are of the same type is analogous to saying that bolts, rivets, and glue spots are the same because they are used to fasten. Such a distinction between "fasteners" and "members" may be important at some point, but we are more interested now in distinguishing bolts from rivets and in determining the relative merits of each in various functional applications.

The designer obviously should know of the existence of bolts and rivets, and should be able to tell one from the other when he gets hit by one. More important, though, he should be able to select the best one for a given purpose. He should know and understand the problems unique to each type. He should know that a bolt is different from a rivet even if both are being used (are functioning) as paperweights. The designer should be able to recognize a nutless bolt held in place by its peen as a special case — a bolt used as a rivet.

An analogous physical classification of modules for computer systems is more difficult for several reasons. We cannot point to a module and describe its shape or color. Size is no help, either: Some subroutines are larger than other programs. Furthermore, the software field has generated a thick fog of jargon, which confuses the issue. Is a PL/I "procedure" the same as an ALGOL "procedure"? Always? One need not have much experience in the field to assume that a FORTRAN "function-type subprogram" and an ALGOL procedure are essentially the same thing. Sometimes, the same word denotes different types of modules, and sometimes the same module is called different names. Every computer manufacturer and language developer seems to create his own unnecessary jargon. How can we penetrate the fog of jargon and objectively classify modules?

16.1 ACTIVATION CHARACTERISTICS

The idea of distinguishing modules by their control or activation characteristics was first suggested by Wegner.[1] When refined, this approach not only provides an objective basis for classifying modules, but also suggests lines for the development of new types of modules.

While other schemes are certainly possible, a three-dimensional characterization of activation and control has proven useful. This involves three (possibly interdependent) factors: time, mechanism of activation, and pattern of control flow. Modules that differ in any one dimension can be regarded as different module types, while modules that are identical in these dimensions are the same type — regardless of the jargon with which they are surrounded.

16.1.1 Time-history

We first introduced the concept of a system's time-history in our discussion of intermodular connections in Chapter 6. A specific module performing a given operation on particular data may become part of the control or activation stream at any point in the system's time-history, although most modules become part of the activation stream at execution time. A "definition-time" module must become part of the activation stream and have its contents and data context determined at the time the programmer writes the code. Obviously, such a module is in-line. The hand-tailored, in-line, unnamed macro-like block that the programmer copies into his code from another source is an example of a definition-time module. We call a module a *segment*.

16.1.2 Activation mechanism

The basic nature or behavior of the mechanism by which a module is activated is another dimension for distinguishing modules. Within this dimension, basic elements have been identified.

The *source* of activation — that is, who does (or can) activate a module — often determines the type of module. Two activation sources are relevant: the *operating environment* and *other modules*. These sources may activate a module synchronously — that is, by explicit command; alternatively, a module may be activated asynchronously — that is, by a signal (trap) or interrupt. Modules activated by an unbroken chain of explicit commands are said to be in the *base load;* those activated by an interrupt are said to be "interrupt modules" or in the *interrupt load,* as are the modules they activate. Clearly, a module may be in both the base load and the interrupt load.

A *conditioned transfer* is a jump out of the current execution sequence with the condition that control eventually be returned to the execution sequence from which the jump was made. The conditioned transfer establishes the mechanism for this return. A conditioned transfer always refers to a target location *explicitly* (by name, address, or other identifier). A *return* always transfers to the location of an instruction in the sequence associated with the most recently conditioned transfer for which a return has not yet been made. Thus, the pattern of conditioned transfers and returns always defines a fully nested set of activations. Such a system is hierarchical since the conditioned transfer establishes its origin as a sequence superordinate to (having control over) the target sequence. Mechanisms for implementing conditioned transfers and returns, as we have defined them here, are numerous and will not concern us now.

A transfer also may be unconditioned — that is, carrying no tacit condition of return. Uncondition*ed* (which could be condition*al*, that is, based on the outcome of a decision; or uncondition*al*) transfers give up responsibility completely; hence, they do not define a hierarchy of subordination. Rather than giving up control (in either a conditioned or unconditioned fashion), the activation of a module sometimes establishes a new control stream, activating the module as a parallel or coordination process. This creation of a separate control stream may be realized either with genuine parallel processing (i.e., with multiprocessing hardware) or with simulated parallel processing (i.e., with the assistance of a multitasking or multiprogramming operating system). The general term *bifurcated transfer* ("forking" transfer) will be used to cover either case.

16.1.3 Pattern of control flow

When activated, most modules begin execution "at the beginning — that is, at the *origin* or (lexically) first executable statement. However, a module may begin execution at the point at which operation was last suspended — and that will be called its *reentry*. A module that begins execution at its reentry, or picks up where it left off, will be called an *incremental module*. Such a module may perform its task incrementally — that is, a portion at a time, one part on each activation. Clearly, incremental and nonincremental modules have very distinct patterns of control flow. Note that the general case (more powerful) is that of incremental execution. Without resorting to programming tricks, an incremental module can be made to function nonincrementally simply by following (lexically) each transfer out of the module with an instruction to transfer to its origin. We will discuss incremental modules in more detail in Chapter 18.

A module may reference another module, not to activate it but rather to check its progress, guarantee completion of a certain point, or otherwise fall in step. This synchronization changes the pattern of control flow; hence, we distinguish *synchronized* (note, *not* synchronous) modules from unsynchronized ones. Any mechanism — a switch, a flag, an "event variable" as in PL/I — may be used to implement synchronizing references. In its strictest sense, the referencing module is the synchronizing module, and the referenced module is the synchronized module (or the other way around in some schools). The point is that synchronized modules, being different animals (or rivets), have their own design problems.

16.1.4 Terminology

The combinations of characteristics in these three basic dimensions yield many different types of modules. Not all have names or are even useful. Figure 16.1 identifies those module types with established names. They also are the most important physically distinct types of modules. We can qualify those names with other factors, such as base-load or interrupt-load subroutines. These are different modules, with (somewhat) different design problems; the interrupt-load subroutine, for example, must be "transparent" and leave all working registers in their original state when it exits. If it makes sense, as with "conroutine," the qualifiers synchronized or unsynchronized may be appended.

The terminology itself warrants explanation. As we pointed out in the Preface, the bias in this book is to favor descriptive, single-word, nonconflicting terms. Whenever possible, common nouns with a broad meaning are not usurped for a narrow technical purpose. Exceptions depend on consistency and precedents in other fields. In Fig. 16.1, the terms in parentheses are less desirable names, even though they may be used fairly widely. In some cases, they are strongly associated with a particular language or a particular computer manufacturer. All of the modules shown in Fig. 16.1 are discussed in the section below, with the exception of subcoroutines, coroutines, and conroutines; these are discussed separately in Chapter 18.

Fig. 16.1 Module types.

Entry mode \ Execution Mode	Nonincremental			Incremental
	Definition time	Translation time	Execution time	
Conditioned				
From environment			PROGRAM (Main routine job step)	SUBCOROUTINE (Demand coroutine)
From modules	SEGMENT (Submodule)	MACRO (In-line or open subroutine	SUBROUTINE (Procedure, subprogram)	
Unconditioned			ROUTINE (Phase, transfer)	COROUTINE
Bifurcated			CONROUTINE (Task)	

16.2 COMMON TYPES OF MODULES

The most common modules are the nonincremental ones. Of those shown in Fig. 16.1, only one is not a module; a *segment* is a kind of "not quite" module. From the point of view of activation characteristics, a segment is a module whose code is copied in-line by the programmer. It is thus entered with condition but becomes part of the activation stream at definition time. Although this may seem a trivial or degenerate case, such an approach to modularity may be useful. A definition-time module may achieve some of the benefits of modularity (especially in terms of avoiding duplicated coding), while minimizing certain costs (notably CPU-time execution costs).

Consider a situation in which some very small function has been identified as being part of a dozen or more different larger tasks. It could be so small that the overhead of calling it substantially exceeds the useful work done by the function itself. If it is used many times, this overhead may be unacceptable. On the other

311

hand, leaving the task to each programmer of each module is a waste of human resources. Each programmer, whether he realized it or not, would be coding and debugging the same sequence as everyone else. Should this turn out to be a tricky and error-prone sequence of code, the cost of duplication could be significant. The hand-tailored segment is thus a good compromise solution. The common operation is coded and debugged once; thereafter, the body of code is copied in-line each time it is needed.

Although segments can be useful, various other forms of modules are far more common: subroutines, programs and functions, and macros. These are discussed in the three subsections that follow.

16.2.1 Subroutines

A subroutine is a module activated at execution time by a conditioned transfer. Its mode of execution is nonincremental. Any module that satisfies these requirements is a subroutine, regardless of its jargon name, provided we find it activated from the execution stream of another module. Two special cases may be distinguished: modules that are subroutines except for the fact that they are activated either by the operating environment or, secondly, from the evaluation stream. These are artificial distinctions, the consequences of which will be discussed in the next subsection.

From a control standpoint, COBOL paragraphs activated by the PERFORM verb are subroutines. So are ALGOL procedures and FORTRAN subroutine-type subprograms. Subroutines are by far the most common module for computer systems. Even languages that do not provide a linguistic mechanism for subroutine activation often provide a method for simulating it — such as the switch, or assigned transfer, features of some languages.

16.2.2 Programs and functions

Many programmers and analysts, who distinguish daily between programs and subroutines in practice, find it difficult to define the two in any rigorous fashion. The following are all common, but *inadequate,* definitions:

- Programs are larger than subroutines. (Clearly, this is not always true!) A program performs a complete function, while a subroutine performs only a partial one. (How is "cosine" any less complete than the first pass of a file update?)

- Subroutines are part of programs; programs include subroutines. (But a program need not have subroutines. "Include" is ambiguous here.)

In truth, the distinction between programs and subroutines is whatever the language/compiler/operating systems conventions make it. In most cases, subroutines are permitted to do certain things that programs are prohibited from doing, and vice versa. Subroutines, as a general rule, can accept arguments, while programs cannot. In many systems, a program can be executed by itself, but a subroutine cannot.

These restrictions lead to very real problems in building systems. In most environments, to implement modules as programs is to choose a dead-end design methodology. Generally, one cannot write a payroll program, then later choose to call it a subprocess in a corporate simulation system. Subroutines with arguments provide considerably more flexibility in this respect. In most second-generation systems, there was no way to imbed programs A, B, and C in a loop — much less have B conditionally executed depending on the value of some output from A. Third-generation systems with sophisticated job control languages represent somewhat of an improvement. However, few — if any — of the existing job control languages compare to the power and simplicity of the following:

```
DO I = 1 TO 23
    CALL A (IN,OUT);
    CALL C (10.2,1);
    IF OUT = 107.9 THEN
        CALL B (IN);
    ELSE
        CALL B (IN + 1)
END;
```

where A, B, and C are subroutines. It is this ability to build larger subroutines from calls on smaller subroutines — and still larger subroutines, in turn — that makes the subroutine so attractive as a basic systems building block.

In the final analysis, all that commonly distinguishes programs from subroutines is that programs are entered from the operating system. However it is implemented, the operating system activates a program (according to the particular job control instructions) with a conditioned transfer of control. It *always* is expected that control will be returned to the operating system's sequence. For a program to retain control clearly would be tantamount to disaster.

In the long run, it is to the advantage of the EDP profession to abolish all distinctions between programs and subroutines. The same module should be activated at the top level of a system, or as a subordinate, depending on the requirements of the task. The easiest approach to this problem is to banish programs by administrative fiat! Every system then could be developed as a subroutine with meaningful arguments. If the operating system is stubborn and will digest only programs, then a small program readily can be written that will do nothing but call a subroutine — a subroutine that is, in fact, the whole system.

The distinction that separates functions and subroutines, though leading to some mathematical elegance in certain proofs, is equally detrimental to software engineering. One way of drawing the line between functions and subroutines is to say that functions take on a value; more precisely, a particular activation of a function may take on a value. For example, the activation of the module sqrt takes on a value that is used in the evaluation (hence, the term "evaluation stream" at the end of the preceding subsection) of the expression

$$z = A + \text{sqrt}(x) - 1.2$$

In structural terms, this is merely a matter of the communication mechanism. Some modules — commonly called functions — are permitted to transmit an output value back to the superordinate without either the superordinate or the subordinate *naming* the value. Another common characteristic is that the functions are not allowed to return other outputs via arguments and parameters. However, this is unnecessary and undesirable.

The context in which a module gets activated implicitly as a result of an attempt to evaluate an expression may be called the evaluation stream. In most programming languages, it is easily — even rigorously — distinguished from the execution stream that flows from statement to statement. Thus, we might say that a function is a subroutine activated from the evaluation stream.

For the programmer who works as a designer and/or an implementer, it is desirable to be able to choose freely the manner in which output values are communicated. It is even useful to have modules only sometimes return values. Or, it might be useful to have the same module operate as a function or as a subroutine, depending on whether its value is of interest to the superordinate. While these abilities may make theoreticians shudder, they are trivial to implement, and they do not seem to be error-prone in use. All that is required is the ability to ignore a value, if assigned but not needed because of activation from the execution stream, and the ability to supply a value if one has not been assigned. The null case — in which a function value is needed but has not been assigned — may be handled by assigning standard default values, or by treating it as an error. A programmer-controlled choice is best.

16.2.3 Macros

Historically, subroutines were called "closed routines" or "off-line subroutines" to differentiate them from something else that was then called a subroutine. The most common term today for an in-line or open subroutine is a macro. A macro is a module (by the strict definition given in Chapter 3) whose body is effectively copied in-line during translation (e.g., compilation or assembly) as the result of being invoked by name; that is, the bounded contents replace the reference to the aggregate identifier. The process of copying in-line, with or without special adaptation called "tailoring," is often called "expansion." A macro is expanded as a result of being invoked. Translation of the macro body into target language may happen before, during, or after expansion, although the current trend is to prefer translation after expansion.

In the terminology used by several computer manufacturers, there is some confusion between macros and subroutines. Let us say that the FETCH "item" ON "file" is a function which performs all necessary housekeeping in order to deliver successive logical items from a particular file — including deblocking, aggregation, and so on. Inclusion of the statement

A: FETCH PAYREC ON PAYROLL

in a program might result in the following expansion:

A: IC033 = IC003 + 1
      CALL SYSFETCH (PAYRSPEC, PAYROLL, 1024)
      MOVE BUFSY (1024, PAYREC)

At execution time, we might find that a block of operating systems code is entered as the result of the call to SYSFETCH. SYSFETCH is not the macro, neither is it part of the macro — no more than SQRT is the subroutine FOO or is part of the subroutine FOO just because we find SQRT used (referenced) in FOO. The FETCH macro happens to call a subroutine named SYSFETCH. Unless there are language restrictions, macros may call subroutines or invoke other macros. Similarly, subroutines may invoke macros. The three lines of code beginning at label "A" in the above example are not the macro FETCH, but just one (of, possibly, many) expansions of it. The macro FETCH exists somewhere as a definition. In its prototype form, a macro looks like a subroutine: It has a declaration of its existence, a list of arguments or parameters, a body of code, and some boundary or boundaries.

Because they are activated at translation time, macros may fill many purposes that subroutines may not. Their contents may be tailored automatically to fit the requirements of a specific invocation. For example, some instructions may be added if a particular argument is present. In their most general form as so-called context-free character-string macros, they may be used literally to change the appearance of the language in which they are defined. The linguistic extensibility features will not concern us in this book — not because they are unimportant or unexciting, but because they do not play a *structural* role in the design task. We will note merely that, besides being a type of module usable much as subroutines, macros may be a way of extending and changing the appearance of a programming language.

At the point when the designer is making a rough cut of the procedural design of a module, it may not be important to him whether a facility is provided through macros, subroutines, or some combination of the two. If he knows that at point QQ1 he wants to, say, degesmilate his data, and if he knows that there exists a module DEGEST that performs that function, then he is really concerned only with showing that it is the function of DEGEST he wants performed at that point. Thus, he would write

QQ1:   DEGEST MY DATA

In short, he does not care whether degesmilating is accomplished by a subroutine, a macro, or a machine instruction. His system will work as long as MY DATA is degesmilated at QQ1. The designer is concerned with the details only if he runs out of storage or execution time in the process of degesmilating his data.

Other things being equal, a system composed entirely of macros will run faster but take more space than a system built from subroutines. It runs faster because linkage and argument communication are dealt with at translation time. It takes more space because each invocation results in a copy of all or part of the body of the macro.

If a programming language uses a common syntax for activating both macros and subroutines, then there is a particularly elegant way of trading off time and storage. Of course, there are myriad ways to speed up systems at the expense of primary memory, and vice versa; most require extensive analysis, recoding, and debugging. However, let us assume that a system is built and debugged as a structure of modules. As it grows, let us imagine that we discover that there is insufficient memory. In such a case, we may simply change the declaration of some of our modules from MACRO to SUBROUTINE and recompile. If the system ran before, it will run now — only slower. It also will take less space. Most important, the effect is automatic and does not require any analysis, recoding, or debugging.

16.3 SUMMARY

It should be clear that macros, functions (in the sense used in this chapter), programs, and subroutines are closely related physical entities. In many cases, it is to the programmer/designer's detriment to emphasize their differences. Ideally, we would like to be able to use them interchangeably, as suggsted in the paragraphs above.

REFERENCE

1. PETER WEGNER, *Programming Languages, Information Structures and Machine Organization* (New York: McGraw-Hill, 1968).

Recursive
Structures

CHAPTER 17

17.0 INTRODUCTION

Nothing in this book so far — least of all the mechanics of the structure chart itself — precludes structures of the type shown in Fig. 17.1, in which the graph for the structure chart has cycles in it. This type of structure is known as *recursive*. Modules F, G, and H all are recursive modules. From a structural standpoint, a recursive module is simply any module M for which we can say that M is subordinate to M. If a module is subordinate, but not *immediately* subordinate to itself, the situation traditionally has been referred to as *simultaneous recursion;* modules G and H in Fig. 17.1 are simultaneously recursive. Although it is traditional to discuss recursion from a procedural or algorithmic viewpoint (for a concise introduction to the subject, consult Barron[1]), it is obvious that recursion is also a structural phenomenon and, therefore, may be explored in terms of structural issues, including structural design.

The weird structures exemplified by Fig. 17.1 can arise either from deliberate design or by accident; they may be sensible, even simple interpretations of many

318

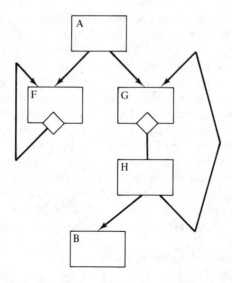

Fig. 17.1 Cyclic (recursive) hierarchical structure.

types of problems, or they may be mistakes. In either case, there will be consequences that must be taken into account by the designer and implementers.

Completing the task of a module by calling the module itself does not mean that an infinite loop will result. Careless or accidental use of recursion (see Section 17.3) *can* result in infinite recursion and those dreadful operating system messages feared by all advocates of recursion: PUSH-DOWN DEPTH EXCEEDED and GARBAGE COLLECTION FAILED. The necessary (but, alas, not always sufficient) conditions for termination of a recursive module are two. First, at least one call in the cycle of subordinates must be conditional — for example, the call on H in Fig. 17.1. Second, the exact values of input arguments may not repeat within recursive calls. The example below in Section 17.1 will clarify how these conditions are met through the appropriate use of recursion.

17.1 FUNCTIONAL RECURSION

Many mathematical functions are or can be defined recursively; that is, the function for a given value is defined in terms of the same function of other values. If we can be forgiven the use of an overused example (well, it *is* simple and familiar), the factorial function can be written in computer Esperanto as:

```
FACTORIAL FUNCTION ARGUMENT N:
    IF N = 0 THEN RETURN 1;
        ELSE RETURN N × FACTORIAL (N-1);
    END:
```

319

The modular structure of this system is obviously that of Fig. 17.2. For this system to work correctly, each reuse of FACTORIAL must employ the proper data context (only the argument N in this example), and return to the proper location defined by the last condition*ed* transfer activating FACTORIAL, whether from within an activation of FACTORIAL or elsewhere. Obviously, if the procedure within module FACTORIAL were to make use of any temporary variables, the right (potentially, different) values for each of these would have to be used in each activation.

The processing overhead requirements are well known to most programmers and analysts; for recursive use, each *reentry* of a module must ensure that the existing data context and control state be preserved (in a LIFO queue or push-down stack), and each return from such a reentry must restore the last data context and control state. These requirements may be met automatically by various major programming languages, including PL/I and ALGOL. The need for such overhead processing is most important to recognize where recursion is unintended.

17.1.1 Recursion, reusability, and reenterability

Some modules perform differently on each activation; this may be useful or problematic depending on the application and on whether the variation in performance was planned. A module that always executes in the same way on each separate activation, as if it were a fresh copy, is said to be *reusable* (or serially reusable). For a subroutine (or function) to be reusable, a correct new data context and control state only need to be established on each entry following a return from the module. This can be accomplished with nothing more than the restriction that the module cannot "have a memory"; that is, there are no variables whose values are retained from one complete activation to the next (OWNed or STATIC variables). *Thus, any recursively usable module is also serially reusable, but not vice versa.* As you can see, reusability is a weaker property than recursivity.

A module is said to be *reenterable* if it can be reactivated correctly at any time, whether or not it has been suspended by a conditioned transfer or return. Reenterability is a stronger property; hence, any module that is reenterable also can be used recursively, but not vice versa. A "pure procedure" — that is, a module

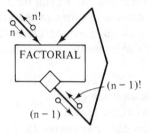

Fig. 17.2 Structure of a recursive factorial routine.

with only constant, executable elements — is one (but only one) way of achieving reenterability.

17.2 RECURSION BY DESIGN

The example of the FACTORIAL module given above suggests one reason why designers might be interested in recursion. Although the gain in that case is very modest, a recursive structure for many kinds of problem will be an especially "simple" solution compared to the iterative alternatives. Sometimes, the best word might even be "elegant." Recursive structures can arise from a pure black-box approach in which the designer makes use of the appropriate black box for accomplishing a particular task, even if the black box is the one still being designed. Besides naturally recursive functions — such as factorial (and its generalization as the gamma function) combinations, and such distributions are the chi square — recursion is appropriate and simplifies processes involving text-processing, language-processing (including compilation), game-playing systems, heuristic optimization techniques, analysis of graphs and networks (e.g., critical path, PERT, transportation networks, and so on), and all forms of structured data. *Structured data* are data containing explicit structural information that relates, by reference, an element of data to other elements of data. The range of applications of recursive structures is very broad and includes many kinds of conventional or business EDP problems.[2,3] Table 17.1 lists some potential applications of recursion.

Figure 17.3 represents an example of one type of structured data, so-called configuration data, representing the configuration of physical systems. There are many processes that might be of interest as applied to this type of data, for example,

Table 17.1 Applications for Required or Useful Recursive Structures

Algebraic and formula manipulation	Language processing and translation
Bill-of-materials and parts explosion	Library cataloging and processing
Compilers and assemblers	List processing
Configuration data	Macro preprocessors
Critical path method and PERT analysis	Mathematical optimization (e.g., "backtrack programming")
Expression evaluation	Network and graph analysis
File inversion	Optimization of code, program simplification
File management and update	Simplification of expressions
Flowcharting programs	Simulation (e.g., traffic networks, electrical circuits, etc.)
Game-playing programs	Sociograms and social network analysis
Genealogical analysis	Statistics and probability
Heuristic programming	String and text processing
Information retrieval	Structure charting and analysis of program structure
Interpreters	Theorem proving
Inventory control and analysis	Work-breakdown data, analysis, updating, reporting

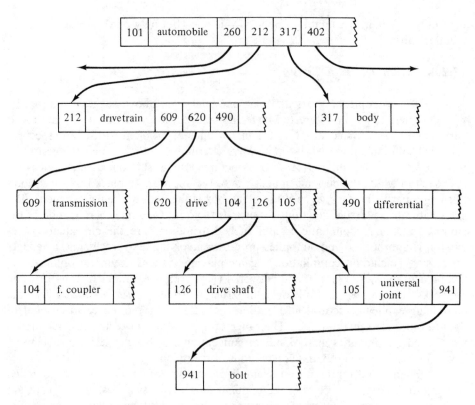

Fig. 17.3 Example of configuration data for an automobile's structure.

a "parts explosion" that lists *all* parts, systems, and subsystems of the given unit. We will try a slight variation on parts explosion, in which all the subsystems of a system that were supplied by a particular vendor are to be exploded, i.e., have all parts listed out. The total count of all components supplied by that vendor is to be reported. The data for a component with a particular identification code, ID, may be obtained by RETRIEVE (ID, DATA); VENDOR (DATA) yields the vendor ID; SUBCOMP (DATA, N) yields the component ID for the Nth immediate subcomponent of DATA if it exists or zero if there is no N^{th} subcomponent. VENDOROUT (DATA) enters the required information into the vendor list report.

For data of the sort shown above in Fig. 17.3, no strictly iterative system will work unless, in part, it simulates recursion through the use of stacks or a system of markers. A recursive structure is straightforward and easy to read. See, for example, the structure on the following page.

```
VENDORREPT:    SUBROUTINE ARGUMENTS SYSTID, VENDID, VENDNAME;
               N = VENDORLIST (SYSTID, VENDID);
               PRINT "VENDOR", VENDNAME, "SUPPLIES", N;
               RETURN;
               END;


VENDORLIST:    RECURSIVE FUNCTION ARGUMENTS COMPID, VENDID;
               RETRIEVE (COMPID, COMPDATA);
               IF VENDOR (COMPDATA) = VENDID
                   THEN RETURN EXPLODE (COMPDATA);
                   ELSE;
                       NUM = 0;
                       I = 1;
                       UNTIL SUBCOMP (COMPDATA, I) = 0 DO;
                           NUM = NUM + VENDORLIST (SUBCOMP
                           (COMDATA, I), VENDID); I = I + 1
                       END UNTIL;
                       RETURN NUM;
                   END ELSE;
               END;


EXPLODE:       RECURSIVE FUNCTION ARGUMENTS VCOMP DATA;
               CALL VENDOROUT (VCOMPDATA);
               NUM = 1;
               I = 1;
               UNTIL SUBCOMP (VCOMPDATA, I) = 0 DO;
                   RETRIEVE (SUBCOMP(VCOMPDATA, I), SUBDATA);
                   NUM = NUM + EXPLODE (SUBDATA);
                   I = I + 1;
               END UNTIL;
               RETURN NUM;
               END;
```

The structure chart for this coding is shown in Fig. 17.4.   Notice how this design directly represents that EXPLODEing a part consists of EXPLODEing each of the subparts.   Producing a VENDORLIST for a part consists of EXPLODEing the part if it is the right vendor, or doing a VENDORLIST of each of the subparts.   The designer has simply invoked the needed function at the appropriate point.

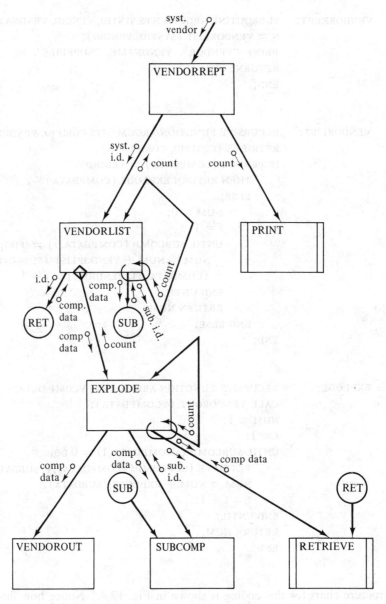

Fig. 17.4 Structure of the system to explode and count all parts supplied by specified vendor.

17.2.1 Recursion and iteration

It is always possible to transform a recursive process into a nonrecursive or iterative process that uses only loops rather than recursive calls. In most cases, this amounts to simulating the recursion by having the procedure do its own explicit stacking and unstacking of the data. It is possible to make some gains in efficiency in this way, but this must be balanced against additional programming of a sort that may be prone to errors, especially as the system is modified. The cost of recursion may be vanishingly small for modules that, for other reasons, are managed dynamically and that have their storage allocated dynamically by the operating environment.

The coding for EXPLORE uses a mixture of iteration and recursion. The loop iterates across the list of immediate subcomponents and recurs down each subcomponent branch. Very often, the structure of the data or the way the data physically are stored and accessed will give a distinct advantage to recursion in one direction rather than the other.[3] The EXPLODE module might be rewritten as follows to iterate down levels and to recur across:

```
EXPLODE:    RECURSIVE FUNCTION ARGUMENTS VCOMPDATA, I;
            NUM = 1;
            UNTIL SUBCOMP (VCOMPDATA, I) = 0 DO;
                CALL VENDOROUT (VCOMPDATA);
                NUM = NUM + EXPLODE (VCOMPDATA, I + 1);
                RETRIEVE (SUBCOMP (VCOMPDATA, I) VCOMPDATA);
            END UNTIL;
            RETURN NUM;
            END;
```

17.3 RECURSION BY ACCIDENT

Functional recursion is not likely to occur unintentionally when a complete structure chart is drawn up in advance; any cycle on the structure chart would be evident. Simultaneous functional recursion can appear accidentally whenever a total design is divided between two or more designers or when the complete structure has not been laid out first. Perfectly good design philosophy, if not guided by good strategy or aided by the structure chart as a tool, can lead to some costly recursion.

The developers of a new operating system might adopt the apparently sensible and innocent philosophy that (1) each separate service shall be implemented as a separate callable module, and (2) all modules requiring a certain service shall make use of the one module that is to perform that service. What could go wrong? Suppose there is to be a single universally used module, LETMAIN, to allocate a block of core storage under the dynamic storage management discipline employed in this sophisticated operating system. If there is insufficient core storage in the running program's allocation, LETMAIN is to put a message to an output device designated in the program's "activation table" via the module MESSOUT. MESS-

OUT, designed by another designer, conforms to the system's modular design philosophy. Of course, before it can write any message to a device, it must set up a message buffer, and of course, *the* module to use is LETMAIN. The structure obviously is recursive without being planned that way. Should LETMAIN ever actually call MESSOUT because the allocation of memory is used up, an infinite recursion of "after you, Alphonse" will result. The potential problem would be self-evident from the structure chart of Fig. 17.5, which *should* have been drawn up before LETMAIN and MESSOUT were programmed.

Uses of recursion may be as near as your next sequential file update. Figure 17.6 illustrates one structure (not *the* structure or even necessarily the best) for updating the items of a sequential file. Looking at this structure from the top down (as the designer must have done when first developing it), we see that the function of updating a file, UPDATE, is composed of an iteration on getting an un-updated item (GETOLDMFREC) and updating it. To UPDATE1REC requires processing all transactions (possibly none) against that record. What do you do if in trying to update the record numbered 136, a transaction to create a record numbered 135 is encountered? The newly created record 135 could also have transactions against

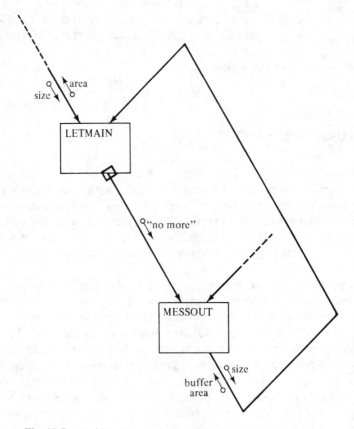

Fig. 17.5   Accidental recursion resulting in a deadly embrace.

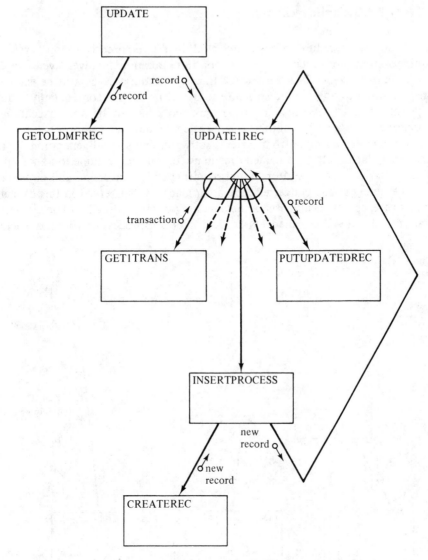

Fig. 17.6 Recursion in a sequential file update.

it. Obviously (?), to process a correct "insert record" transaction, you must create the record, then completely update it. There is already a module in the system that will perform the latter function, namely UPDATE1REC. The resulting recursive structure works!*

* In all fairness, a recursive structure for this problem is overkill, since the nesting can never correctly go to more than one level. But the procedures *would* be fairly straightforward to write.

17.3.1 Dynamic recursion

For any procedure to be recursive, all that is required is a loop (cycle) in condition*ed* transfers of control.   (By contrast, iteration involves cycles in *un*-condition*ed* transfers.)   The condition*ed* transfers need not necessarily be explicitly written subroutine calls for the structure to be recursive and consequently require the special facilites for recursion.   Interrupts and switching between execution of one user's active task and any other task operate as conditioned transfers.

In another example from systems software, one second-generation operating system (which shall go unnamed) made use of a master routine to PRINT on an on-line printer — a nontrivial operation requiring code conversion and direct control of the timing of the converted tabulating machine that served in this capacity. User software, as well as all parts of the operating system, printed on-line via PRINT. Among the modules that called PRINT were interrupt processing routines, such as

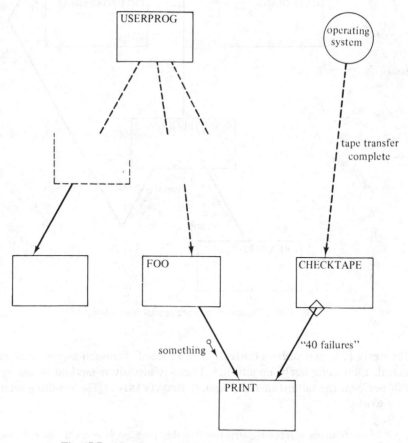

Fig. 17.7   Module shared by base load and interrupt routine.

CHEKTAPE, the routine that intercepted the "magnetic tape transfer complete" signal, checked for parity error, and reread or rewrote the record if necessary. A long series of parity failures on the same record would result in a call to PRINT to tell the operator that something was awry. The structure of this system is portrayed in Fig. 17.7.

Since PRINT can be called by the main processing stream and from CHEK-TAPE, it is said to be in both the base load and the interrupt load. *Any module that can be activated from both the base load and any interrupt load (that is, both synchronously and asynchronously from the operating environment) is potentially dynamically recursive!* An interrupt can occur at any time, including during some use of PRINT by the base load. The interrupt itself, which must return to the point interrupted, functions as a conditioned transfer. The dynamic recursion is clear in Fig. 17.8.

In our example, since on-line printing is slow relative to tape transfer, there is some not insignificant probability of the dynamic recursion shown. It is unlikely that this situation will develop on just the 40th successive parity failure; but if it does, the return location for PRINT to go back to FOO gets clobbered and an infinite merry-go-

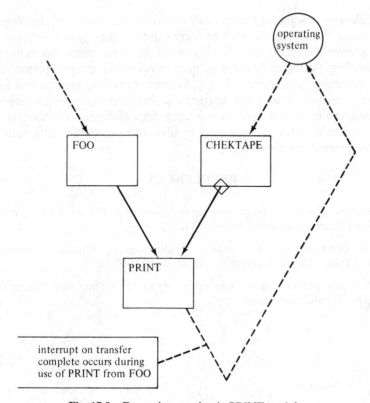

Fig. 17.8 Dynamic recursion in PRINT module.

round is established between parts of PRINT and CHEKTAPE. As the reader can guess, such infinite loops *did* occur in using this operating system (Murphy's Law again) without leading to a correction. Why? Because correcting all of these dynamic recursions would require either (a) multiple copies of all routines on both base and interrupt loads (wasteful!), or (b) interrupt lock-out during execution of all such routines (unacceptable!), or (c) making such routines properly recursively usable, which would, of course, be inefficient to say nothing of requiring too much work. The bugs remained through all umpteen versions of the operating system!

Dynamic recursion exists whenever a module (1) is shared by two or more tasks, even from different jobs, which can be among active jobs at the same time, (2) is used by routines handling different interrupts or asynchronous processes, or (3) is reachable from both base and interrupt loads. Usually, these modules are implemented as pure procedures to meet correctly the requirements of dynamic recursion; with proper design of the operating environment, recursivity can be sufficient.

17.4 SUMMARY

Recursive or cyclical hierarchical structures are useful for the simple realization of many kinds of problems. In fact, if the designer merely judiciously pursues a top-down design by transform analysis or some other function-centered strategy, invoking the use of modules as black boxes wherever appropriate, recursive structures inevitably will result — if the designer waits long enough and blackens all his boxes. Sooner or later, the designer will find himself drawing an arrow from one module down in the hierarchy to one somewhere above it. Whether intentional or not, recursion requires housekeeping to save and restore the data context and control state on each reactivation.

REFERENCES

1. D.W. BARRON, *Recursive Techniques in Programming,* 2nd ed. (New York: MacDonald and American Elsevier, Inc., 1975).

2. LARRY L. CONSTANTINE, "Commercial Applications of Symbolic Processing and Structured Data," *Data Processing Magazine,* April 1967.

3. LARRY L. CONSTANTINE and V. DONNELLY, "PERGO: A Simplified Project Management Tool," *Datamation,* October 1967.

Homologous
and
Incremental
Structures

CHAPTER 18

18.0 INTRODUCTION

In designing the modular structure of systems to solve varied classes of problems, the designer often has difficulty selecting an appropriate top level or determining what is to be in charge of what, or which processes are to be afferent, which efferent. These decisions are necessitated by the use of conventional modules, such as subroutines, that might be arranged in a hierarchy of subordinates and superordinates. The choices can be critical, in part, because modules linked by hierarchical mechanisms behave differently as viewed from above than from below.

In Chapter 16, we introduced the notion of a typology of modules based on time-history, activation mechanism, and pattern of control flow. Such a typology points the way to module types and modular structures that avoid some of the problems of conventional hierarchical systems. In this chapter, we will consider some unconventional structures that can greatly simplify both implementation and structural design.

18.1 HOMOLOGOUS SYSTEMS

The questions of which module is in charge and which is the subordinate can be avoided altogether by employing structures that are not hierarchical. In this way, no design decisions need to be made regarding such matters as choice of afferent, efferent, or executive modules.

Homologous,* or non-hierarchical, systems arise from any control relationship that does not define a hierarchy of control responsibility. All modules related solely by homologous relationships have the same degree of control or responsibility, since the receipt of control by such a coordinating transfer relinquishes full responsibility for whatever level of control the activating module possessed.

Responsibility appears to be a vague and informal term, but the concept can be made precise by noting that every outstanding unreturned subordination carries the *obligation* for eventual return — an obligation not under control of the currently active subordinate module. An active module may surrender control (canceling a subordination), or activate new modules as subordinates with responsibility to return to the current module. Alternatively, it can activate new modules as coordinates, with responsibility for return to the superordinate (if any) or to the current module.

Obviously, it is possible for only a portion of a system to be homologous — giving rise to "mixed" systems. Normally connected (as contrasted with pathologically connected) mixed systems are defined only if the definitions (and implementation) of homologous relationships are such that they are consistent with and do not violate subordinations.

Homologous structures result from connections that transfer control without an implicit return condition. A series of ordinary *routines* or program steps connected by direct transfer (e.g., GOTO) to a named entry point would comprise one kind of homologous system. Another type involves the use of so-called incremental modules.

18.2 INCREMENTAL MODULES

In the more common cases found in real-world systems, a module (e.g., subroutine) performs one complete instance of a distinct task on each activation. Unless the module is pathologically connected, each activation physically begins execution at the origin, the first executable statement. Although internal coding may cause an immediate branch to some other part of the module and the destination of the branch may vary from activation to activation, this is an internal procedural property.

We can hypothesize a type of module that executes only some portion of its code (and/or function) on each activation — that is, a module that proceeds incrementally. In keeping with the characteristics already established in Chapter 3

---

* Homologous is established terminology for horizontal, rather than hierarchical, structures in the typology of organizations and groups. See for example, Eric Berne's work.[1]

for true modules, the exact portion to be executed is invisible to the activating module, i.e., the next portion to be executed is determined by the incremental module, not its activator. This means that, to the activator, an incremental module can appear to be a black box as much as a subroutine can. As with all modules, this will depend, in the final analysis, on the quality of design and coding! Incremental execution makes it *possible* to decouple one module more completely from the internal state and state maintenance mechanisms of another module.

18.2.1 Coroutines

The coroutine may have been invented almost concurrently by several people, though the credit usually goes to Conway,[2] who first published a paper on the concept. For an interesting history of the development of the coroutine, as well as several programming examples, see Knuth.[3] The coroutine is a very basic module type, possibly every bit as important as the subroutine.

In the abstract, a coroutine is a module whose point of activation is always the next sequential statement following the last point at which the module deactivated itself by activating another coroutine. Thus, the entry point of the coroutine floats. It must be stressed that a coroutine does not (normally) have more than one entry, unlike a multiple-entry (compound) subroutine. The coroutine has a single entry point whose value varies with time. Each entry of a particular coroutine z commences execution at the point defined by the entry. Each entry of another coroutine from z establishes a new value of z's entry: the next sequential statement in z. This will be when z is next entered.

The operation of coroutines is most easily understood by assuming a typical form of implementation. Each coroutine may be thought of as having associated with it an "entry locator": a device that always will contain a current value of the coroutine's entry. The entry locator is assumed to be initialized to the origin of the module; i.e., when a coroutine is activated for the first time, it actually does begin at the beginning. Thus, Fig. 18.1 conceptually represents the coroutine z in its initial state. z will be activated by an appropriate reference to its entry locator, which serves as its identity interface. We will use the statement ENTER. (The characteristics incremental or nonincremental are internal details of a module. By using ENTER for either type, the detail remains hidden to other modules.)

A cotransfer from one coroutine to another (mixed systems will be discussed later) is conceptually a two-step process. The first step is to set a new value for the entry locator of the currently active module. The second step is to transfer to the location defined by the entry locator of the coroutine to be activated.

In Fig. 18.2 are two coroutines, called NULL and CIPHER. In NULL is a loop that executes, alternately, three different variations on the NULL function: the first starting at A, the second at B, and the third at CIPHER uses two NULLifying steps in another loop. Successive activations of NULL will result in values of the entry locator of S, B, C, D, B, C, D, ... Successive activations of CIPHER, on the other hand, result in values of its entry locator of X, Y, Z, Y, Z, Y, Z, ... Neither module

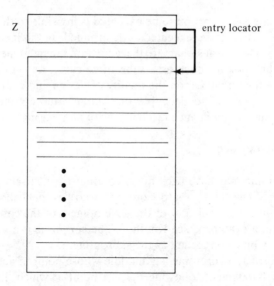

Fig. 18.1 Conceptual representation of a coroutine in initial state.

needs to "know" the number of sections in the other — or the ratio of occurrences, or which section is next to be performed. Each coroutine has full control over its process. Since neither is in control of the other nor has more responsibility, the name coroutine is indeed appropriate.

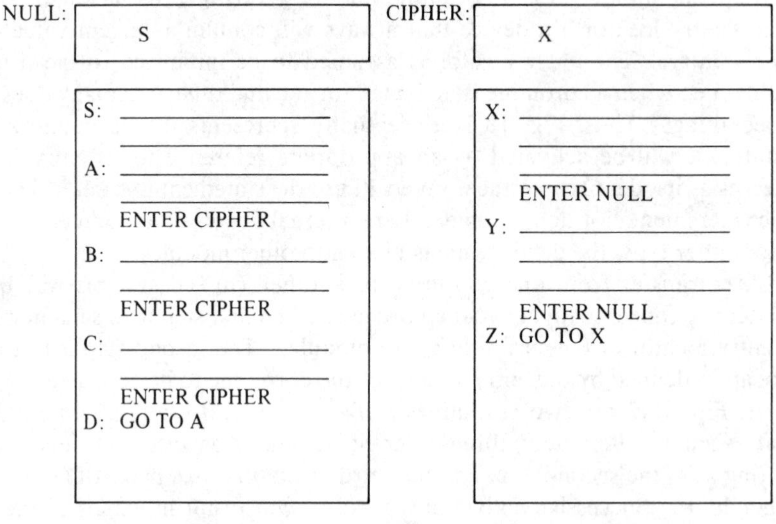

```
NULL:  ┌──────────────────┐    CIPHER: ┌──────────────────┐
       │        S         │            │        X         │
       └──────────────────┘            └──────────────────┘

       ┌──────────────────┐            ┌──────────────────┐
       │ S: _____   │            │ X: _____   │
       │    _____   │            │    _____   │
       │ A: _____   │            │    _____   │
       │    _____   │            │    ENTER NULL    │
       │    ENTER CIPHER  │            │ Y: _____   │
       │ B: _____   │            │    _____   │
       │    _____   │            │    _____   │
       │    ENTER CIPHER  │            │    ENTER NULL    │
       │ C: _____   │            │ Z: GO TO X       │
       │    _____   │            │                  │
       │    ENTER CIPHER  │            │                  │
       │ D: GO TO A       │            │                  │
       └──────────────────┘            └──────────────────┘
```

Fig. 18.2 Conceptual representation of coroutines NULL and CIPHER.

334

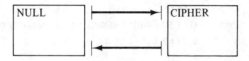

Fig. 18.3 NULL-CIPHER system using standard graphic notation.

Consider the complications that would arise if NULL and CIPHER had to be designed as a single integral process. The relative execution ratios would have to be reflected in the procedure. The entire procedure might have to be recoded to accommodate a change in the number of unique segments for any one of the two processes. In Fig. 18.3, the system of NULL and CIPHER is represented by using standard graphics. Note that this coroutine chain is linked by references in both directions.

18.2.2 Brief application of coroutines

Consider the module DO, which performs some processing on each incoming record on a file. The process performed by DO requires accessing the next record in, say, two places within the code; that is, the algorithm is linear rather than iterative with respect to two distinct usages of an incoming record. We shall assume that the DO process is complex in itself, though the details need not concern us here. Its code is shown, in outline form, in Fig. 18.4.

Suppose the required records reside on three magnetic tape drives — which we will call "unit 1," "unit 2," and "unit 3" — and which are to be merged according to the following discipline: one record from unit 1; two records from unit 2; then one record from unit 3 unless it is an exception type, in which case it should be preceded by another record from unit 1.

The code for the merge discipline, though not really very complicated, is not the sort of thing we wish to have duplicated throughout our system. There are too many opportunities for error. Moreover, the process of getting the next record in a merged stream is a well-defined function and is appropriately implemented as a separate module. The most straightforward approach is to specify a coroutine named NEXTREC:

NEXTREC:	COROUTINE
MERGE:	GET RECORD FROM UNIT 1 INTO REC
R1:	ENTER DO (REC)
L1:	GET RECORD FROM UNIT 2 INTO REC
R2:	ENTER DO (REC)
L2:	GET RECORD FROM UNIT 2 INTO REC
R3:	ENTER DO (REC)
L3:	GET RECORD FROM UNIT 3 INTO REC

```
                        IF EXCEPTION-TYPE THEN
L4:                             GET RECORD FROM UNIT 1 INTO REC2
R4:                             ENTER DO (REC2)
                        ENDIF
R5:                     ENTER DO (REC)
                        GO TO MERGE
```

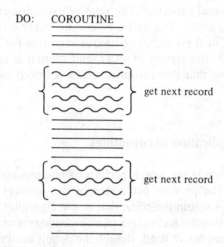

Fig. 18.4   Outline of coding for the DO coroutine.

The nature of the merge discipline is obvious from the above code. If NEXTREC were implemented as a subroutine, the instructions at R1, R2, R3, R4, and R5 would have to be replaced by switch settings followed by RETURN statements. At the entry to NEXTREC, a five-way branch would dispatch to L1, L2, L3, R5, or MERGE. This is the simplest analogy we can draw with a subroutine; it may be regarded as a simulation of a coroutine operation through a coding trick.

Several points are important. First, the coroutine structure *permits* truly independent procedural design of each coroutine in the chain. The only inter-modular relationships that must be taken into account are those involving demands for, or delivery of, data. Thus, a coroutine always can be written in such a way that it simply enters a "donor" coroutine when it needs the next item of data; similarly, it enters a "receiver" coroutine when it has prepared an item of output.

Of course, any module that has both its input and output functions available as subroutines can be written in a similar fashion. However, it is obvious that this cannot be done for *all* modules in a system; some modules will be in a subordinate position. For example, the afferent subroutine does *not* control its own output; the efferent subroutine does not determine the point of input requests in the code — input is always made available to the efferent subroutine at its origin. However, conflicting requirements for control over input and output processes can be resolved through a homologous structure using coroutines.

336

Such structures are not only homologous but symmetrical with respect to control. Thus, NEXTREC behaves like, or appears to be, a subroutine to DO, while DO functions as if it were a subroutine to NEXTREC. Clearly, this is *not* recursion of the sort that we discussed in the previous chapter. A complete, recursive performance of the entire DO process is not being activated (which was, in turn, activated by DO); only the next *step* in the whole process is being called for. Unlike the recursive process, the coordinate process need not "unwind" through a set of returns resulting from nested calls.

18.2.3 Subcoroutines

The NEXTREC coroutine functions properly for each of the two (or N) required references in DO. But obtaining the next record in a merged sequence is a function quite likely to be of general use in the system. Suppose that there is another module, DO2, which may be used at times to process input records. In general, whether DO or DO2 is to be used may be known only by DO or DO2 or perhaps by another module. A given activation of NEXTREC must deliver its output to either DO or DO2, depending on which activated it to obtain an item of input. If NEXTREC is a coroutine, it must know the criteria determining which module to reenter; that is, it must execute either the statement to enter DO or the one to enter DO2 — it cannot enter both.

What is needed is an incremental module, which can be subordinated and which will resume whatever module calls it. Such a module is known as a *subcoroutine*. Although it has also been called a "demand coroutine"[4] (performing its function on demand for any module) and a "subordinated coroutine," the word subcoroutine is a more compact term carrying the proper implications.

A subcoroutine looks like an ordinary subroutine to its superordinate — it is entered by a conditioned transfer — but it has a floating entry point like a coroutine. As with subroutines, the return location is best thought of as being stacked. The subcoroutine deactivates itself by executing a RESUME statement which resumes its (unnamed) superordinate process. This RESUME of an implicit module (the last one to call) establishes a new value for the subcoroutine's entry locator. Thus, the next statement following the last executed RESUME serves as the entry point for the next call to the subcoroutine.

18.2.4 Input-output event ratios

The advantages and applications of incremental modules also can be illustrated through consideration of the flow of data through conventional hierarchical nests of subroutines. Any transform, such as x in Fig. 18.5a, can be characterized by the ratio of incoming data elements, or events, to outgoing data events. In the simplest case, x might require a single *a* to produce one *b*. The input-output event ratio is said to be one to one. In such a simple case, the transform x could be as easily implemented as an afferent subroutine, an efferent subroutine, or, for that matter, a subroutine in any position in the hierarchy. In cases of non-simple

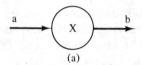

(a)

Fig. 18.5a   Simple transform bubble.

input-output event ratios, a subroutine has a preferred direction of data flow because it is in control of subordinate, but not superordinate, events. If transform x were to require several inputs for each output *b*, it would be easier to implement as an afferent subroutine than as an efferent one. A many-to-one event ratio might also result from fan-in, as in transform y in Fig. 18.5b. As an afferent module, the procedure for transform x would simply assemble as many *a* elements as needed, transforming these into a single *b* to be returned. Because a call always enters it at the origin, an efferent subroutine would have to keep track of some intermediate information about each *a* until the right number was received to produce a *b* to be passed down to a subordinate. Each type of data flow through a module implies that some input-output event ratios can be programmed without any complications being introduced due to the position of the subroutine, while other ratios will be somewhat less straightforward to implement.

The reader can verify that the event ratios that can be implemented most directly for each type of data flow through a module are as follows:

Afferent subroutine:	1 to 1, many to 1
Efferent subroutine:	1 to 1, 1 to many
Transform subroutine:	1 to 1
Coordinate (top level) subroutine:	1 to 1, 1 to many, many to 1, many to many

Any event ratio other than one to one requires additional coding in a transform module! Note that no coding problems would occur with any event ratio if every module could be written as a top-level module, which is exactly what the use of coroutines and subcoroutines permits. Where input-output event ratios are variable rather than fixed, the degree of difficulty in coding is even more marked.

18.3 APPLICATIONS OF COROUTINES AND SUBCOROUTINES

For many applications, the use of incremental structures permits more straightforward translation of the problem structure as expressed in a data flow

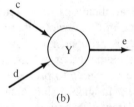

(b)

Fig. 18.5b   More complex transform bubble.

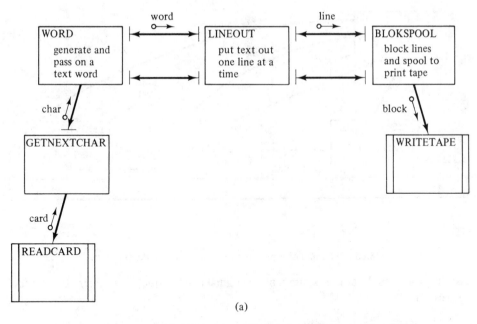

(a)

Fig. 18.6a Example of bidirectional linkage in a linear coroutine chain.

graph than would be possible with strict hierarchies of subroutines. Appropriate applications are characterized by state dependent or sequential decision processes, asynchronous or parallel processing, variable input-output event ratios, or event ratios incompatible with a module's position in a hierarchy. Almost all instances of text- and language-processing fall into one or more of these areas. Even such a mundane routine as an input deblocker is simpler as a subcoroutine than as a subroutine because of its one-in-to-many-out event ratio. Provided communications are handled normally, incremental modules actually are easier to maintain and modify independently than conventional modules.

The usual use of coroutines is to have bidirectional linkages, as in Fig. 18.6a, which communicate data in one direction. Circular coroutine chains also have uses in simulating parallel processes. The structure in Fig. 18.6b actually was used to permit separate programming of routines to manage simultaneous operations of several mechanisms on a computer-controlled machine tool. Each module transfers to its adjacent coroutine whenever it otherwise would have nothing to do, because it had just output something or was waiting for a completion signal from the machine tool. Each of the operations had its own unique dynamic characteristics and special programming problems; by using coroutines, these could be kept separate. The subsystem could be activated by a call to either of its three coroutines; that is, these appear to be subroutines to CONTROL, which is returned to when all processes indicate they are done.

Another, more complex, application using coroutines and subcoroutines is shown in Fig. 18.7. Note how incremental modules are used for sequential de-

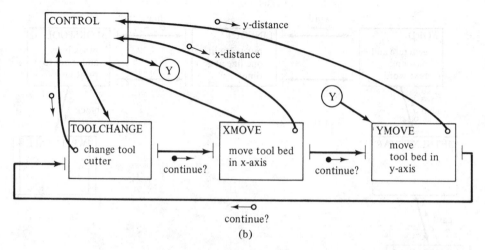

Fig. 18.6b Example of a unidirectional linkage in a coroutine cycle.

cision processes like the statement recognizer and stack compiler for "infix" expressions.

18.3.2 Implementation of incremental facilities

Few contemporary languages supply facilities for declaring and using co-routines and subcoroutines, but they readily can be added to most languages having macros or macro preprocessors. Even though such implications are apt to be less than elegant, they still may simplify programming.

Subcoroutines are the more useful of the two types and also the more easily added, as they require no special methods for handling activation records for separate procedures to be used incrementally. Briefly, the following facilities are required:

(a) a macro statement to "declare" a subcoroutine that looks like and translates into a normal procedure/subroutine declaration, but adds a declaration of an invisible label variable or switch to serve as entry locator, plus an inserted GOTO depending on the switch as the first executable statement; the initial value of the switch is the first programmer-written executable statement, that is, the one following the switched GOTO

(b) a RESUME macro that translates into a "set switch to next-statement" followed by a RETURN

(c) if static or OWNED label variables cannot be used, then the entry locator can be carried as an input argument added to the argument list by a CALLing macro

340

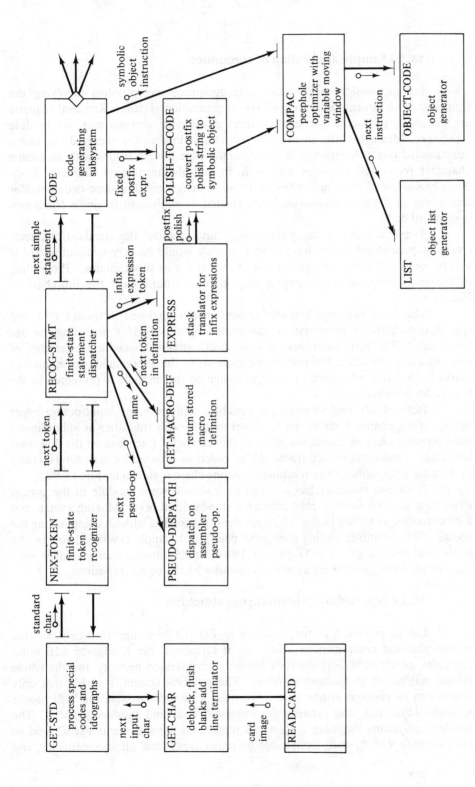

Fig 18.7 Principal modules in a one-pass compile-and-go system for a simple language.

18.3.3 Sample application of coroutines

Let us consider a primitive language-processing problem involving the front-end of an information retrieval/report generation system. Retrieval requests are obtained, character-by-character from a message concentrator via module NEXCHAR. Messages enter in two different character codes, a standard one and a nonstandard one. A message in nonstandard code always begins with an escape character *(ec)*. All messages end with an end-of-transmission character *(eot)*. Some characters of the nonstandard code are to be ignored and some two-character ideographs in the nonstandard code are treated as equivalent to single characters in standard code.

The remainder of the system only "understands" the standard character code. A procedural design for a STDIZE module would be very straightforward if STDIZE could call NEXCHAR and the rest of the system as subordinates. Proceeding in the most simple-minded, step-by-step manner would yield the flowchart of Fig. 18.8a.

The input language includes quoted matter enclosed in quotes (' ') and special two-character abbreviations designated by a period(.) preceding the abbreviation. The retrieval/report system itself, RETREP, accepts a character of input on each activation, but it does not understand the abbreviations or quotation marks. The straightforward procedural design of this module is presented in the Fig. 18.8b flowchart.

Both STDIZE and XPAND have variable, many-to-many input-output event ratios. They cannot both be the top-level module with the other as subordinate; implementing them as coroutines resolves this conflict. Each box on the flowchart invoking a predefined procedure would be coded as a coroutine transfer (ENTER) to the adjacent routine. The resulting coroutine chain is shown in Fig. 18.9a.

Even this structure has a defect in it should some module in the system other than RETREP need to read expanded standardized text. Making STDIZE into a subcoroutine as shown in Fig. 18.9b resolves this conflict without complicating the coding. The resulting coding (see next page) is a simple transliteration of the procedural designs of Figs. 18.8a and 18.8b, and is demonstrably simpler than what would be required if either or both modules had to be a subroutine.

18.3.4 Separability of homologous structures

Let us assume that the structure of Fig. 18.9b is implemented, but that certain practical complications arise. As it turns out, the Kludgevac 616 mini-computer on which the system runs has only very limited memory and the whole system will not fit in memory at once. The retrieval system is so big that only XPAND can be resident at one time. We need a two-pass system that will handle message traffic and later retrieve the requested data and produce reports. The Kludgevac Systems Engineer suggests we replace all the statements P1, P2, and so on, in STDIZE with "punch a character on paper tape," and all statements R1, and

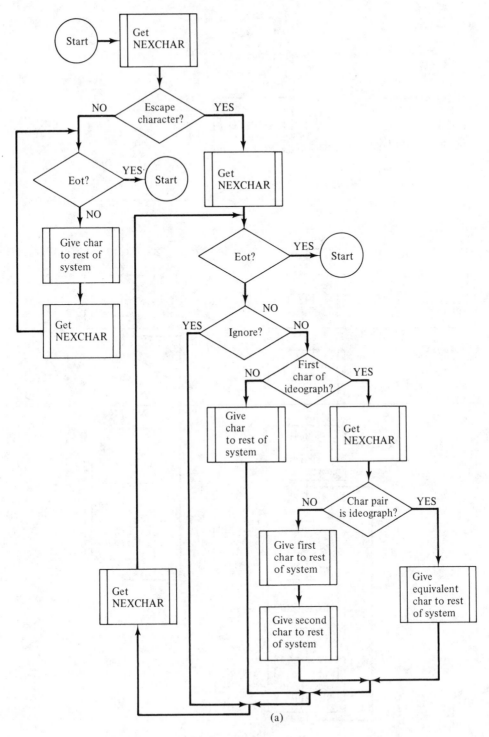

Fig. 18.8a Flowchart of module STDIZE to convert all incoming code to standard character set.

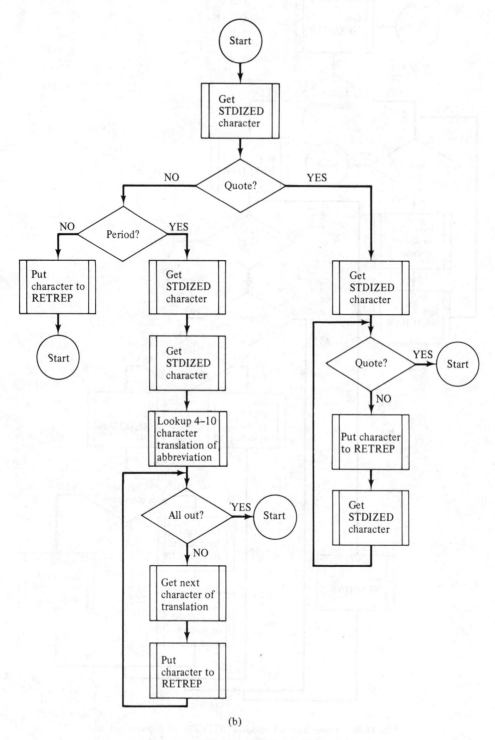

(b)

Fig. 18.8b Flowchart of module XPAND to remove quotes and expand abbreviations.

so on, in XPAND with "read a character from paper tape." The system then will punch a tape of standardized text, which can be torn off and read in when the second pass is loaded at the end of the day. Will it work? Yes! if the system in its one-pass version also worked. This property of coroutine chains can be (and has been) exploited in making the same compiler work in one, two, or more passes, depending on available memory.

```
      STDIZE:   COUROUTINE
                CALL NEXCHAR (CH)
                IF CH = ec
                    THEN
                      CALL NEXCHAR (CH)
                    UNTIL CH = eot
                      DO
                        IF LOOKUP (CH, IGNORETABLE)
                          THEN
                          ELSE
                            IF LOOKUP (CH, IDEOGRAFTABLE(1))
                              THEN
                                CALL NEXCHAR (CH2)
                                IF LOOKUP (CH2, IDEOGRAFTABLE(2))
                                  THEN
        P1:                         XPAND (IDEOGRAFTABLE(3))
                                  ELSE
        P2:                         XPAND (CH)
        P3:                         XPAND (CH2)
                                  ENDELSE
                              ELSE
        P4:                     XPAND (CH)
                              ENDELSE
                            ENDELSE
                      ENDUNTIL
                    ELSE
                      UNTIL CH = eot
                        DO
        P5:               XPAND (CH)
                          CALL NEXCHAR (CH)
                        ENDUNTIL
                    ENDELSE
                END
      XPAND:    SUBCOROUTINE ARGUMENTS CHAROUT
        R1.     STDIZE (CHAR)
                IF CHAR = ' " '
                    THEN
```

```
R2:          STDIZE (CHAR)
             UNTIL CHAR = ' " '
               DO
                 CHAROUT = CHAR
                 RESUME
R3:          STDIZE (CHAR)
             ENDUNTIL
           ELSE
             IF CHAR = ' . '
             THEN
R4:            STDIZE (CH(1))
R5:            STDIZE (CH (2))
             EQS = LOOKUP (CH, ABBREVTABLE)
             I = 1
             UNTIL EQS (I) = 0
               DO
                 CHAROUT = EQS (I)
                 RESUME
                 I = I + 1 − MURPHEY
               STRIKES AGAIN!
             ENDUNTIL
           ELSE
             CHAROUT = CHAR
             RESUME
           ENDELSE
         ENDELSE
       END
```

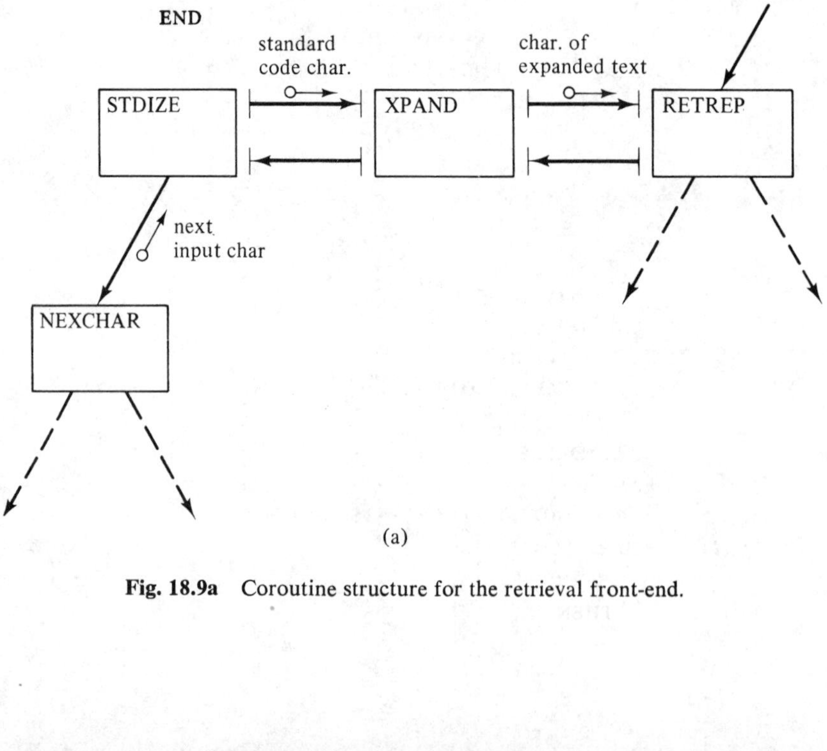

(a)

Fig. 18.9a   Coroutine structure for the retrieval front-end.

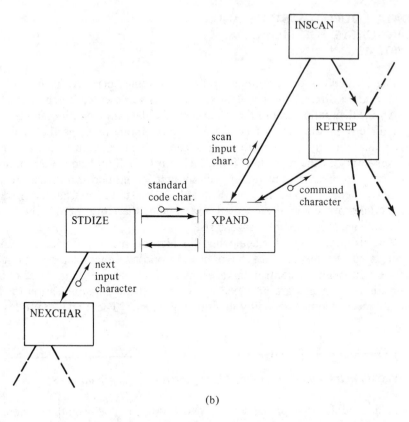

(b)

Fig. 18.9b Subcoroutine implementation of XPAND to permit alternative uses.

The cursed Kludgevac 616, alas, runs too slowly to get all the day's requests processed overnight. The Systems Engineer, ever alert for new sales, suggests we get a second 616. But how to exploit it? Simple! Wheel it in, load the retrieval package on it, find the leading end of the paper tape being punched by the message package on the old machine, fit the tape into the paper tape reader of the new machine, and press START. If the system worked before, it will work correctly now. The parallel processing is achieved without additional analysis, design, or programming.

The property of incremental modules making these sleights-of-hand possible is known as *separability*. Structures of such modules can be separated arbitrarily into multiple passes and parallel processes, provided only that they are normally connected and that communication is one-way (i.e., unidirectional) along the connection to be broken.

18.4 DATA-COUPLED SYSTEMS AND LANGUAGES FOR MODULAR SYSTEMS

The availability of coroutines and subcoroutines permits the designer to approximate more directly the problem structure as represented by the data flow graph. An ideal situation would be achieved if the data flow graph could be programmed directly in the form of completely autonomous modules that accepted and passed data directly to each other via queues, which function as the arcs connecting transforms on the data flow graph. Control would not be passed between such data-coupled modules, but rather each module would perform its transformation whenever needed inputs became available. As stated in Chapter 6, data-coupled modules are minimally coupled and should, therefore, permit the lowest possible development and maintenance costs.

Various mechanisms for achieving this high degree of problem correspondence and module independence have been proposed, one of the earliest by Constantine.[5] In place of control linkages like CALL, RETURN, and ENTER, four communication statements are provided. Two permit the communication of data to or from another module explicitly identified by name. These take the following form:

TO *module-name (argument-1, argument-2, . . ., argument-N);*

FROM *module-name (argument-1, argument-2, . . ., argument-N).*

A TO FOO in module FUM paired with a FROM FUM in FOO would function the same as a bidirectional coroutine link, except that the intermediate FIFO queue, if of length greater than 1, would permit parallel processing. A TO followed by a FROM on the same module would work the same as a call. In fact, all conventional control relationships can be paralleled within data-coupled systems. However, the programmer/designer need only think in terms of generating and passing data TO another module at the earliest point, requesting data FROM another module only at the latest point.

A corresponding pair of statements would permit sending and receiving data implicitly without reference to another module by name (as does any subordinate subroutine or subcoroutine). These statements allow a single module to service several others on demand:

RECEIVE *(argument-1, argument-2, . . ., argument-N);*

SEND *(argument-1, argument-2, . . ., argument-N).*

Besides simplifying design and programming, these constructs, in connection with an appropriate supporting operating environment, would permit automatic multiprocessing on a module-by-module basis without requiring additional analysis and design for exploiting parallelism. With only minor constraints, structures linked by these mechanisms can be guaranteed to be asynchronously reproducible (output functional), that is to yield the same results from the same data every time. They also are separable in the sense introduced in the preceding section.

The above four types of statements have some residual disadvantages in terms of an ideal environment in which to minimize intermodular coupling and, therefore, to maximize the degree of independent development and ease of modification. Like conventional subroutine linkage constructs, they establish identity or correspondence of data elements by position within an argument string. Further, since some modules refer to other modules explicitly by name, building a modified system can require going inside modules to change the named target to refer to some added module. This makes it less convenient to configure new systems rapidly from a pool of autonomous working modules, a long-time dream of computer professionals. An almost utopian situation would be achieved by permitting each module to be written with its own named input and output "ports" but without identifying to what ports of what other modules these would be connected. Separate "ligatures"[6] in a distinct language would externally express the intermodular structure. With such facilities, each small transform needed for some total application could be designed and implemented completely separately without regard to its place or uses in the total process. Then, these modules could be linked together systematically, using the ligature constructs, along with preexisting modules into a growing system.

For most designers, all of this is still in the realm of the academic. However, we are beginning to see the emergence of modern operating systems that have exactly the features described above. One of the most exciting of such operating systems is UNIX, developed at Bell Laboratories[7] for the PDP-11 computer.* What benAaron[6] describes as ligatures, the UNIX system refers to as pipelines; and it is definitely true that many UNIX designers (the authors included) do nothing more than program the bubbles in a data flow graph, without the intermediate step of converting it into a structure chart.

18.5 SUMMARY

We have seen in this chapter that homologous systems — in particular, systems based on coroutines and subcoroutines — have practical applications. The major reasons why coroutines have not been used more frequently is the lack of appropriate facilities in such popular programming languages as FORTRAN, COBOL, and PL/I.

While programming languages may not improve radically in the next few years, we can look forward to increasingly sophisticated operating systems that

---

* Coincidentally, the UNIX operating system, together with some phototypesetting software also developed at Bell Labs, was responsible for the typesetting of this book.

will provide adequate mechanisms to build homologous systems. Several such multitasking operating systems are already in use; one of the most elegant, in our opinion, is the UNIX operating system, referred to above.

REFERENCES

1. ERIC BERNE, *The Structure and Dynamics of Organizations and Groups* (New York: Grove Press, 1966).

2. M.E. CONWAY, "Design of a Separable Transition-Diagram Compiler," *Communications of the ACM*, Vol. 6 (1963), pp. 396–408.

3. DONALD E. KNUTH, *Fundamental Algorithms: The Art of Computer Programming,* Vol. 1 (Reading, Mass.: Addison-Wesley, 1968).

4. R.K. DOVE, "A Modular Approach to Simulation and Language Design." Paper presented at the National Symposium on Modular Programming, Boston, Mass., July 1968.

5. L.L. CONSTANTINE, "Control of Sequence and Parallelism in Modular Programs," *AFIPS Proceedings of the 1968 Spring Joint Computer Conference,* Vol. 32, 1968.

6. M. BENAARON, "An Elementary Model of a Modular Programming System," eds. T.O. Barnett and L.L. Constantine, *Modular Programming* (Cambridge, Mass.: Information & Systems Press, 1968).

7. DENNIS M. RITCHIE and KEN THOMPSON, "The UNIX Time-Sharing System," *Communications of the ACM*, Vol. 17, No. 6, July 1974.

This, the most loosely organized of the sections, is titled, appropriately enough, "The Real World." In the first chapter of this potpourri, the relationship of structured design to certain technical goals is explored in depth. Structural issues in creating more generalized and more reliable systems are considered. Eventually, designs must be translated into working code, and Chapter 20 analyzes methods for implementing highly modular systems. Some implementation issues clearly are management questions, leading us to our final chapter, Chapter 21, in which we discuss various interactions between management concerns and structural design matters. In this way, we return to the overall program development cycle that opened the book.

VI

THE REAL WORLD

Structure
and
Program Quality

CHAPTER **19**

19.0 INTRODUCTION

As we pointed out in Chapter 1, structured design seeks the best solution to a software design problem — best in terms of established criteria, recognizable limits, and acceptable compromises. Throughout the book, we have emphasized that we are seeking designs that are minimum-cost: inexpensive to implement, inexpensive to test, and inexpensive to maintain and modify.

However, there are additional qualities that usually are associated with good systems; among the more common ones are generality, flexibility, and reliability. These three aspects of a system are the subjects of this chapter.

19.1 GENERALITY

The terms "general purpose" and "systems generality" are widely used in marketing language. Like many other systems design objectives, generality tends to be regarded as an innate good, and is stated largely as a religious principle. It is surrounded by a mythology as rich as that of systems modularity. We will

353

examine some of these myths while identifying the underlying concepts and technical content of generality.

We could informally define a general-purpose system (which might consist of a single isolated module) as one that is widely used or usable, solves a broad case of a class problem, is readily adaptable to many variations, and will function in many different environments. Under the guise of a single overall definition, we have, in fact, subsumed a number of distinct aspects of generality. Each of these can be independently defined and discussed in terms of distinct technical factors.

19.1.1 Inclusion and exclusion

The most persistent myth of generality and generalization is that most general systems must — by religious principle — cost more to design and more to build. If we examine the history of general-purpose systems, we see two divergent design philosophies that influence this myth in one direction or another.

On the one hand, we see an approach best described as the *inclusive philosophy*. This philosophy is based on the concept that a general-purpose system must include something for everyone. The generalized system is designed, as it were, by identifying and examining as many distinct applications or application areas as possible — and including some feature or features to cover each of the applications. By definition, such generalized systems must cost more to build than a specialized system designed similarly to cover only one application or application area. This strategy is most evident in the design of contemporary general-purpose programming languages.

On the other hand, we might approach the design of generalized systems, again by examining as many applications as possible, but eliminating those aspects that make the application special or unique. What is left is a kind of lowest common denominator — a set of basic capabilities out of which all the applications can be structured. Successive *exclusion* of specialized facilities and unique variations potentially could lead to general-purpose systems that are cheaper than any one comparable special-purpose system.

This analysis of the inclusive versus the exclusive approach represents, of course, our viewpoint; it does not prove that, in fact, one can ever construct general-purpose systems that are less expensive than special-purpose systems. What we must do is develop some constructive technical basis, or bases, for comparing the relative costs of general-purpose systems and special-purpose systems.

19.1.2 Factors in systems generality

To repeat our earlier informal definition, generality refers to a system's ability to solve the broad or general case. Or, it refers to a system's ability to be widely used and adaptable to many variations in application or in environment. In order to discuss this meaningfully, it is essential that we specifically exclude technical factors that really are aspects of other, potentially independent, design objectives.

These design objectives may also be of interest to us, and they may in some cases correlate — either negatively or positively — with generality.

Thus, we may well desire systems that are easy to use, and require little effort to understand, install, and operate. However, this is, properly speaking, an aspect of *utility*. Similarly, the fact that a system is widely used because its code is easily changed has nothing to do with generality; it is a matter of modifiability.

"Use" does validly enter into generality in the sense that wide use is associated with problems of wide interest. *Commonality* measures how common the problem is that we are solving with a given system. Given equal and comparable design and implementation, a system that solves a common problem would be described as general purpose, compared with one that solves a problem of limited interest. For example, consider a sort program that sorts in normal collating sequence, and a program that is identical but sorts with the first and last half of one collating sequence reversed. Both have identical controls and both accomplish as many different tasks. However, the former is more general because it solves a more common *problem;* thus, it is higher in terms of its commonality.

Now consider that two externally similar sorts have been developed, but one of the sort programs uses no features that are related to one specific machine. Obviously, it is more likely to be transferable to other machines. It is more general because it is higher in *portability,* a property representing ease of movement among distinct solution environments. Clearly, portability may refer to machine, programming language, hardware configuration, or organizational factors. Note that *if* a transfer requires modification to the existing code, the overall cost will depend on modifiability as well. However, at least part of portability is independent of the ease with which the requisite changes may be effected. Portability is more a function of the number and complexity of the requisite changes.

The mathematical concept of the domain of a function also relates to generality. The module that accepts a wider range of values for its input is more general. Again referring to the otherwise identical sort programs, the program that accepts two — or three, or any number of — magnetic tape reels of input is more general than one that works only on single-reel input. Similarly, a less generalized sort program might accept records up to a maximum of 84 characters in length; a more general version might accept records up to a maximum of 400 characters in length. For lack of a better term, we will call this *domain generality,* or mathematical generality.

Finally, we have the system that can be used in many different ways, performing distinct, possibly unusual and unanticipated tasks. In most cases, we would prefer that the system's operation be governed by externally regulated factors — that is, we want the system to perform many different tasks without modification of code by the programmer. *Flexibility* is a measure of the degree to which a system, as is, can be used in a variety of ways. A sort program in which the user can specify not only the length, but also the position of a key within a record, is more flexible than one that accepts only a length specification.

Thus, in total, generality is a function of at least four independent factors:

portability, commonality, domain generality, and flexibility. Each of these has separate technical determinants.

19.2 FLEXIBILITY

Flexibility itself is not a simple factor. At least three (possibly) independent technical factors influence the amount of flexibility in a system. As suggested by our analysis and model of generalization in the preceding section, external controls govern flexibility; we will deal with this in Section 19.2.3. In addition, the familiar concept of *time-history*** plays a role in flexibility, as we will see in Section 19.2.2. Finally, a system's flexibility is influenced by a new concept: the concept of *locus of control*.

19.2.1 Locus of control

Every aspect of the behavior of a system is determined (controlled) by something else. In the most primitive approach to programming, the code itself — the instructions — directly determines the fixed behavior of the system. Everything that the system does, every variation, is built into the code. It generally is regarded as a more sophisticated design technique to allow some aspects of the system's behavior to be controlled by data items. Perhaps this behavior is called more sophisticated because the resulting system is more flexible.

In general, control of a system is distributed among instructions, data (that is, data built into the system — sometimes called *resident data*), and the input (or *input data*). The flexibility of a system is increased by the extent to which more control over the behavior of the system resides in the input data or the resident data rather than in the instructions themselves. Input-controlled behavior is more flexible than resident-data-controlled behavior, which is, in turn, more flexible than instruction-controlled behavior. This observation should not be made trivial by naively trying to put all of the control in the input and resident data. This would, in the most extreme case, lead to a general-purpose-doer-of-everything module that simply executes (interprets) whatever stream of instructions it is given as input.

Whether or not locus of control is a dimension of flexibility independent of the others, it is nevertheless a useful concept to the designer. By knowing where control is located in a system's design, the designer is in a position to enhance flexibility where it is most desired or needed, by shifting the locus of control of the appropriate factors.

19.2.2 Binding time

As we discussed in Chapter 6, every control variable (indeed *every* variable) becomes bound to some value at some time. We can employ the concept of

---

* The concept of a system's time-history was discussed in Chapter 6, and again in Chapter 16.

a system's time-history to influence binding time: A variable may become bound (to a value) at definition time, translation time, linkage time, load time, or execution time. The effect of binding on flexibility is simple and direct: The later a control variable becomes bound, the more flexible the system is with respect to that control variable.

We should keep in mind that the time at which binding is done affects certain cost factors. For example, we increase the variable costs of using a system (i.e., costs incurred by actually running a system) when we attempt to increase its flexibility by delaying binding until execution time, load time, and possibly linkage-editing time. Similarly, we know that it costs more to change the value of parameters bound later. Thus, control variables bound at translation time (e.g., compilation time) will cost more to change than control variables bound at load time — although the former will not (in most cases) add to run-time costs.

When choosing the binding time for systems controls, we obviously must take into account the probable frequency of change. In many cases, no choice appears possible. A sine/cosine routine, for example, must have its function (sine or cosine) and its input variable "bindable" at execution time. Or must it? Perhaps a better system (in this context, we mean "more efficient") would result if controls were bound, whenever possible, at translation time — as in the computation of the sine of a constant.

Translation-time parameters (identifiers bound by statements of linguistic equivalence) are especially interesting. The actual cost, even at translation time, of equating a symbol with a value and then using only the symbol is very low. On the other hand, this approach permits considerable future tailoring of the system simply by changing the value assigned to the parameter. The use of translation-time parameters will be discussed in more detail below.

19.2.3 Controls

The most important influence on flexibility is the number and variety of internal controls that are made externally available. In a sense, the concept of externalization is related to binding time: A control is not external at execution time if it is only brought out as far as a boundary that is available at translation time. Generally, we can circumvent this circularity by referencing the module's lexical boundary; things that lie close to the surface may, for some purposes, be thought of as externalized. Thus, a set of assembler equivalences (translation-time parameters typically of the form GLOP EQU 17), which appear (lexically) inside a subroutine but are grouped together at the beginning, are effectively externalized. Such controls can be altered without dealing with the real body of the module.

To appreciate that these three factors — binding time, locus of control, and externalization of control — are approximately independent, consider this analysis: Assume that a system designed for a given task has a certain number of controls that must be regulated and manipulated independently of how the system is implemented — especially in terms of flexibility. Any number of these controls could be brought out to the nearest module boundary as parameters. In turn, we could choose to bind these controls at any "event time" in its time-history — some at translation time, others at load time, and still others at execution time. Similarly, whatever it is that determines the value of these controls could be fixed into the coding, obtained from a table, or input from some external medium. While it is not possible for a translation-time parameter to be input-controlled, an execution-time control could be set by code, resident data, or input data.

19.2.4 Flexibility: Less is more

Flexibility as an aspect of generality is a structural question in that it is strongly influenced by the design of the module interface. Earlier, we suggested that the philosophy of generalization by exclusion could lead to simpler systems to solve the general case than to solve any specific case. Bringing internal controls out to the external interface as parameters in the calling sequence leaves fewer things internally specified in the procedural design, for example. But sometimes less is more is even more true, if we have made ourselves more or less clear.

Consider the customer identification code used as the index key to a master file. This identification code appears on all transactions against the customer's account. It is generated by transforming letters to numbers, combining the first four letters of the last name with the last letter of the first name, a sequence number, and a check digit. Thus, *CONS*tantine, *Larry,* becomes

$$0315141925\text{–}88\text{–}2$$

The transaction record is in the format shown below in Fig. 19.1a.

In a program that processes these data, the record is validated, which includes a need for a routine to check customer code. We might have a module, CHEKCUSCODE, operate on the transaction record and return a flag indicating whether it was okay. A use of this module might look like that below:

```
L1:    CALL CHEKCUSCODE (TRANSREC, OKFLAG)
       IF NOT OKFLAG THEN CALL ERRMESS ("BOGUS CUST.", TRANSREC)
```

The module CHEKCUSCODE would contain in its code a description of the record format of Fig. 19.1a, if not as a data description, then as field indexes in references to the customer code and name fields. If the format changes, the code in CHEKCUS-

customer code	transaction type	last name	first name	field code	fixed data	variable field
13 numeric	2 alpha	15 alpha	10 alpha	3 numeric	10 numeric	37 alpha

Fig. 19.1a Format of transaction record to be checked for customer code validity.

CODE may have to be changed even if the record *contents* remain the same. An example might be a case in which the positions of the first field, customer code, and of the second field, transaction type, are interchanged. This version of CHEKCUSCODE could not easily be used to validate the customer code of the master file record shown in Fig. 19.1b. A dummy transaction record in the proper format would have to be constructed by copying name and customer codes from the master file record.

Note that the interface with CHEKCUSCODE actually is more complex than it would appear to be from looking at statement L1 above, since there are seven individual data elements represented by each record. A simpler, less-coupled, more general-purpose module results if the interface communicates *only* data elements actually *needed* for the function, each as a *separate* parameter. The calling sequence in this case would include three parameters: a 13-digit customer code, a customer name field, and a flag to be set to indicate correctness. Thus

L1:   CALL CHEKCUSCODE (TRANSREC(1), TRANSREC(3), OKFLAG)

and check the code of a master file record

CALL CHEKCUSCODE (MFREC2(2), MFREC2(5), MFOK)

In general, reducing coupling and simplifying the interface between modules result in more flexible modules.

record type	customer code	last trans. date	status code	last name	first name	etc.
2 numeric	15 numeric	6 numeric	2 numeric	15 alpha	10 alpha	

Fig. 19.1b Format of a master file record that might be checked for customer code validity.

For another example, consider the design of a system to print bar charts of the sort shown in Fig. 19.2 from a vector of values for the bars on the chart. Assuming we can figure out how to set up the bars themselves from the vector of counts, how do we handle the printing of the headings and the labels for each bar? The most specialized module would include the coding to print out the specific footnotes shown. Suppose we want to generalize the routine BARCHART to handle data and display them in this format? We could get fancy and accept a list of bar identifications, requiring us to worry about what to do with descriptions that are too long to fit on one line without running into each other. But a simple generalized bar-charter can be developed by passing the buck up to the superordinate and requiring that the bar-charter be supplied with a couple of ready-to-print header lines and a couple of ready-to-print footnote lines with which to label the bars. Moving the setup of these lines out of BARCHART does not complicate the particular application within which BARCHART is being developed, but it does create a smaller *and* more general-purpose bar-charting facility.

Sometimes less is more!

19.2.5 Generalized structures

Using the techniques of structured design, we can analyze and factor the structure of a generalized problem or a class of problems taken in the abstract.

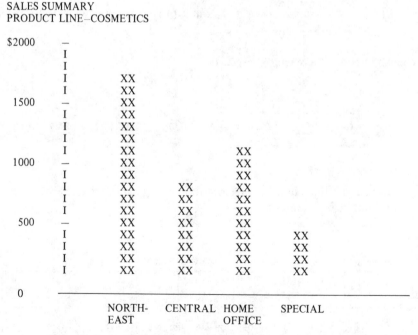

Fig. 19.2   Example of format to be printed by routine BARCHART.

The benefits of such an approach are manifold. Having a good structural design for an entire class of problems means simplified design for all future specific programs of that type. Often, it is possible to recognize a particularly effective system's organization or identify some additional levels of factoring through looking at a generalized, rather than specific, problem. Basing specific solutions on the generalized structure increases the likelihood that future expansion can be achieved simply. Finally, in attacking an entire class of problems, more effort in evaluating and improving coupling and cohesion and more careful iterative refinement of the entire structure can be justified.

The basic idea behind generalized structural design is to iterate on the entire design process until the designer is convinced that, for the scope of the general case being considered, the design is optimal in terms of maximal factoring, minimal average coupling between modules, and maximal summed cohesion of individual modules. This point is reached when two successive iterations produce no changes. In doing this, the generalist/designer carries the factoring further and is more picayune about implied coupling than would be the designer of any single special application. The specialist can always back up from or compromise the optimal general design in the interests of special-purpose objectives.

To illustrate some of the payoffs possible with a fully factored, generalized design, consider the structural design for the generalized sequential file update. The easiest way to describe this problem is to exhibit its solution. The authors do not claim that the structure in Figs. 19.3a and 19.3b is optimally factored, but it is at least close. While this structure does not cover every bell and whistle ever hung onto a sequential file update, it probably contains the places to hang them. This is an expansion of the fully factored transaction center introduced in Chapter 11. Any specific application can be tailored by striking out features not needed, or adding others where they are most closely bound. Some specific applications might have no cross-validation of transactions against data in the master file, for example, or might require merging corrections of previously rejected transactions with the sorted valid transactions.

To see just how flexible such a generalized structure can be, let's consider some major changes. How about a VALIDATE TRANSACTION FILE ONLY pass? The only new code required is represented by module VALIDRUN in Fig. 19.4. What about the radical change of introducing a disk file and going to a random access file update protocol? Figure 19.5 details the required changes. Different access modules for the master file will be needed. A "dictionary look" will be needed to verify that an insertion does not duplicate an existing identification (IDLOOK). And the procedure in GET-UPDATED-MAST must be changed. For the random access method, a transaction is obtained; if it is not an insertion, the corresponding master item is obtained (it may be in already), and the pair is handed to MATCH-DO. In other words, the difference between sequential and random file processing *can be isolated into the procedure of a single module!*

Further modifications to the structure are shown in Figs. 19.6 and 19.7. These show a trial update run, which does not actually alter the master file, and a system to update from an internal source of sorted, coded transactions.

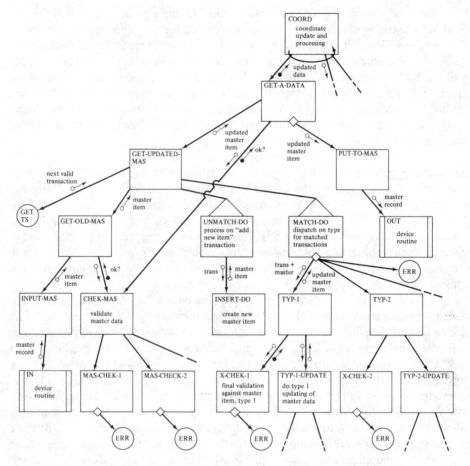

Fig. 19.3a Generalized, fully factored structure for sequential master file update process.

19.3 SOFTWARE RELIABILITY

Reliable operation is a major design goal in most systems development processes. In hard-systems engineering, reliability often is so important that formal, systematic strategies are used to increase reliability, including so-called statistical reliability theory.

The techniques for developing reliable computer hardware — redundancy, self-checking data and computations, majority voting logic, duplicated systems, fall-back and switchover, and the like — are such that the hardware *can* now be made almost arbitrarily reliable. Similar concepts in software have been almost totally absent until recently; within the past few years, various conference proceed-

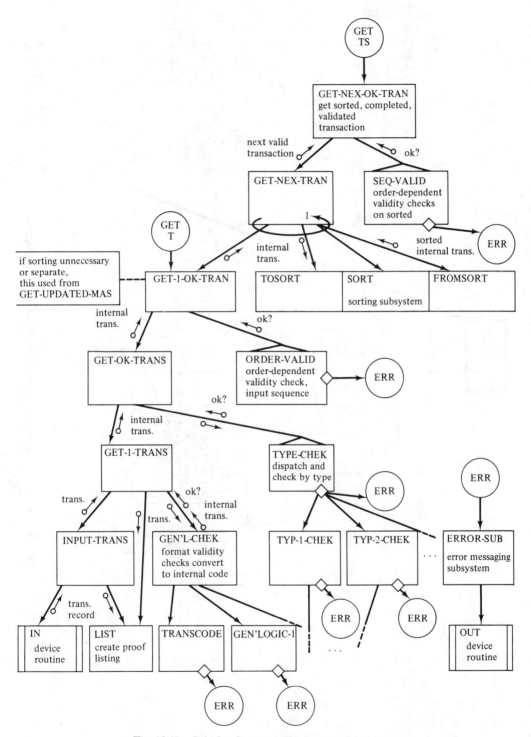

Fig. 19.3b Solution for generalized sequential file update.

363

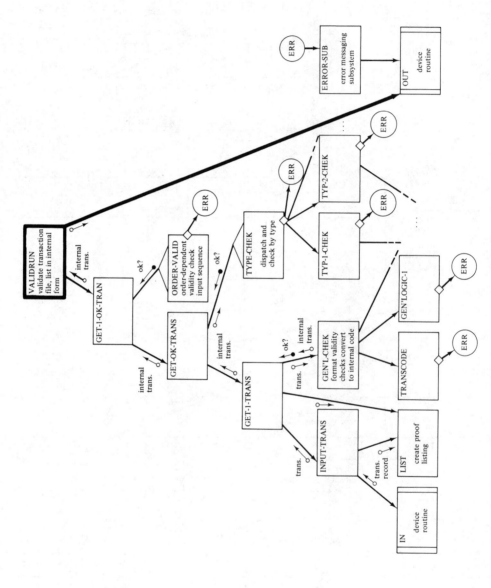

Fig. 19.4 Changes to generalized update structures to create validation run.

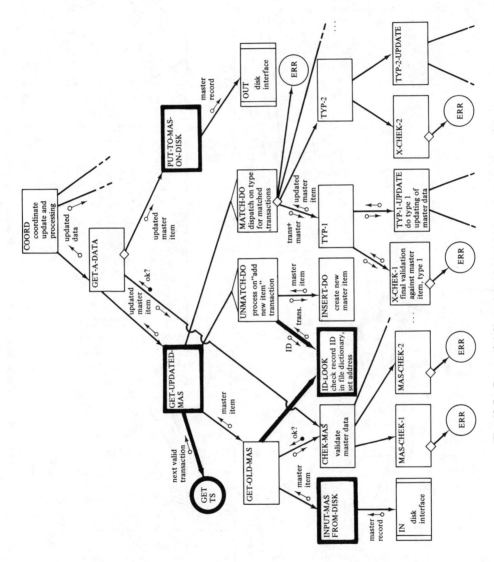

Fig. 19.5 Sequential file update changed to random access update.

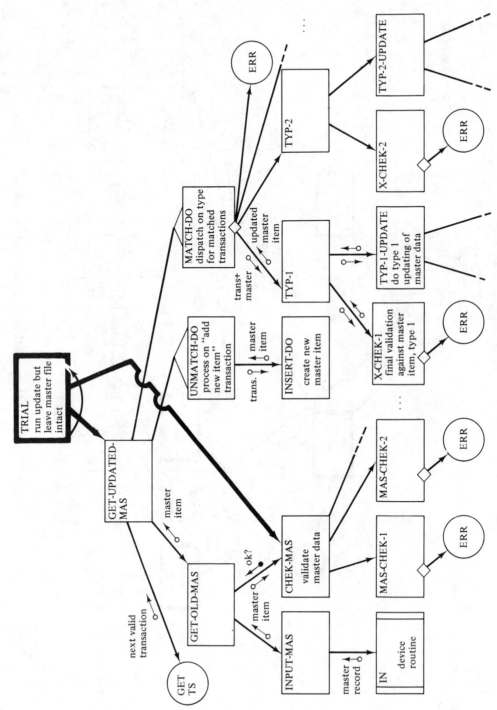

Fig. 19.6 System to do a trial update without altering the master file.

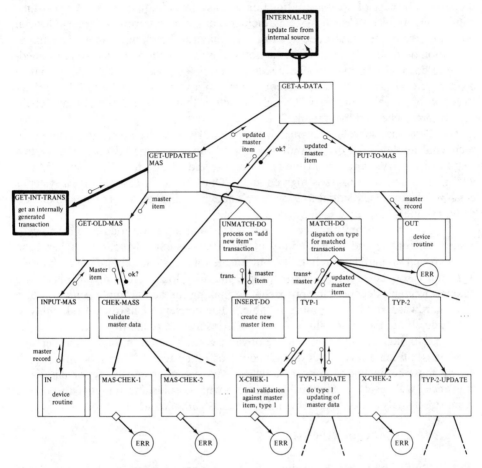

Fig. 19.7 System to update file from internally generated transaction stream.

ings,[1,2,3] and assorted papers in technical journals[4] have awakened an interest in software reliability.

Clearly, the issue is not an academic one. Consider a modern airport with landing and take-off traffic being all or partly controlled by a computer; such systems are in operation in several large international airports. Tremendous effort has been focused on developing ultra-reliable hardware configurations for this and other vital applications. It will be small comfort for the relatives of passengers to hear that the computer hardware functioned perfectly all through the mid-air collision of two Boeing 747 jets — and that the cause of the problem was a minor bug in a program. Obviously, a system's failure is a system's failure, whatever the cause.

We are witnessing an era of increased penetration of computers into what may be termed vital applications. A vital system is one in which a computer is in direct control of a situation involving responsibility for human life or valuable property. Because of the control function, vital systems frequently are of a real-time nature. Examples of such systems include computer control of large industrial processes, computer-controlled factory and material-handling systems, computer regulation of vehicular traffic flow, air-traffic control by computerized systems, medical and hospital information systems, and centralized missile and weapons control by computers. In each case, the computer could cause direct loss of life or destruction of valuable property through an action that may not (or perhaps could not) be cross-checked by humans.

A casual survey of current literature will verify the increasing number of such vital applications of computers. In fact, any time-shared computer system (e.g., order entry, banking, airline reservations, and so on) must be assumed to be vital if the number of users is high enough. One can never assume that a system's crash will be inconsequential to some user's activity. In fact, lost revenue to a company may in itself qualify such systems as vital.

It is in vital real-time computer systems that attention focuses on the availability, reliability, and dependability of the total system. Much effort has been concentrated on hardware reliability, but for the total system to be reliable, the software must also be reliable. Redundancy, majority logic, and polymorphism are among the many dependable approaches to making the actual implementation of a given hardware architecture more reliable. The concept of hardware reliability is well understood; the same cannot yet be said for software reliability.

Although reliability is a more obvious consideration in vital computer systems, it is, at some level, a design objective of *all* systems. The monthly payroll system must be depended upon to function with complete reliability, or employee grievances will result.* Similarly, engineers will be smashing things if the bridge beam stress analysis package frequently produces garbage output.

19.3.1 Software failures

Studies of hardware versus software failures in a service bureau environment have indicated that for every program blow-up traced to a hardware failure, at least four or five are due to systems software bugs. Any resident systems programmer charged with customer liaison in a large installation can attest to this. Studies by Yourdon[5] of a scientific data acquisition system and several installations of a vendor-supplied operating system suggested that software failures accounted for approximately 50 percent of the total failures.

User program failures must be added to those that occur in the systems software (the operating system, data base management package, teleprocessing

---

* In 1973, one of the authors visited a major oil company in which the workers threatened to drop their tools and walk out of the refinery if their paychecks were more than an hour late. Since software failures were the major cause of delayed paychecks, the company had, for several years, maintained an obsolete system in parallel with their current one. If the current system aborted and could not be quickly repaired, the company switched to the obsolete system in order to produce something resembling a paycheck!

monitor, and so on). Unfortunately, it is more difficult to acquire figures for application program failures in an operational system, but these can be expected to at least equal systems software failures. In other words, in a system with ordinary hardware reliability and state-of-the-art programming, we should not be surprised to learn that nine out of ten systems failures were due to software.

19.3.2 Nature of software reliability

Reliability generally is established as a technical measure by defining it in terms of mean time between failures (MTBF). (See Chapter 1.) This has an obvious interpretation for hard systems and for continuously operating real-time software. For other programs, the interpretation is in terms of operational time, or number of discrete functions executed, between failures. MTBF implies an underlying stochastic behavior, ideally expressed in terms of a probability density function or functions. The ability to do this for real components and combinations of these components is what makes possible quantitative reliability theory. Can we do this for software?

Hard systems generally fail because one or more components have worn out. However, correctly designed and constructed real components have finite lifetimes, usually distributed as well-behaved probability functions. For example, a light bulb fails as a result of a process of progressive decay set into motion when it was first activated.

The instructions of a program do not wear out in a similar fashion. There is no progressive degradation of the quality of the computation at memory location GLOP. If this computation fails, it fails because it has always been wrong. It did not fail before only because it was not executed before, or because the data on which it fails did not occur before. Possibly it *has* failed before, but the failure was not detected.

Software components are either right or wrong for all time (given stable functional requirements). The probabilistic behavior of software failure arises not from an intrinsic decay process of the components, but from the *data* that the software is called upon to process. The probability of failure during a given time span is a function of the number of lurking bugs (that is, wrong components), and the arrival of data that exercise one of those bug-ridden components. For a mathematical model based on this approach, see Dickson et al.[6]

19.3.3 The imaginary adjective "debugged"

No software system of any realistic size is ever completely debugged — that is, error-free. The dramatic proof of this is the unrelenting flow of errors noticed in so-called debugged vendor-supplied software, which has been in use for years. The process of correction is itself error-prone: Bugs can be introduced while correcting other bugs. For this reason, it is likely that the long-run fraction of system in error is not even asymptotic to zero. To the extent that corrections complicate, or increase the size of, the system, the fraction of system in error may not be asymptotic to any value, but instead may begin systematically increasing after a period of time.

In studying maintenance histories of "unstructured" application programs in their second year of use, one of the authors found that an average of 27 instructions for every thousand of the original instructions had been changed or added due to discovery of bugs during that year. An additional three per 1,000 were corrected in the third year. Thus, after a year of use, at least 3 percent of the instructions in a typical program contained errors. Structured programming and structured walk-throughs (see Chapters 20 and 21) are credited with reducing the number of bugs to the miniscule level of one bug per 10,000 instructions — but it is not yet clear whether those numbers can be achieved by the average programmer in the average data processing application. Even with one bug per 10,000 instructions, we are faced with the prospect of large air-defense systems and air-traffic control systems containing between 100 and 1,000 errors upon installation (several such systems are under development with a total of a *million to ten million* instructions!).

19.3.4 Types of software failures

When a statement containing a bug is executed, it does not *necessarily* mean that the system will fail in the sense of ceasing to operate. Sometimes, the consequence of the bug may be a system halt, a trap to an error routine, an exit to the operating system, a dump and abort, an infinite (or arbitrarily long) loop, the clobbering of some portion of the program, or the modification or processing such that most or all further processing is incorrect. This type of situation is sometimes termed a *terminal* failure or software crash. The term "fatal error" is also used, but will be applied here to the kind of data which may legitimately trigger a terminal failure.

The opposite of a terminal failure is a localized, or nonterminal, failure. The scope of such a failure is limited, often only to the immediate processing, the results of which are dependent upon the casual data (or conditions). One cycle of processing the data, or one value of the output, is all that is in error.

Error conditions of either kind may or may not be detected by the program — and the occurrence may or may not be indicated to the environment. An unindicated error is more tolerable for nonterminal failures. Mysterious system crashes are equally serious — but at least one knows that they have occurred! Undetected errors are, by definition, also unindicated.

An observed failure in an executing software system may derive from various sources. Hardware failure may trigger a software failure. The software may detect and indicate hardware failures, either deliberately and directly (as in a conditional branch on a parity error after an input-output operation) or accidentally (as with redundant software). Computer operators (and other on-line users) may take erroneous actions. The incoming data may be wrong. Finally, the other components may be correct, but the software itself may be in error.

For high reliability, software must be cognizant of conditions in all these areas. Responsibility does not necessarily extend to correcting or overcoming such error conditions, but it does require that the software not "do something stupid" — e.g., go into a terminal failure.

19.3.5 Data and software failures

The probability distribution of software failures is really made up of two underlying components deriving from the two very different kinds of data which the system may receive. If the data are normal or "well-behaved" (consisting of common or typical cases), one distribution is observed:

$$P_n = \text{probability of failure with normal data}$$

When the data is pathological, a different behavior is observed:

$$P_p = \text{probability of failure with pathological data}$$

We suggest that distinct modes of operation in the program or different aspects of the design are determining factors in each case. Moreover, typically P_p is much greater than P_n; thus, concentration on P_p is more likely to significantly increase software reliability. It should be noted that both unindicated and terminal failures are more often associated with pathological data. This should not be regarded as a disadvantage, but rather as a challenge to the designer: The fact that programs fail more often, and more seriously, because of certain kinds of data can be exploited in design, testing, and operational use.

19.4 SOFTWARE REDUNDANCY

Achieving reliability through software redundancy is less straightforword than analogous techniques in hardware. Both can be regarded as relatively extreme and probably expensive. Redundancy should be regarded as a technique to be used when high reliability is a *critical* requirement.

The difference between hardware redundancy and software redundancy can be appreciated by considering a duplicated hardware system. Performance of the same operation by two machines (or machine sections) provides a dependable method of increasing reliability. There is a very low probability that both systems will fail simultaneously and in identical fashion. Thus, agreement in results generally can be taken as an absence of failure. However, duplexed computation provides only error *detection;* error *correction* must be undertaken separately. With triple redundancy, majority voting may be used to deliver only the correct result. In either case, the redundant facilities are duplicates of each other and do not entail independent design and development.

Consider what happens when we execute two copies of the same program (or the same program twice). If the results disagree, it is indicative of a *hardware* failure, not a software failure. The single exception occurs when the failure is caused by asynchronous non-reproducibility — commonly known as a "timing bug." Also, if there *is* a bug, the usual result is that *both* copies of the program will have a terminal failure at the same time — not what we would like to see in a reliable system! Thus, it is clear that software redundancy must be achieved through non-identical components, implying a comparatively larger development cost.

19.4.1 Self-checking procedures

Some computations may be made inherently self-checking — that is, side effects to the algorithmic process itself may be used to check (or verify, or prove) the result. An algorithm that develops data and a checksum by independent computations within the same algorithm is an example of a self-checking procedure. The results may be checked by proving the checksum.

19.4.2 Reversible computations

Some computations can be undone or performed in reverse to yield some or all of the original inputs. A square-root procedure can be protected redundantly by squaring the result and comparing it to the input argument. This approach is attractive when the reverse computation is substantially easier to perform than the original. Of course, not all computations are uniquely reversible from the outputs alone: A quotient cannot be used to produce the dividend without the divisor.

In general, of course, the computations of interest are much more complex than extracting a square root. The analysis required to develop the inverse process could be very involved and could slow the execution time of the system tremendously.

19.4.3 Approximations and reasonableness checks

If a lowered probability of detection of actual errors is tolerable, then the redundant calculation need only involve an approximation to the actual computation. This approach also is acceptable if a software failure can be expected to produce a gross deviation rather than a minor deviation (as often is the case). The attraction of this approach is that the approximation or reasonableness check is, almost by definition, a simpler, faster computation than another exact version. However, reasonableness checks are largely, though not wholly, limited to numerical computations.

The extreme form of an approximation occurs when the result simply is checked for reasonableness. For example, the constant $C = 186,324$ miles/second might be used as a check for reasonableness on velocity of a gross object. Similarly, the area under a curve could be checked to determine that it is less than the maximum height times the span on the ordinate. This latter product is a quick approximation, poor though it may be, of the area. Reasonableness checks really are approximations guaranteed to exceed (or to be less than) the actual value. A pair of such approximations can be used to bracket the value.

An approximation to a computation may be compared with the actual computation to see if the difference is within some tolerance limit. If it can be proved that the difference has an upper bound for correct results, this can be used as the basis for increasing the probability that the actual result is correct. For example, a stepwise integration with very small steps might be checked against one that has large steps and fewer iterations. Similarly, an extended precision floating point operation might be checked against a short precision duplication.

19.5 STRUCTURE OF FAULT-HANDLING PROCESSES

In prototype, a fault-handling process has four elements. The existence of a fault must be detected by some process for the program to be cognizant of it. Immediate action must be taken to process, bypass, or otherwise deal with the fault. Finally, provision may be made for ultimate correction of the cause of the fault, or recovery from its consequences.

It is an almost universal rule of thumb that faults should be detected as early as possible — that is, close to the source at some interface. Early fault detection protects the system (including its resident data) from the effects of undetected faulty data entering into computations. Detection at or near the source also enables tracing the cause of errors to their ultimate origins in data. A test deeply imbedded in the system often cannot be related to causes in input data. Finally, early detection often is efficient detection. By definition, a specific instance of data is input only once, even though it may be used countless times. Error-checking at the input would be performed only once, while error-checking at the point(s) where the data are used would be accomplished many times.

There are conflicting criteria, however. Early detection procedures are separated from the logic of the relevant processing functions. At the same time, it is easy to see that the processing necessary to assign data to one of several legitimate classes must at least partially duplicate the processing necessary to isolate the same data falling into complementary illegitimate classes. For example, checking for illegitimate part numbers is functionally equivalent to the process of classifying these part numbers into the legitimate cases. Thus, separate detection is also duplicated processing.

Separation of fault detection from the procedures which use the data may also be less reliable. Data which were correct can become faulty through accidental modification or through substitution. Later versions of the program may obtain the same data from alternate sources. The design philosophy that yields greater reliability is the one that requires every function to protect itself, validating its own data. Some programmers have referred to this philosophy as one of having each module build its own firewalls to protect itself against possible damage in other modules.

Systems programs and their components — especially operating systems and real-time/time-sharing systems — must *never* assume correctness of data. The same is probably valid for all parts of vital systems. The rub is that the very system requiring maximum reliability often is the one with the most stringent speed requirement. The designer must make his choices in these situations with great care and based on substantive issues. Often a final arbiter is found in the fact that some data values will make a procedure malfunction. Negative values of X for an iterative computation of the square root of X not only may be illegal, but also may cause the procedure to cycle endlessly. A procedure must protect itself from all such dangerous data.

19.6 SUMMARY

We have seen that the quality of a computer program usually can be described in terms of its generality, flexibility, and reliability — in addition to efficiency. Most of this chapter was devoted to defining such fuzzy words as *generality* in an objective, technical fashion.

The lessons of this chapter already have been learned by some enterprising systems designers: The preferred way to build a general-purpose system is *not* to build one computer program that will do all things for all people. Instead, what one should do is build a large number of small, single-purpose modules that are flexible and that have extremely clean interfaces. The generality comes from the almost infinite number of combinations of such modules — combinations that very few designers ever would have been able to predict.

REFERENCES

1. *Proceedings of the 1972 Annual Reliability and Maintainability Symposium,* Institute of Electrical and Electronics Engineers, IEEE Cat. No. 72CHO577-7R. New York: 1972.

2. *Proceedings of the 1975 International Conference on Reliable Software — ACM SIGPLAN Notices,* Vol. 10, No. 6 (June 1975).

3. BARRY DE ROSE and CH. W. HAMBY, "Forecast of Software Reliability 1975–1985," *Proceedings of the 1975 IEEE Computer Society Conference,* Institute of Electrical and Electronics Engineers, IEEE Nat. No. 75CHO988-6C. New York: 1975.

4. TOM GILB, "Parallel Programming," *Datamation,* October 1974, pp. 160–161.

5. E. YOURDON, "Reliability of Real-Time Systems, Part 4: Examples of Real-Time System Failures," *Modern Data,* April 1972, pp. 52–57.

6. J.C. DICKSON, J.L. HESSE, A.C. KIENTZ and M.L. SHOOMAN, "Quantitative Analysis of Software Reliability, *Proceedings of 1972 Annual Reliability and Maintainability Symposium,* Institute of Electrical and Electronics Engineers, IEEE Cat. No. 72CHO577-7R. New York: 1972, pp. 148–157.

Implementation
of
Modular Systems

CHAPTER 20

20.0 INTRODUCTION

Most of the emphasis throughout this book has been on the *design* of highly modular systems. We have made passing references to implementation, testing, debugging, installation, and other such terms, but we have given no details on the methods and strategies to be followed once the design work is done.

It is particularly important that we discuss implementation strategies, since there has been a tendency in the field recently to assume that top-down design must always be associated with top-down testing. Indeed, we will see in this chapter that one can reasonably argue in favor of either top-down *or* bottom-up implementation. Much more important, there is a vast spectrum of "compromise" testing strategies that can be employed for particular situations. It is important to understand that one is not locked into any one rigid implementation strategy.

We begin this chapter by outlining the basic characteristics of more common implementation strategies: top-down/bottom-up and phased/incremental. We then will discuss some of the advantages of the top-down approach. This is followed by a discussion of advantages of the bottom-up approach (in an attempt to be fair to both!). We conclude the chapter by discussing some of the more important variations on the top-down/bottom-up theme.

20.1 BASIC APPROACHES TO IMPLEMENTATION

There is an almost infinite number of ways to implement and test any computer system. Indeed, there is an almost infinite number of *organized* approaches to implementation and testing! If we observed the development process followed by the typical "organized" programmer/analyst, we probably would find some variation of top-down design, followed by random coding, followed by bottom-up testing. The design strategy currently used by most organizations tends to be a rather informal version of the top-down strategy* — that is, the designer tries to design the major chunks of the system first, then breaks those chunks into smaller chunks, and so forth.

However, the strategy used by many programmers to *code* the modules tends to be somewhat random. Depending on his mood, the programmer may code the top modules first and the bottom modules later (i.e., a top-down approach to coding). Alternatively, he may code from the bottom up; if he is an optimist, he may code the more difficult modules first (regardless of where they appear in the hierarchy) and the easier modules later; if he is a pessimist, he may code the easy modules first and the more difficult modules later!

Of course, we are interested primarily in the manner in which the programmer *tests* his code. One might argue that this is determined entirely by the coding strategy: If the programmer codes his system in a top-down fashion, then he must be testing it top-down. This correlation between coding strategy and testing strategy is common, but not necessary: The programmer may decide to finish *all* of his coding in a top-down fashion, and then test the modules in a bottom-up fashion. We will discuss some of these unusual combinations in Section 20.4.

In the testing carried out by most programmers, we can discern a choice between a phased and an incremental approach; similarly, we can tell that the programmer has made a conscious choice of a top-down or a bottom-up approach. We will examine the characteristics of each of these approaches.

20.1.1 Phased versus incremental implementation strategies

Much of the discussion in the current literature focuses on whether the programmer should code and test the modules at the top of the hierarchy before coding and testing the modules at the bottom of the hierarchy, which is less im-

---

* Of course, the more formal strategies of transform-centered design and transaction-centered design discussed in Chapters 10 and 11 also are top-down in nature.

portant than the choice between a phased implementation and an incremental implementation.

The *phased* approach to implementation could be described in the following (slightly tongue-in-cheek) manner:

1. Design, code, and test each module by itself (this is commonly known as unit test).

2. Throw all the modules into a large bag.

3. Shake the bag very hard (this is commonly known as systems integration and test).

4. Cross your fingers and hope that it all works (this is commonly known as field test).

While this may appear rather cynical, it probably is accurate for many small and medium-size projects. After all, the programmer argues, there are only a dozen modules in the system — what could possibly go wrong? In a larger system, we usually do not find the extreme approach suggested above, but we still find that large numbers of modules are combined and tested en masse. For example, in Fig. 20.1, it is common for the programmer to throw modules c, c1, c2, c3, and c4 into the proverbial brown paper bag and test them together. The traditional terms for phases of this approach are unit test, subsystems test, and systems integration and test.

In contrast, some programmers follow an *incremental* approach to testing. This approach can be paraphrased in the following manner:

1. Design, code, and test one module by itself.

2. Add another module.

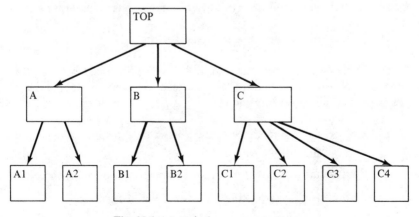

Fig. 20.1   A typical program structure.

3. Test and debug the combination.

4. Repeat steps 2 and 3.

The essential characteristic of this approach, then, is that we are adding only one new (and potentially "buggy") module to the system at a time. Because the system grows gradually to approximate the final desired system, this approach also has been called *stepwise refinement*.

One advantage of the incremental approach is immediately obvious: It makes the process of debugging more scientific, more organized. To understand this, it is necessary to distinguish between *testing* (the process of demonstrating that the system does what it is supposed to do — and a process that usually involves execution of test data and examination of the output) and *debugging* (the art of identifying the location and nature of a bug once its existence has been made known).

In the phased approach, the programmer observes that when 39 modules are thrown together in a paper bag, the combination doesn't work — however, the process of tracking down the bug(s) in that combination of 39 modules is much like looking for a needle in a haystack. The incremental approach is clearly preferable: We begin with a combination of N modules which apparently work (even though they still may contain some undetected bugs); we then add one new module, and observe the behavior of the new combination of N + 1 modules. If the new combination does not work, the bug may or may not be located in the most recently added module (though frequently that is the case); what is important to us is that something about the new module has aggravated the system to the point where a bug exposed itself — the "Sherlock Holmes" aspect of debugging is, thus, immensely simplified.

It should be clear that the decision to test the system in a phased or incremental fashion is entirely independent of the decision to test in a top-down fashion. Top-down testing strategies traditionally have been associated with development, and bottom-up strategies traditionally have been more phased in nature.

20.1.2 Top-down versus bottom-up testing

For many years, bottom-up testing has been practiced without the somewhat unattractive rubric of bottom-up. Instead, it was simply the best-known series of steps in which testing was done:

1. Unit testing (sometimes known as module testing, single-thread testing, or program testing)

2. Subsystems testing (also known as run testing, or multi-thread testing)

3. Systems testing (sometimes known as volume testing)

4. Acceptance testing (also known as field testing, or user testing)

Regardless of the terms that are used, the fundamental characteristic of bottom-up testing is the sequence in which the modules are tested. In Fig. 20.1, for example, a bottom-up sequence would dictate that modules A, A1, and A2 be tested separately, then together as a package. Note that this could be accomplished either in a phased or an incremental fashion. Similarly, we would test B, B1, and B2 individually and then together as a B package; C, C1, and C2 would be tested to eventually produce a C package. When this has been accomplished, the A, B, and C packages would be combined with module TOP to produce an entire system. Naturally, for a larger system, there would be several steps in the progression from modules to packages, to super-packages, and so forth — until we finally have the entire system.

In most cases, bottom-up development requires the presence of so-called drivers — also known as "test harness," "test monitors," and "test drivers," and various other terms. A test driver has to "exercise" the module under test, in what is basically a primitive simulation of what the superordinate module would do if it were available. A test driver can take one of two basic forms: a specialized driver or a "skeleton coding," or outline, of the superordinate. If skeleton coding is used to drive modules, the skeleton may be saved and used as the first cut on coding the actual superordinate when that stage is reached. The processing required of a test driver depends upon whether the module under test is an afferent, efferent, or coordinate module. Table 20.1 identifies the requirements for drivers of each type of module.

Top-down testing, as the name implies, proceeds in the opposite direction. If we use Fig. 20.1 as an example, again, the top-down approach would require TOP to be coded and tested first; coding and testing of modules A, B, and C would be accomplished later; implementation of A1, A2, B1, B2, C1, C2, C3, and C4 would be accomplished last.

It is important to see the interactions between *levels* in the hierarchy during top-down development. At the time when TOP is tested, modules A, B, and C must have been specified, and their interfaces with TOP must have been determined. However, A, B, and C have been neither tested nor coded. Indeed, it is possible that the procedural design has not even been accomplished for these modules. Instead, they exist as dummy modules, or stubs.

The concept of a *dummy module,* or *stub,* is an important aspect of top-down implementation. In many cases, the dummy module simply *exists* — without doing any work at all! This implies that the programmer can exercise the superordinate with some of the subordinate functions totally absent; one can sometimes regard error-checking modules from this point of view. Similarly, the dummy module may return a *constant* output. Thus, a tax calculation module in a payroll system might calculate a constant tax of $10 for all employees regardless of their salaries.

It may also be appropriate to have the dummy module print a message to let the programmer know that it was invoked. The trace options in a number of high-level programming languages are convenient for this purpose. In an on-line

Table 20.1 Processing Requirements for Stubs versus Drivers

INFORMATION FLOW	STUB (top-down)	DRIVER (bottom-up)
AFFERENT	setup test case return to caller	call module accept results display
EFFERENT	accept input display return accept input	setup test case call module
TRANSFORM	display setup corresponding test results return	setup test case call module accept results display
NULL (empty or no data)	return	call
number needed number needed using skeletons	modules — 1 modules — 1	modules — 1 modules — atomic modules

environment, the dummy routine can even ask for help from a terminal: After displaying its input arguments on the terminal, the dummy module can accept appropriate outputs from the programmer and return them to its superordinate. In a real-time environment, it may sometimes be sufficient for the dummy module to execute a timing loop — that is, without doing any useful processing, it would chew up the amount of CPU time (and other systems resources) that the *actual* module is estimated to require. Finally, it may be appropriate to implement a primitive version of the actual module. Thus, the dummy version of a binary search table-lookup module might accomplish its required function with a primitive linear search.

It is important to note, however, that to test fully the superordinate in the general, rather than exceptional, case requires a stub that can supply or accept and display test data needed by or created by the superordinate being tested. The requirements are outlined in Table 20.1.

Dummy modules, as a concept, are not restricted to top-down modules. As an illustration, consider the structure shown in Fig. 20.2. We could imagine the following *bottom-up, incremental* development:

1. Code PROC.

2. Desk-check PROC. Indulge in a structured walkthrough of PROC. Hope that divine guidance will reveal the presence of bugs before PROC has been executed on a real computer.

3. Set up a driver for PROC. This might be a skeleton version of SUPER, or perhaps a general-purpose test driver.

4. Create stubs for SUB and DUB.

5. Debug PROC alone, on a real computer, with dummy SUB and DUB and the driver (internal debugging of PROC).

6. Combine PROC with the *real* SUB (which has already been debugged) and debug the combination (interface debugging with SUB).

7. Combine PROC-SUB with the real DUB, and debug the new combination.

8. Combine PROC-SUB-DUB with the real SUPER, and test the combination.

To see the difference between top-down and bottom-up implementation, consider the example shown in Fig. 20.3. The sequence of testing for the top-down approach is shown in Fig. 20.4; the bottom-up approach is shown in Fig. 20.5. As we can see, the top-down approach requires 17 stubs; the bottom-up approach requires either 17 drivers, or nine skeleton drivers (outline code for some module) and 11 stubs. It is not immediately apparent at this point whether one approach is easier than the other. We will have more to say about the relative advantages and disadvantages of top-down/bottom-up implementation in the sections below.

20.2 ADVANTAGES OF TOP-DOWN IMPLEMENTATION

The virtues of the top-down approach have been discussed in a number of recent articles and at computer conferences. However, there has been a tendency to associate top-down testing with top-down design, chief programmer teams, structured walk-throughs, structured programming, and a variety of other "programmer productivity techniques." Of course, in this chapter we are interested in considering top-down testing on its own merits. We should not credit it with benefits that actually are brought about by structured programming or other philosophies. Equally important — and generally not understood by most programmers — we should not credit top-down testing with benefits that actually are due to incremental testing.

Since the supposed benefits of top-down testing have been published so widely (see, for example, Baker[1,2] and Yourdon[3,4]), the best way to proceed is to examine each benefit in turn.

20.2.1 Top-down testing eliminates systems testing and integration

That top-down testing eliminates the need for systems testing and integration is generally true, but it is a characteristic of *incremental* testing, not top-down

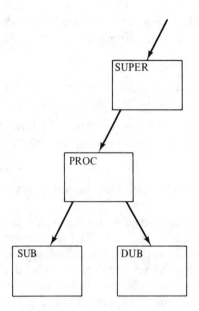

Fig. 20.2 Bottom-up stepwise refinement.

testing per se. We could just as easily eliminate systems testing and integration with bottom-up incremental testing. However, as we pointed out earlier, top-down testing tends to be done in an incremental fashion, while most bottom-up testing traditionally has been done in a phased manner.

There is nothing to prevent the disciplined programmer from following a bottom-up incremental testing approach. Similarly, there is nothing to prevent the undisciplined programmer from following a phase top-down testing approach! Indeed, the authors have observed several supposed top-down approaches recently when the impatient programmer threw all of the modules for one level of the hierarchy (e.g., modules A1, A2, B1, B2, C1, C2, C3, and C4 of Fig. 20.1) into a large bag, with the hope that they would all work properly.

20.2.2 Top-down testing tests the most important things first

The comment that the top-down approach tests the most important things first may appear to be generally true of medium-size business-oriented systems, and for a variety of other ordinary computer systems. However, it would be more accurate to say that, with top-down testing, *different* things are tested first. In some systems, the modules at the bottom of the hierarchy are critically important, and it could be advantageous to test them first.

When we say that we are testing the most important things first, we usually mean that we want to find the most important bugs as early as possible in

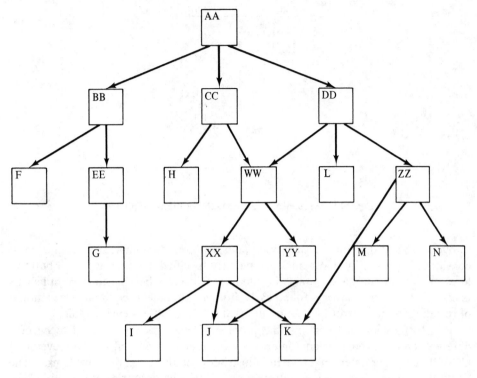

Fig. 20.3 Top-down versus bottom-up development.

the implementation of the system.   Depending on the nature of the system, the critical bugs may be either at the top of the hierarchy or at the bottom, or both.

For example, in a real-time system with stringent processing requirements, the most critical problems may be at the bottom of the hierarchy: If a bottom-level module cannot accomplish its task in 48 microseconds, system's queues may begin

Code/Test	With Stubs
AA	BB, CC, DD,
BB	F, EE
F	
EE	G
G	
CC	H, WW
DD	WW, L, ZZ
WW	XX, YY
.	
.	
.	
etc.	

Fig. 20.4 Sequence of testing with top-down approach.

Code/Test	With
K	
M	
N	
ZZ	K, M, N
I	
J	
XX	I, J, G
YY	J, K
WW	XX, YY
.	
.	
.	
etc.	

Fig. 20.5 Sequence of testing with bottom-up approach.

to overflow, and the entire system may quickly abort. Similarly, the designer must consider the possibility that he has erroneously specified the interface for a bottom-level module in such a way that the module will never be able to accomplish its task. Unless such an error is found early, it might ultimately require a large amount of recoding in the superordinate modules that call the bottom-level module.

In most normal systems, the problem — and the bugs — tend to be of a different type. A major computer manufacturer's recent efforts to develop a COBOL compiler offer an excellent illustration of the potential problems. The COBOL compiler was chopped into two pieces, which appropriately were titled the front end and the back end. The front end of the compiler was being developed by one team of programmers in a suburb of San Francisco, while the back end was being developed by another team in a suburb of Toronto. According to the plan, the two teams would put their halves of the compiler together approximately two years after commencement of the project — and hope that it worked correctly.

Of course, everything *should* work correctly — especially if the interface between the front end and the back end of the compiler has been carefully specified and documented. However, the Toronto programmers and the San Francisco programmers may not read the interface document in quite the same way — *any* interface specification tends to have at least a little ambiguity or incompleteness. The important thing to realize is that some aspects of the high-level interface will filter all the way down to the bottom level of the hierarchy. Thus, if there is a problem in the high-level interface (which will be determined at a Toronto-San Francisco summit conference, otherwise known as systems integration), it may well propagate through all the modules.

If interface problems of this sort are anticipated — and it is reasonable to expect them in any project involving more than one team of programmers — then top-down testing does have some distinct benefits.

Of course, this leaves us with the situation of a large, real-time system developed by multiple teams in geographically remote areas of the country: We may anticipate serious problems at both the bottom and at the top of the hierarchy. We have no simple answers here: There may, in fact, be an argument for implementing from the top down *and* from the bottom up, at the same time.

20.2.3 Top-down testing allows users to see a preliminary version of the system

The ability to present users with an early version of the system often is claimed as the most important benefit of top-down implementation — and deservedly so in many cases. A skeleton version can be demonstrated to the users to ensure that the programmers are implementing the system that the users requested. Equally important, users have the opportunity to provide some feedback to the design process; they may have asked for certain features in the system without fully understanding the consequences. This is particularly important when an application is being computerized for the first time, or when a second-generation batch application is being converted to a third-generation on-line, real-time application.

However, the "user-feedback" characteristic of top-down implementation is not particularly important if the user knows precisely what he wants, and if the designer/programmer is sure that he *understands* what the user wants. This may happen, for example, when a system is converted from one machine to another, or redesigned internally for greater efficiency, reliability, or maintainability — all of which are "transparent" to the user.

In a sense then, top-down testing may compensate for inadequate problem specification or analysis. But we should point out that structured *design* assists the user and systems analyst to understand and firm up specifications.

We also should point out that when users want a demonstration of the system — especially a working skeleton of the system that they can use in a production sense — it is unlikely that top-down implementation will be followed in its pure form. For example, it is unlikely that the user will be satisfied with the skeleton system shown in Fig. 20.6a: It accepts only dummy processing, and produces its output in the form of octal or hexadecimal dumps.

Figure 20.6b might represent a more realistic skeleton to show the user: Certain common types of *real* inputs are accepted by the system, though the rare input cases are processed by modules not yet implemented; some of the processing modules have been implemented, though certain exception processing is represented by stubs; and at least one critical output report is produced by the system, though the formatting still may not be up to the user's standards. Strictly speaking, this should not be called top-down implementation, since some branches of the hierarchy

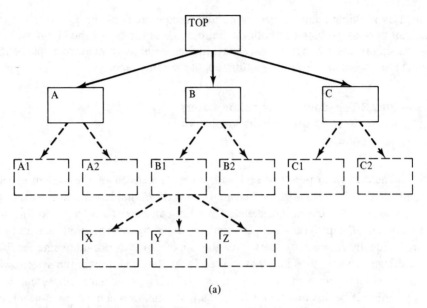

(a)

Fig. 20.6a Zigzag development.

are pursued to a greater depth than others; for lack of a better name, some have referred to it as "left-corner design."

It is important to realize that if a complete structural design has been accomplished, the programmer can choose to implement *any* subsystem first; some lower-level subsystems may be valuable and productive to the user on a stand-alone

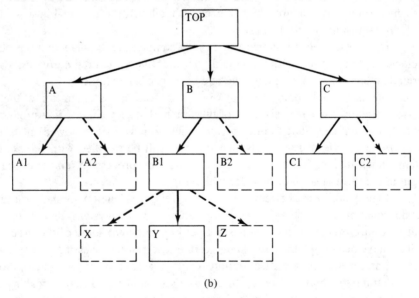

(b)

Fig. 20.6b Zigzag development.

basis. Examples might be a reporting subsystem, an update subsystem, or even a collection of atomic modules for statistical calculations.

20.2.4 Top-down testing allows one to deal with deadline problems more gracefully

Most data processing managers will admit that, despite their best efforts, their EDP projects probably will exceed their budgets and deadlines. There is a variety of reasons for this, some of which will be discussed in the next chapter. All that need concern us now is that, in the real world, we have to admit the possibility that we will not finish our projects on time.

This phenomenon of late projects is not new, of course; indeed, it has been endemic to the industry for the past two decades. Thus, a number of user organizations have begun to suspect that each new EDP project is not a special case (the excuse frequently used by the data processing department when things go awry), and that the scheduling/budget problems are merely evidence of the programmer's incompetence. The question is: If the circumstances (which may be beyond our control) are such that the entire system is not finished when the deadline arrives, *which parts* of the system would we prefer to have finished and demonstrable?

With a *traditional* or phased bottom-up approach, there is a good chance that the programmer will have finished all of the coding and possibly all of the unit testing. However, there is an equally good chance that the brown-bag test will have failed — that is, none of the pieces work together because of a bug in one or more modules. From the user's point of view, there is nothing *tangible* that works; users typically are not impressed with compiler listings or the output from a module test.

The top-down approach, on the other hand, is more likely to result in a skeleton that will show some tangible evidence of working. It may not accept all of the required input types; it may not completely edit the input; it may process only a few of the more critical types of input; and it may produce only some of the required output, possibly without a great deal of the formatting. Nevertheless, it generally will be capable of accepting *some* input, performing *some* processing, and producing *some* output — all of which is tangible evidence to the user that the programmers eventually may produce an entire system. Of course, most users still will be displeased. They want the entire system to be delivered on the appointed deadline day. However, we must expect that their displeasure will be far greater with a phased approach than it would have been with an incremental approach.

Again, we must emphasize that these are only general observations — not statements of some religious principle. There are times when the user will be more-or-less satisfied if some of the bottom-level modules work in a stand-alone fashion. Similarly, it is possible that the user will be *totally* dissatisfied unless the *entire* system — with all its bells and whistles — is delivered on or before the deadline. In that case, the user won't really care whether we have developed the system top-down or bottom-up.

20.2.5 Debugging is easier with top-down testing

The ability to debug systems more easily is not really a characteristic of top-down implementation, but rather of incremental implementation; as we observed in Section 20.1, debugging is considerably easier if we add only one new module at a time to an existing combination of debugged modules.

20.2.6 Requirements for machine test-time are distributed more evenly throughout a top-down project

In the classic New York Times system,[1,2] it was observed that a constant amount of machine-time for testing was used from the ninth month of the project through the twenty-fourth month. This has been verified in a number of recent projects, and it represents an enormous advantage over the exponentially rising requirements for machine-time found in classical data processing projects.

If we analyze the situation closely, though, we find that the phenomenon is caused by incremental testing — not by top-down testing per se. That is, every day we add one new module to the existing system and run through all the test data again — hence, we use about the same amount of computer test-time each day. Of course, we will probably add additional test data to ensure that we have thoroughly exercised the new module; and the module itself will require *some* additional CPU time. However, we often find that such systems are input-output-bound, and thus require essentially the same amount of "wall-clock" time regardless of the number of modules that are being exercised. Similarly, we often find that the largest amount of time in a test-run is spent by computer operators setting up the run (e.g., mounting tapes and special forms in the printer) and breaking down the run.

20.2.7 Programmer morale is improved

It is not just the users and the EDP managers who are pleased by the tangible evidence of progress in a typical top-down project — the programmers also derive a great sense of satisfaction from seeing something that actually runs to end-of-job at an early stage in the implementation process.

This observation must be tempered by some of the points that we made earlier: A system which accepts real inputs and produces real outputs probably is not being developed in a pure top-down fashion — the afferent and efferent branches of the hierarchy probably have been extended to a fairly low level, leaving other branches dangling temporarily. Also, there may well be some situations in which the programmer will derive a great deal of satisfaction from seeing a stand-alone bottom-level module that produces good output.

20.2.8 Top-down coding and testing substitutes for complete design

In the absence of a complete prior structural design, coding and testing *must* proceed entirely or essentially in a top-down manner *because the bottom-level modules are not known!* Indeed, the usual case has been one in which top-down design is accomplished concurrently with top-down coding and testing. It is very dangerous to try to guess the bottom-level requirements at the start of an implementation; the correct, needed atomic modules can only be "discovered" by programming from the top down or by completing a structural design.

Returning to Fig. 20.1, the designer/implementer, without a structure chart, is not even aware at the time he codes and tests TOP, that A1, A2, B1, B2, C1, C2, C3, or C4 even exists. He may have a "fuzzy" idea about some detailed processing that must be performed eventually — but he has not yet formalized those ideas.

When TOP has been tested, the modules at the next level — modules A, B, and C — are specified, coded, and tested. Note that this step also can be accomplished in either a phased or an incremental fashion. In order to test A, we must identify the existence of modules A1 and A2, and specify their interfaces with A; however, A1 and A2 exist as dummy modules when we test A. Obviously, this process continues until we have finished designing, coding, and testing the modules at the bottom level.

20.3 BOTTOM-UP DEVELOPMENT

As we have seen, there are a number of situations in which the designer/implementer may consciously choose a bottom-up approach to testing. Perhaps the best justification for bottom-up development is the system whose low-level modules are critical in some sense. However, most systems have only a few critical modules, and one could argue that after those modules have been tested, the project should return to a top-down approach.

20.3.1 Bottom-up development as a function of resources

Another common justification for bottom-up development is based on the scheduling of programmers. A structure chart for a typical system often resembles a pyramid, with relatively few modules at the top and relatively large numbers of simple modules at the bottom. Thus, the manager might argue that the bottom-up approach is preferable, because it allows him to assign large numbers of programmers to work, in parallel, on the bottom-level modules.

In theory, this is true; in practice, we often find serious interface problems between the multitude of bottom-level modules. This usually is not the fault of the bottom-up approach per se, but rather because of the almost irresistible urge to accompany it with a phased approach: All of the programmers throw their modules into a *very* large paper bag and hope that the resulting jumble will accomplish some useful processing. Appropriate use of the management ideas introduced in the next chapter can avoid most of these problems.

There are situations in which the programming manager finds that a large number of programmers have been assigned to his project, against his wishes, on the first day of the project. One might argue that this would never happen in a rational organization; we can only observe that (a) it is a mistake to think that most organizations are rational, (b) contractual commitments with one's customers may require that the programmers be assigned to the project as soon as it has been authorized, and (c) the manager may feel that if he does *not* assign the people to his staff when the project starts up, then he runs the serious risk that they will not be available when he needs them. Such a situation is likely to influence the manager to pursue a bottom-up development approach — because it enables him to put the programmers to work more quickly.

While these problems tend to influence the manager to pursue a bottom-up approach, it probably is more accurate to say that such problems lead to a phased approach. Thus, if there is no machine-time for testing, there is a good chance that the programmers will write all of their code with little or no testing — and, then, in a last-minute rush, all of the modules will be thrown together for a system's test.

20.3.2 Bottom-up approach required for generalized atomic modules

Occasionally we find that the bottom-up approach is the only way in which we can generate appropriate test data for low-level modules. In Fig. 20.7, for example, suppose we have just developed low-level module Bn, and that we wish to test it in a top-down fashion. This means that we must be able to invent an appropriate number of variations of a_1 data elements that will be converted to a_2 elements. These will be converted eventually to a_n data elements, then to b_1 elements, and ultimately to the b_n elements with which we test our module Bn.

The problem is that it may be very difficult to invent an appropriate number of a_1 elements that will generate an acceptable sample of b_n elements; quite possibly, all of the distinct a_1 elements that we are capable of thinking of (or generating with a test driver) will only generate two or three distinct b_n elements. Consequently, we may decide to follow a bottom-up testing approach, using a driver in place of module Bk. This assumes, of course, that a driver would be capable of generating an adequate sample of b_n data elements directly.

20.4 VARIATIONS ON THE TOP-DOWN AND BOTTOM-UP APPROACHES

As we have seen, the programmer often is required to make a choice between top-down and bottom-up testing; he also must choose between a phased ap-

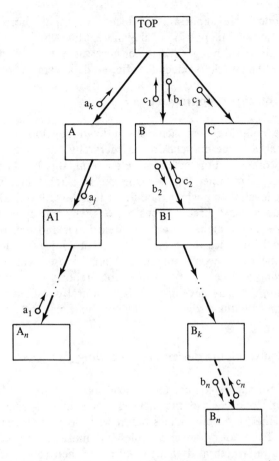

Fig. 20.7 Testing problems with the top-down approach.

proach and an incremental approach, the latter being highly preferable for all but the most simple projects. What may not be obvious is that there are *many* different approaches — indeed, an entire spectrum — available to the programmer. Some of the more common "compromise" approaches are discussed below.

20.4.1 The extreme approach: Design, code, and test a level at a time

When we first introduced top-down testing in Section 20.1, we suggested that the design, coding, and testing of the N + 1 level of a hierarchy could not commence until the Nth level had been completed. This could be regarded as a radical top-down approach; unfortunately, it is impractical if applied literally. In Fig. 20.6a, for example, it is impractical to assume that the programmer could effectively test TOP if *all* of the subordinate modules were stubs. Furthermore, if we wish to introduce *real* input and produce *real* output, there is an implicit assumption that at least some portion of the afferent and efferent branches have been carried to a low level (although this is not necessarily true: A dummy version of module A in Fig. 20.6a could produce the afferent data element from a test file).

20.4.2 The zigzag approach

A more common approach to top-down development is suggested by Fig. 20.6b — that is, some branches of the hierarchy have been pushed down to a lower level than others. For lack of a better term, this has been called a zigzag approach[3] — the programmer hops around the hierarchy, first pushing module A to the next lower level, then pushing module B1 to a lower level, and so on.

There are at least three obvious reasons why this approach is likely to be taken. First, the requirement to deal with real input and real output, as we suggested earlier, will influence the programmer to develop some legs of the afferent and efferent branches. Second, pressures from the user will dictate that certain types of processing and certain types of output reports be completed as early as possible. Finally, a zigzag development is a natural consequence of several programmers working on the project simultaneously: Some programmers are faster than others.

20.4.3 Finishing the design before coding

Earlier, we suggested that the radical approach to top-down development involved designing one level of the hierarchy at a time — and then immediately writing code for the top-level modules before one has the faintest idea of the number and nature of the bottom-level modules. A more conservative approach suggests that the entire structural design should be finished (and perhaps documented in the form of a structure chart) before coding and testing commence. When implementation *does* begin, it can proceed in a top-down fashion — the difference is that the programmer knows what lies ahead of him (or below him in the hierarchy) as he codes each module.

There are advantages and disadvantages of this conservative approach. Perhaps the most important advantage is that it affords the designer an easier method of altering and refining the design before he begins writing code. That is, when he reaches the bottom level of his structure chart, he may observe that a minor change — propagated through the entire structure — would greatly enhance the quality of the design. If he is working with a structure chart, it usually is a simple matter of erasing a few lines and drawing a few others. If he already has committed himself to code, he faces the more arduous task of recoding, recompiling, and retesting code. More important than the physical labor involved is the psychological reluctance to change that which already works: The programmer's normal instinct is to leave it alone!

Thus, we might argue that one of the disadvantages of the radical approach

— known by some cynics as "designing it as you go" — is that it is less likely to be modified during implementation. This is particularly important when several programmers are working on the system simultaneously. If they are following the radical approach, they frequently will miss the opportunity to fan-in to common low-level subordinate modules. Even if they become aware of the opportunity, they are less likely to change their code — especially if it appears to work already — than if the opportunity had been recognized while drawing the structure chart. Thus, the result is likely to be a number of similar low-level modules, which may add significantly to the problems of efficiency (because of increased memory requirements) and maintainability.

On the other hand, performing a complete structural design for a large system is a time-consuming affair — during which there is no tangible evidence of progress, at least not in a form that would be appreciated by most users. As we pointed out earlier, one of the advantages of the radical approach or the zigzag approach is that it provides tangible evidence of progress to the user — which can be extremely important if the project starts to fall behind schedule.

There is another aspect of the user interaction that may argue against the conservative approach. As we suggested, many users do not really know what they want from the system, or do not understand the consequences of the system they have specified. Thus, we run the risk of performing a time-consuming and expensive systems analysis, and a time-consuming structural design — only to find when we begin implementing the system, that it is *entirely* unacceptable to the user. The more fickle the customer, the stronger the argument for a "design on the fly" approach; the less fickle the customer, the stronger the argument for the conservative approach. However, it is crucial to recognize that only a complete prior structural design can maximize cohesion and factoring, while minimizing intermodule coupling. Thus, the previously designed structure emerging from the conservative approach also is the most modifiable. Unless the customer rejects the *entire* system (very improbable!), the prior structural design will be most easily adapted to fit the real but unstated user needs.

20.4.4 Mixed approaches

A review of Table 20.1 will suggest the possibility for a mixed strategy, which minimizes the task of creating or specifying stubs and test drivers. Note that the driver for an afferent module is simpler than an afferent stub, and that the stub for an efferent module is simpler than a driver. (Transform modules, once again, are the stubbrn holdouts!) The simplest testing would result from proceeding bottom-up on afferent branches and top-down on efferent ones. This amounts to testing and debugging from inputs through outputs. One reason this input-output strategy is easier is that most testing (with exceptions as noted in Section 20.3.2) can make use of real input for test data rather than internal tables and generated data.

Many mixtures of top-down and bottom-up are possible and practicable.

Guided by a structure chart, a system even could be sensibly implemented by step-wise refinement from the middle outward, starting with module B in Fig. 20.1 and adding TOP, B1, and B2 one at a time!

The essential thing is that the choice of implementation strategy be made rationally rather than as a matter of religious principle. With a complete structure chart available in advance, the greatest possible latitude in workable options is achieved. With a highly factored, cohesive, uncoupled design, errors in structural design are most easily corrected, even in the coded modules themselves, and testing and debugging become possible with minimal interactive effects between various parts of the design. Structured design thus fits well with any disciplined coding, testing, and debugging strategy.

20.5 SUMMARY

We have seen in this chapter that design and implementation often are inter-twined; it is important to keep in mind that there are many different ways of com-bining design and implementation. A conservative approach to building systems would be to accomplish almost all of the design before any implementation begins; a more radical approach would allow implementation to begin as soon as a small amount of design was accomplished.

Much of the attention in the popular EDP literature today is focused on the distinction betwen top-down and bottom-up implementaion. We have discussed the advantages and disadvantages of both approaches in this chapter — but, more important, we have stressed that the key to successful implementation is *incremental* testing.

REFERENCES

1. F.T. BAKER, "Chief Programmer Team Management of Production Programming," *IBM Systems Journal,* Vol. 11, No. 1, 1972, pp. 56–73.

2. F.T. BAKER, "System Quality Through Structured Programming," *AFIPS Proceed-ings of the 1972 Fall Joint Computer Conference,* Vol. 41, Part 1, 1972.

3. EDWARD YOURDON, *Techniques of Program Structure and Design* (Englewood Cliffs, N.J.: Prentice-Hall, 1975).

4. EDWARD YOURDON, "A Brief Look at Structured Programming and Top-down Pro-gram Design," *Modern Data,* June 1974, pp. 30–35.

The
Management
Milieu

CHAPTER **21**

21.0 INTRODUCTION

Ultimately, the designer works within an environment that includes, among other strange creatures, the manager. Often, the professional will find himself at odds with management over what he sees as technical issues, but what management obviously sees in another way. In this chapter, addressed both to managers and to designers, we will examine some ways in which technical design and management decisions interact. We will see that many seemingly purely management prerogatives determine the technical factors of a system in subtle ways. Moreover, for systems design to be effective — not just in terms of theoretical systems goals, but in terms of the actual goal of building better systems — some of our technical objectives will have to be bent to accommodate the exigencies of the real world in which politics is a decisive force.

In the face-off between managers and professional systems designers, the odds favor management — especially since few computer professionals are truly professional. Even if the professional argues that a proposed method is technically unsound or that some other alternative is optimal, he often does not have a rigorous, formal discipline to back him up. Equally damned is the manager who has the intuition to see the value of finishing a complete structural design before writing any code, but who ends up in a debate on programming style because he lacks proofs and theories. However, with the amount of literature that has been published recently on various aspects of structured design and structured programming, we can no longer be very sympathetic to this excuse. We will be even less so as more rigorous theory and more conclusive empirical evidence builds from here.

The basic questions to be asked in this chapter are: Should management understand anything about the concepts of structural design? How does structural design help the manager accomplish his job more effectively? We will be concerned, as we have been in several previous chapters, with the job of dispelling myths. Overall, it will be necessary to discard the myth that the technical and the managerial aspects of systems development are separable. In reality, they are not.

21.1 THE IMPACT OF MANAGEMENT DECISIONS ON THE TECHNICAL ASPECTS OF A PROJECT

Obviously, the technical aspects of a project affect the resource utilization. A poorly designed system may require twice as many programmers for implementation as a well-designed, highly modular one. However, it is less obvious that the converse is true: Resource utilization, determined largely by management, can have a strong influence on the technical aspects of the project.

As an illustration, consider the plight of a large national conglomerate involved in building a multi-company, totally integrated, on-line, real-time management information system. Their design-on-the-fly approach was clearly creating problems and, in the long run, would almost certainly lead to considerable duplicated effort. A consultant was brought in to study the situation; he suggested that they needed a complete structural design prior to any coding, and he explained what this entailed. The proposal was vetoed on the grounds that the complete structural design was so enormous that it would take more than the three years budgeted for the entire design *and* implementation to be completed.

Now, clearly this is faulty reasoning! The code for the system contains all of the information in the structure chart, plus a great deal more. Indeed, no model of the system can contain more information than is in the code since that *is* the whole system. If it would take more than three years of effort by the whole staff to design the system, then certainly it would take *much* more to code it!

The real question is whether the cost (in dollars or time) of doing a complete, detailed design and then coding exceeds that of just coding from the top. As a rule, additional design time saves implementation time, primarily by reducing debugging. Indeed, the savings almost always substantially exceed the cost of the additional design. This trade-off cannot be continued without limits, of course: Past a certain optimum point, additional design effort, while tending to improve the system, will not always reduce total cost — and may even increase it as refinements and extensions continue to be introduced.

Figure 21.1 illustrates the presumed behavior of total systems development cost as a function of design effort. With no prior design (especially design of a structural nature), the cost can be expected to be very high. More design (prior to coding) reduces cost at an increasing rate. The initial flatness of the curve to the left of point A is largely conjectural. It appears that too little design may be almost as bad as none at all; subminimal design could even increase the total cost somewhat — we simply do not have sufficient evidence to know as yet.

Between A and B, the greatest gains are possible. Functionally, B probably corresponds to a complete design of a highly modular structure following the intrinsic problem structure, plus corresponding designs for data structure and interfaces. Neither design optimization nor many iterations of the design are implied at that point. As more design is added, we get an improved system at little increase in cost. Over some fairly broad range (shown as points B to C on the diagram), the total cost falls to, or near to, the minimum. It then begins to rise slowly, due to diminishing returns and to elaboration of the system.

One aspect of the model shown by Fig. 21.1 has, in fact, been verified; under-budgeting of design increases total system's cost. As experiments, a few parallel developments of systems have been accomplished — and, among other things, the ones with greater design effort were implemented at lower total cost. This is vitally important to the systems analyst or the manager: Underbudgeting of design, or premature termination of the design effort may be responsible for overrun of budget and time estimates for the project.

It is argued frequently that the iterations (or refinements) of design are "too expensive" — that is, revisions, refinements, and improvements to the structure of a large modular system are difficult and time-consuming. Certainly, there is an

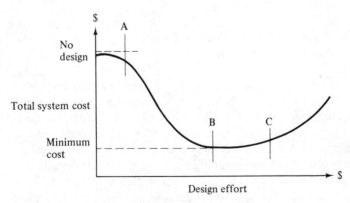

Note: Ordinate and abscissa are not on the same scale.

Fig. 21.1   Behavior of total development cost as a function of design expenditures.

element of truth in this: In a large-scale system of, say, 100 or more modules, a single iteration of the design may involve massive rearrangement of modules and interfaces. On the other hand, the corresponding changes would cost many times more once the system has been committed to code. Expensive though such changes may be, they will never again be so cheap.

Of course, some design iterations may involve refinements that would *not* be made if the system were already committed to code — for they represent options or marginal refinements and extensions. Failure to make these improvements during design probably is not serious. What *is* serious is the failure to develop, through successive iterations, an adequate, implementable system, thus *necessitating* expensive trial-and-error revisions during the implementation and debugging of the system. These types of design failures most commonly show up during the so-called systems integration and test phase that we mentioned in the previous chapter. On large-scale projects, this is normally one of the largest costs — precisely because of insufficient design and planning.

Many of these points were raised in Chapter 20, where we discussed various approaches to the implementation and testing of a system. What we wish to emphasize in this chapter is that many of these problems are exacerbated by management pressures of one sort or another. For example, as the apparent or expected cost of a system goes up (or as time and budget constraints become tighter), there frequently is management pressure to solve the problem through allocation of greater resources. If one programmer can finish a job in two years, then two programmers can finish it in one year — or so the reasoning goes.

Brooks[1] refers to this as the "mythical man-month"; that is, programming managers often make the assumption that people and time can be freely interchanged. This is roughly equivalent to suggesting that nine women can produce a baby in one month. In the programming example mentioned above, it is likely that the two programmers will take two years to solve a problem that *one* programmer would have solved in two years.

21.1.1 Project organization and modular structure

At the 1968 National Symposium on Modular Programming,[1] consultant George Mealy gave a particularly dramatic example of the mythical man-month problem. His story involved his experience in IBM's development of OS/360. At one point, the project had approximately 50 technical people assigned to it. An analysis of progress-to-date and the projected size of the system revealed that it would take twice as long as it should to complete, and consume half again as much resources as had been allocated. This is the picture illustrated in Fig. 21.2, the dotted line showing projected resource utilization. By doubling the staff, the project management hoped to be able to follow the dotted line.

The staff was doubled, redoubled again, again, and nearly a fifth time — and yet the performance was worse than that projected with 50 people! In retro-

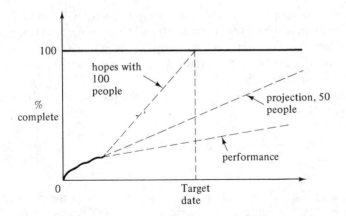

Fig. 21.2 Representation of the effect of Mealy's Law.

spect, it appears that the only stratagem with much promise of completion on time, within budget, and with a sound technical product would have been to cut the staff in half, retaining the 25 best people. The larger staff created a more complex system (some would say inordinately so, but we will leave that for history to judge!) and created more management problems.

In formal terms, we can state Mealy's Law like this:

There is an incremental person who, when added to a project, consumes more energy (resources) than he or she makes available. Thus, beyond a certain point, adding resources (people) slows progress in addition to increasing the cost.

The components of this effect are myriad. Since the incremental man must learn about the project, someone must train him. He must communicate with other team members, and thereby introduces additional managerial and technical interfaces. We do not say he will do no productive work. Presumably, his own overhead does not consume all of his own resources — but when we add up what he uses from everyone else, the project loses.

There are other ways of looking at Mealy's Law. The authors recall the story of a programmer assigned to write an application program on a small 12-bit minicomputer. His estimate of six months to complete the job was deemed unacceptable to his boss. When the manager assigned another programmer to the project in hopes of speeding it up, the original programmer responded, "But two programmers won't fit in there!"

There is another common problem that can be traced to management decisions; we'll call it the Thousand Module Effect. If you turn 1,000 programmers loose on the same project *before a total structural design has been completed,* one thing is reasonably certain: There will be at least 1,000 modules in the final system (counting probable duplicates), since two programmers "will not fit in one module." Indeed, there will be 1,000 modules *even if it is only a 150-module problem.* A number of large vendor-supplied operating systems, as well as some massive data processing systems developed by various U.S. government and military agencies, will attest to this phenomenon.

In more general terms, we can describe the phenomenon above as a variation of Conway's Law:*

> *The structure of a system reflects the structure of the organization that built it.*

Thus, if a system is developed (with design done in a seat-of-the-pants fashion) by 1,000 chimpanzees, we can expect a system with 1,000 modules — with extreme coupling and cohesion problems. If a system is designed by two groups in geographically remote locations, the final system probably will reflect that *management* organization rather than the inherent problem organization. If the design work is done initially by one person, or by a small, tightly knit team of professionals, there is some hope that the final system will reflect that tight-knit unity. Actually, Conway's Law has been stated even more strongly:

> *The structure of any system designed by an organization is isomorphic to the structure of the organization.*

Thus, if there are two subsystems designed by different designers or design teams who do *not* communicate with each other, by definition, the subsystems will not communicate with each other or make common use of shared facilities. Connections between subsystems always will reflect some communication between the organizations that designed them.

21.1.2 Design of large-scale systems

Circumventing Mealy's Law and Conway's Law can prove very difficult for large applications. The complete structure chart for an information system comprising 50,000 lines of source coding would have perhaps as many as 1,200 boxes on it. If it could be drawn at all, it would cover an entire wall. Very few systems of this order of size have been implemented from complete prior structural designs. Comprehension of such a vast structure is difficult, and its development by any formal strategy is tedious and error-prone.

There are three primary reasons for doing a single integrated design of the structure of an entire application area or larger system, rather than subdividing the

---

* So-named by participants at the 1968 National Symposium on Modular Programming.

design effort. First, a subdivision of the design effort determines the interfaces between major subsystems by managerial fiat with the frequent result that the major subsystems are excessively coupled. The design efforts under such circumstances cannot really proceed independently any more than can later maintenance and modification of the highly coupled subsystems. Second, the subdivision of structural design usually determines an ultimate *packaging* into programs or "suites" of programs that is suboptimal and much less convenient or efficient than the packaging that would be possible after a complete overall structural design. Third and most important, subdividing the structural design work inevitably leads to duplicated programming because opportunities for fan-in are missed in all but the most elementary cases, such as in computing square root.

Particularly expensive are the cases where a slight change in assumptions in one structure and minor changes in the arrangement in another would make possible sharing of entire subsystems and deep nests of modules. These opportunities can only be recognized in an integral design or separate designs undertaken with extensive interaction between designers. We all know that as programmers and systems analysts we are forever reinventing the wheel; subdividing structural design helps make this waste possible. For example, it has been estimated that the integral design of a single union compiler that would compile FORTRAN, ALGOL, PL/I, and COBOL for a single machine would result in a program only about 25 percent larger than that of the PL/I compiler alone. The more usual situation is that FORTRAN A-level, B-level, and z-level compilers were all designed and implemented separately. The analogies in the average user's applications are obvious and equally painful.

What does the project manager for a large effort do to get unstuck from between "the rock and the hard place"? Several organizations have found an approach that permits subdividing the structural design effort into manageable subprojects while minimizing the negative effects cited above. A data flow graph for the entire system or application area is drawn up. To keep that task within bounds, the data flow is presented at a fairly high or abstract level. This data flow is examined to assure that it is complete, correct, and the simplest model of the problem for the level of detail employed.

The overall data flow graph is analyzed to identify more or less independent subgraphs that have the fewest transitions (flow lines) connecting to the remaining graph, where these transitions involve uncomplicated data sets or small information volumes. Each essentially independent (uncoupled) subgraph then becomes the initial input to a separate structural design project. If duplicate design or replication in code is to be avoided, there must be frequent mutual design walkthroughs and continual cross-checking between the various designers or design teams. Careful comparison of the subgraphs may suggest areas of potential shared facilities. In this way, maximal fan-in can be achieved even between subsystems designed separately.

It is possible to employ an iterative design approach which yields high-quality structural designs in general and is especially indicated for subsystem design of a project segmented in the manner outlined above. The subgraph is first refined, then used to derive a complete structure by transform-transaction analysis. Understanding of the problem gained during the design is then used to develop a *new* data flow graph for the subsystem, and the design process is repeated. Typically, significant improvements continue to develop through six or seven iterations. The final subgraph can be used to refine and correct the total system's data flow graph.

More than anything else, the problems discussed in this section seem to emphasize the advantages of completing the structural design before any substantial coding takes place. In Chapter 20, we discussed some situations in which one could justify coding at an earlier stage; however, most normal projects would benefit from complete prior structural design.

21.2 MANAGEMENT BENEFITS OF PRIOR STRUCTURAL DESIGN

There are several management benefits to be gained from the design/ implementation approach that has been suggested in earlier sections and chapters. While there are some valid arguments for the radical approach to top-down implementation discussed in Chapter 20, we nevertheless suggest, for the sake of management, that a complete (or nearly complete) structural design be accomplished first, using all of the principles of coupling, cohesion, transform-centered design, and others previously discussed. When this has been accomplished, we suggest that coding and testing be accomplished in an *incremental* fashion; circumstances will dictate whether the basic implementation approach should be top-down or bottom-up or some combination. It can be assumed that nearly all modules in the resulting design are small (in the sense presented in Chapter 9) and independent (i.e., uncoupled).

21.2.1 Reliable cost estimating

One of the most difficult aspects of managing/developing systems is predicting, *in advance,* the requirements for people time, machine test time, and other resources. This will always be a difficult problem, and there is no magical approach that will guarantee precise cost estimates.

However, observe that estimating is an exercise in human problem-solving. Human beings have a limited capacity for dealing with complex problems — and estimating budget and manpower requirements for a million-statement system is certainly a complex problem! The probable error in any estimate will vary with the complexity of the problem being estimated. Since human errors rise with problem size, estimates on big problems will have more error in them than estimates on smaller problems. Because estimation errors deviate randomly, the laws of statistics guarantee that the total error in a summed estimate will be less than the sum of the errors in all the little estimates comprising it.

If most of the modules are truly independent of each other and the system is implemented in an incremental fashion (always adding one more small, independent module), the cost relationships are all additive. Thus, the sum of all module development costs closely approximates the total system's development cost. With a complete prior structural design of small independent modules implemented incrementally, errors in cost estimation can therefore be reduced substantially. Moreover, the estimating process is simplified.

The drawback is that these reductions in probable error are realizable only *after* the structural design is completed. This points to the advantages of two-phase design and implementation contracting. Even where delayed cost estimating is not possible, an accurate estimate provided upon completion of the design can be useful to management as a check against the previous estimate, and can supply fairly reliable figures on which to base possible reconsideration of the decision to implement all or part of the system.

21.2.2 Improved scheduling, improved planning

One of the advantages of a prior structural design is that every module to be programmed is identified and specified in advance. In addition, possible perturbations on the high-level modules (as a result of design problems in the low-level modules) have been resolved before coding begins. Thus, it should be relatively smooth sailing once the coding begins.

In addition, prior structural design makes it easier for the manager to schedule adequate, but not excessive, personnel and machine requirements. Indeed, this is one of the disadvantages of the radical top-down approach discussed in Chapter 20: The managers (and the programmers) rarely know what lies below the surface of the modules on which they currently are working.

21.2.3 Parallel development of acceptance and validation criteria

On any large project, it is important to develop test data, acceptance criteria, and benchmarks in parallel with the development of the system itself. With a prior structural design, this is possible because the functional requirements of every module are known before the coding/testing begins. With the radical top-down approach, this is considerably more difficult since the functional requirements for some of the modules will not be known until midway through the project.

This is not to say that acceptance criteria are impossible to develop with the radical top-down approach. The designer, the systems analyst, and the user must identify different versions of the system, each one of which will have certain features present, certain features absent, and certain features in a primitive form. This requires rather delicate coordination between several different parties — and, in the authors' experience, it often breaks down completely. Because of impatience or frustration, the user frequently announces to the analyst and the programmer that he does not wish to discuss acceptance criteria until the entire system has been specified.

21.2.4 Better project monitoring and control

Most data processing projects are accompanied by milestones that are used by management to gauge the progress of the project. There are two problems with most milestones. The primary one is that they do not represent *tangible* evidence of progress. Thus, we often see a milestone of "95 percent of the code has been written," which most programmers will claim to have accomplished on the second day of the project! Also, the milestones often are too far apart: The manager only learns at six-month intervals whether he is ahead of or behind schedule.

As we pointed out in Chapter 20, the top-down incremental approach has the advantage of providing tangible evidence of progress: A real skeleton system can be demonstrated on a real computer. Indeed, *any* incremental approach can be considered tangible, in the sense that the programmer should be able to supply test data to demonstrate that some combination of modules works.

However, the problem with the radical top-down approach is that the manager has difficulty judging the proportion of *finished* modules to *unfinished* modules. For all he knows, the modules that have been completed may represent only the tip of the iceberg. By having a complete prior structural design, the manager can more readily — and more precisely — judge the fraction of the *total* system that has been accomplished. Indeed if 76 of 100 small, uncoupled modules have been implemented by stepwise refinement and have passed acceptance tests, then the job is approximately 76 percent complete. In practice, this type of simple linear projection has proven to be as good as rather fancy project management systems projections.

It also should be clear that the incremental approach affords the opportunity for more frequent milestones. Indeed, it might be more appropriate to use the phrase inch-pebbles to describe the checkpoints that can be established at the completion of each module.

21.3 PERSONNEL MANAGEMENT FOR IMPLEMENTING MODULAR SYSTEMS

Finally, a few remarks about the problems of personnel management in large modular systems: As a number of articles in popular journals have pointed out for several years, one of the supposed advantages of modularity is that it gives the manager the opportunity to assign different programmers to different pieces of the system. But does this actually work? Do the programmers really accept it?

Consider the structure shown in Fig. 21.3. We might imagine that it represents a programming task large enough to require six or eight programmers. How should the manager assign programmers to work on different parts of the system?

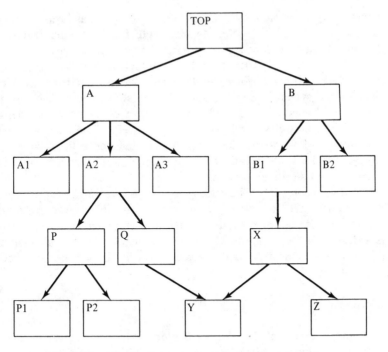

Fig. 21.3 Personnel management for management systems.

There seem to be three basic approaches, each with its own advantages and disadvantages.

One approach is to assign a complete subsystem — perhaps the A subsystem — to an individual programmer. This has the advantage of enabling the programmer to see the big picture. He derives more job satisfaction knowing that he is working on a substantial piece of the system. On the other hand, the manager runs the risk that the design of the A subsystem will drift from the original structural design. Even worse, the drift may not be discovered until the programmer has finished the entire subsystem. This is particularly true if the programmer works on his code in a vacuum, isolated from the other programmers on the project. When he finishes, we run the risk that there will be interfacing problems with module TOP and with module X.

Another approach is to assign individual programmers to work on individual modules. Thus, the manager might assign one programmer to work on module Z; another programmer might work strictly on module TOP. This has the advantage of better control: If one programmer gets behind schedule, writes terrible code, or quits, the consequences are limited to one module. On the other hand, this approach has a definite psychological disadvantage: It makes the programmer feel that he is a small cog in a very large machine. He frequently finds it difficult to become motivated by the challenge of working on his own module.

Finally, we have the suggestion of assigning a team — perhaps two or three programmers — to work on a subsystem. This approach has been referred to recently as "adaptive teams," "egoless teams," "chief programmer teams," and a variety of other terms. It seems to stem largely from the studies and writings of Weinberg.[3] One of the advantages of this approach is that the members of the team see the overall scheme; they should derive satisfaction from working on a major piece of the system. Because several programmers are involved, there is more of a chance for control. It still is possible, of course, that the design may drift, but it is less likely if several people are involved. The team approach also has the advantage of involving the programmers in each other's code. This is usually formalized by such techniques as structured walk-throughs, in which the programmers read and critique each other's code.

Recently, the tendency has been towards the team approach. However, we must emphasize that the overall development is much more manageable if the team is presented with a structural design before it commences work. If the team practices a design-on-the-fly approach, it may be very difficult to estimate its time and manpower requirements — and the team may develop a system that suffers from Conway's Law.

21.4 SUMMARY

The major theme of this chapter has been that management decisions can influence the technician's ability to develop a good design, and vice versa: The kind of design carried out by the technician can have an important impact on the manager's ability to schedule, budget, and monitor his project.

It has been our experience that careful attention to the principles of structured design makes it far easier for the manager to develop accurate schedules and budgets — for precisely the same reason that structured design enables the technician to develop, test, and maintain his system more easily. Developing a schedule and budget for a large, complex system is an extremely difficult *human* problem-solving process; developing a schedule and budget for a number of small, independent modules is considerably easier, and considerably less error-prone.

REFERENCES

1. FREDERICK P. BROOKS, JR., *The Mythical Man-Month* (Reading, Mass.: Addison-Wesley, 1975).

2. TOM O. BARNETT, ed., *Proceedings of the National Symposium on Modular Programming* (Cambridge, Mass.: Information & Systems Press, 1968).

3. GERALD M. WEINBERG, *The Psychology of Computer Programming* (New York: Van Nostrand Reinhold, 1971).

APPENDICES

Structure Charts:
A Guide

Appendix A

The purpose of this guide is to describe standard charts, how to develop them, and how to read them. The standards promulgated here are the cumulative result of feedback from many users over a period of nearly ten years. They are intended to be consistent, theoretically sound, but most importantly, maximally useful. It should be noted that these standards differ in a few significant ways from those that IBM supports. (The portions that differ are flagged with a triple asterisk and refer to the notes on page 435.) Our experience indicates that the graphics presented in this Appendix significantly increase readability of structure charts and decrease the probability of errors in the design process.

Note on graphics: *The symbology of the structure is designed to be drawn with the aid of the standard Flowcharting Template (IBM, ANSI, and ISO standards). Generally, some semblance of compatibility is retained to make learning the new meanings easier.*

409

I. EXPLANATION OF SYMBOLS IN STRUCTURE CHARTS

The complete standard for structure charts includes, in a single inter-related set, facilities for representing all possible structural features of programs in any known programming language/environment. In any one programming context, a designer/programmer would expect to use only a subset of the standard.

A. Pieces of systems

The basic building blocks of modular computer systems are modules. There are many kinds of modules. Some, like PL/I PROCEDURES, are activated out-of-line. Others, like COBOL PARAGRAPHS, may be executed in-line. All modules in any programming language have certain properties in common.

1. A module consists of a set of lexically contiguous statements; that is, statements comprising the module are written together, sequentially.

2. A module has an identifier by which the entire module, all of its lexically included statements, may be referenced as a single piece.

A module may or may not be referred to by its identifier (although usually it will be, at least once). A module may receive and transmit data as parameters in a calling sequence such as TIME-RECORD in the statement

CALL PROG2 USING TIME-RECORD.

or a module may communicate data via fixed cells or a common-data region. No matter how it is activated or is given data, if a piece of system consists of adjacent statements with an overall unit-name or identifier, it may be called a module.

A module is represented by a simple rectangle with the module name in the upper-left corner:

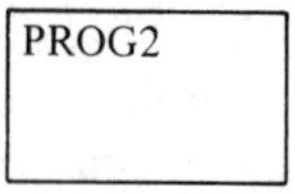

```
┌─────────────┐
│ PROG2       │
│             │
│             │
└─────────────┘
```

Fig. A.1

Such a picture represents *any* kind of module. Sometimes it is desirable to distinguish between special physical types of modules. For example, a module defining a named macro (to be inserted in-line at compile- or translation-time when invoked by its name) may be distinguished from other types. A macro, to be distinguished, is represented by the following:

410

Fig. A.2   ***(1)

Any previously written or pre-existing module may be represented by striping. For example, the system-supplied subroutine SQRTF

Fig. A.3

and the library macro procedure XREAD

Fig. A.4   ***(1)

Any module, regardless of type, may contain in its defining statements both executable and nonexecutable elements. A module whose only contents are data (e.g., a NAMED-COMMON region in FORTRAN) would be shown thus:

Fig. A.5   ***(1)

Often, the operating system or machine environment itself behaves as a unit of a system to and from which both control and data may be passed. To show the operating environment, this symbol is used:

Fig. A.6

B. Connections

In a system, a connection is a reference to an object by its identifier (name, address, label, index and so on). An intermodular connection exists whenever a reference appears within one module to an identifier not defined (or *first* defined, or caused to exist) within the module, but elsewhere. When the reference is to the identifier of another module, the connection is called *normal,* and is shown as an arrow pointing to the box representing the module whose identifier is being referenced. For example, within module DISTANCE is found the code

411

.

.

.

SUMSQRS = XDIF**2 + YDIF**2
ZDIS = SQRTF (SUMSQRS)
IF (ZDIS-TOL) 14, 15, 15

.

.

.

The above includes a reference (underlined) to the identifier of module SQRTF. In this case, the context of the reference is that of using SQRTF as a function subroutine. Intermodular connections in the context of normal subroutine "calls" are as follows:

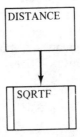

Fig. A.7

The data being passed as arguments are shown as an annotation to the connection for a "call." The small annotating arrow shows the direction of *flow* of the data. Thus

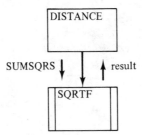

Fig. A.8

Or a footnote table may be used. Thus

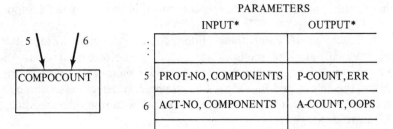

Fig. A.9

The names or identification given for data flowing as parameters to and from sub-routines are the names as used in the call*ing* module, that is the "actual" rather than "dummy" parameter list.

Often, it is useful to distinguish between parameters that are normal data to be operated upon, from parameters that are elements of control — e.g., switch settings, exception flags, error or end-of-data indicators, and so on. A small dot on the tail of any arrow indicates "control," a small circle indicates "data." Thus

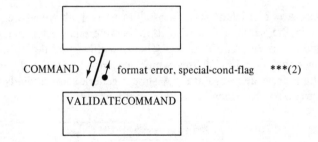

COMMAND   format error, special-cond-flag   ***(2)

Fig. A.10

Annotations on the connection and a parameter footnote table may be intermixed to produce a chart that is both uncluttered and readable, as well as complete. Thus

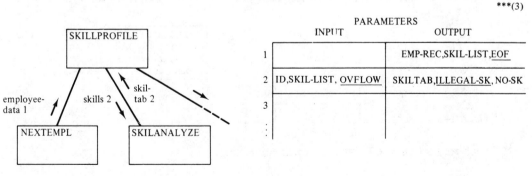

***(3)

Fig. A.11

* Input *to* subordinate, output *from* subordinate.

Note that control parameters have been underlined in the parameter footnote table.

1. Pathological Connections: Intermodular references to identifiers other than the external names of modules are called "pathological" and are shown as arrows originating within the box for the referenc*ing* module and terminating within the box for the referenc*ed module*. For example, a direct reference by module SEARCH to a data element by its name INPVECTOR, within another module, BUILD-VECT, is shown thus:

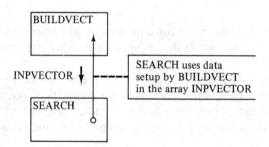

Fig. A.12

The conventions are consistent with those introduced above: The direction of the connection is the same as the direction of reference (pointing), i.e., from referencing module to referenced object (here, within module BUILDVECT); the annotation shows the direction of flow which may not be in the direction of connection; the small circle denotes data. A simple generalization yields the form for a direct transfer (GOTO) to a location *within* another module:

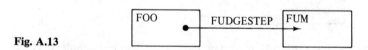

Fig. A.13

An intermodular modification of code, such as an ALTER from one COBOL section to another or an assembly language address substitution, is shown as

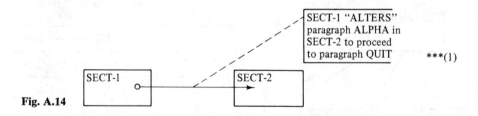

Fig. A.14

Such connections are known as *hybrid* connections.

2. Common Environments: References to commonly held data, such as FORTRAN COMMON or PL/I EXTERNAL names, are pathological connections that present special problems in graphic representation. Consider, for example, a COBOL program with several SECTIONS. All of the data in a COBOL program are defined in a single, globally accessible DATA DIVISION and all data are communicated pathologically, i.e., by direct reference. The structure chart quickly becomes cluttered with pathological data connections, as shown below:

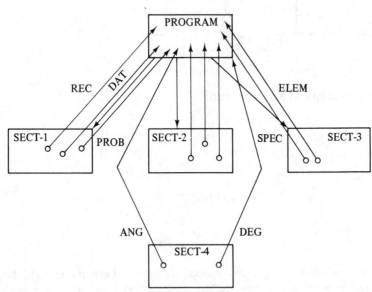

Fig. A.15

which would hide other important structural features. A "connector" is used for this reason (and anywhere else to clarify the chart). Thus

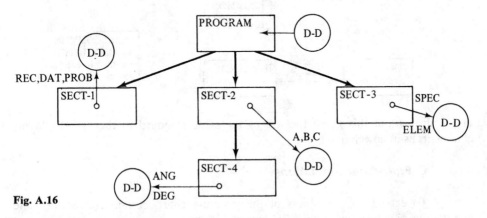

Fig. A.16

A connector represents a graphic break, exactly as in a flowchart; thus, the two structures below are identical:

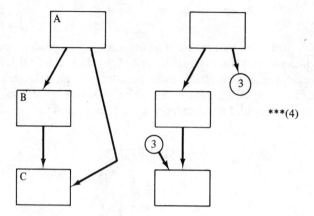

Fig. A.17

***(4)

Off-page connectors also may be used:

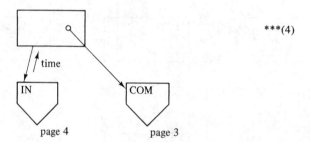

***(4)

Fig. A.18   page 4   page 3

Each named, labeled, or logically grouped collection of commonly held data may be represented by a named "data only" module distinct from any other module; thus,

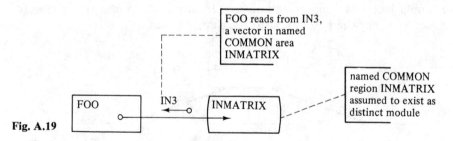

Fig. A.19

(Note throughout this guide the use of the same standard method of displaying comments as in flowcharts.)

C. Procedural annotations

To extend the usefulness of the structure chart, certain conventions and annotations representing procedural aspects of the program are used. Wherever possible, connections are ordered left-to-right (less often, top-to-bottom) as they emerge from the referencing module in the same order in which they usually would be accessed (used, executed):

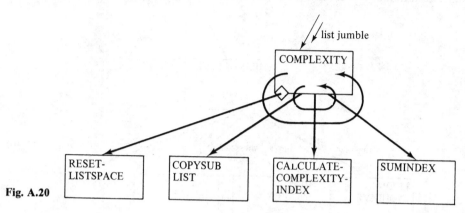

Fig. A.20

The above figure represents, *by convention,* that the expected order of calling is RESETLISTSPACE, COPYSUBLIST, CALCULATECOMPLEXITYINDEX, SUMINDEX. In developing the initial structure chart, it may not always be possible to observe this convention at all times as the structure changes.

When intermodular references are used repeatedly within an iterative procedure (loop), a procedural annotation encompassing the references may be added as in Fig. A.20, which indicates that COPYSUBLIST, CALCULATECOMPLEXITYINDEX, and SUMINDEX are executed repeatedly within an inner loop, which is in turn within a loop with RESETLISTSPACE.

Conditional access (use, execution) to intermodular connections is shown by enclosing the point of reference in a diamond (decision symbol) as in the case of the call on RESETLISTSPACE, which will be made contingent on the outcome of some decision process. This decision annotation may embrace several references. By convention, these are assumed to be used in alternation; that is, they are alternative outcomes of the decision. Thus, a dispatch on transaction type to one of several modules is shown as follows:

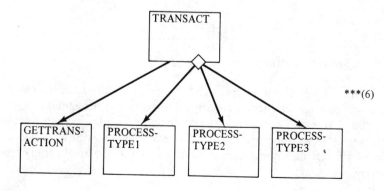

***(6)

Fig. A.21

If more than one connection is accessed as the result of one outcome, these may be shown as originating at the same point. For example, each of two outcomes resulting in two calls could be shown as

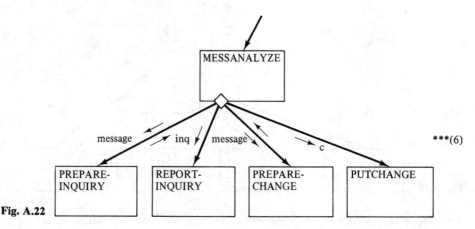

***(6)

Fig. A.22

Such procedural detail is really beyond the structural model itself, but can make the structure chart easier to interpret. Generally, reference should be made to the flowcharts or other procedural documentation to obtain details of the procedural interrelationships between modules.

Procedural annotations may be used with any type of connection; for example

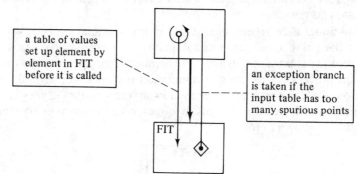

Fig. A.23

D. Special symbols

This section discusses graphics for more unusual or sophisticated structural features that may not be encountered by all programmer/designers.

Some transfers of control take place automatically, asynchronously, or concurrently with established processes. These are shown with a dashed connection. Examples are activation on program interrupt (sequence break, trap) from the operating environment.

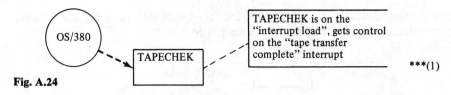

Fig. A.24

TAPECHEK is on the "interrupt load", gets control on the "tape transfer complete" interrupt

***(1)

A parallel "call" of a "subroutine," such as CALL . . . TASK B in PL/I, could be represented as in Fig. A.25:

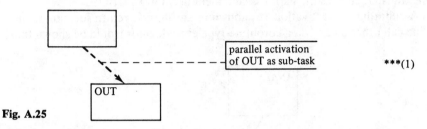

parallel activation of OUT as sub-task

***(1)

Fig. A.25

In some programming languages, it is possible to transfer control unconditionally to a complete module, by name; that is, a normal but unsubordinated transfer of control (e.g., "GOTO section-name" in COBOL, or "TRANSFER subprogram-name" in ICETRAN). This is shown in a logically consistent manner as

Fig. A.26

***(1)

The comparable case for data, in which data (but *not* control) are communicated normally to or from the identity interface of a module, has not been implemented, but has been proposed. This would be represented as

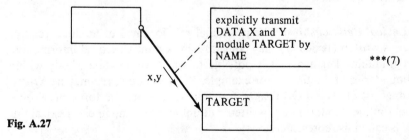

explicitly transmit DATA X and Y module TARGET by NAME

***(7)

Fig. A.27

1. Coroutines: When activated by name, a coroutine always resumes at the next sequential statement following *the point at which* control was last transferred out. This is known as incremental execution. An "entry locator," reset on each exit, serves as an intermediary for any activation of the coroutine. Thus, a coroutine transfer consists of (a) resetting the source module's entry locator, and

(b) transferring to the location defined by the target module's entry locator. These characteristics are suggested by the following graphic:

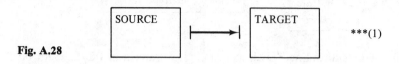

Fig. A.28

This models an intermodular reference to the identifier TARGET in the context of a coroutine transfer, such as the PROCESS statement in B8500 COBOL.

A subordinated activation (establishing an implicit return location as in a subroutine call) that enters via a coroutine-type entry locator would be shown thus:

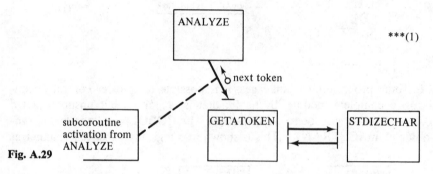

Fig. A.29

which makes GETATOKEN a *subcoroutine* of ANALYZE. Of course, the return from GETATOKEN to ANALYZE resets the entry locator of GETATOKEN.

(Note that a module is a certain type only in relation to some other module and that this typal relationship is defined by the connection. Thus, GETATOKEN is a coroutine to STDIZECHAR.)

2. *Lexical Relationships:* The positional relationships of modules relative to each other as written (lexically) may constitute important structural information. In many programming languages, it is possible to write one module wholly within the lexical boundaries of another. For example, PL/I PROCEDURES may be written nested, as may ALGOL. FORTRAN function-statements (a form of a one-statement subroutine module) are written within another module. Lexical inclusion, as it is called, is represented thus:

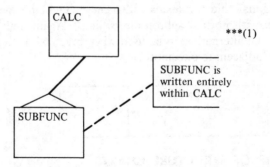

Fig. A.30

***(1)

Note that lexical inclusion is shown independently of all other relationships, e.g., in a COBOL program with three sections:

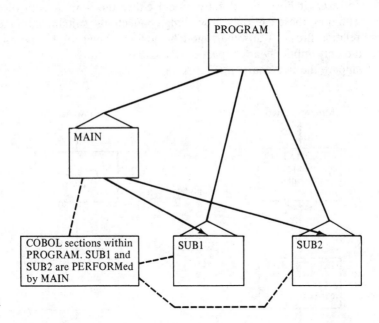

Fig. A.31

Where practical, lexical inclusion is shown with lighter lines than physical connections.

Lexical adjacency — modules written contiguously — may be shown, where it is significant, with a simple horizontal line. (Note: No arrow!)

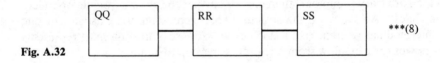

Fig. A.32

***(8)

421

A vertical or diagonal line for lexical adjacency should be avoided to prevent possible confusion with normal subroutine calling. Again, light lines should be used if practical. An alternative, to be used when practical, is to place the module symbols physically adjacent to one another:

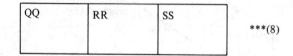

***(8)

Fig. A.33

II. RELATIONSHIP OF STRUCTURE CHARTS TO OTHER PROGRAM MODELS

The structure chart models the physical (referential) structure of a modular system. However, it does not directly model either the flow of control or data, since, by definition, these can only flow along connections; suitable annotations reveal these relationships. A flowchart models the flow of control, but nothing of the data flow and only implicitly any aspect of referential structure.

Compare the two charts in Fig. A.34:

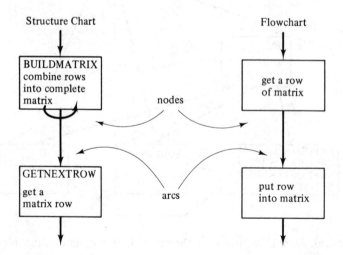

Fig. A.34

The "nodes" in the structure chart always are physically recognizable modules conforming to a rigorous, although unrestrictive, definition (see p. 37). The nodes of a flow chart are processing steps and may correspond to the processing of a single statement, an arbitrary group of statements, or any part or all of a module or collection of modules. An "arc" on the structure chart represents the existence of one or more intermodular references of a single type. An arc of the flowchart represents that control will (or can) flow from one processing step to another.

A. Data flows

A data flow represents successive transformations of data and the data dependencies interrelating these transformations. The nodes are processes that map one set of data into another; an arc represents that an output set of one transformation is required by another:

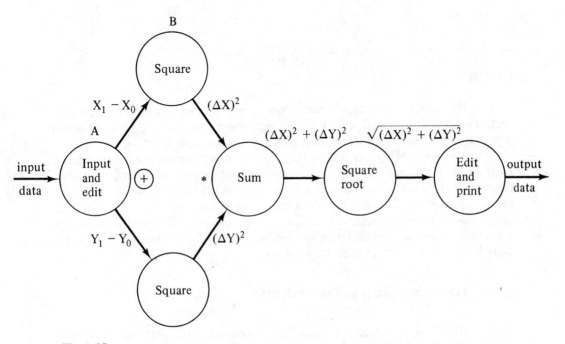

Fig. A.35

The notation $\oplus$ (known as disjunction, denoted by "exclusive or") means that only one of the juxtaposed data sets is produced (or needed) per performance of the transformation. The notation * (known as conjunction) means that all of the juxtaposed data sets are produced (or are needed) per performance of the transformation.

The data flow defines the required order intrinsic to the task, but does not show the flow of control nor the modular structure. It is a diagram that more closely can model the intrinsic structure of problems than can either the structure chart or the traditional flowchart.

Data flow may be modeled to various levels of detail, as shown below:

423

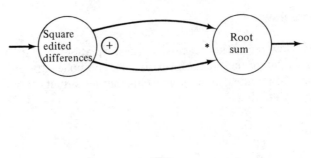

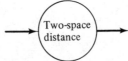

Fig. A.36

It should be clear that to fully model a problem and its programmed solution, data flow, referential structure, and procedure must all be represented (as well as the structure-format of the data on which the program is defined).

The relationships among the three models of a program can be appreciated from a careful study of Fig. A.37. Take note that (a) each module in the structure chart has (or may have) a flowchart for its internal procedure (two of these flowcharts are shown); (b) each flowchart reveals only one level of the structural relationships, viz, the subordinate modules to be called; (c) the flow of data through the modular structure satisfies the requirements inherent in the data flow model, but there is not a simple mapping between the two.

B. Structure charts and HIPO charts

IBM has introduced a design and documentation aid they call **HIPO** (Hierarchical-Input-Process-Output). The structure chart *supplants* the HIPO hierarchical representation (also known as the "visual table of contents," or VTOC), but the HIPO representation of relationship of inputs to outputs is a useful adjunct to structure charts.

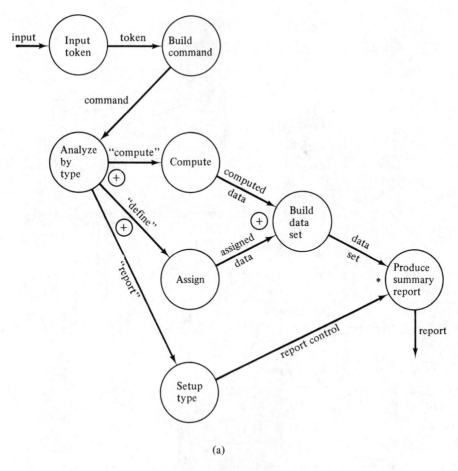

(a)

Fig. A.37a   Data flow (program graph) for the Expensive Desk
Calculator interpreter program.

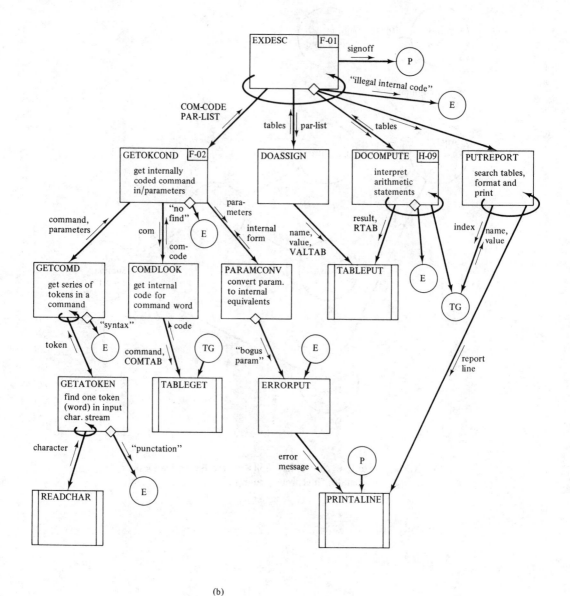

(b)

Fig. A.37b   Structure chart for the Expensive Desk Calculator.

426

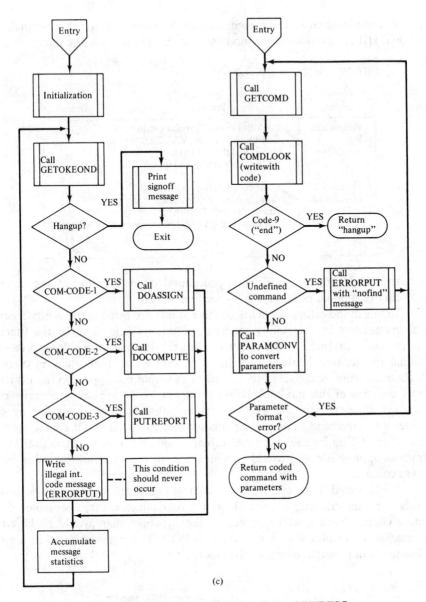

Entry

Initialization

Call
GETOKEOND

Hangup?

YES

Print
signoff
message

Exit

NO

COM-CODE-1

YES

Call
DOASSIGN

NO

COM-CODE-2

YES

Call
DOCOMPUTE

NO

COM-CODE-3

YES

Call
PUTREPORT

NO

Write
illegal int.
code message
(ERRORPUT)

This condition
should never
occur

Accumulate
message
statistics

Entry

Call
GETCOMD

Call
COMDLOOK
(writewith
code)

Code-9
("end")

YES

Return
"hangup"

NO

Undefined
command

YES

Call
ERRORPUT
with "nofind"
message

NO

Call
PARAMCONV
to convert
parameters

Parameter
format
error?

YES

NO

Return coded
command with
parameters

(c)

Fig. A.37c   Flowcharts for two modules of EXDESC.

427

A completed structural design, such as shown in Fig. A.37b, may include a "functional HIPO" chart for some modules.   Such a chart looks like this:

HIPO-09   MODULE DOCOMPUTE

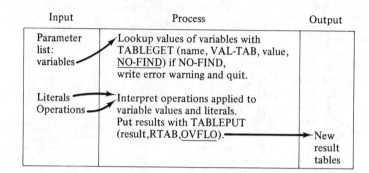

Fig. A.38

This functional HIPO becomes a non-procedural documentation of the *function* (transform) of module DOCOMPUTE — see Fig. A.37b.

Inputs in the calling sequence of this module are listed in the INPUT column, output parameters in the calling sequence of this module (and/or the function value returned) are listed in the OUTPUT column.   The PROCESS column states the functional relationship between data listed as INPUT and that listed as OUTPUT. Data obtained from or delivered to subordinates would not appear in the INPUT or OUTPUT columns of this module's HIPO chart but would appear as parameters in ersatz CALL statements in the PROCESS column; that is, transformations by subordinates are referenced as aspects of this module's PROCESS.   Of course, in turn, the functional HIPO for each such subordinate would list its parameters as INPUT or OUTPUT as appropriate and would explain the subordinated transformation in the PROCESS column.

When keyed to a structure chart, control inputs and outputs should be distinguished by underlining, consistent with the parameter footnote table of the structure chart.   Each module symbol on the structure chart would be keyed by page number or identifier to a particular HIPO.   This may be done in a small window in the upper-right corner of the module box:

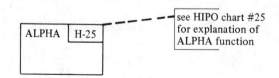

Fig. A.39

Since the interior of the box is often crowded, it is acceptable to key to HIPOs or flowcharts outside the box at the upper-right corner.   (This corner avoids most interference with connections and procedural annotations.)

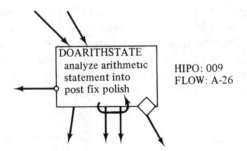

HIPO: 009
FLOW: A-26

Fig. A.40

A. Style

The purpose of a structure chart is to present an easily understood picture of an entire system. Clarity in the portrayal of salient structural features is the important goal. Most often, these ends are advanced through style, which is both consistent and intuitive. In a sense, the aim is to convey information on structure in such a way that the first quick impression is also the correct interpretation.

B. Hierarchy

The arrangement of elements in layers is known as hierarchy, an essential property of nearly all kinds of systems. By causing a module to behave as a sub-function whose execution is bracketed by the execution of the superordinate, sub-ordinating relationships establish a basic hierarchy of control in any program structure. Subroutine calls, macro invocations, and subcoroutines calls all are subordinating relationships.

The function and behavior of a system is clearer when superordinate modules appear above their subordinates on the page. Modules related by any sub-ordinating connection should be displaced vertically with respect to each other, the subordinate below the superordinate. Thus, Fig. A.41a is better styled than is Fig. A.41b, even though both model the same structure.

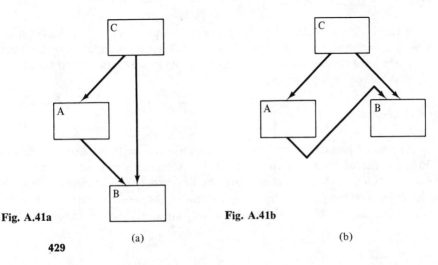

Fig. A.41a   **Fig. A.41b**

(a)   (b)

Similarly, non-subordinating (coordinating) relationships establish modules as being at the same level in the control hierarchy. Examples of coordinating relationships are the coroutine transfer and direct normal transfer (GOTO module by name). The relationship between such modules is clearest when they are shown at the same level on the page. Thus, the mixed (hierarchical and homologous, or non-hierarchical) structure chart of Fig. A.42 shows good style in presenting these relationships.

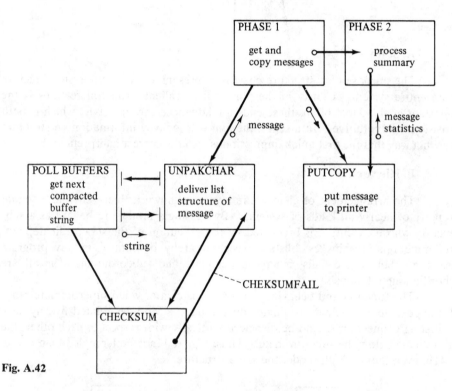

Fig. A.42

Because pathological connections violate (depart from) both hierarchical and homologous relationships, the position of a module's representation on the page should not be determined by them. An example is GOTO label CHEKSUMFAIL or the reading of message statistics in Fig. A.42.

C. Order

As part of procedural annotation, connections usually are arranged left to right in the order of their expected use by the referencing module. Sometimes, particularly when a module has many subordinates, it may not be possible to show all connections emerging along the lower margin of the module symbol. Experience has shown that the most easily read arrangement in this case is to use the margin of the module symbol beginning in the upper-left corner and proceeding counterclockwise around the margin. Thus, the arrangement in Fig. A.43:

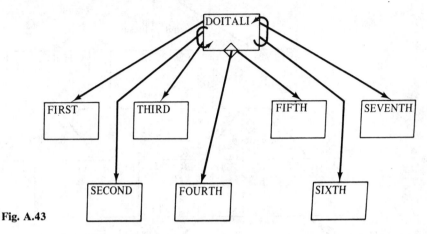

Fig. A.43

Note also in this example that when space is at a premium, not all modules subordinate to the same module are necessarily shown at the same level in the chart.

Since it often corresponds to expected order of usage, inputting subordinates are commonly placed to the left of processing subordinates, which are to the left of outputting subordinates. Consistent use of this rule creates inputting branches that are tilted toward the upper right, and outputting branches tilted the other way: Thus, input data flow toward the northeast and output data toward the southeast. Charts that can be made to conform to this convention are particularly easy to follow and interpret. An example, in abstract form, is shown in Fig. 44 below, with the flow of data indicated by the usual annotations. Note how easily the eye follows successive transforms of the same stream of data.

The lexical order of connections in the source code for the referencing module, the expected order of use, and the input-process-output order may conflict. In this case, one should choose the arrangement that most clearly represents what the system does. For permanent documentation purposes, the lexical order, being an objective physical feature of the module, is probably the best choice.

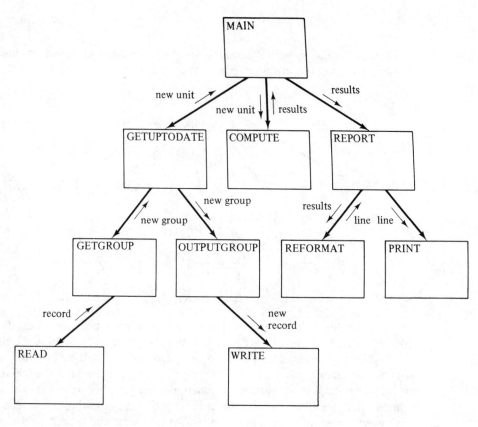

Fig. A.44

D. Multiple connections

Any number of connections of the same type from one module to another may be represented by a single line on the chart, showing simply that the modules are connected in a particular manner. Especially in the case of subroutine calls from one module to another, only one line almost always would be shown. For example, what is usually important is only that REPORT makes *some* use of RE-FORMAT. There are times when this practice of using only one line to represent one *or more* connections is impractical or unclear. For example, each use of module FOO from FUM may involve different actual parameters. Or a module might use another module in two or more completely different contexts. Whenever the resulting structure chart would be clearer, each connection from one module to another specific module should be shown separately. In Fig. A.45 below, the same report module, STATPUT, is used in three different ways by PERSYST; each of these is shown separately. Note, however, that no clarity would be added by showing three separate pathological data connections for EMP-ID, EDUC, and SKIL-LIST.

432

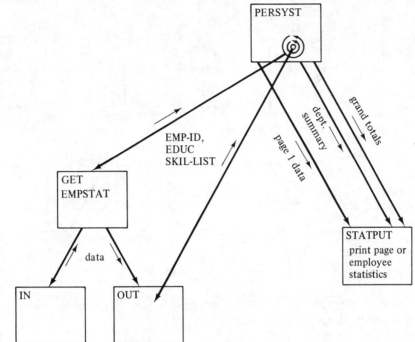

Fig. A.45

E. Crossing and connections

In general, one should avoid lines that cross in a structure chart, as this is messy and sometimes confusing. Connectors usually are used; but where the two ends of the connection are close, as in the example above, crossing lines may be preferable. The standard form of crossing may be used, as shown in Figs. A.45 and A.46.

Fig. A.46

When using connectors, you should observe certain rules. It is permissible to show several "to" connectors that refer to the same target. For example

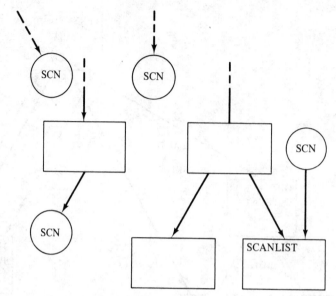

Fig. A.47

The converse, one "to" connector referring to several different targets, as in Fig. A.48 below is *not* permitted.

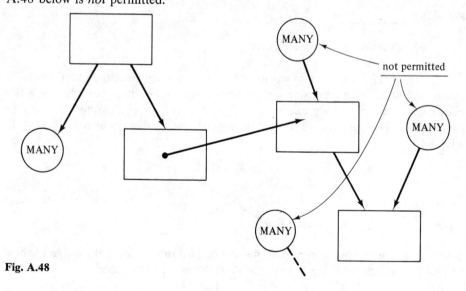

Fig. A.48

Off-page connectors should refer from one page to another, but not back again. That is, each separate page of a single structure chart should, if possible, present the structure of a complete, self-contained substructure. Both on-page and off-page connectors should use mnemonic, rather than arbitrary, identifiers to simplify reading the chart. Page numbers for off-page connectors should be added as an annotation.

Modules with many uses scattered throughout the structure, such as an error message module, present special problems. The structure chart will be easiest to understand correctly when each such commonly used module is shown at the bottom of the chart, separated from the rest of the structure. A connector with a clear mnemonic identifier should be used wherever the module is to be referenced. For example:

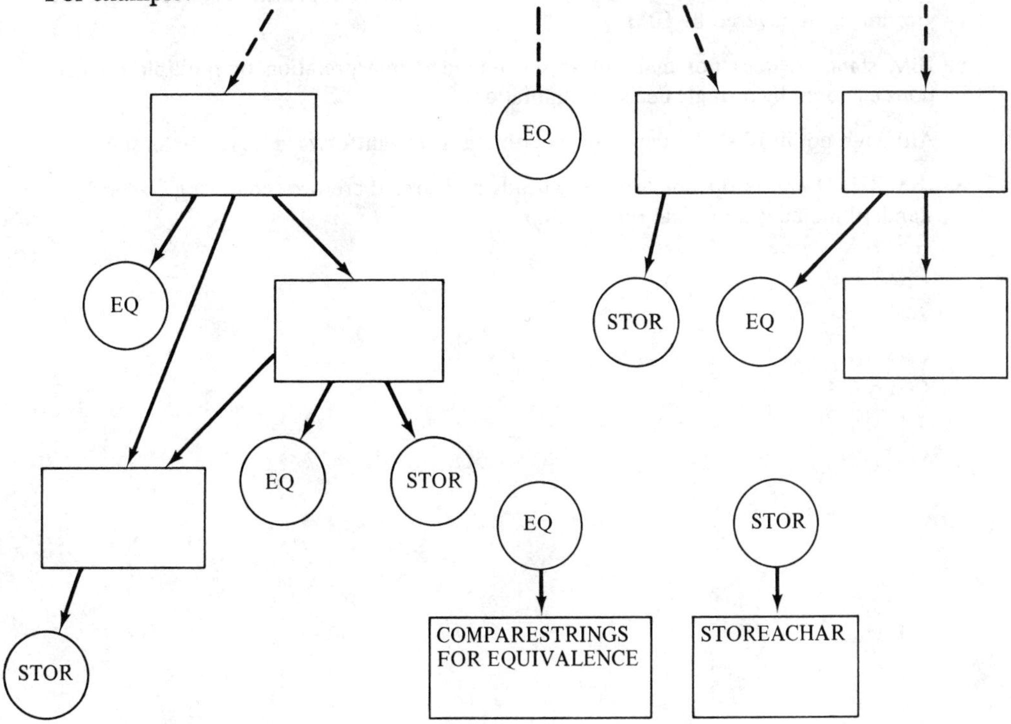

Fig. A.49

Never repeat the same box (module symbol) on a chart, even when representing multiple usage. Each distinct module should appear once, and only once, on the structure chart of the system, unless it specifically is intended that more than one version of the same module is to be implemented, in which case, an explanatory comment is essential. Multi-page structure charts are much harder to read and understand than are multi-page flowcharts, unless great care is taken in their construction. It is better to use a larger piece of paper than to separate a structure onto several pages. For design work, a large sheet of paper or a chalkboard is a must.

EXPLANATORY NOTES

1. Graphic symbol is not in IBM standard as presented in W.P. Stevens, G.J. Myers, and L.L. Constantine, "Structured Design," *IBM Systems Journal,* Vol. 13, No. 2 (May 1974), pp. 115–139.

2. IBM standard provides only the unspecified (tail-less) annotating arrow.

3. IBM standard does not provide for mixing direct and footnoted annotation of parameters.

4. Use of connectors is not covered in IBM standard.

5. Neither the "data only module" symbol nor its use to represent common data environments is covered by IBM.

6. IBM standard does not make clear the intended interpretation of multiple connections enclosed by a single decision annotation.

7. Although not in IBM standard, this notation is a straightforward logical extension.

8. IBM HIPO charts do not use arrowheads and are, therefore, confusing. The IBM standard includes no lexical relationship.

Summary

of

Standard Graphics

for Program

Structure Charts

Appendix B

I. FUNDAMENTAL ELEMENTS

This section is meant to clarify the basic logic of the complete graphic model of program structure for two reasons: to aid you in learning the model and to suggest generalizations or extensions through combinations of fundamental elements.

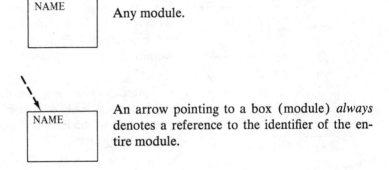

Any module.

An arrow pointing to a box (module) *always* denotes a reference to the identifier of the entire module.

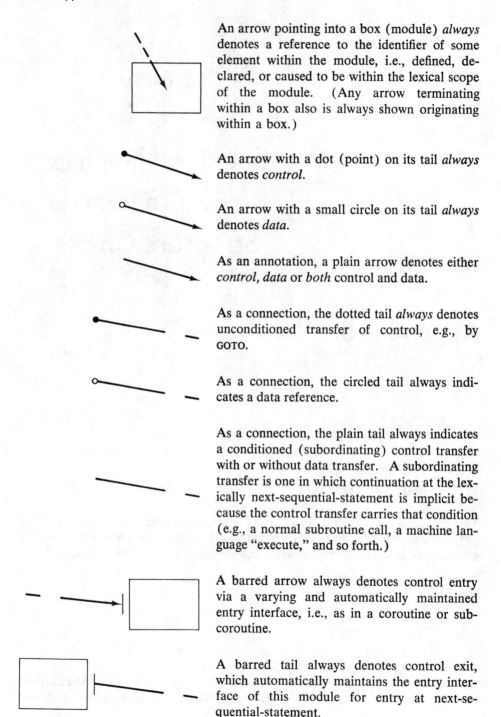

An arrow pointing into a box (module) *always* denotes a reference to the identifier of some element within the module, i.e., defined, declared, or caused to be within the lexical scope of the module. (Any arrow terminating within a box also is always shown originating within a box.)

An arrow with a dot (point) on its tail *always* denotes *control*.

An arrow with a small circle on its tail *always* denotes *data*.

As an annotation, a plain arrow denotes either *control, data* or *both* control and data.

As a connection, the dotted tail *always* denotes unconditioned transfer of control, e.g., by GOTO.

As a connection, the circled tail always indicates a data reference.

As a connection, the plain tail always indicates a conditioned (subordinating) control transfer with or without data transfer. A subordinating transfer is one in which continuation at the lexically next-sequential-statement is implicit because the control transfer carries that condition (e.g., a normal subroutine call, a machine language "execute," and so forth.)

A barred arrow always denotes control entry via a varying and automatically maintained entry interface, i.e., as in a coroutine or sub-coroutine.

A barred tail always denotes control exit, which automatically maintains the entry interface of this module for entry at next-sequential-statement.

MODULES AND ENTITIES

E-1:   Any module, regardless of physical or activation characteristics. See defintion, page 410 of Appendix A. When other types of modules are distinguished, the symbol is used for a normal subroutine.

E-1.1:   Any predefined or pre-existing module. Striping may be added to other module symbols, that is, E-3.

E-2:   Any module consisting solely of data elements.

E-3:   A macro. Any module inserted or expanded in-line at compile-time (or transaction-time) when invoked by name.

E-4:   The operating environment within which the program runs, including, but not limited to, the operating system, monitor, system task management, the hardware itself, and so on.

E-5:   Any physical input-output device/medium/file referenced by identifier; e.g., CARD-READER-2.

CONNECTIONS

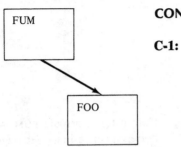

C-1:   Subordination, normal. A reference to FOO exists in FUM in the context of an invocation that subordinates FOO to FUM, i.e., a subroutine call, function reference, or macro invocation.

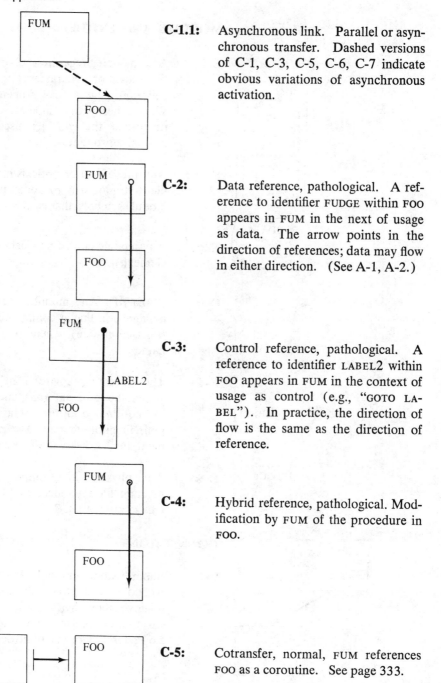

C-1.1: Asynchronous link. Parallel or asynchronous transfer. Dashed versions of C-1, C-3, C-5, C-6, C-7 indicate obvious variations of asynchronous activation.

C-2: Data reference, pathological. A reference to identifier FUDGE within FOO appears in FUM in the next of usage as data. The arrow points in the direction of references; data may flow in either direction. (See A-1, A-2.)

C-3: Control reference, pathological. A reference to identifier LABEL2 within FOO appears in FUM in the context of usage as control (e.g., "GOTO LABEL"). In practice, the direction of flow is the same as the direction of reference.

C-4: Hybrid reference, pathological. Modification by FUM of the procedure in FOO.

C-5: Cotransfer, normal, FUM references FOO as a coroutine. See page 333.

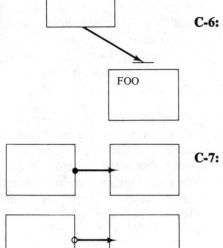

C-6:   Subordinated   cotransfer,   normal. FUM references FOO as a subordinate, which is entered via an entry locator maintained by FOO on resumption of any subordinating task.

C-7:   Transfer,   normal.   Unconditioned (unsubordinated) transfer of control to FOO by name.

Data transfer, normal. Transmission of data to or from FOO by name without transfer of control. See Section 18.5.

ANNOTATIONS
Information Flow

A-1:   Information flow.   Notation adjacent to any connection indicates the direction of flow of information (data and/or control). The description may consist of identifiers, narrative description, and/or numbered footnote references (see A-4). Usually used for parameters to and from modules. Identifiers are those appearing in the referenc*ing* module, that is, the actual rather than dummy parameters.

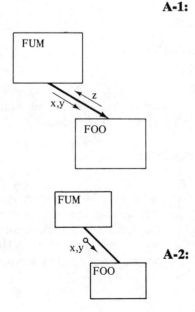

A-2:   Data flow.   As in A-1 except only denoting data. (Here: Input parameters x and y to FOO.)

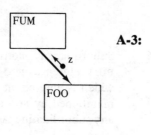

A-3: Control flow. As in A-1, except only control or elements of data used to communicate control information are denoted. Here: Flag z, an output (return) parameter of FOO.

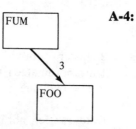

A-4: Footnote reference. Index number of an entry in a parameter footnote table as shown. The input and output columns list, respectively, the parameters going to and from the referenced module. (Here: As in entries for A-1, A-2, and A-3.)

PARAMETERS

	INPUT	OUTPUT
1		
2		
3	x,y	z
4		
.		
.		
.		

COMMENTS

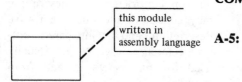

A-5: Comment. Any explanatory appendation. Note the dashed line without an arrowhead.

PROCEDURE

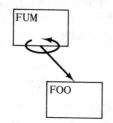

A-6: Iteration. The reference indicated is imbedded in a looping procedure. It may be used to enclose the origination of any connection. (Here: Repeated use of FOO as a subroutine.)

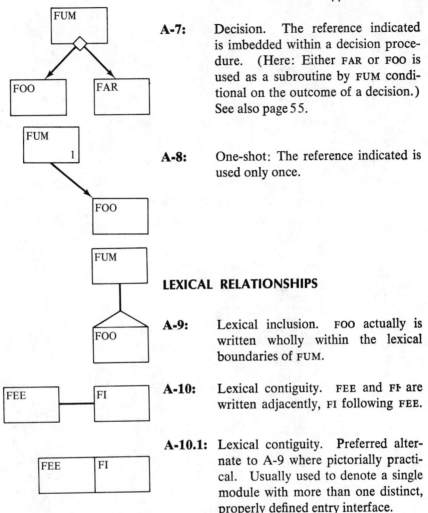

A-7:   Decision. The reference indicated is imbedded within a decision procedure. (Here: Either FAR or FOO is used as a subroutine by FUM conditional on the outcome of a decision.) See also page 55.

A-8:   One-shot: The reference indicated is used only once.

LEXICAL RELATIONSHIPS

A-9:   Lexical inclusion. FOO actually is written wholly within the lexical boundaries of FUM.

A-10:   Lexical contiguity. FEE and FI are written adjacently, FI following FEE.

A-10.1:   Lexical contiguity. Preferred alternate to A-9 where pictorially practical. Usually used to denote a single module with more than one distinct, properly defined entry interface.

Glossary

access	to make use of a reference; that is, to execute the statement in which the reference is contained.
accessibility of information	one of three aspects of an intermodule interface that can affect its complexity.
adjacency	a term used to describe modules that execute one right after the other. Used as a low-priority packaging criterion.
afferent data element	a high-level element of data that is furthest removed from physical input, but that still constitutes input to the system.
afferent flow	a flow of data from low-level subordinates upward to higher-level superordinates.
afferent module	a module that obtains input from its subordinate and delivers it upward to its superordinate.

445

aggregate	a contiguous group of statements, bounded by boundary elements.
aggregate identifier	the identifier associated with an entire aggregate.
A-level module	a second-level "action" module created as part of the transaction-analysis strategy.
alternate returns	a module linkage convention that allows the subordinate to return to a location other than the normal return location.
anticipatory loading	an automatic storage management discipline that loads modules into memory before they actually are invoked, based on knowledge of the hierarchy of modules in the system.
associative principle	a principle or concept used by a designer in associating processing elements together in a single module.
atomic module	a module with no subordinates; a bottom-level module.
automatic packaging	the dynamic determination (usually by an operating system) of which modules should be loaded into primary storage, and which modules should be overlaid and/or written onto secondary storage.
balanced systems	systems that are not input-driven or output-driven; such systems usually have a fairly deep hierarchy of modules to obtain inputs and to deliver outputs.
base load	a set of modules activated by an unbroken chain of explicit commands.
bifurcated transfer	a transfer of control to a module such that a separate control stream is created; this is accomplished with genuine parallel processing, or with simulated parallel processing (i.e., with the assistance of a multitasking or multiprogramming operating system).
binding	a common synonym for cohesion. In this book, binding is used exclusively to describe the process of assigning a value or referent to an identifier.
binding time	the point, in the development life cycle of a program, at which a value or referent is assigned to an identifier; binding time is a factor influencing degree of coupling.
black box	a system (or, equivalently, a component) with known inputs, known outputs, and generally a known transform, but with unknown (or irrelevant) contents.

bottom-up testing	a testing strategy in which bottom-level modules are tested first, and then are integrated into higher-level superordinates. Usually contrasted with top-down testing.
boundary clash	in the Jackson data-structure design technique, a particular form of structure clash, usually caused by the blocking characteristics of physical input-output devices.
boundary element	a statement or other element of a language which serves to define the lexical limits of groups of statements and allows the statements so bounded to be used as a single entity for some purpose.
bubble chart	synonym for data flow graph.
business systems analyst	a common term used to describe a person whose job it is to talk to the end-user of a computer system, and to document that user's needs so that an appropriate computer system can be developed.
call by name	a means of passing data to a module by passing the address of the data.
call by value	a means of passing data to a module by passing a copy of the data.
central transforms	central system's functions which take relatively digested data (afferent data elements) as input streams, and which then create major output streams (efferent data elements).
CIPO	a specific (obsolete) model of systems organization; the acronym, CIPO, stands for *C*ontrol-*I*nput-*P*rocess-*O*utput.
coding	the process of writing the computer instructions after procedural design has been carried out by a programmer, after structural design has been carried out by a designer, and after specifications have been developed by a systems analyst.
cohesion	the degree of functional relatedness of processing elements within a single module.
coincidental cohesion	the lowest of seven levels of cohesion, used to describe a module whose processing elements have no constructive relationship to one another.

commonality	a measure of how common the problem (or application) is that we are solving with a given system; one of the factors in program generality.
common-data environment	a means of describing data such that the data can be accessed by any module in a system.
common-environment coupling	a form of coupling that occurs whenever two or more modules interact with a common-data environment.
communication analysis	a refinement of a completed structural design, in which appropriate means are chosen for communication between modules — e.g., intermediate files, subroutine arguments, external variables, and so on.
communication structure	the structure of a program defined by the relationship of transmission and reception of data.
communicational cohesion	one of seven levels of cohesion that occurs when all of the processing elements of a module operate upon the same input data set and/or produce the same output data; this is the lowest level of cohesion at which there is a relationship among processing elements that is intrinsically problem-dependent.
complexity of interface	one of the factors influencing coupling between modules. The complexity of the interface is approximately equal to the number of different items being passed — the more items, the higher the coupling.
computer systems analyst	a common synonym for "systems designer." Used to describe the person who is concerned with the structural design of a computer system, once its specifications have been determined by a business systems analyst.
conceptual structure	the structure of a program defined by the relationships existing in the programmer's mind.
conditioned transfer	a jump out from the current execution sequence with the condition that control eventually be returned to the execution sequence from which the jump was made, i.e., a subroutine call.
connection	a reference in one part of a program to the identifier of another part (i.e., something found elsewhere). See intermodular connection.

conroutine	a nonincremental module activated by a bifurcated transfer. Also known as a task.
content-coupling	a strong form of coupling that occurs when some or all of the contents of one module is included in the contents of another.
control structure	the structure of a program defined by references which represent transfers of control.
control-coupling	a form of coupling that occurs whenever there is any connection between two modules that communicates elements of control.
Conway's Law	an observation by Mel Conway that the structure of a system reflects the structure of the organization that built it.
coordinate flow	a flow of data from a subordinate upward to its superordinate, and then downward from the superordinate to some other subordinate.
coordinate module	a module primarily concerned with coordinating and managing the activities of subordinates. Frequently referred to as an executive module.
coordination	a form of indirect control in which one module involves itself in the procedural contents of another; for example, a subroutine that assembles data elements into compound elements for a superordinate, sending a flag to the superordinate indicating whether its return is either to request an additional data element or to deliver a completed compound item.
coroutine	a module whose point of activation is always the next sequential statement following the last point at which the module deactivated itself by activating another coroutine.
cost of debugging	the cost of everything the programmer does in the development of a program beyond the initial writing of the code, the first compilation or assembly, and the last test-run (the one that confirms that the system is acceptable).
cotransfer	the activation of a coroutine.
coupling	a measure of the strength of interconnection between one module and another.

data flow graph	a graphic tool used to represent the flow of data streams through successive transforms.
data-coupling	a form of coupling caused by an intermodule connection that provides output from one module and that serves as input to another module.
data-structure design	a type of design strategy that derives a structural design from consideration of the structure of data sets associated with the problem.
debugging	the process of identifying a bug's location and nature.
decoupling	any systematic method or technique by which modules can be made more independent.
demand coroutine	a synonym for subcoroutine.
demand loading	a form of storage management in which nonresident modules are loaded into primary storage only when they actually have been invoked by some other module. Usually contrasted with anticipatory loading.
demodularization	the process of compressing all of one module (or, on occasion, part of one module) into another. Usually carried out as part of the process of optimizing the performance of a system.
design	to plan the form and method of a solution.
design principles	very broad principles that generally work in the sense that they favor increasing quality for decreased development cost.
device-centered design	an informal (obsolete) design strategy, which focuses on a physical input-output device and its interface as the organizing principle for placing processing elements within a module.
device-coupled communication	a form of pathological communication in which modules pass data to one another through some secondary storage device, rather than passing the data through superordinates.
direct pathological connection	a form of pathological connection in which a module refers directly to an identifier contained within another module.
disposable modules	a maintenance strategy in which modules are thrown away and rewritten if they are discovered to contain bugs or inadequacies.

D-level module	one of the four levels of modules specified by the transaction analysis strategy. D-level modules are bottom-level "detail" modules, which are responsible for carrying out the details of the actions required to complete a transaction.
domain generality	one aspect of generality in a computer program. A module with a large domain — i.e., which accepts a wide range of values for its input — is more general than one with a smaller domain.
downward compression	a form of compression in which a superordinate module is copied in-line in the body of its subordinate; usually carried out as part of a process of optimizing the performance of a system.
driver	a primitive simulation of a superordinate module, used in the bottom-up testing of a subordinate module.
dummy module	a common synonym for stub. A dummy module provides a primitive simulation of a subordinate, and is used in the top-down testing of a superordinate.
dynamic control	a packaging mechanism in which the programmer specifies to the operating system when a load unit actually should be brought into primary memory.
dynamic integrity	used to describe the dynamic behavior of a black-box module; a module with dynamic integrity is stable and dependable, and carries out the same function each time it is invoked.
dynamic recursion	a form of recursion that exists wherever a module is shared by two or more tasks that can be among active jobs at the same time, is used by routines handling different interrupts or asynchronous processes, or is reachable from both base and interrupt loads.
efferent data element	a data element that is furthest removed from the physical outputs and that still may be termed outgoing.
efferent flow	a flow of data in which a superordinate passes a data element to its subordinate, which then passes it downward to its subordinate.
efferent module	a module that receives its input from a superordinate, and that delivers its output to a subordinate.

exclusion	a strategy for designing generalized systems in which the designer examines as many applications as possible, but excludes those aspects that make the application special or unique.
explosion point	the point in data flow graph at which data streams separate (explode).
factoring	a process of decomposing a system into a hierarchy of modules.
fan-in	the number of superordinate modules which refer to a specified subordinate.
fan-out	the number of immediate subordinates to a specified module.
feasibility study	a study, normally conducted at the beginning of a systems development project, to determine the likelihood that a system can, in fact, be built within the constraints of time, manpower, and budget.
filter transform	a type of data flow graph "bubble" (transform) that separates a stream of input data into a stream of good data and a stream of bad data, passing on the good.
flexibility	a measure of the degree to which a system, as is, can be used in a variety of ways.
fully factored systems	systems in which all actual processing (or computation or data manipulation) is handled by bottom-level atomic modules, and in which all non-atomic modules consist only of control and coordination.
functional cohesion	the strongest form of relationship between processing elements in a module; occurs when every element of processing is an integral part of, and essential to, the performance of a single function.
functional recursion	a means of defining certain functions, mathematical and otherwise; the value of such functions, for a certain input, is defined in terms of the same function of other inputs.
functional requirements	a precise description of the requirements of a computer system; includes a statement of the inputs to be supplied by the user, the outputs desired by the user, the algorithms involved in any computations desired by the user, and a description of such physical constraints as response time, volumes, and so on.

functional specification	a synonym for functional requirements.
functionality	a synonym for cohesion.
function-centered design	an informal design strategy that attempts to derive a system whose modules all represent single, self-contained functions.
general system design	an informal description of the work carried out by the computer systems analyst: designing the major elements of the data base, the major components of a system, and the interfaces between them.
generality	a measure of the degree to which a system exhibits the properties of a general-purpose system.
general-purpose system	a system that is widely used or usable, that solves a broad case of a wide class of problems, that is readily adaptable to many variations, and/or that will function in many different environments.
gray box	a system that does not have all of the desirable properties of a black box, but whose contents do not have to be completely understood in order to be used.
head routine	a top-level subroutine or subcoroutine, or a module whose data comes in from below and goes out below; a coordinate module.
heuristic	a specific rule of thumb that usually works but is not guaranteed.
HIPO chart	an acronym for *H*ierarchy-*I*nput-*P*rocess-*O*utput, developed by IBM to document the structure of systems. Similar in some ways to structure charts.
homologous system	a system developed with any control relationship that does not define a hierarchy of control responsibility; i.e., a non-hierarchical system.
hybrid-coupling	a strong form of coupling that occurs when one module modifies the procedural contents of another module.
identifier	the name, address, label, or distinguishing index of an object in a program.
identifier space	all identifiers defined over a given lexical scope.
identity interface	the interface associated with the aggregate identifier of a module or segment.

implicit structure	structure based on implicit control and data relationships for which there are no references (connections).
inch-pebbles	a useful term for describing small milestones in a computer project.
inclusion	a strategy for designing general-purpose systems that operates by identifying and examining as many distinct applications as possible and including some feature or features to cover each of the applications.
incremental implementation	a testing/implementation strategy for adding a new (potentially buggy) module to a tested collection of modules, and then testing the new combination.
incremental module	a module that begins its execution at the point at which operation was last suspended, e.g., a coroutine or sub-coroutine.
independence	a term used to describe pairs of modules: Two modules are said to be independent if each can function completely without the presence of the other.
information hiding	a design heuristic developed by D.L. Parnas: Modules are formed in such a way as to hide from the rest of the system assumptions about the solution that are likely to change.
initial boundary	the lexically first boundary element that begins a module or segment.
input-driven system	a term used to characterize a system that obtains all of its inputs in elementary, (raw) physical form at or near the top of the hierarchy.
input-output coupling	a synonym for data-coupling.
interface	the point in a module or segment elsewhere referenced by an identifier at which control or data is received or transmitted.
intermodular connection	a reference from one module to an identifier in a different module.
interrupt load	the set of modules activated by an interrupt.
interrupt module	a module activated by an interrupt.
intramodular functional relatedness	a synonym for cohesion.

item-centered design	an informal (obsolete) design strategy that associates in one place all processing for a given item of incoming data.
job step	a common (vendor-dependent) term used to describe a physically executable unit of code.
lateral compression	a process of combining two or more procedurally adjacent modules into a single module; usually carried out as part of a process of optimizing the performance of a system.
lexical	of or pertaining to the program as written, as it appears in a program listing.
lexical inclusion	the property of one object (usually module or segment) being wholly contained within the lexical boundaries of another.
lexical order	the order in which statements appear as written.
load module	a common (vendor-dependent) term used to describe a physically executable unit of code.
load unit	a common (vendor-dependent) term used to describe a physically executable unit of code.
localization	a technique of decoupling affected by subdividing the data elements communicated through a common environment into a number of regions common to a smaller number of modules.
locus of control	a means of describing the extent to which control over the behavior of a system resides in the input data or in the resident data, rather than in the instructions themselves. The flexibility of a system generally is increased as the locus of control shifts away from the instructions and toward the input data and/or the resident data.
logic design	the design of the procedural logic within a single module.
logical cohesion	one of the weakest of seven levels of cohesion. A module is said to be logically cohesive if its processing elements can be considered members of the same logical class of similar or related functions.
macro	a module whose body is effectively copied in-line during translation (e.g., compilation or assembly) as a result of being invoked by name; that is, the bounded contents replace the reference to the aggregate identifier.

maintainability	the extent to which a system can be easily corrected when bugs are discovered during the system's productive lifetime.
maintenance	the correction of bugs that are discovered in a system during its productive lifetime.
Mealy's Law	the observation, by George Mealy, that there is an incremental person who, when added to a project, consumes more energy (or resources) than he or she makes available.
mechanically segmented	a term used to describe a system whose structure is largely determined by mechanical restrictions such as memory page size and real-time response constraints.
merge point	a point in a data flow graph where data streams fan-in (merge).
minimally connected	a term used to describe a system whose connections are restricted to fully parameterized (with respect to inputs and outputs) conditioned transfers of control to the single, unique activation/entry/origin/interface of any module.
modifiability	the ability of a system to be changed or enhanced to meet the needs of a user during the system's productive lifetime.
modification	the act of changing or enhancing a system to meet the changing needs of a user during the system's productive lifetime.
module	a contiguous sequence of program statements, bounded by boundary elements, having an aggregate identifier.
module strength	a synonym for cohesion.
monolithic	of, pertaining to, or behaving like a single piece; minimal modularity.
morphology	shape; particularly with respect to the structure of a system.
mosque shape	a characteristic shape of well-designed systems; also referred to as a cigar or a flying-saucer shape.
normal connection	a reference to an aggregate identifier of a module.
normally connected	a term used to describe a system that is minimally connected except for one or more instances of (a) multiple

entry points to a single module, provided that each such entry is minimal with respect to data transfers, (b) control returns to other than the next sequential statement in the activating module, provided that the alternate returns are defined by the activating module as part of its activation process, or (c) control is transferred to a normal entry point by something other than a conditioned transfer of control.

ongoing debugging   a synonym for maintenance.

order clash   in the Jackson data-structure design technique, a particular form of structure clash that occurs when a program must deal with input data sets that have been sorted in a different order.

output-driven system   a system in which the top-level module produces the output of the system in elementary (or raw) form.

overlay   a common (vendor-dependent) term to describe a physically executable unit of code.

packaging   the assignment of the modules of a total system into sections handled as distinct physical units for execution on a machine.

pancake structure   an informal term used to describe a system with very few intermediate levels of executive modules. The few executive modules that do exist in such systems usually are characterized by a high span of control.

pathological connection   a reference to an identifier other than the aggregate identifier of a module (i.e., a reference to an object within the module).

phase routine   a term for a module that is activated by name by an unconditioned transfer of control; that is, as a next step rather than as a subordinate.

phased implementation   a form of testing/implementation in which several untested modules are combined together at once, and the collection tested for correctness.

P-level module   one of the four levels of modules created by the transaction analysis strategy. The P-level module is the program-level module that receives a transaction and dispatches it to the appropriate T-level subordinate to completely process the transaction.

pointer   an entity containing or having the value of an identifier.

portability	a property of a program representing ease of movement among distinct solution environments.
procedural analysis	a set of criteria to determine which modules must be in the same load unit for the sake of efficiency; normally considered part of the process of packaging.
procedural cohesion	an intermediate degree of the seven levels of cohesion; a module is said to be procedurally cohesive if its processing elements are elements of a common procedural unit, either an iteration or decision process.
procedure-centered design	an informal (obsolete) design strategy in which the design of a system is derived from procedural representations (for example, flowcharts) of a system's operation.
processing element	any part of the task performed by a module — not only the processing accomplished by statements executed within that module, but also that which results from calls on subordinates.
program	a system composed of precise, ordered statements and aggregate. Sometimes used informally as a synonym for module. Often used in the context of packaging decisions; that is, a program is often regarded as the smallest unit of a system than can be manipulated (initiated, loaded into primary memory, overlaid, and so on) by the operating system.
program development process	a complete process of analyzing the requirements of a system, carrying out the structural design, writing the code, and testing the resulting product.
program inversion	in the Jackson data-structure design technique, a procedure for converting a pair of coroutines into a superordinate-subordinate relationship. Used primarily as a means of dealing with structure clashes in a programming environment that does not support coroutines.
program specifications	a precise description of the requirements of an individual program: It includes a statement of the inputs to be supplied to the program, the outputs desired, the algorithms involved in any computations, and a description of such physical constraints as execution speed, memory limitations, and so on. Sometimes used as a synonym for functional requirements.

programmer   an informal term used to describe the person who designs and writes the programming instructions to implement a module. In some organizations, programmers also are responsible for the structural design of the system, and occasionally even for the analysis of the user's requirements.

prologue/epilogue processing   "Overhead" processing normally required upon first entering a module, and just prior to exiting from the module. Such processing usually includes saving and restoring of hardware registers, establishing the scope of identifier definition within the module, and so on. The prologue/epilogue processing often requires a considerable amount of CPU time (and memory), but usually is transparent to the programmer and designer; it usually is an issue only when optimization needs to be carried out.

recursion   the act of invoking a module as a subordinate of itself; a recursive module is one that calls itself.

reenterable   a synonym for reentrant.

reentrant   a module is reentrant if it can be reactivated correctly at any time, whether or not it has been suspended by a conditioned transfer or return.

reference   the use (appearance lexically) within some part of a program of an identifier of a program entity.

referent   the object identified in a reference.

referential structure   the structure based on all references (connections) within a program.

reliability   a measure of the quality of a program or system; sometimes expressed as mean-time-between-failures.

resident data   data built (e.g., compiled) into a program.

reusable module   a module that always executes in the same way on each separate activation, as if it were a fresh copy of the module.

reversible computation   a computation that can be undone or performed in reverse to yield some or all of the original inputs.

SAPTAD   an acronym for an earlier version of the transaction analysis strategy. SAPTAD, developed at Bell Telephone of Canada, is an acronym for *System-Application-Program-Transaction-Action-Detail*.

scope of control	the scope of control of a module consists of the module itself and all of its subordinates.
scope of effect	the scope of effect of a decision is the collection of all modules containing any processing that is conditional upon that decision.
scope of identifier definition	the lexical region (scope) over which an identifier is defined and carries a given meaning.
segment	an aggregate with no aggregate identifier.
self-checking procedure	a computation that can be made inherently self-checking — that is, side effects to the algorithmic process itself may be used to check (or verify, or prove) the result.
semantic element	an aspect of processing related to the action that a transaction requires.
sequential cohesion	one of the strongest of the seven levels of cohesion. A module is said to be sequentially cohesive if the output data (or results) from one processing element serve as input data for the next processing element.
serially reusable module	a synonym for reusable module.
side effects	processing, or activities, unrelated to a module's primary function.
simultaneous recursion	a structure that results from a module being a subordinate, but not an immediate subordinate, of itself. For example, if module A calls module B, and module B calls module A, then A and B are said to be simultaneously recursive.
singular function	a function, or module, that is invoked only once during the execution of the entire system; also known as "once-only" modules, or "one-shot" modules.
skew	a feature of the morphology or shape of a system that occurs when a few high-level executive modules have many levels of subordinates, while most of the executive modules have none or only a few levels of subordinates.
software redundancy	redundancy achieved by coding two (or more) distinct implementations of the modules of a system (presumably by different people).

software reliability   a measure of the quality of a program or system; sometimes expressed as mean-time-between-faliures.

span of control   a module's span of control is the number of its immediate subordinates; fan-out.

span of control flow   the number of lexically contiguous statements that a programmer must examine before he finds a black-box section of code that has one entry point and one exit point.

statement   a line, sentence, or other similar well-defined construct of a programming language that defines, describes, or directs one step or part of the solution of the problem.

static control   the ability to specify which modules (or portions of modules) constitute load units; an aspect of packaging.

static integrity   used to describe the static behavior of a black-box module; a program has more static integrity to the extent that its behavior can be characterized in terms of a set of immediate inputs, a set of immediate outputs, and a simply stated relationship between the two.

stepwise refinement   a synonym for incremental implementation.

strategy   a procedure or plan in which to imbed the use of tools, principles, and heuristics to specify systems parameters in order to increase technical objectives.

structural design   the design of the structure of a system: the specification of the pieces (e.g., modules) and the interconnection between the pieces.

structure charts   a documentation technique for illustrating the modules in a system, and the interconnections between modules.

structure clash   in the Jackson data-structure design technique, the existence of multiple sets of data which do not have a one-to-one correspondence at all levels of the data structures.

structured analysis   a set of guidelines and techniques that assists a systems analyst in stating functional requirements of a system in logical terms.

structured data   data which itself contains explicit structural information that relates, by reference, an element of data to other elements of data.

structured design	a set of guidelines and techniques that assists a systems designer in determining which modules, interconnected in which way, will best solve a well-stated problem.
structured programming	a set of guidelines and techniques for writing programs as a nested set of single-entry, single-exit blocks of code, using a restricted number of constructs.
stub	a primitive implementation of a subordinate module; normally used in the top-down testing of a superordinate module.
subcoroutine	an incremental module which can be subordinated and which will resume whatever module calls it.
subroutine	a module activated at execution time by a conditioned transfer.
synchronized module	a module which references another module, not to activate it, but to check its progress, guarantee completion of a certain point, or otherwise fall in step.
syntactic element	an aspect of processing related to the form that a transaction takes.
system flowchart	a physical version of a data flow graph; i.e., a diagram that shows physical inputs and outputs to a system, as well as the physical processing units (job steps, runs, and so on) that transform the data.
system specification	a synonym for functional requirements.
systems analyst	an informal term for a person whose job it is to analyze the user's needs, and to then derive the functional requirements of a system.
systems development life cycle	a synonym for program development process.
technical objectives	technically based measures of quality which generally relate consistently to the overall goals of least-cost or maximum-gain.
technical parameters	non-evaluate measures of a system — that is, merely descriptions of certain aspects of a system.
temporal cohesion	one of the lower of seven levels of cohesion. A module is said to be temporally cohesive if all occurrences of all elements of processing in the module occur within the same limited period of time during the execution of the system.

terminal failure	a software error that causes a system to completely stop functioning.
test harness	a synonym for driver.
test monitor	a synonym for driver.
testing	a process of demonstrating that a system carries out its function as specified.
Thousand Module Effect	an informal observation that if 1,000 programmers are assigned to develop a system before a structural design has been completed, then there will be at least 1,000 modules in the resulting system.
T-level module	a third-level module derived by the transaction analysis strategy. A T-level module, or transaction-level module, is responsible for completely processing a transaction.
top-down design	an informal design strategy in which the major functions of a system are identified, and their implementation expressed in terms of lower-level primitives; the design process is then repeated on the primitives, until the designer has identified primitives of a sufficiently low level that their implementation can be expressed trivially in terms of available program statements.
top-down testing	a testing/implementation strategy in which high-level modules are tested before low-level modules; this usually requires the use of stubs to provide a primitive simulation of low-level modules in order to be able to test the higher-level superordinate modules.
transaction	any element of data, control, signal, event, or change of state which causes, triggers, or initiates some action or sequence of actions.
transaction analysis	a design strategy in which the structure of a system is derived from an analysis of the transactions the system is required to process.
transaction center	a portion of a system that can (a) obtain transactions in raw form, (b) analyze each transaction to determine its type, (c) dispatch on type of transaction, and (d) complete the processing of each transaction.
transaction-centered design	a synonym for transaction analysis.

transform	the transformation of some input data into some output data; a mapping of inputs into outputs; the function of a module; the representation of a transform on a data flow graph.
transform analysis	a design strategy in which the structure of a system is derived from an analysis of the flow of data through a system, and of the transformations of data.
transform flow	a flow of data into a module (as an input parameter from a superordinate) and then out of the module (as an output parameter to the superordinate) such that the input data is transformed into the output data.
transform module	a module with transform flow.
transform-centered design	a synonym for transformation analysis.
unconditioned transfer	a transfer of control from one module to another with no tacit condition of return.
upward compression	a form of compression in which a subordinate module is placed in-line in its superordinate; i.e., in which the body of the subordinate replaces the calling statement in the superordinate.
user	an informal term describing the person, persons, or organization that expects to benefit from the development of a computer system.
utility	the extent to which a system is easy to use, easy to install, easy to operate, and easy to understand.
virtual memory	a hardware mechanism present on many third-generation and fourth-generation computers that permits a degree of automatic packaging.
white box	the opposite of a black box: a system whose contents must be understood in order to be usable.

INDEX

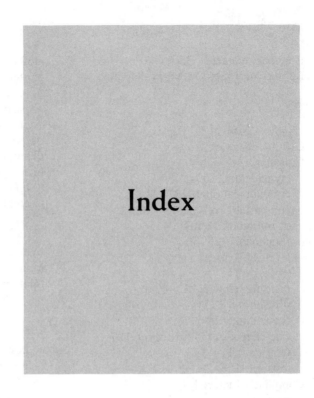

Index